MAGIC

THE UNTOLD STORY OF U.S. INTELLIGENCE AND THE EVACUATION OF JAPANESE RESIDENTS FROM THE WEST COAST DURING WW II

David D. Lowman

FORMER SPECIAL ASSISTANT TO THE DIRECTOR, NATIONAL SECURITY AGENCY

ATHENA PRESS, INC.
www.athenapressinc.com

Library of Congress Cataloging-in-Publication Data

Lowman, David D., 1921-1999
  Magic : the untold story of U.S. intelligence and the evacuation of Japanese residents from the West Coast during WW II / by David D. Lowman.
        p. cm.
Includes bibliographical references.
  ISBN 0-9602736-1-1 (alk. paper)
 1. Espionage, Japanese--United States--History--20th century.
 2. Japanese Americans--Evacuation and relocation, 1942-1945.
 3. World War, 1939-1945--Military intelligence--Japan.
 4. World War, 1939-1945--Cryptography. I. Title.
  D810.S7 L68 2000
  940.54'8752--dc21

                                          00-009704

The paper used in this publication meets the minimum requirements of the American National Standard for Information Sciences—Permanence of Paper for Printed Library Materials, ANSI Z39.48-1992

First Edition: February 2001
Printed in the United States of America.

Cover design by: Kerry Ellen Pate and Sam Allen
Layout by: Sam Allen

ISBN 0-9602736-1-1

With love and appreciation to my wife of fifty years,
Eleanor Sather Lowman, the devoted mother of our two children,
Jeff and Janell, and my best friend

ABOUT THE AUTHOR

David Daniel Lowman was a career intelligence officer for the National Security Agency, retiring as Special Assistant to the Director. During his service he received numerous commendations and honors including the Exceptional Civilian Service Medal, NSA's highest award.

A native of Washington state, he served with the Army in the South Pacific during World War II. After the war he attended Stanford University where he met his future wife, Eleanor. After graduation they married and moved to Washington D.C. where he joined the National Security Agency and studied for a doctor of jurisprudence from George Washington University. She joined the CIA while getting a master's degree in Russian history.

During his service with NSA David Lowman rose rapidly through the ranks fielding a wide variety of assignments as a linguist, educator, negotiator, lecturer, and liaison with U.S. business, Congress and foreign officials and diplomats.

After retirement from NSA he served as a consultant on the declassification of World War II intelligence documents. He testified as an expert witness on this subject four times before congressional committees and federal courts. He was a popular speaker and writer on the subject of signal intelligence and its role in the Pacific War.

CONTENTS

Publisher's Preface

From late 1940 until the attack on Pearl Harbor on December 7, 1941 American leaders had access to sensitive intelligence gained from intercepted and decoded message traffic between Japan and its stations in the United States. That intelligence revealed the existence of widespread Japanese espionage operations, particularly on the West Coast. Because of its sensitivity, the intelligence was given a cover name, MAGIC, and only a select few were given access to it.

When war came the decision to evacuate Japanese residents from the West Coast was largely based on MAGIC intelligence. Since protection of this intelligence source was critical to the war effort, a cover story was developed to justify the evacuation, which eliminated Japanese espionage and potential sabotage efforts, without revealing our cryptologic success.

After nearly sixty years of questioning and hindsight, the government's cover story seems far less plausible today than it did during the early days of the war. This has led many to believe that our government's motivations during the evacuation were less than honorable.

The issue of evacuation was problematic from the outset because about two thirds of those evacuated were U.S. citizens, mostly the children of Japanese citizens. Citizen children enjoyed certain rights under the U.S. Constitution which alien parents, after the declaration of war, did not. Instead of separating families to accommodate an idealized concept of justice, the decision was made to evacuate everyone.

When President Roosevelt authorized the evacuation he observed that there would probably be "some repercussions" and urged the Secretary of War to "Be as reasonable as you can."

Considerable effort was made during and after the evacuation to provide for the material needs of evacuees and to compensate them for their losses. Crops in the field were purchased, land leases were transferred, personal property was stored and cars were bought by the Army at Blue Book value. After the war additional payments were made to settle claims against the government for losses resulting from evacuation. Seditious and treasonous conduct by large numbers of Japanese residents was not prosecuted.

To be sure, it was a difficult time, but it was a difficult time for millions of others whose lives were forever changed by the requirements and sacrifices demanded by war. For many Japanese residents evacuation and life under government care provided much needed relief from trials and threats they faced on the West Coast.

Thirty-five years after the evacuation a large-scale release of MAGIC intelligence was made which provided credible justification for the evacuation, justification which the wartime cover story lacked. Although this intelligence was readily available, it was ignored by those who had begun a movement in the mid-1970s to obtain punitive damages from the U.S. government for human suffering.

In the days of national doubting following the end of the Vietnam War considerable headway was made convincing the American public that the government, acting irrationally and not from military necessity, had perpetrated a civil rights outrage worthy of redress.

In 1980 Congress established the Commission on Wartime Relocation and Internment of Civilians to investigate the World War II incident. In 1983 the Commission's findings were presented to Congress without any reference to MAGIC and its relationship to the evacuation. Since that time, in an effort to obtain money and to rewrite history, there has been an unrelenting effort to recast the reasons for the evacuation solely in terms of racism, war hysteria and lack of political will. In short, the 1942 cover story has been ceaselessly attacked while the real reasons for evacuation as revealed by MAGIC intelligence are ignored or denied.

This book by David D. Lowman, which is published posthumously, tells the fascinating story of MAGIC. It also tells a story characterized by a Japanese-American scholar as one of "intellectual dishonesty, moral posturing and political opportunism." It is a book that will interest those who never could quite believe the worst that was said about our wartime leaders and the motivations of our country.

Lee Allen
Publisher
July 4, 2000

INTRODUCTION

This book describes one of America's greatest intelligence feats, the breaking of Japan's highest level diplomatic and espionage codes and ciphers in 1940. Cover named MAGIC because it was so astounding in its achievement it seemed magical, this book describes how that near miraculous accomplishment relates to a current national issue—Japanese reparations.

Recently declassified MAGIC intelligence, which was processed and distributed during 1941 and early 1942, clearly supports President Roosevelt's controversial wartime decision to issue Executive Order No. 9066 which served as the authority to evacuate more than 112,000 residents of Japanese descent from the West Coast of the United States at the beginning of World War II. In addition to MAGIC, the President had available to him alarming assessments from the U.S. intelligence community which reported large-scale disloyalty, espionage, and potential sabotage by U.S. residents of Japanese ancestry.

The cumulative total of this intelligence revealed to the President and his key advisers the specter of subversive nets up and down the West Coast, controlled by the Japanese government, utilizing large numbers of local Japanese residents, and designed to operate in a wartime environment. Because of this intelligence all people of Japanese ancestry, aliens and citizens alike, in early 1942 were ordered to evacuate strategic areas along the West Coast of the United States. The situation on the West Coast was perceived by our wartime leaders and the U.S. intelligence community to be a major security hazard to the U.S., and so dangerous that extraordinary measures were required, a decision the legality of which the Supreme Court would uphold in 1944.

Now, years later, the U.S. Congress has passed legislation to give an official apology and to award $20,000 to anyone of Japanese ancestry who was evacuated, relocated, or interned during World War II. This includes the thousands of children who accompanied their parents, the 6,000 babies born in the camps, the 4,300 evacuees who attended colleges in the East during the war, the thousands who refused to sign a loyalty oath, and the many thousands who, at their own request, were returned to Japan. Total cost to the taxpayers is more than $1.25 billion.[1] This monetary award is punitive damages for human suffering, which is being assessed against U.S. taxpayers (most of whom were unborn in 1942) because our wartime government allegedly acted on the evacuation issue without any legitimate cause or reason and in bad faith.

In a complete turnaround, and over the objections of the Department of Justice, President Reagan signed the reparations bill into law on August 10, 1988. Thus, lost in a maze of misinformation and fraudulent concealment, a well-meaning government has succeeded in rewriting our country's history.

The case for reparations from Congress and damages in the courts rests almost entirely on the findings and conclusions of the congressionally authorized Commission on Wartime Relocation and Internment of Civilians. This commission, with members appointed by the President and the Congress, was charged to investigate the circumstances surrounding President Roosevelt's signing of Executive Order No. 9066 on February 19, 1942 which authorized the evacuation. The stated purpose of the executive order was to protect against espionage and sabotage.

For whatever reason, the Commission and its large staff, after more than two years of hearings and investigation, in its formal report to Congress in February 1983, *Personal Justice Denied*,[2] managed to overlook all the intelligence on the subject which it was charged to investigate. Yet, this same intelligence was the reason Executive Order 9066 was issued by the President in the first place.

Incredibly, none of the reports of the intelligence community was mentioned nor were any of the broken code revelations from MAGIC considered. Together,

---

[1] The eventual cost was over $1.64 billion.

[2] Commission on Wartime Relocation and Internment of Civilians, *Personal Justice Denied*, 2 vols. (Washington D.C.: GPO, 1982-83; reprint, The Civil Liberties Public Education Fund and the University of Washington Press, 1997). All references to *Personal Justice Denied* in this book refer to the 1997 edition.

these messages and reports were the most important and authoritative intelligence available to the U.S. government at that time on this issue. By design, or ignorant of all of this official intelligence, the Commission concluded that there was no evidence of espionage by West Coast Japanese residents. Therefore, said the Commission, President Roosevelt's motives, and those of his key wartime advisers, in authorizing the evacuation were based solely on political and racial considerations combined with war hysteria. A misinformed media, along with the Congress and the public, accepted these findings without question as the whole truth.

Seldom has any major event in U.S. history been as misrepresented as has U.S. intelligence related to the evacuation. It has been twisted, distorted, misquoted, misunderstood, ignored, and deliberately falsified by otherwise honorable people.

The facts are that the entire U.S. intelligence community in late 1941 and early 1942 was unequivocal in warning of widespread, ongoing espionage operations controlled by the Japanese government on the West Coast of the United States. Intelligence assessments, based on broken Japanese codes and ciphers, stated in detail how undercover Japanese naval officers were working with local Japanese on the West Coast, and how Japanese consulates had recruited Japanese residents to spy on U.S. military installations and the movement of ships, airplanes, and troops. Japanese-Americans were reported by the Japanese government itself to be in factories, airplane plants, and the armed forces for subversive purposes. The intelligence community detailed how Japanese clubs, labor organizations, legitimate business groups, certain associations and societies, and hundreds of individuals had been organized into widespread interlocking espionage nets designed to continue the flow of information to Japan after it went to war with the United States.

All these reports were available on a continuing basis to key decision makers in the government, including the President. The intelligence itself was a composite from the Office of Naval Intelligence, the Army Military Intelligence Division, the Federal Bureau of Investigation, and the code breaking services of the Army Signal Corps and the Office of Naval Communications.

Collectively, this group represented the best intelligence available to the United States on the threat posed by Japanese residents on the West Coast when Executive Order 9066 was signed on February 19, 1942. Although opinions differed on how to handle the situation, every one of these sources agreed that there was a major security problem on the West Coast which required immediate action. And it is particularly significant that none of the key, high-level officials with authorized access to MAGIC intelligence opposed mass evacuation.

Now, in this book for the first time the actual intelligence which guided President Roosevelt and his key wartime advisers in making their historic decisions on this issue has been collected and made available to the public. Part II of this book includes over one hundred intercepted and decoded Japanese government espionage messages, some of them smoking guns. In Part III are twenty-four reports, assessments, wrap-ups, and memoranda issued at the highest levels of the U.S. intelligence community. These fascinating documents contain both MAGIC and other intelligence derived from traditional methods such as wiretaps, informants, and observation, all directly related to the West Coast exclusion laws.

World War II and intelligence buffs, along with those interested in knowing the true story behind Executive Order 9066, will have a field day browsing through all this material.

No pretense is made that this book is a definitive statement on the moral, legal, economic, or sociological aspects of the evacuation and relocation of people of Japanese ancestry from the West Coast at the start of World War II. Those issues are discussed here only in the most general terms. If the reader desires to pursue these subjects in more depth, there are many reference materials available. This book is about the intelligence which prompted the evacuation decision, intelligence which the Commission on Wartime Relocation and Internment of Civilians said did not exist. I also hope to lend some support to upholding the honor and reputations of those high-ranking government officials who relied and acted on this intelligence in a manner which they perceived at that time to be in the best interests of our nation at war.

In early 1942 the country appeared to be faced with a dangerous espionage situation on the West Coast, and perhaps an unmanageable one, at a time when the military outlook was, to say the least, bleak. The decision to evacuate was not made without evidence and in bad faith. The United States government did not act shamefully, dishonorably, and without cause or reason as charged. Years of hindsight may cast doubts on the wisdom of the evacuation decision, but the intelligence illustrated in this book will provide ample proof that the decision was made honestly and with what seemed *at that time* to be complete justification.

David D. Lowman

August 1989
Honolulu, Hawaii

PART I
THE BACKGROUND

CHAPTER 1

The Executive Order

On February 19, 1942, more than two months into World War II, President Franklin Delano Roosevelt signed one of the most controversial documents in U.S. history—Executive Order 9066.[1] With a few strokes of his pen he gave Secretary of War Henry L. Stimson absolute power to exclude anybody from designated areas within the United States. Congress quickly backed up Executive Order 9066 with appropriate legislation known as Public Law 503. In a series of proclamations by the War Department over the next few months the western half of Washington and Oregon, the entire state of California, and the southern part of Arizona were all designated exclusion areas. The reason given for the order was military necessity, i.e., the fear of espionage, sabotage, and fifth column activities. That these were the major concerns of the administration were put forth unmistakably in the very first sentence of Executive Order 9066:

> The successful prosecution of the war requires every possible protection against espionage and against sabotage to national-defense material, national-defense premises, and national-defense utilities....

Although the order did not specify who would be excluded from the designated areas, it was widely understood that it was directed at the approximately

---

[1] See text of Executive Order 9066 on page 335.

58,000 Italian and 22,000 German aliens, and, most of all, at the 112,353 people of Japanese ancestry, citizens and aliens alike, then residing on the West Coast. Contrary to what many people believe, Executive Order 9066, which was only a one-page document, did not say anything whatsoever about putting people who were evacuated into relocation centers. At the time this was not contemplated.

When Executive Order 9066 was signed in February 1942, the military outlook was alarming. Only ten weeks earlier the Japanese Empire had viciously and without warning attacked Pearl Harbor. A good part of the U.S. Fleet was sunk or left barely afloat. Following up on their surprisingly easy success at Pearl Harbor, Japanese forces were advancing victoriously on all fronts; they appeared unstoppable. That great British bastion of power in the Orient, Singapore, had surrendered along with an entire British army. Bataan was about to fall, and the loss of the Philippines and all American and Philippine forces in those islands was a foregone conclusion. India was threatened as Allied troops were being forced out of Burma. Japanese troops were already en route to conquer the Dutch East Indies. Hong Kong had capitulated, and it was all China itself could do to keep from complete disintegration under the Japanese onslaught. Wake Island and Guam had surrendered, and their American defenders were now prisoners of war.[2]

In Europe the situation was equally bad. After having brought most of the continent to its knees, Hitler's armies were within sight of Moscow. England was hanging on desperately and hoping for a miracle.

But it was in the Pacific where the U.S. was most vulnerable. Alaska, Hawaii, and the West Coast all lay exposed to Japanese air and naval power. With considerable justification there was widespread fear of a Japanese attack on any or all of these areas, although U.S. military chiefs thought that an actual invasion of the West Coast was unlikely. Nonetheless, the Japanese navy controlled the Pacific Ocean and was capable of moving in force almost anywhere it chose. Japanese submarines were beginning to operate off the West Coast, and on February 23 a Japanese submarine surfaced and shelled the oil facilities near Santa Barbara, California.

Today, decades later, knowing the crushing defeat Japan eventually suffered, it is difficult to imagine what it was like in the early days of World War II when

---

[2]   The magnitude of Japanese aggression was dramatically described by President Roosevelt in his speech before Congress on December 8, 1941. "Yesterday, the Japanese government also launched an attack against Malaya. Last night, Japanese forces attacked Hong Kong. Last night, Japanese forces attacked Guam. Last night, Japanese forces attacked the Philippine Islands. Last night, the Japanese attacked Wake Island. This morning the Japanese attacked Midway Island."

everything was going Japan's way. In those first few, uncertain months the danger of attack was very real, and so was the fear. Japan's rampaging forces in just a few months had overrun more of the earth's surface than had any other nation in history, and were on the verge of bringing almost half of the world's population under Japanese domination.

With the United States moving as rapidly as possible to shore up its Pacific defenses and to gear up for the bloody battles which lay ahead, there was both suspicion and concern within the U.S. government over the actions and loyalty of the large Japanese population in the U.S. What had happened in the countries overrun by Japan was not encouraging. In China, Hong Kong, and Southeast Asia the resident Japanese had sided completely with the attacking Japanese armed forces. Moreover, the conquering troops treated all resident Japanese as reunited brethren rather than part of the local population, and this was more than reciprocated by the local Japanese when they welcomed the troops with flags and nationalistic fervor. In the Philippines there were about 30,000 Japanese residents on Mindanao Island alone, almost all of whom appeared to have completely gone over to the invaders, offering to serve as guides and interpreters, or to be useful in other ways.

The Japanese resident population in the United States was largely concentrated along the West Coast, primarily in California where, according to the 1940 census, they numbered 93,717 or about 1.6 percent of the total population. The other large concentration was in Hawaii where they numbered 160,000 and composed about 40 percent of the entire population of the Hawaiian Islands.

While there was some anxiety about the Italian and German aliens residing in what were considered strategic areas, most of the concern focused on the Japanese because of their suspected loyalty to the Japanese Emperor, and because whatever threat there was of invasion, real or imagined, was from Japan, not Germany or Italy.

For many years the Italians and the Germans had been melting into the general population. Most had become thoroughly Americanized, and people thought of them as normal, everyday Americans but this was not the case with the Japanese. Of course, simply being Oriental accounted for much of the difference when it came to assimilation; but it was more than that. Within the U.S. the Japanese were truly a unique group.

Although 148 contract laborers had arrived in Hawaii from Japan as early as 1868, Japanese immigration to America did not begin in significant numbers until 1885 as a result of a proposal made in 1881 by the Hawaiian king, David Kalakaua, to Japanese Emperor Meiji. Under the terms of the agreement the Japanese government would select contract laborers to be sent to

Hawaii to work in the sugar cane fields. Originally, contracts were for three years, and it was anticipated that at the conclusion of their contracts the workers would return to Japan. Eventually, about half of them did return. The other half remained, although not necessarily as field hands. When Hawaii was annexed by the United States in 1898, Hawaii's contract labor laws were voided; thereafter, the Japanese simply entered as immigrants.

In 1885 mass immigration began with the arrival of 994 Japanese in Honolulu. By 1930, 180,000 had reached Hawaii. Immigration to the mainland of the United States commenced shortly after the first Japanese landed in the Hawaiian Islands, with more than 2,000 arriving during the 1880s, 6,000 in the 1890s, and more than 100,000 in the first decade of the twentieth century.

Concern over the ever-mounting numbers of Japanese arriving in the United States led to the so-called Gentlemen's Agreement in 1907 which was supposed to slow down Japanese immigration.[3] Nevertheless, between 1907 and 1924 another 159,675 entered the continental United States. In 1924, restrictive laws governing Japanese immigration (and other nationalities as well) were passed, and thereafter few Japanese entered the country. Altogether, approximately 450,000 Japanese came to Hawaii and the continental United States. Of these, based on passport studies, almost half returned to their homeland.

Unlike immigration from Europe, the Japanese influx was predominantly male, seven times as many males as females in 1890, and twenty-four times as many males as females in 1906. This led to the practice of picture brides, who must have been the most courageous of all emigrants, coming to Hawaii and the mainland to marry men they had never seen. They came in impressive numbers, 14,376 to Hawaii alone between 1907 and 1923.

One of the most overlooked implications of this mass immigration was that it largely occurred during the reign of Emperor Meiji, who ruled Japan from 1868 to 1912. During the Meiji period Japan moved from being a feudal isolationist country to a modern world power. It was a period of intense ultra-nationalism, traditionalism, and militarism. Almost overnight Japan became a force to be reckoned with. To the amazement of almost everyone, Japan defeated China in 1895 and Russia in 1905. The Japanese Empire grew by astonishing dimensions. Worship of the Emperor as a divine leader of the Japanese race reached new heights. It was from this political and social environment that the Japanese emigrated from Japan to the U.S. As a well-known

---

[3]   The agreement called for the Japanese government to deny emigrant passports to Japanese laborers except those who had relatives or previously established interests in the United States.

writer in Japan, Yasuo Wakatsuki, observed, "If you want to see Japan of the Taisho Era (1912-1926) go to Brazil; if you want to see Japan of the Meiji Era (1868-1912), go to America."

Although the Nisei, second-generation Japanese born in the U.S., were undergoing an assimilation process which was never achieved by their foreign-born parents, Issei, a huge gulf of misunderstanding and mistrust remained between the rest of the American population and those of Japanese ancestry at the beginning of World War II. The Japanese appeared as a monolithic bloc unto themselves, speaking their own language, attending their own, separate schools at the end of the regular public school day, organizing themselves into a seemingly endless array of societies and associations, publishing their own newspapers, practicing a strange and little understood religion, and sending their children, whenever possible, back to Japan for schooling where they were thoroughly indoctrinated by the Japanese government. Japanese children sent back to the homeland for schooling were called Kibei and often returned, in the words of University of Hawaii sociologist, Andrew Lind, "more fanatically Japanese in their disposition than their own parents." Since about 20 percent of the Nisei had been sent back to Japan for their schooling, the implications involved were not inconsequential.

By attending Japanese schools in the U.S. students were regularly subjected to indoctrination. Teachers were often brought in from Japan, and many taught the ultra-nationalism that had become increasingly strident in that country. As a high school student in 1939, Daniel Inouye, the present U.S. Senator from Hawaii, was thrown out of his Japanese school when he objected to the pro-Japan, anti-American rhetoric of his teacher who taught his Japanese-American students that their first allegiance was to Japan, not the United States: "You must remember that only a trick of fate has brought you so far from your homeland, but there must be no question of your loyalty. When Japan calls, you must know that it is Japanese blood that flows in your veins."[4]

On the economic level, particularly in California, the Japanese incurred the enmity of many because of their willingness to work long hours for less pay. Further resentment arose when they began to compete successfully as small businessmen and farmers. Their very virtues were turned against them.

Thus, often rejected by their adopted country, and clinging tenaciously to their own culture and kind, the Japanese remained a little understood island in the mainstream of American society. By far the most damaging perception

---

[4]   Daniel K. Inouye with Lawrence Elliott, *Journey to Washington* (Englewood Cliffs, NJ: Prentice-Hall, 1967), pages 36-37.

of them in 1942 by the general population was that they would never assimilate and that their loyalty to their homeland and Emperor remained unshaken.

Of the more than 112,000 Japanese residents on the West Coast in February 1942, 40,869 were enemy aliens[5] and 71,484 were American-born citizens. However, more than half of the American-born Japanese were also citizens of Japan. They had dual citizenship. Estimates of dual citizenship vary widely, and are complicated because of a change in Japanese law in 1924.

Most reliable researchers, however, believe that roughly 50 to 60 percent of the Nisei (U.S. citizens) had dual citizenship on the eve of World War II. The Dies Committee told Congress, "It has been conservatively estimated that about 75% of the Nisei, or American-born Japanese, have dual citizenship." This figure seems too high. In Hawaii, where the figures are probably more accurate, Professor John Stephan of the University of Hawaii concluded that out of 119,316 Nisei, 73,281, or 60 percent, had dual citizenship. In all likelihood the percentages for the mainland were very close to those in Hawaii.

Prior to 1924, according to Japanese law, all children born of a Japanese father were Japanese citizens no matter where they were born. The law was changed in 1924. Thereafter, children born in the U.S. were Japanese citizens for the first two weeks of their life, but lost that citizenship unless their parents registered them at the Japanese consulate within the two-week period. Of course, by U.S. law anyone born in the United States was a U.S. citizen. Most

---

[5] The term "enemy alien" has a specific legal meaning derived from the Alien Law enacted in 1798: "Whenever there is a declared war between the United States and any foreign nation or government... all natives, citizens, denizens, or subjects of the hostile nation or government, being of the age of fourteen years and upward, who shall be within the United States and not actually naturalized, shall be liable to be apprehended, restrained, secured and removed as alien enemies." The Supreme Court in *Johnson v. Eisentrager* said, "Executive power over enemy aliens, undelayed and unhampered by litigation, has been deemed, throughout our history, essential to war-time security.... The resident enemy alien is constitutionally subject to summary arrest, internment and deportation whenever a 'declared war' exists."

On December 7, 1941 President Roosevelt issued Presidential Proclamation No. 2525, "Alien Enemies—Japanese" stating "...all natives, citizens, denizens or subjects of Empire of Japan being of the age of fourteen years or upwards... are termed alien enemies," and issued instructions concerning their status and conduct.

In recent years this wartime classification has been ignored by those seeking redress. The term "permanent resident alien" has been substituted, implying that those Japanese citizens in the United States during the war were somehow protected by the constitutional safeguards that would normally apply in times of peace. For a discussion of this subject see, William H. Rehnquist, *All the Laws but One: Civil Liberties in Wartime* (Knopf, 1998).

Under the provisions of the Civil Liberties Act of 1988 Japanese citizens, enemy aliens during the war, were awarded $20,000 payment on the same basis as citizens without regard to their involvement in pro-Japan activities.

Japanese parents registered their children with the consulates after 1924 because there appeared to be no disadvantages to being a dual citizen, and there were certain benefits to having Japanese citizenship because of property ownership and inheritance laws in Japan. A big potential problem was that dual citizens could be drafted into the Japanese armed forces. And some Japanese-Americans who went to Japan were, in fact, drafted into the Japanese army.

For the most part, these fine distinctions were ignored by the Japanese government and, unless it had some legal reason for singling out a specific citizenship status, it referred to all Japanese living abroad as Doho, literally, compatriots, and considered all of them extensions of the Japanese nation. When war broke out the average age of born-in-Japan first generation, Issei, was fifty-five years; the average age of their American-born children, Nisei, was seventeen.

While the Caucasian population as a whole distrusted and was highly suspicious of the local Japanese, most of these concerns were based on surface considerations rather than on any actual evidence, let alone proof. Immediately following the attack on Pearl Harbor rumors ran wild: the local Japanese were signaling to ships offshore; they were hoarding arms; factories had been sabotaged; food grown on their truck farms had been deliberately poisoned. It wasn't just the rednecks of the day who distrusted the local Japanese, it was almost everybody. Military base commanders, officials from all three Pacific Coast states, some of the most respected names in the media such as Walter Lippmann, and the entire West Coast congressional delegation all demanded that the Japanese, both citizens and aliens, be removed from strategic areas along the West Coast.

Unfortunately for the Japanese, they had largely settled in areas near air-fields, shipyards, military bases, and important ports. This, of course, was perceived by many as having been done by design rather than as a natural consequence of the agricultural and fishing activities in which they were engaged. The pressure on the U.S. government to do something about the Japanese was intense.

Most of the many rumors about the Japanese living along the West Coast turned out to be untrue, but practically everybody at the time believed them. In later years while the real intelligence remained classified, these stories were revived to show how foolish people were who believed that the local Japanese were involved in any disloyal acts.

The government, however, did not operate on rumors. It had more concrete evidence. U.S. intelligence in late 1941 and early 1942 was unequivocal in warning of large ongoing espionage operations controlled by the Japanese government on the West Coast of the United States. This information, produced by the U.S. intelligence community, told of the recruiting of Japanese residents for espionage by all Japanese diplomatic posts in the United States. It noted that: (1) whole colonies of Japanese such as at Terminal Island near Los Angeles were hotbeds of espionage and potential sabotage; (2) a number of Japanese businesses, clubs, and labor organizations had been converted into espionage units; (3) specified types of local Japanese organizations and associations were certain to be given espionage and sabotage functions; (4) 25 percent of all Japanese-Americans were of doubtful loyalty, and a much higher percent of the Issei; (5) approximately 3,500 Japanese residents could be expected to act as agents and saboteurs; (6) several thousand Japanese-Americans educated in Japan (Kibei) were so dangerous to U.S. security that they should be placed in immediate custodial detention; (7) ports, airfields, and military bases were under observation by local Japanese who reported back to the Japanese government; (8) there were Japanese-Americans located in the U.S. armed forces, factories, and airplane plants for subversive purposes; and, (9) that U.S. cryptanalysts had succeeded in breaking certain high-level Japanese codes and ciphers which revealed a steady stream of U.S. national defense information was being transmitted back to Tokyo. It was further reported that this information had been gathered by espionage nets established by the government of Japan along the entire West Coast of the United States.

This alarming intelligence was a composite produced by the Office of Naval Intelligence (ONI), the Army G-2 or Military Intelligence Division (MID), the Federal Bureau of Investigation (FBI), the intelligence services of the Army Signal Corps, and the Office of Naval Communications, plus a private assessment from Lieutenant Commander K. D. Ringle, ONI's leading expert on the Japanese situation on the West Coast. Collectively, this group provided the best intelligence available to the United States on the threat posed by the Japanese population on the West Coast when Executive Order 9066 was signed on February 19, 1942.

Every single one of these sources agreed that the West Coast Japanese did indeed present a threat to the security of the United States. There was a difference of opinion on the solution. J. Edgar Hoover (but not his FBI West Coast field offices), and Lieutenant Commander Ringle (but not the Office of Naval Intelligence), thought that after an initial roundup of approximately 10,000 suspects only a careful watching of the remainder would be necessary. Ringle proposed that boards be established to decide individual cases. Both the Army and the Navy felt that to organize and to administer such a program would amount to nothing more than a cumbersome half-measure and was not at all a practical solution to the immediate threat.

In any event it is clear that the motivating force behind the evacuation was the intelligence being fed on an almost daily basis to the President and his key advisers. The picture presented was a dangerous and perhaps unmanageable situation on the West Coast, which had been declared a war zone, at a time when the military outlook was, to say the least, bleak.

John J. McCloy, Assistant Secretary of War under Roosevelt, and until very recently, the only man alive from the President's inner circle on the evacuation, testified that U.S. intelligence was the reason Roosevelt signed the evacuation order.

Removal and/or arrest based on suspicion alone was legally sufficient to take reasonable actions regarding the Issei who were, by definition, enemy aliens. It was settled law that the Constitution did not afford the same protection to enemy aliens as it did to U.S. citizens.

By the time of the Pearl Harbor attack the FBI had compiled long lists of German, Italian, and Japanese aliens to be arrested who had something in their record indicating possible disloyalty to the United States or allegiance to the enemy.

On December 7, 1941 President Roosevelt issued Presidential Proclamations 2525, 2526 and 2527 regarding the status, directing the conduct and issuing regulations for enemy aliens of Japan, Germany and Italy respectively. Large numbers of these enemy aliens were arrested and confined by the Department of Justice. Later as individuals they appeared before review boards composed of leading citizens and were evaluated as to their loyalty and threat to the security of the country. Generally, they were either interned for the duration of the war, paroled or released.

Those interned for the duration were placed in special Department of Justice internment camps. The largest such camp at Crystal City, Texas held aliens from all three enemy nations as well as others.[6]

The fires at Pearl Harbor were still smoldering when the FBI went into action. By December 10, 1941 FBI Director J. Edgar Hoover announced that

---

[6]   Though it is common today to use the term "internment" to describe all facilities relating to the evacuation of persons of Japanese ancestry, internment camps should not be confused with relocation centers which were run by the civilian War Relocation Authority and had as their objective the resettlement of evacuees in areas of the U.S. outside the West Coast exclusion area. Internment camps were run by the Department of Justice and held only enemy aliens who had been deemed security risks and their U.S. citizen family members who chose to stay with them. The government went to considerable effort to accommodate this arrangement. During the war 10,995 Germans, 16,849 Japanese and 3,278 Italians were interned. Among the Japanese interned were 5,589 who voluntarily renounced their U.S. citizenship thus becoming enemy aliens.

1,291 Japanese (367 in Hawaii and 924 in the continental United States), 857 Germans, and 147 Italians had been taken into custody.

The law was clear insofar as enemy aliens were concerned, but left open the question of Japanese-Americans about whom there was also hard evidence of disloyalty and subversive activities. As early as December 22, 1941 the FBI felt that most of the "bad" aliens had been arrested (a poor estimate as it turned out) and the problem now was with the Japanese who were American citizens.

In Hawaii martial law was declared shortly after Pearl Harbor and control of the islands was turned over to the military. However, on the West Coast citizens could only be arrested and held as provided under the U.S. Constitution with its full range of protection. Bearing this in mind the FBI had started gathering evidence which would hold up in a court of law, and already had its first Japanese-American sedition case ready for prosecution, but the Attorney General dismissed it, and ordered the FBI not to proceed against citizens. In an FBI memo dated December 22, 1941 Hoover expressed his disagreement with this policy, saying, "You had to teach some of those fellows a lesson."[7]

Presumably, the monumental effort to apprehend, indict, and prosecute what appeared to be a great many Japanese-American cases in the midst of a war, without revealing intelligence sources, and at the same time trying to defend the West Coast against attack in the face of ongoing espionage, was not only beyond all reason, but also very likely beyond the country's counter-espionage and judicial capabilities.

Within just a few weeks after Pearl Harbor the U.S. had taken several thousand enemy aliens into custody about whom there was evidence of disloyalty, but it had not yet touched the Kibei, the American citizens educated in Japan, who everybody agreed were the most dangerous security problem of all, and who numbered in the thousands.

If the intelligence community was to be believed, and it was, the investigatory and legal implications of proceeding against possible traitors in this group alone was staggering. Even Lieutenant Commander Ringle, the naval officer constantly quoted as an expert on the Japanese situation on the West Coast by the Commission on Wartime Relocation and Internment of Civilians, was at a loss what to do about the Kibei. His solution: "In spite of their legal citizenship and the protection afforded to them by the Bill of Rights, they should be looked upon as enemy aliens and many of them placed in custodial detention." But this was illegal and could not be done under the Constitution.[8]

---

[7]   See J. Edgar Hoover memo of December 22, 1941 on page 224 for a view of the situation at that time. Reference on page 225.

[8]   See Ringle memo of January 26, 1942, page 315. Reference on page 317.

To the top brass in the government total evacuation seemed to be the only effective and ready solution, and was regarded by them as a legitimate wartime measure taken to defend the nation with what appeared at that time to be adequate justification. In 1944 the Supreme Court would agree with this reasoning.[9]

The U.S. government had hoped that after the signing of Executive Order 9066 most Japanese would simply move eastward, out of the exclusion areas, and whatever problems there were would then be solved. But this was a naive hope. Many of the uprooted Japanese didn't speak English; money was a problem with some; they had no jobs or homes to which they could go; few had relatives or friends in the East; and most states to the east were openly hostile to them.[10]

Almost immediately it became obvious that the government would have to step in and organize this mass exodus.

It wasn't only the United States which evacuated its Japanese residents, alien and citizen alike, from exposed areas. The British removed all people of Japanese ancestry from Singapore, sending them to India. All Japanese in the Fiji Islands were sent to New Zealand where they were detained for the duration of the war. Subsequent information revealed the Japanese army planned to use Japanese residents living in Fiji to help govern the Islands. On February 15, 1942 Mexico removed all of its Japanese residents from Lower California and away from the coastal areas of continental Mexico. Sixteen Latin American countries interned more than 8,500 Axis nationals. In January 1942 the Canadian government began relocating the 20,096 people of Japanese ancestry from its West Coast in British Columbia. Unlike the United States, however, the Canadian government did not allow them to return to the West Coast until 1949 and encouraged them to remain in eastern Canada or to return to Japan which some 4,000 did. Canada was determined to break up the heavy concentration of Japanese along its western shores. Toronto, with only 135 Japanese-Canadians in 1941, had a population of 11,690 Japanese-Canadians thirty years later.

In Hawaii, in the weeks following the attack on Pearl Harbor on December 7, 1941, the FBI took into custody 1,450 Doho.[11] Between 1941 and 1945, 1,875 Japanese were sent to the mainland, 1,118 to relocation centers, and the

---

9   *Korematsu v. United States*, 323 U.S. 214-248: Oct. Term 1944 .

10   In those confusing times opposition to resettlement in other Western States also came from the Japanese community. See Japanese American Citizens League of Ogden, Utah March 25, 1942 letter to Governor Herbert B. Maw of Utah, requesting that West Coast Japanese not be resettled in their area, page 342.

11   Compatriots of Japan.

remainder to Department of Justice internment camps. But there was no mass evacuation even though both President Roosevelt and Secretary of the Navy Frank Knox continued to fret over what they regarded as a dangerous situation in Hawaii. A steady stream of proposals poured in from Washington: evacuate everyone of Japanese descent from Oahu to one of the other Hawaiian islands; ship all Japanese residents to the mainland; ship up to 20,000 of them to the mainland; and there were still other suggestions on how to handle what was perceived as a continuing security threat.[12]

But each new proposal presented practical problems to the authorities in Hawaii. Persons of Japanese descent constituted a substantial part of Hawaii's labor force. To have removed them from Oahu to another island— Molokai was the one mentioned—would have involved shipping problems, massive construction problems for living areas, utilization of scarce building materials and even scarcer labor, huge support problems, and probably would have resulted in having to search for workers to come from the mainland to ease the labor shortage on Oahu. For example, 90 percent of all the carpenters on Oahu were of Japanese ancestry. Their evacuation back to the mainland would have caused a major problem to both the local economy and to various defense projects as well.

All of these logistic and economic realities combined with the fact that martial law had been declared in Hawaii, giving the military a large degree of control over the civilian population, caused the military commands in Hawaii to be less anxious about mass evacuation than would otherwise have been the case. Consequently, the Army command in Hawaii resorted to foot dragging that ultimately, by design or by accident, succeeded, despite continual prodding from Washington to do something. Not until April 1943 did Washington finally give up on some kind of a Hawaiian evacuation. In a neat twist, it turned out to be a military necessity to keep the Japanese in the Hawaiian Islands.

No such shipping and labor problems existed in Alaska to save the Alaskan Japanese from evacuation. The entire resident Japanese population of Alaska, numbering 230 people, was evacuated to the mainland of the United States.

Colonel Karl R. Bendetsen was the man chosen by the Army to be in charge of the evacuation on the mainland. Lieutenant General John L. DeWitt,

---

[12] One of the first indications of a desire to intern Japanese residents is found in an FBI memo from Edward A. Tamm to the Director, December 21, 1941, in which Tamm reports on a meeting with the Assistant to the Secretary of War, McGeorge Bundy. Bundy told Tamm that the President, in a cabinet meeting a few days before said he wanted all Japanese aliens but not citizens in Hawaii "interned at once." The timing of this order, being less than two weeks after Pearl Harbor, reveals no racial motivation. See page 345.

Commander of the Western Defense Command (WDC), gave Bendetsen his orders in the presence of John J. McCloy, Assistant Secretary of War, and General George Marshall, Chief of Staff of the Army. They were as follows:

> I hereby delegate to you, Colonel Karl R. Bendetsen all and in full my powers and authority under Executive Order 9066, which, in turn, have been delegated by the President to the Secretary of War, by the Secretary of War to the Chief of Staff, and by the Chief of Staff, to the Commanding General of the Western Defense Command and Fourth Army.... No military guards will be used except when absolutely necessary for the protection of the evacuees. You will, to the maximum, take measures to induce voluntary evacuation and relocation, providing assistance. For those who do not relocate themselves, comfortable transportation will be provided to temporary assembly centers. Families will not be separated, medical care, nutrition for children and food for adults will be provided....[13]

The evacuation proceeded. Those people of Japanese ancestry living on the West Coast of the United States were added to the ever growing list of unfortunate and often tragic happenings brought about by World War II. Initially, voluntary migration was encouraged but it soon became evident that this wouldn't work.[14] Consequently, General DeWitt, whose Western Defense Command (WDC) embraced all the Pacific Coast states as well as five other western states, stopped voluntary evacuation on March 29, 1942. Thereafter, the evacuation was carried out under Army supervision with the evacuees reporting to Army-operated assembly centers and then proceeding onward to relocation centers. The first areas ordered to be evacuated were Terminal Island in the Los Angeles harbor and Bainbridge Island near Seattle. These were probably first on the list because of two enciphered Japanese government messages intercepted in May 1941 which outlined an extensive espionage effort in these two areas utilizing local Japanese residents.[15]

On June 7, 1942 the Western Defense Command completed the evacuation of more than 100,000 persons of Japanese ancestry from Military Area No. 1

---

[13] The unusual circumstances of this delegation of authority: the presence of the Assistant Secretary of War, the Chief of Staff of the Army, the Commanding General of the Western Defense Command and a stenographer to record the lineage and details of the charge seem to indicate a desire to establish an unambiguous legal basis for the action and an intention to handle the situation as humanely as possible.

[14] Approximately 9,000 individuals evacuated voluntarily.

[15] See messages #067, May 9, 1941, p. 147 and #45, May 11, 1941, p. 148.

which included the western half of Washington, Oregon and California, and the southern half of Arizona.[16] Evacuation from Military Area No. 2 which was the eastern part of California was completed in August 1942.

The evacuation itself was a model of efficiency: commercial buses and passenger trains, including Pullman cars for the aged and sick, were provided; baggage was carefully transported; hot meals were served; the Army even supplied diapers for babies.

Once the displaced Japanese arrived in the relocation centers they became the responsibility of the civilian-run War Relocation Authority (WRA). Milton Eisenhower, a Department of Agriculture official and the brother of General Dwight D. Eisenhower, was the man chosen by the President to be the first director of the War Relocation Authority.[17] After about three months Eisenhower was replaced by Dillon Meyer, another official from the Department of Agriculture, who remained head of the WRA until it was disbanded at the end of the war.

With the help of the WRA about 30,000 evacuees eventually moved from the relocation centers to other states, out of the West Coast exclusion areas. The majority of the remainder, however, faced with the uncertainty of relocation, language difficulties or an inability to work, chose to stay in the ten hastily established relocation centers where they remained until the end of the war, making the best they could of a bad situation. Testimonials after the war by evacuees who lived in the relocation centers praised the WRA for its understanding and sensitive handling of a most difficult situation.

---

[16] The presence of the coastal portions of California, Oregon and Washington in the exclusion area to protect against espionage and possible sabotage of shipping and war industries is fairly intuitive. However, the inclusion of southern Arizona defies understanding without access to MAGIC messages #44, January 30, 1941, p. 146 and #93, June 2, 1941, p. 151 which call for a shift of espionage operations to Mexico in the event of war and the use of Mexicali as the point of access to Mexico.

[17] The circumstances surrounding Eisenhower's appointment give some insight to the President's situation at the time. They also leave little doubt about who made the decision and gave the orders for evacuation. Eisenhower in his book, *The President is Calling* (Doubleday, 1974) p. 95 described the meeting. "He was blunt. His first words were: 'Milton, your war job, starting immediately, is to set up the War Relocation Authority to move the Japanese-Americans off the Pacific Coast. I have signed an executive order which will give you full authority to do what is essential. The Attorney General will give you the necessary legal assistance and the Secretary of War will help you with the physical arrangements. Harold' - he nodded at the Budget Director - 'will fill you in on the details of the problem.' He looked back at the paper he had been reading, and I realized the interview was over. My mind was full of half-formed questions, I turned to leave. The President looked up at me again and said: 'And, Milton... the greatest possible speed is imperative.'"

In December 1944 the exclusion laws were removed, and the war ended in August 1945. People the world over heaved a sigh of relief and picked up their lives as best they could. President Ford rescinded Executive Order 9066 on February 19, 1976.

Recognizing that many evacuated Japanese had suffered economic hardships, the U.S. Congress in 1948 enacted the American-Japanese Evacuation Claims Act. This legislation authorized compensation for "any claim" for damages to or loss of real or personal property which was a reasonable consequence of the evacuation or exclusion of persons of Japanese ancestry resulting from government actions taken during World War II.

Ultimately, 26,568 settlements were achieved. The number of claims actually settled was considerably larger since many of the claims covered not one person but entire families. A total of over $37 million was paid by the U.S. government in compensation pursuant to this Act.[18] The Act specifically stated that payment was a full discharge of the United States and its agents with respect to all claims arising out of the evacuation issue.

Today there are about 800,000 Americans of Japanese ancestry in the United States, and there is universal recognition that the nation is richer for their presence. Japanese culture is respected and admired. Indeed, sushi bars have become as American as pizza parlors and taco stands. Contrary to the predictions of many in 1941, fourth and fifth-generation Japanese have thoroughly integrated into the American scene.

For those Americans unaware of what was revealed to our wartime leaders in the broken Japanese codes, and the warnings of the 1942 intelligence community, it is difficult to understand what could have prompted the U.S. government to take such drastic action as eventually resulted from Executive Order 9066. This is especially true when viewed from the perspective of the late 1980s because those actions were directed against a people and a race who are today widely regarded as one of the country's best acquisitions.

The evacuation was a long time ago. It was another world then. What happened, happened. The evidence of subversive activities which swung the pendulum on the evacuation decision cannot today be swept under the rug and erased from history by simply writing a new scenario. The documents in Parts II and III of this book, the broken codes and the intelligence reports, are the realities which guided that decision, and all the opprobrium heaped on the 1942 U.S. government, and the accusations, denunciations, and denials, are not going to change that one whit.

---

18   In the year 2000 this would be over a quarter billion dollars.

Assembly Centers

"The evacuation itself was a model of efficiency: commercial buses and passenger trains, including Pullman cars for the aged and sick, were provided; baggage was carefully transported; hot meals were served; the Army even supplied diapers for babies."

National Archives

March 31, 1942, Salinas, California—Baggage is being assembled to be taken by truck to the Salinas Assembly Center.

National Archives

May 8, 1942, Hayward, California—Evacuees prepare to move by chartered bus to the Tanforan Assembly Center. Baggage was taken to the center by truck.

National Archives

May 2, 1942, Byron, California—Main street of small town in the farming district on morning of evacuation. Six bus loads of residents of Japanese ancestry were checked in and taken to the assembly center at the Turlock Fairgrounds, 65 miles away.

National Archives

April 6, 1942, Arcadia, California—Evacuees of Japanese ancestry arriving at the Santa Anita Assembly Center in their own automobiles.

National Archives

March 31, 1942, Salinas, California—A young evacuee of Japanese ancestry identifies her baggage at this assembly center prior to transfer to a relocation center.

National Archives

March 31, 1942, Salinas, California—Baggage belonging to evacuees at the assembly center.

National Archives

April 8, 1942, Pomona, California—Workmen erecting barracks for evacuees of Japanese ancestry at assembly center on Pomona Fairgrounds.

National Archives

April 6, 1942, Arcadia, California—Special food formulas are prepared for babies at Santa Anita Assembly Center.

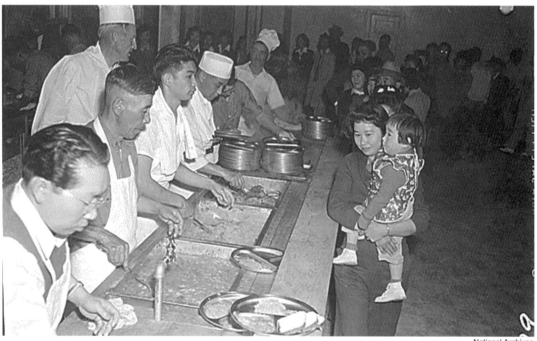

National Archives

April 6, 1942, Arcadia, California—Cafeteria-style dining halls assure promptness in serving meals at Santa Anita Assembly Center.

April 6, 1942, Arcadia, California—Lunch time at the Santa Anita Assembly Center.

April 6, 1942, Arcadia, California—To insure cleanliness and to protect health, modern dishwashing apparatus is used to sterilize dishes for thousands of meals at Santa Anita Assembly Center.

Relocation Centers

"[Evacuees]...faced with the uncertainty of relocation [to states outside of the exclusion area], language difficulties or an inability to work, chose to stay in the ten hastily established relocation centers where they remained until the end of the war, making the best they could of a bad situation."

National Archives

Tule Lake Relocation Center, Newell, California—A view showing the artistic way in which some evacuees decorated the exterior of their barracks to make them more homelike.

National Archives

A long pass and the dust flies over the football field at the Topaz Relocation Center in Utah.

National Archives

Topaz Relocation Center, Utah—This indomitable golfer keeps his form by first preparing a short course and then spending all of his spare time with his irons and putting clubs.

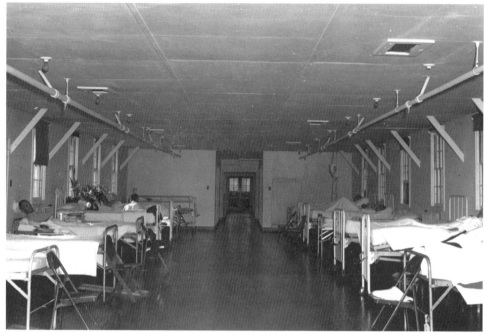

National Archives

Tule Lake Relocation Center, Newell, California—Hospital Ward 1.

National Archives

Tule Lake Relocation Center, Newell, California—Hospital Laboratory.

National Archives

Tule Lake Relocation Center, Newell, California—A close up of hogs eating garbage at the hog farm. The garbage is brought to the farm by trucks from the center.

National Archives

Tule Lake Relocation Center, Newell, California—A view in the slaughter house. Hogs grown in the evacuee-run hog farm are slaughtered here for consumption by the residents of the center.

National Archives

Tule Lake Relocation Center, Newell, California—Mr. Nakamura, poultry caretaker, and former farmer of Sacramento, California, feeds four-month old chickens. The chickens grown here will furnish the residents of the project with all their eggs and chicken meat.

National Archives

Tofu factory at Tule Lake Relocation Center, Newell, California operated by the Tule Lake Co-Op.

National Archives

High school class at the Tule Lake Relocation Center taught by Mrs. John Moursund.

National Archives

Nursery school class at Topaz Relocation Center, Utah.

Tule Lake Relocation Center—The office of the Tulean Dispatch, the center's newspaper.

Tule Lake Relocation Center, Newell, California—There were three Co-Op canteens in the center which carried general merchandise of all kinds. This scene shows a cosmetics and stationery counter.

National Archives

This beauty parlor is operated by Tule Lake Co-Operative Enterprises, Inc. Patrons were charged a nominal fee.

National Archives

Tule Lake Relocation Center, September 1944—Student queen and her attendants at the Tri-state Carnival.

Woodie Ichihashi band playing for a dance at the Tule Lake Relocation Center, November 1943.

Japanese-Americans at Topaz Relocation Center celebrate with a big New Year's Eve party on December 31, 1944.

CHAPTER 2

MAGIC INTELLIGENCE

In one of the most remarkable achievements of World War II, U.S. cryptanalysts had succeeded by the fall of 1940 in breaking all the Japanese diplomatic codes and ciphers. The Japanese believed these to be their most secure crypt systems and entrusted to them not only their diplomatic traffic but also their espionage communications.

It was called America's greatest intelligence feat. A joint congressional committee said it shortened World War II and saved thousands of American lives. It was also directly responsible for bringing about one of the greatest social upheavals in modern U.S. history, the uprooting of more than 112,000 people from their farms, homes, jobs, and businesses based solely on their ancestry. Yet, withal that, it is little known and even less understood. Its name is MAGIC and largely because of it President Roosevelt signed Executive Order 9066.

MAGIC was the cover name given in 1941 to the exploitation of the worldwide communications of the Japanese foreign ministry by U.S. Army and Navy radio intelligence units. It was so named by one of the directors of Naval Intelligence who thought such a bonanza could only have been conjured up by magicians.

MAGIC belongs to the most esoteric and prolific source of intelligence in the history of our nation. It is called communications intelligence or, in jargon, COMINT.

COMINT is the analysis and exploitation of an opponent's radio communications. This involves intercepting his messages from the airwaves or any other way you can get them, and then breaking his codes and ciphers through cryptanalysis in order to read the underlying plain text. ELINT, or electronic intelligence, is a related field and is concerned with electronic emissions such as those from radar. The two together are often grouped under the general term, signals intelligence, or SIGINT.

A code is the substitution of a group of letters or digits for a word, phrase, or whole thought. A cipher is the substitution of individual letters or a rearrangement of these letters according to a prearranged plan. Codes are usually manual. Complex ciphers are generally machine systems.

Even when a crypt system hasn't been broken and the text cannot be read, COMINT can be produced through analyzing "the externals" of intercepted messages. The study of call signs, message routing, volume, priorities, and frequency allocations is called traffic analysis, and in military communications can result in knowing your enemy's order of battle and location and movements of various units, particularly when combined with radio direction finding techniques which can pinpoint the location of a transmitter many hundreds of miles away.

Within the MAGIC complex there were fourteen separate crypt systems used by the Japanese foreign ministry. Of these the Japanese considered the *crème de la crème* to be a machine cipher which was used almost exclusively at embassy level. They called it *97-shiki O-bun In-ji-ki* which meant alphabetical typewriter, but in Japanese communications it was referred to simply as "the machine." The *97* was an abbreviation for the year 2597 of the Japanese calendar, corresponding to 1937 in the western calendar.

To encipher an outgoing message the communications clerk typed the plain text onto an electric typewriter, the signal went into "the machine," was automatically enciphered, and then typed out on a second typewriter in cipher form. The reverse procedure was followed for incoming messages. Each day a new set of identical keys was fed into all machines so that they would be in "sync" with each other.

The U.S. name for this crypt system and its accompanying machine was PURPLE. Traffic first appeared in this cipher in March 1939, replacing a predecessor system called RED which had been in existence since at least 1932. Decrypts of messages from the RED machine revealed that an expert named Okamoto was being sent from Tokyo to all major Japanese embassies for the express purpose of installing the new machine.

The PURPLE and RED systems were the two highest-grade systems within the MAGIC complex. RED was being gradually phased out but was still used by the Japanese, who committed the crucial error during this interim period of enciphering the same message in both the RED and PURPLE systems. Since the RED system was already exploitable, this gave U.S. cryptanalysts a wedge into PURPLE.

Next, in order of complexity were two hand systems: the first was termed *TSU* by the Japanese and called J-19 or the Consular Code by the U.S., the other was named *OITE* by the Japanese and PA-K2 by the Americans.

The ten remaining systems were little more than abbreviation codes to save transmission costs, specialized bank codes, and so on, all of little or no intelligence value.

Far and away the most important of all these crypt systems was PURPLE which was used at embassy level and J-19 employed at the consulate level. When Tokyo ordered its diplomatic posts in the Allied countries to destroy their high-grade codes and ciphers five days before the Pearl Harbor attack, these were the ones smashed and burned. Only the relatively simple PA-K2 was left for Japanese diplomatic posts to communicate with during the last few days before the war. One Japanese "machine" was to be retained in the Washington D.C. embassy just long enough to decipher the fourteen-part Japanese message breaking off relations with the U.S. which was supposed to have been delivered to Secretary of State Cordell Hull one-half hour before the attack on Pearl Harbor.

Tokyo told its ambassador in Washington that this message was so secret that the regular clerks and secretaries should not be allowed to prepare it. The harried diplomats took so long to get the message ready that it wasn't handed to Hull until fifty minutes after the attack on Pearl Harbor.

Meanwhile, U.S. cryptanalysts had already snatched the Japanese message from the airwaves, deciphered it on the PURPLE machine, and delivered it to Secretary Hull. When the Japanese diplomats were finally able to deliver their own message breaking off relations with the U.S. to Cordell Hull, he had to pretend that he was seeing it for the first time. Of course, he had already read it and had also been informed that the Japanese had attacked Pearl Harbor. Trembling with rage, it was all that Hull could do to restrain himself before the Japanese envoys.

This kind of intelligence was available to top-level U.S. government officials on a continuing basis because of the exploits of a legendary group of intelligence specialists.

Shortly after PURPLE made its appearance in 1939 a special team of cryptanalysts from the Army's Signal Intelligence Service (SIS) was organized to tackle the incredibly difficult task of solving the PURPLE system. The team was led by William F. Friedman who was generally acknowledged to be the world's greatest cryptanalyst. After eighteen months of exhausting mental labor the team broke the PURPLE system and created an analog machine which deciphered the Japanese messages.[1]

Without ever having seen the original Japanese apparatus, the American cryptanalysts built one whose maze of electronic circuitry did exactly the same thing as *97-shiki O-bun In-ji-ki*.[2]

But the sustained pressure on the team over so long a period took its toll. Friedman collapsed from exhaustion and emotional strain and had to be hospitalized for almost four months.

The Japanese considered the PURPLE system to be absolutely unbreakable. After the war those Japanese who were involved with "the machine" refused to believe that it had been broken by analytic means. They went to their graves believing someone had betrayed their system to the Americans.

Since RED, J-19, and PA-K2 had also been broken, the solution of PURPLE meant that all the messages in the worldwide communications network of the Japanese foreign ministry, called MAGIC, were now readable, and they remained so throughout the entire war. Of course, keys[3] had to be recovered, and there were adjustments in some of the systems, but we knew the underlying structure, and were able to maintain readability on all the MAGIC crypt systems with only occasional lapses.

Sandwiched among the diplomatic messages sent between the United States and Tokyo were hundreds of espionage messages. Foreign ministry communications were the conduit for sending espionage messages between agents in the United States and the Japanese organization primarily responsible for gathering intelligence on the U.S., the Third Bureau of the Naval General Staff, the Joho Kyoku, or Naval Intelligence. Analysis and reporting on the United States was accomplished by the Third Bureau's Fifth Section which was responsible for intelligence on the Western Hemisphere, and was by far the largest and most important section in the Third Bureau.

Normally, agents from the Third Bureau were naval officers who worked underground, often posing as language students, and who operated independently from the Japanese diplomatic posts in the country to which they

---

[1]   While William F. Friedman was in overall charge of the effort, it is generally recognized today that Frank B. Rowlett was the individual most responsible for breaking the PURPLE code and building the amazing machine which gave U.S. leaders access to Japan's most guarded secrets during the entire war.

[2]   See Frank B. Rowlett, *The Story of Magic* (Aegean Park Press, 1998) for a fascinating description of the effort that went into building the PURPLE analog machine.

[3]   The settings of the machine were changed daily to increase security of the system.

Courtesy: National Security Agency/National Cryptologic Museum

A photograph of the team that broke the PURPLE system and built the PURPLE analog machine. Left to right: Frank Bearce, Dr. Solomon Kullback, Capt. Harrod Miller, Louise Nelson, William Friedman, Dr. Abraham Sinkov, Lt. L.D. Jones, Frank Rowlett (absent: John Hurt).

Photo by Sam Allen

This machine on display at the National Cryptologic Museum at Ft. Meade, Maryland was built using off-the-shelf components. The telephone stepping switches and intricate wiring can be seen on top. It cost the U.S. government $684.65 to build and gave the United States access to Japan's highest-level diplomatic communications.

had been assigned. But within the United States, MAGIC messages indicated an almost complete fusion between the two organizations. Of course, the foreign ministry itself was no novice at intelligence and easily fit in with the overall plans for intelligence gathering. Diplomacy was the main occupation of the embassy, but the consulates' job was to work with the local Japanese population, thereby placing them in a particularly valuable position to implement Japan's espionage plans.

Intelligence derived from Japanese army and navy communications whose codes and ciphers were also broken during the war by U.S. cryptanalysts in a separate program, was given the code word ULTRA. This made for some awkwardness since the same code word was also used as the designator for all high-grade radio intelligence in Europe. To add to the confusion, toward the end of the war in the Pacific the terms MAGIC and ULTRA began to be used interchangeably. But both cover names continued to serve their main purpose which was to alert those cleared to receive it that the intelligence being reported came from the broken crypt systems of the enemy and was, therefore, of the highest possible validity, and that it was to be handled in special security channels.

Together, the twin accomplishments of MAGIC and ULTRA gave the United States an almost unbelievable advantage over the Japanese. They were responsible in large measure for some of America's most spectacular successes of the war in both the Pacific and in Europe.

During the 1944 presidential race, Thomas E. Dewey, Roosevelt's opponent, threatened to make the surprise attack on Pearl Harbor a campaign issue. Alarmed that this might somehow reveal our success against Japanese codes, General George Marshall, the Army Chief of Staff, on his own initiative and without the knowledge of the President, sent a hand-carried letter to Dewey. At Marshall's insistence Dewey had to agree before he opened the letter that he would never make any unauthorized disclosures of its contents. In the letter Marshall made his case:

> In brief the military dilemma is this: The most vital evidence in the
> Pearl Harbor matter consists of our intercepts of the Japanese
> diplomatic communications. Over a period of years our cryptograph
> people analyzed the character of the machine the Japanese were using
> for encoding their diplomatic messages. Based on this a corresponding
> machine was built by us which deciphers their messages. Therefore,
> we possessed a wealth of information regarding their moves in the
> Pacific....

Our main basis of information regarding Hitler's intentions in Europe is obtained from Baron Oshima's [the Japanese ambassador] messages from Berlin reporting his interviews with Hitler and other officials to the Japanese government. These are still in the codes involved in the Pearl Harbor events.

To explain further the critical nature of this set-up which would be wiped out in an instant if the least suspicion were aroused regarding it, the battle of Coral Sea was based on deciphered messages and therefore our few ships were in the right place at the right time. Further, we were able to concentrate our limited forces to meet their naval advance on Midway when otherwise we almost certainly would have been some 3,000 miles out of place. We had full information on the strength of their forces in that advance....

Operations in the Pacific are largely guided by the information we obtain of Japanese deployments. We know their strength in various garrisons, the rations and other stores continuing available to them, and what is of vast importance, we check their fleet movements and the movements of their convoys. The heavy losses reported from time to time which they sustain by reason of our submarine action, largely result from the fact that we know the sailing dates and routes of their convoys and can notify our submarines to lie in wait at the proper points. All operations in the Pacific are closely related in conception and timing to the information we secretly obtain through these intercepted codes.[4]

After reading Marshall's letter Dewey agreed to drop Pearl Harbor as a major campaign issue. And he was as good as his word.

What was the nature of this amazing World War II intelligence which "guided our actions in both the Pacific and in Europe," "shortened the war," "saved thousands of lives," and was "the finest intelligence in our history"? And how did the U.S. happen to be in this fortuitous position at this critical time? Was it just happenstance or was there more to it than that?

Indeed there was. Behind these intelligence successes in World War II were twenty-five years of colorful history, rivaling any spy novel. Codes and

---

4   See *Sources in Cryptologic History, Number 3, The Friedman Legacy: A Tribute to William and Elizebeth Friedman* (Center for Cryptologic History, National Security Agency, 1992) pages 232-236 for the full text of the letter.

ciphers have fascinated mankind since people first learned to communicate with each other, but during World War II the entire science of cryptology was developed and practiced on a scale theretofore beyond imagination. In spite of its mechanization, cryptanalysis has retained its aura of the mystique and the occult. Indeed, the areas where governments perform their cryptanalysis are still known as black chambers.

Once it got started, the U.S. took to COMINT with unmatched energy, skill, and imagination. From 1920 through 1945 the U.S. performed miraculously in COMINT, and the bulk of that effort was directed against Japan. Both the U.S. Army, and especially the U.S. Navy, considered Japan to be our most likely future enemy. As a result, the communications of Japan were relentlessly exploited by the U.S. No other nation was subjected to such exploitation, and the results changed history.

This country's official entry into the modern COMINT business began in 1917 during World War I with the formation of a newly created cryptologic section of the Military Intelligence Division known as MI-8. Its chief was Herbert O. Yardley. In a business known for its eccentric personalities he stood out. He was a combination genius and con-artist. In 1913, when twenty-four years old, he started to work in the State Department as a $17.50-a-week telegrapher, having learned the skill as a boy in his father's office at the local railroad station.

Fascinated by all the coded messages he saw flowing in and out of the State Department, he decided to study cryptanalysis. Searching everywhere for information, he managed to find several books on the subject at the Library of Congress and devoured them. For practice he worked on encoded State Department messages. To his amazement he was able to break into the codes. He caused near panic within the department by writing a hundred page memorandum titled, "The Solution of American Diplomatic Codes."

Shortly thereafter the United States entered World War I. Yardley talked his way into a commission as a lieutenant and was made chief of MI-8. With a staff of about 150 people, mostly clerks, mathematicians, and linguists, all hired and led by Yardley, and learning as they went, MI-8 enjoyed moderate success throughout the war, enough so that it was decided to maintain a peacetime cryptanalytic effort after the war ended.

Under deep cover, Yardley, now a major, and some of his key people moved to New York City in 1919. They operated out of a four-story brownstone house on East 38th just off 5th Avenue. Their cover story was that they compiled commercial codes. The operation was jointly funded by the State and War Departments. In 1919 the War Department was the predecessor of what was to become the Department of the Army, and there was no such position as the Secretary of Defense.

During the next ten years Yardley and his people broke the diplomatic codes of *forty* different countries, an incredible accomplishment. Included were such major powers as Brazil, China, England, France, Germany, Mexico, Spain, the Soviet Union, and Japan. As the messages of all these countries passed between their foreign ministries and their diplomatic posts in the U.S., they were intercepted from the airwaves or covertly obtained from the telegraph companies. Sometimes they were obtained by break-ins and bribery. When a particular crypt system was reading, Yardley's organization would decode the messages, translate them, and send them on to the Departments of War and State.

In 1921 and 1922 there was a major disarmament conference in Washington D.C. The great naval powers of the world consented to limit the size of their navies according to an agreed upon ratio. There also were to be limitations on the types of ships and their armament. Additionally, there was to be an agreement on which of the many islands in the Pacific formerly owned by Germany and now mandated to Japan could be fortified. Japan wanted no part of such a conference but was forced by world opinion to participate. During the conference the Japanese delegation was closely controlled by the home government. Tokyo sent coded messages to its delegation telling them exactly what they were to try and achieve and what their absolute minimum position would be.

Yardley, who had personally broken the Japanese code, decoded hundreds of intercepted Japanese messages, had them translated, and passed them along to the American delegation. As he later said, "stud poker is not a very difficult game to play after you've seen your opponents hole card." Needless to say, Japan's minimum position is exactly what she got. Thereafter, the ratio for naval tonnage allowed Great Britain, the United States, and Japan was set at 5-5-3 in that order.

In 1928 Herbert Hoover was elected president. His Secretary of State was Henry L. Stimson. In the course of events Stimson was briefed on Yardley's organization, and he was outraged. He could not believe that the U.S. would stoop to such underhanded activities. His view was summed up in the famous remark later attributed to him, "Gentlemen do not read each other's mail." He then abruptly withdrew State Department's support of Yardley's operation. (This is the same Henry L. Stimson who, in 1942 as President Roosevelt's Secretary of War, was instrumental in removing 112,000 people of Japanese ancestry from the West Coast of the U.S. based almost entirely on reading intercepted Japanese messages transmitted during 1941.) Without the cooperation of the State Department, the War Department was forced to terminate Yardley's entire program in 1929.

Furious at having his operation shut down, Yardley retaliated by writing the most famous book in the history of cryptology. There had never been anything like it. *The American Black Chamber* created a sensation when it appeared in 1931. He told everything. The State Department, of course, promptly disavowed any knowledge of Yardley's activities, and indignantly denied that it had read Japanese messages during the Washington Arms Conference of 1921-22. State's protest of innocence was somewhat difficult to maintain since Yardley included in his book copies of the actual messages.

Written in a popular style, the book sold extremely well in the U.S. but twice as many copies were bought in Japan. In less than one month alone 30,000 translations of the book were sold. Major newspapers in Osaka and Tokyo serialized the book, and 138 copies were sent out to Japanese embassies and legations around the world as required reading. There was a cabinet crisis, and several suicides. Newspaper headlines blazed, "Treachery at the Washington Conference." It was, altogether, a humiliating experience for Japan, but only a taste of what was to come.

Yardley wasn't finished. He put together another book titled, *Japanese Diplomatic Secrets*. By this time, however, the U.S. government was ready. Congress passed a new law making it a crime to divulge any non-authorized information on cryptology. The government seized Yardley's manuscript, and prospective publishers were warned away. Interestingly, the government lawyer involved in all this was a young district attorney named Thomas E. Dewey whose next encounter with COMINT was a startling letter from General Marshall in 1944.

Yardley next proceeded to write several spy novels with cryptanalysis as a background. One of them was made into a movie called "Rendezvous" starring William Powell and Rosalind Russell, both of whom became good friends with Yardley.

His next move was from Hollywood to China as a special employee of Chiang Kai-shek, hired for the sole purpose of training Chinese cryptanalysts to break into Japanese military codes and ciphers. Although he was under deep cover, the Japanese learned of his presence and tightened up their communications security; but to no avail. Yardley and his Chinese trainees broke into some nineteen Japanese army systems, relatively low-grade systems, but still quite an accomplishment. Ever one to make a buck, he later sold these solutions to the U.S. for a reported $10,000.

Yardley next appeared in Canada working on agent systems for the Canadian government. Henry Stimson, now Secretary of War under Roosevelt, notified Canada in no uncertain terms that they could expect no intelligence cooperation from the U.S. so long as Yardley was on their payroll.

The U.S. had just broken into the PURPLE system and there was no way that it was going to risk that knowledge with Yardley. Reluctantly, Canada fired him.

This ended Yardley's career in cryptanalysis and he turned to his second love, poker. His book, *The Education of a Poker Player*, remains a classic. So far there have been fourteen printings and it has sold well over 100,000 copies.

Yardley died in 1958 and was buried in Arlington Cemetery with full military honors. Thus passed one of the most colorful personalities in U.S. history.

While all this hubbub was going on among the Army, State, and Yardley, the Navy, keeping a low profile, was quietly building its own COMINT capabilities against Japan. In the U.S. Navy COMINT was the responsibility of an organization with the intriguing title OP-20-G, which was located within the Office of Naval Communications.

The Navy entered the field in the early twenties by the most direct route of all, surreptitiously breaking into the Japanese consulate in New York City and photographing all the code material. With this running start the U.S. Navy's COMINT efforts prospered. By 1926 it had broken the main Japanese navy crypt system, called the Flag Officers' Code. From time to time over the next fourteen years the Japanese navy changed the code, but its principles were known, and each time the U.S. Navy managed to solve the new system without too much difficulty.

This happy situation prevailed all during the 1930s. Every three years the Japanese held massive naval maneuvers to test out their tactics and equipment. From intercept sites in China and aboard U.S. naval ships OP-20-G managed to intercept most of the Japanese fleet's message traffic while it was on maneuvers. Based on this data the U.S. Navy was able to develop details on the design, speed, armament, and capabilities of Japanese warships. Having this information enabled the U.S. to keep one step ahead of the Japanese by modifying the design of its own ships, and adjusting its tactics to counter those of the Japanese.

All this came to a crashing halt in late 1940 when the Japanese navy, preparing for war, introduced a new operational crypt system of extreme complexity. It was given the designator, JN-25. OP-20-G worked feverishly on it throughout 1941 and just when they were beginning to achieve some success, the Japanese, a few days before Pearl Harbor, changed JN-25 along with their entire call sign system.

To add to OP-20-G's problems, the bread and butter Japanese Flag Officers' Code was changed during 1940 and was never read again, the only major Japanese crypt system the U.S. failed to break. Fortunately, the Flag Officers' Code had been made so difficult to use that the Japanese themselves gave it up in 1942.

Thus, all the major Japanese naval crypt systems were basically unreadable for the year preceding Pearl Harbor.

It took the U.S. Army cryptanalytic effort until the mid 1930s to recover from the Yardley fiasco. In the interim, William F. Friedman and his high-powered group which had been working with considerable success in developing ciphers and codes to protect U.S. communications, slowly began easing Signal Intelligence Service (SIS) back into the cryptanalysis business, but it only worked diplomatic traffic. Because of a lack of accessibility there simply were no intercepted Japanese army communications available to them, so SIS had to be content for the time being to concentrate on intercepted diplomatic messages.

To recap where America stood insofar as COMINT was concerned on the eve of the Pacific War: The U.S. Navy had had great success with Japanese naval codes and ciphers from the mid-1920s up until late 1940, but was practically shut out on all major systems during 1941. The U.S. Army had expended little or no effort on Japanese army crypt systems for a number of years preceding the Japanese attack on Pearl Harbor.

But there was a big ace in the hole—MAGIC—and it supplied practically all of the U.S. intelligence we had on Japan during 1941.

MAGIC was the most reliable of several sources which indicated that war was imminent. Japanese diplomatic messages prior to Pearl Harbor, especially during late November and the first week in December, made it abundantly clear that Japan had abandoned hope for a diplomatic settlement and was preparing for war with the U.S. Those Japanese who were to run the carefully constructed espionage nets in the U.S. from Latin America were ordered in early December to leave for their posts in Mexico and South America. A final deadline was given to the Japanese ambassador for negotiations with the U.S. because after November 29, 1941 "things are automatically going to happen." There were numerous hints of momentous events about to unfold, and everyone was "to prepare for the worst."

Arrangements for ships to evacuate Japanese nationals from the U.S. were underway. A series of special newscast code phrases on the weather were devised by Tokyo which were intended to let its diplomats and agents know when relations with the U.S., Great Britain, or the Soviet Union were broken. Tokyo informed its ambassador in Berlin on November 30, 1941 that further negotiations with the U.S. were pointless and to notify Hitler and Ribbentrop that war would break out with the Anglo-Saxons "far quicker than anyone dreams." When all this and more was added to such classic war indicators as out-of-schedule call sign and crypt system changes accompanied by instructions to destroy cryptologic data and to burn all classified documents, it could mean only one thing: war.

And MAGIC was so interpreted by the highest authorities in Washington. Instructions were given to field commanders warning them that war with Japan could happen momentarily, that an aggressive move by Japan in any direction was a possibility, and that Washington desired that the first hostile action be taken by the Japanese. American diplomatic posts in areas likely to be overrun by the Japanese were ordered to destroy their crypto materials.

MAGIC and Pearl Harbor are inseparable. One cannot be studied without the other. Moreover, any history or study of what happened at Pearl Harbor written prior to 1977, by which time all of the important MAGIC was declassified, is probably obsolete.

Although this is not a book about Pearl Harbor, it is impossible to discuss Japanese spying in 1941 without some mention of the espionage messages sent between Honolulu and Tokyo. Accordingly, these messages are included in Part II.

In 1946 a joint congressional committee completed a ten-month, painstaking investigation of what happened at Pearl Harbor. It is perhaps the finest study of its kind ever made. On page 253 of the committee's final report is the following statement: "The committee has been intrigued throughout the Pearl Harbor proceedings by one enigmatical and paramount question: Why, with some of the finest intelligence available in our history, with the almost certain knowledge that war was at hand, with plans that contemplated the precise type of attack that was executed by Japan on the morning of December 7th, why was it possible for a Pearl Harbor to occur?"[5]

There will never be a completely satisfactory answer to this question, but after reading the MAGIC messages associated with the Pearl Harbor attack, the author guarantees the reader will have new perceptions and yes, new questions to ponder on this endlessly fascinating subject.

It is also true that no study of Executive Order 9066 and the evacuation of people of Japanese ancestry from the West Coast can be made without examining MAGIC intelligence in detail and without a full understanding of the nature and handling of MAGIC.

It was because of MAGIC that the U.S. government decided in early 1942 to evacuate all persons of Japanese ancestry from the West Coast of the United States. In January 1941, as revealed in MAGIC communications, the Japanese embassy and all eight of its consulates in the U.S. were ordered to begin establishing espionage nets designed in such a fashion as to be able to function in a

---

5   Congress, Joint Committee on the Investigation of the Pearl Harbor Attack, *Pearl Harbor Attack: Hearings Before the Joint Committee on the Investigation of the Pearl Harbor Attack*, 79th Congress, 1st. Sess., November 15, 1945-May 23, 1946, 23 vols. (Washington D.C.: GPO, 1946).

wartime environment. Detailed intelligence requirements were promulgated, and all diplomatic posts were directed to recruit agents, including first and second-generation Japanese. Success in their efforts was transmitted back to Tokyo in May 1941 by West Coast consulates stating that there were now reliable Japanese in airplane factories and in the U.S. armed forces who would gather information, and that other local Japanese residents were keeping watch on military posts and bases, and that shipyards, airfields, and ports were under observation.

During the latter half of 1941 hundreds of messages containing ship and aircraft movements, armed forces data, airplane and arms production on their way to Tokyo sent in the MAGIC crypt systems were intercepted by the U.S. These messages revealed that the Japanese government had succeeded in establishing subversive nets all along the West Coast, subservient to Japan, manned by local first and second-generation Japanese residents, and organized to operate after war broke out between Japan and the United States. MAGIC corroborated similar information obtained by other components of the U.S. intelligence community using traditional intelligence collection methods.

The Joint Congressional Committee in its investigation of the Japanese attack on Pearl Harbor, looking beyond Hawaii, made the following observations about MAGIC:

> With extraordinary skill and watchfulness the intelligence services of the Army Signal Corps and the Navy Office of Communications broke Japanese codes and intercepted messages between the Japanese Government and its spies and agents in all parts of the world and supplied the high authorities in Washington with reliable secret information respecting Japanese designs, decisions and operations at home, in the United States, and in other countries.

and through MAGIC:

> ...Washington authorities learned that Japanese spies and agents, directed by the Japanese Government were collecting and transmitting to Tokyo an immense amount of exact and detailed information respecting military and naval installations....

As incredible as COMINT had shown itself to be during peace, it was to reach even higher pinnacles during the Pacific Conflict.

Just prior to the Battle of the Coral Sea in May 1942, Navy cryptanalysts were able to regain partial readability of the main Japanese navy operational code, JN-25. Fortunately, enough of the code was readable to smoke out Japanese plans to seize Port Moresby. Based on COMINT, Admiral Nimitz alerted Task Force 17 which was able, at the last possible moment, to stop the Japanese drive. Although considered a draw by most historians, the Battle of the Coral Sea marked the first time the Japanese juggernaut had been halted.

One month later, in time for the Battle of Midway, in early June 1942, the U.S. Navy was able to read about 90 percent of the JN-25 messages.[6] It was from this COMINT that Admiral Nimitz knew Admiral Yamamoto's overall plan and most of the important details about his huge fleet bearing down on Midway. The Battle of Midway, the turning point of the Pacific War, was an out and out intelligence victory. As General Marshall said in his letter to Thomas Dewey, without COMINT the U.S. Fleet would have been some 3,000 miles out of place.

As the war went on COMINT kept pouring forth. OP-20-G became so efficient at breaking Japanese ship location and ship movement codes that U.S. submarine captains began to complain if the Japanese convoys didn't appear in their periscopes exactly when scheduled. All submarine skippers were required to sign an oath never to reveal the ULTRA secret as long as they lived. When an ULTRA was received—identified by the first word in the dispatch— the decoding officer was required to stop and call the captain. Only he was allowed to read an ULTRA message.

During World War II OP-20-G cracked approximately seventy-five Japanese naval crypt systems. Admiral Nimitz once estimated that the resulting COMINT was worth an entire extra fleet to him, perhaps too conservative a judgment.

In April 1943 one of the most dramatic incidents of the war occurred, the shoot down of Admiral Yamamoto, Japan's greatest hero and the commander of the Combined Fleet. He was making an inspection of Japanese bases in the Southwest Pacific and his aides sent out a message giving his precise itinerary, times, mode of transportation, everything, all in the JN-25 code. There was the

---

6   The JN-25 code was broken on March 13, 1942. However, on May 27, 1942, about a week before the Battle of Midway, a new cipher system (Baker 9) was introduced by the Japanese and temporarily made the code unreadable. This forced the Navy to depend on traffic analysis and direction finding for last minute intelligence on Japanese operations. For a detailed account of COMINT in this period of U.S. Navy history see Frederick D. Parker, *A Priceless Advantage: U.S. Navy Communications Intelligence and the Battles of Coral Sea, Midway and the Aleutians*, United States Cryptologic History, Series IV, World War II, Vol. 5 (National Security Agency, 1993).

risk that if he was shot down the Japanese might deduce that the U.S. was reading their code, but it was too big a prize to let go. A story was concocted that coast watchers had obtained the flight data, and sixteen P-38s flew almost 400 miles to make a precise intercept over Bougainville Island. Yamamoto's plane and another Betty bomber were shot down. Thus, because of COMINT, the planner of Pearl Harbor first lost his country's greatest naval battle at Midway, and then lost his own life.[7]

Surprisingly, it was in Europe that MAGIC scored some of its biggest intelligence coups. The Japanese ambassador in Berlin was Hiroshi Oshima, a lieutenant general in the Imperial army and a baron in the Japanese nobility. He spoke German fluently and was the pet of Adolph Hitler and the darling of the German general staff. They told him everything. He was invited to field tests of all the major new weapons of the Third Reich where he was given specifications and production data. Hitler told him his plans for submarine warfare, for defending Italy, and for the buzz bombing of England.

A few months before the Allies landed on the beaches of Normandy, Oshima and his staff were given an inspection tour of the defenses of northern France. Oshima transmitted back to Tokyo meticulous details on the number and types of artillery, siting of machine guns, methods for emplacing anti-tank guns, and the varying depths of defense zones at strategic points. Included were the command structure and the disposition of German forces all along the coast. Hitler himself briefed Oshima on his planned tactics to counter the Allied invasion. Oshima faithfully reported all he had learned to Tokyo using the PURPLE system. As soon as these messages were intercepted they were decrypted, translated, and forwarded straight to Eisenhower, Churchill and Roosevelt. They were so valuable to Allied invasion planning that General Eisenhower later asked to meet the people in the Army's Signal Intelligence Service who had produced this intelligence so that he could personally thank them for their accomplishments.

Oshima was an inexhaustible source of information, transmitting back to Tokyo almost every significant bit of information in the Third Reich right up until Germany surrendered. All of his messages were enciphered in the PURPLE system and all were routinely intercepted and read by the U.S. General Marshall referenced this when he told Thomas E. Dewey in 1944 that our best source of information on Hitler's intentions came from Japanese messages.

When the war was over Oshima was tried as a war criminal and given a life sentence. He was paroled in 1955 and granted clemency in 1958. For his

---

7   See Carroll V. Glines, *Attack on Yamamoto* (Orion Books, 1990) for an excellent account of the Yamamoto shoot down including the intelligence background.

contribution to winning the war in Europe we probably should have given him a medal.

Japanese army communications became readable in 1943 when we began to intercept large volumes of its traffic, and remained so until the end of the war. Just as COMINT had helped the U.S. Navy in the great sea battles, so it was with the land battles against the Japanese army. In Brisbane, Australia, Signal Intelligence Service established a forward COMINT processing unit specifically designed to support General MacArthur. It moved with MacArthur's headquarters and accompanied him on his advance to Hollandia, New Guinea, and then to Leyte in the Philippines. Known as the Central Bureau, the unit grew to an astonishing 4,000 men throughout the Southwest Pacific area by the end of the war. A report prepared for the Military Intelligence Service in Washington D.C. stated that the Central Bureau provided MacArthur with "precise information as to the location, composition and activities of Japanese forces, both in front line positions and in rear areas." The reports also include information about the arrival of rein-forcements, casualties, and statements as to U.S. activities, dispositions and intentions, as well as of Japanese intentions. It was this kind of intelligence which led to a remark first attributed to his G-2 and then to MacArthur that, "Never in military history did an army know so much about an enemy prior to actual engagement."[8]

Near the end of the war Japanese messages described in detail the suicidal defense measures being prepared and what U.S. troops would have to face if they invaded the main Japanese islands. Fuel and aircraft were being con-served for kamikaze missions. A July 1945 message stated, "Air strategy is to be based on total suicide air attacks." The most experienced pilots were to use old biplanes whose wood and fabric frames made them more difficult to pick up on radar. Fighter planes, dive bombers, and torpedo planes were being

---

[8]   In addition to the success derived from the herculean efforts of the cryptologic units in the Pacific luck sometimes played an important role. In January 1944 thanks to an alert engineer of the Australian 9th Division who was sweeping for mines, the entire cryptologic library of the Japanese 20th Division was found in a steel box buried near a stream bed. Individual pages of the sodden and moldy mass were carefully dried out in commercial cooking ovens. From the time of the recovery till the end of the war about 2,000 Japanese army messages were recovered, decrypted and processed each day. One of the first was a message from a Japanese lieutenant reporting that the 20th Division codes had been destroyed, thus possibly securing his place in history as the individual making the greatest single contribution to Allied victory in the Pacific. For a more detailed discussion of Central Bureau operations see *The Quiet Heroes of the Southwest Pacific Theater: An Oral History of the Men sand Women of CBB and FRUMEL,* Sharon A. Manekied. United States Crytologic History, Series IV, Vol. 7 (National Security Agency, 1996).

converted to kamikaze aircraft. Less than a month before the first atomic bomb was dropped a message to all Japanese field commanders told them to emphasize suicide attacks. Eight hundred Japanese demolition frogmen utilizing a new type of diving suit were organized and ready to blow themselves up on the bottom of ships. Forty squadrons of suicide crash boats were ready to attack. Two-man submarine crews were being trained to blow themselves up beneath U.S. ships. One thousand men were trained and ready to ride on top and steer surface launched torpedoes into Allied ships. Fourteen special landing forces of 1,000 men each were activated whose mission was to strap explosives to their bodies and hurl themselves against U.S. tanks.

All this intelligence was, of course, available to President Truman and surely must have influenced his decision to drop the atomic bomb. If there had been an invasion, a blood bath of indescribable dimensions for both Japanese and Americans would have taken place.

After the atomic bombs were dropped Japanese messages related the devastating effects of these bombs and the utter sense of frustration by the Japanese high command. There were frantic queries about the status of Japan's own atomic bomb project, and discussions on defense measures to be taken against future atomic bomb attacks.

Finally and fittingly, just as MAGIC had disclosed Japan's war intentions in 1941, it revealed in August 1945 Japan's desperate attempts to negotiate peace. MAGIC provided the first hard intelligence that the Japanese were ready to surrender when instructions to the Japanese ambassador in Moscow disclosed that terms about to be proposed by Japan were tantamount to unconditional surrender; the only caveat was that the integrity of the Imperial household be maintained. Thus ended twenty-five years of continuous U.S. communications intelligence against Japan, much of which helped shape the history of the world during that period.[9]

---

[9] For a short period after the war the U.S. intercepted Japanese foreign office traffic in PURPLE code. A foreign service circular on September 13, 1945 to Stockholm, Lisbon and Bern, for example, said in part, "Since the Americans have recently been raising an uproar about the question of our mistreatment of prisoners, I think we should make every effort to exploit the atomic bomb question in our propaganda...." This strategem, in one form or another, continues to this day.

CHAPTER 3

Magic Operations and Declassification Operations

Traditionally, the COMINT operations of the U.S. Army and Navy have not been performed within the Army G-2 or the Office of Naval Intelligence as one would suppose. To be sure there is a close relationship, but separate commands are involved. To further confuse the uninitiated, operational and technical control (interception, processing, and distribution) of COMINT does not always follow command lines. This has come about because successful COMINT requires central direction from a highly technical base to coordinate multiple efforts, provide technical backup, and to maintain extensive file data. Fragmented COMINT doesn't work. It is essential that forward cryptanalytic units and intercept sites be nourished continuously with technical support and guidance. Part of that overall control is to insure that both national level customers and field commanders are supported with appropriate COMINT on a timely basis. Unfortunately, that didn't always happen in pre-World War II days. Distribution of intelligence in 1941 was badly mismanaged and may have cost us dearly in lives and ships on the morning of December 7, 1941.

During World War II the Navy's OP-20-G conducted its COMINT operations within the Office of Naval Communications. The Army's COMINT activities were the responsibility of Signal Intelligence Service which was organizationally located in the Signal Corps.

Step number one in any COMINT operation is to obtain copies of the target country's communications. For OP-20-G this presented no great problem insofar as Japanese navy communications were concerned since they were almost entirely manual Morse and transmitted in the high frequency range. As long as the intercept site was in the right location, and the signal had enough power behind it, these messages could easily be plucked from the airwaves.

Japanese army traffic was more difficult to collect because of the low powered transmitters used. When American and Japanese army forces began to have contact with each other on a large scale the collection picture changed, and Signal Intelligence Service was able to obtain enough message volume to perform successful cryptanalysis on Japanese army communications. But this did not happen until 1943.

MAGIC presented a different kind of intercept problem. Diplomats had to communicate with their foreign ministry in the home country, but in practically every country in the world they were forbidden to have their own communications facilities within the host country. Consequently, correspondence with the home office had to be through diplomatic couriers who simply carried the correspondence back and forth, a very time consuming process, or through international mail facilities which were both slow and untrustworthy, or, best of all, by using the facilities of private international commercial telegraph companies. In the U.S. this meant such companies as RCA Global and Western Union International.

When the Japanese diplomats in the U.S. wished to send a message to Tokyo using the telegraph companies, first they had to have it encoded or enciphered within the confines of the embassy or the consulate using Roman letters. Then they hand-carried it to the cable company, paid the discounted diplomatic rate, and out the message went. When it arrived in Tokyo the cable company office there delivered it to the foreign ministry which sorted out its own messages based on serial numbers and then forwarded on those messages intended for the Third Bureau (Naval Intelligence). The opposite procedure was followed for telegrams going the other direction.[1]

This procedure worked very well for most foreign governments' important communications where timeliness was a factor. It was fast, relatively inexpensive, and reasonably secure if your crypt systems were good. This kind of communication did, however, pose a problem for the COMINT people. The cable companies were given that name because a large share of the telegrams they forwarded went at least part of the way via undersea cables, and in those days could not be intercepted while they were in that mode. Almost every country in the world solved that sticky intercept problem by requiring the cable companies to turn over to the host government a copy of all messages sent or received by a foreign government.

---

[1]   The background of this book's cover is a reproduction of one such message.

In the United States this was against the law. Section 605 of the Federal Communications Act of 1934 made it a crime for any cable company to give a copy of one of its customer's messages to anyone, including the U.S. government, even if that customer happened to be a foreign power with whom America was about to go to war. All the cable companies were well-versed in this law, and under normal conditions scrupulously followed the law. It was also technically illegal for the U.S. to intercept the cable company's messages off the airwaves if either end of the transmission was located in the U.S. or one of its possessions. The powers in Washington, however, particularly General George C. Marshall, considered that to be a legal nicety overridden by national defense needs.

Fortunately, international commercial messages traveling between the United States and Japan did not always go by cable. Many of them were simply sent through the ether via high frequency Morse code or printer, and could be easily copied by anybody. For those messages that did travel over cables, U.S. intercept operators were clever enough to get most of them when they were retransmitted between the cable heads and the receiving station. Of 227 messages pertaining to Japanese-American negotiations sent between Tokyo and Washington from March to December 1941, all but four were intercepted by the United States.

To intercept MAGIC and other communications Signal Intelligence Service and OP-20-G controlled sixteen major listening sites located in the Philippines, Guam, Hawaii, the Canal Zone, and the West and East Coasts of the continental U.S.

All intercepted MAGIC traffic had to be forwarded to Washington D.C. for processing. Time delays in moving the messages from most of the intercept sites back to Washington were a continuing headache. In some cases intercepted traffic was simply forwarded by mail which sometimes arrived in Washington as much as several weeks after it had initially been copied. Although registered mail was approved for classified information, this presented ONI with a problem when it was discovered that out of a total of 198 postal employees in Hawaii, fifty-one of them had dual American-Japanese citizenship and the foreman in the registry section was a Japanese alien. As a result of this discovery, registered mail for the fleet stationed in Hawaiian waters was routed directly to the Pearl Harbor Navy Yard as a security measure.

Other traffic was enciphered in U.S. crypt systems and radioed back to Washington. This presented a potential security problem because if the Japanese intercept service was to deduce that the U.S. was collecting and forwarding their foreign ministry traffic, they might also reason that it was having some cryptanalytic success against these particular communications.

Secure teletype was being installed at a few of the intercept sites, but as of December 7, 1941 only the Navy site at Bainbridge Island in Puget Sound and the Army's site in San Francisco actually had it in place.

Although too late to help in collecting the flow of pre-war MAGIC between the U.S. and Japan, the intercept problem for other diplomatic traffic sent via international commercial circuits was neatly solved during the war when all such traffic was screened by military censors located at the cable companies as part of the wartime censorship program. Under this program a copy of all the messages of foreign intelligence targets was turned over to U.S. military intelligence.

MAGIC was exploited in Washington because of the mind-set that it was solely diplomatic and because of perceived operational and security hazards in decentralizing it to the field. The one exception to this was the Navy unit located at Cavite in the Philippines. Cover named CAST, this unit copied the high priority Tokyo-Berlin and Tokyo-Moscow circuits. The original idea was to send a PURPLE machine to them so that they could separate the wheat from the chaff, thus cutting down the amount of intercept forwarded to Washington and thereby lessening the risk that the Japanese might be tipped off about U.S. interest in their foreign ministry traffic. As it turned out all the messages were important. There was little or no chaff to be winnowed out. From its analytic center in Washington D.C. OP-20-G supplied CAST with the daily changing PURPLE keys on an especially secure Navy circuit called COPEK.

Direct MAGIC intelligence support to General MacArthur and Admiral Hart, Commander of the Asiatic Fleet, was only a secondary reason for sending a PURPLE machine to CAST. Surprisingly, MAGIC apparently didn't make much of an impression on either of these two gentlemen during 1941. When questioned after the war, MacArthur seemed to be a little vague about MAGIC, but was lavish in his praise for ULTRA.

MAGIC was deemed to be diplomatic because it was passed in the crypt systems of the Japanese foreign ministry and transmitted between diplomatic posts. Thus, the reasoning went, it was diplomatic and that kind of intelligence was to support the State Department and other high level officials in Washington. Only they could fathom what the wily Japanese striped-pants representatives were talking about and only they could determine the significance of diplomatic intelligence and take appropriate actions. It certainly wouldn't do, according to them, to have every overseas military command running about with its own interpretation of what the diplomatic situation was.

Historically, the State Department has always frowned on any kind of direct delivery of diplomatic COMINT to the military even though it was the military which produced the intelligence in the first place. If the military commands needed to know information like this, the State Department would tell them. What no one seemed to grasp in 1941 was that a very large part of MAGIC was not diplomatic. A good share of it was espionage intelligence involving U.S. military forces, movements, installations and activities and, therefore, primarily of interest to the military commands wherein these subversive acts were taking place.

Later in the war COMINT distribution was handled far better, and when Ambassador Oshima transmitted military data back to Tokyo on the defenses of Normandy and new German weapons in the PURPLE system, this MAGIC intelligence went directly to General Eisenhower. The same kind of MAGIC support to military commanders also came to be true in the Pacific, even though MAGIC continued to be processed in Washington throughout the entire war. Given the nature of MAGIC this was probably the best way to handle it from a purely technical standpoint, provided the field commands were kept informed of MAGIC intelligence on matters within the scope of their responsibilities.

Signal Intelligence Service and OP-20-G had their headquarters and processing units in government buildings in Washington at the start of the war, but both were relocated along with their operations to former girls schools: OP-20-G to a Nebraska Avenue site in Washington D.C., and Signal Intelligence Service to Arlington Hall just across the Potomac in northern Virginia.

For the first six months of the war OP-20-G not only worked with Signal Intelligence Service in processing MAGIC, but also worked closely with its cryptanalytic groups at Pearl Harbor and Cavite on Japanese naval systems.

Signal Intelligence Service had field collection sites but its cryptanalytic efforts against Japanese systems during 1941 were located only in Washington D.C., and concerned exclusively with MAGIC. This wasn't by choice. SIS would have preferred to work on Japanese army systems in addition to MAGIC, but it was impossible to intercept enough Japanese army messages even to identify the types of systems being used. The nearest intercept site SIS had in 1941 was in the Philippines and that was too far away to intercept the low-powered Japanese army transmitters then in use. But all that changed in 1943 when U.S. troops began large-scale operations against Japanese forces in the Southwest Pacific. With plenty of traffic to work with SIS commenced full scale analysis and exploitation of Japanese army crypt systems.

By 1943 the entire worldwide U.S. COMINT effort was in full swing. At the beginning of the war there were about 1,500 people collecting, analyzing, and reporting on COMINT. By the end of the war there were almost 20,000. Of course, not all of these people were exploiting Japanese communications. OP-20-G and SIS, in close collaboration with the British, also worked on the communications of Germany and its European allies, and both organizations had responsibilities to develop and maintain secure U.S. crypt systems.

Almost everybody had to be trained in accelerated programs because there were no cryptanalysts or traffic analysts in civilian life, and precious few Japanese linguists who could be cleared for top secret COMINT. To cope with the situation hundreds of especially selected students with high aptitude were trained in intensive courses during the war, and while the graduates of these crash programs were able to handle the job, there was always a shortage of really first-rate, experienced analysts and Japanese linguists.

In the language area there was, however, an untapped reservoir, the Nisei. In late 1943 a number of them who had had special training in the Japanese language began arriving in the Pacific area. They had been largely recruited right out of the relocation centers. It was the Navy's and the Marines' policy not to use them in their operations, but the Army assigned them to its Military Intelligence Service where they performed a number of valuable functions such as translating captured diaries and documents, interrogating prisoners of war, and translating low-level, plain-text voice intercepts. Because of security considerations, no one of Japanese ancestry was ever allowed in MAGIC or ULTRA operations. As a result, the Nisei were never permitted to work in any of the intelligence centers where they might be exposed to MAGIC or ULTRA or learn of its existence.[2] This severely limited their usefulness. Nonetheless, they did ease the translation burden considerably by allowing fully cleared translators to concentrate on highly classified intelligence.

In Washington there was plenty of work for everyone. MAGIC messages rolled in at a rate of 50 to 75 a day but got as high as 130. With an amazing lack of interservice rivalry, OP-20-G worked Japanese messages transmitted on odd days and SIS did so on even days. Since there were usually more messages than could be processed, priorities had to be established. In general, PURPLE messages, particularly those between Washington D.C. and Tokyo, were decrypted and translated first, followed by the Consular Code, J-19, and then the relatively simple PA-K2. This was based on the usually correct theory that high-grade intelligence is most likely to be sent in high-grade crypt systems. To some extent this was tempered by giving certain links high priority no

---

[2]   There seems to have been at least one exception to this general rule. Clarence Yamagata, a Hawaiian Nisei, served as a linguist with Central Bureau. He was particularly helpful explaining formal Japanese usage since he was fluent in spoken and written Japanese. Yamagata was highly regarded by those who served with him and the unclassified history of Central Bureau, *Signal Intelligence Service Record*, written in 1945, was dedicated to him. A photograph of Yamagata with twenty other linguists can be found on page 54 of *The Quiet Heroes of the Southwest Pacific Theater*.

matter what crypt systems were used. In addition to decrypting and decoding, a constant cryptanalytic effort had to be maintained in order to recover daily changing keys and periodic changes in the crypt systems. There were never enough COMINT cleared translators, and the pressures on everyone were intense. PURPLE traffic was usually decrypted the same day it arrived by simply running it through the analog machine. J-19 took longer because it was a manual operation, the keys changed every day, and sometimes, if there was not enough volume, key recoveries were extremely difficult to achieve.

To process PURPLE, eight analog machines were constructed at the Naval Gun Factory in Washington D.C. at a cost of $684.65 each, possibly the best buy the government ever made. OP-20-G and SIS in Washington had two each. One was at Cavite. Two were sent to the British. The eighth one was originally intended for the Navy cryptanalytic group at Pearl Harbor, but it also ended up with the British. Even if a PURPLE machine had been sent to Pearl Harbor it wouldn't have helped to read those critical messages passing between the Japanese consulate in Honolulu and Tokyo during the critical few days prior to the Pearl Harbor attack because the Japanese consulate in Honolulu didn't have "the machine." It used J-19 and PA-K2 which the Navy unit at Pearl Harbor could easily have read if it had been given that mission. If it had, the entire course of the war might well have been changed.

As one might expect, the intelligence contained in MAGIC was so important and so fragile that the entire operation was shrouded in secrecy rivaled only by that accorded to the development of the atomic bomb. Initially, full knowledge of MAGIC was restricted to the Secretary of War, the Army Chief of Staff, the Chief of Army War Plans, the Army Director of Military Intelligence, the Secretary of the Navy, the Chief of Naval Operations, the Chief of the Navy's War Plans Division, the Director of Naval Intelligence, the Secretary of State, and the President of the United States, the most elite power group of that time.

Working closely with SIS and OP-20-G, Colonel Rufus F. Bratten, Chief of the Army's Far Eastern Section in its Military Intelligence Division, and Lieutenant Commander Alwin D. Kramer of ONI's Far Eastern Section selected the messages to be hand-carried by them to the select group of high-level recipients in Washington D.C. MAGIC was put in special pouches and hand-carried to those who had been "anointed." While Lieutenant Commander Kramer or Colonel Bratten stood by, the chosen few unlocked the pouch with a special key, read the MAGIC material, put it back in the pouch, and then locked it up again. MAGIC was never mentioned over the phone. Special care was taken to guard against leaving any notes or memos concerning MAGIC where any unauthorized person might see them.

An average of twenty-five messages each day were selected for distribution. The important espionage messages were included in the folder along with the diplomatic messages.

The President received his MAGIC information in a variety of ways during 1941. At first, selected messages were placed in his folder. Then, as volume grew, gists were made. When the President was briefed by those key advisers who were cleared for MAGIC they often incorporated it into their briefings. When things got really tight in November the President asked to start seeing the actual messages again because he was afraid that the gists or the briefings might leave out something that he would be interested in seeing.

The original list of those cleared for knowing the full story on MAGIC was established by General Marshall, Army Chief of Staff, and Admiral Stark, Chief of Naval Operations, in January 1941. Although the list kept expanding during the year, both officially and unofficially, it remained limited to people in Washington D.C. There was a general policy that the existence of these messages and our ability to decode them should be confined to the least number of people possible, and that no distribution should be made outside of Washington.

Even J. Edgar Hoover, Director of the Federal Bureau of Investigation, who was in Washington, was excluded from the list. That didn't mean that he was unaware of MAGIC intelligence. The FBI was kept informed of the contents of the most important MAGIC espionage messages in a "sanitized" form. Sanitizing COMINT was widely practiced in order to use the intelligence without disclosing its true origin, and thus gain a far broader distribution than would be otherwise possible. Sanitizing was accomplished by attributing the information to a "highly reliable source" and the content of the message was paraphrased to prevent any possible comparisons with the original. The FBI, Office of Naval Intelligence, and Military Intelligence Division all used sanitized MAGIC in their intelligence reports and estimates. Almost all the intelligence published by these organizations, as shown in Part III, is heavily laden with sanitized MAGIC. After comparing these reports with copies of intercepted Japanese messages displayed in Part II, the extent to which the intelligence community relied on MAGIC becomes readily apparent.

A "highly reliable source" was about as good a rating as you could get for intelligence, only COMINT being higher. But even so this validity never had the intelligence impact of holding in your hand an exact copy of a top secret message sent only a few hours before by a cabinet level official in the Japanese Empire utilizing his nation's most secure crypt system.

After Pearl Harbor all COMINT distribution was reorganized. The war brought about fundamental changes in almost every aspect of COMINT.

ULTRA increased tremendously and the character of MAGIC intelligence changed, becoming increasingly military and administrative in nature. Communications between Tokyo and the Axis countries now provided the bulk of MAGIC intelligence and it tended to be heavily military in nature. MAGIC continued to produce solid diplomatic intelligence between Tokyo and the big neutrals such as the Soviet Union and Spain as these countries maneuvered for position with the tide of battle.[3]

The occupation of other countries by Japan produced a whole new field of what was transmitted in MAGIC. Within the conquered territories of the Empire, MAGIC codes and ciphers were used by Japanese civil administrators and "diplomatic representatives" to correspond with each other and with Tokyo. There was a variety of good intelligence in these communications, ranging from ship cargoes and budget matters to the state of local agriculture, but it was a far cry from the kind of MAGIC still being produced in other parts of the world.

In June 1942 OP-20-G pulled out of MAGIC processing in Washington in order to devote all of its Pacific resources to working against Japanese navy crypt systems. Signal Intelligence Service took on the entire responsibility for processing and reporting on MAGIC for the remainder of the war. It also did something sorely needed, it completely revamped MAGIC distribution. In addition to making entire messages available to those customers who required that kind of service, SIS developed a daily synopsis of MAGIC called the "MAGIC Summary" in which all the important MAGIC messages were either gisted or compiled into report form. By this time the character of MAGIC had changed so much that even the State Department didn't object to gisting and distributing intercepted messages which were sometimes purely diplomatic in nature.

When some Japanese army crypt systems were solved in 1943 a flood of new intelligence suddenly became available. To take full advantage of this new source of COMINT, SIS moved fully-supported cryptanalytic units into the field and began participating, along with OP-20-G, in combined operations such as the Joint Intelligence Center Pacific Ocean Area (JICPOA) in Hawaii. Additionally, SIS began providing direct intelligence support to General MacArthur and to his subordinate Army commands in the Southwest Pacific area through the Central Bureau in Brisbane.

In Washington, SIS began publishing a military supplement to the daily MAGIC summaries. General Marshall was so impressed with the level of intelligence produced by these newly-broken Japanese army crypt systems

---

3   In the Pacific Theater ULTRA referred to intelligence gained from breaking military and naval codes. MAGIC was derived from diplomatic codes.

that he sent copies of the MAGIC Military Summaries to President Roosevelt with the recommendation that the President read them on a regular basis. Distribution of COMINT during the war years bore little resemblance to the almost paranoid handling of it in 1941. Yet, withal this, the extraordinary level of secrecy required for COMINT was maintained while getting near-maximum use out of the intelligence.

All Japanese consulates in the U.S. and the embassy were shut down on December 7, 1941 when Pearl Harbor was attacked. After that there were no longer any official Japanese messages passed between the U.S. and Tokyo. That phase of MAGIC forever disappeared; but it did not mean that the espionage problem vanished. If it were that simple the U.S. could have shut down the consulates months earlier and solved everything. The problem was that MAGIC had already disclosed that the Japanese government, anticipating this exact eventuality, had given specific instructions that the espionage nets on the West Coast were to be constructed in such a way as to be able to function after war was declared. The nets were to continue to operate even though the diplomatic posts were no longer there to direct the effort and to serve as a communications relay. The reports in Part III make it quite clear that the intelligence community continued to struggle with the espionage problem subsequent to December 7, 1941 after the consulates were closed. *It was only after the evacuation of Japanese residents that the U.S. intelligence services finally ceased reporting the existence of large-scale espionage on the West Coast.*

Actually, from a purely intelligence point of view, the U.S. was better off when the consulates were open because this provided a MAGIC window to keep tabs on what the Japanese were doing. In June 1941 all twenty-four German consulates were shut down and the Italian ones were closed in July. The reason given was that they were involved in spying. Not being able to read their codes had a good deal more to do with the closures than the reasons given to the public. The U.S. allowed the Japanese consulates to remain open when we had absolute proof that they were involved in spying, and were recruiting Japanese residents for espionage. Still, they were allowed to remain open right up to the last minute. The reason they were not closed, of course, was the intelligence community's reluctance to give up MAGIC. If the flow of correspondence between the U.S. and Tokyo had been cut off, our vision of what the Japanese were up to along the West Coast would have been considerably dimmed.

After Pearl Harbor, espionage information about the United States in MAGIC communications became limited to Japan's attempts to use Latin America as a base for spying against the United States and the fascinating story of Spain's espionage efforts in the U.S. on behalf of Japan.

MAGIC intelligence on the Spanish connection was obtained by monitoring Japanese diplomatic communications between Madrid and Tokyo. For a price, one week after Pearl Harbor, Spain agreed to perform espionage in the United States for Japan. The Japanese ambassador in Madrid was kept informed by the Spanish foreign minister of Spain's activities in the U.S. and given espionage data obtained there by Spanish agents. Over a period of about six months during 1942 at least eighty Spanish espionage reports containing information on convoys and related military data were sent to Madrid from the Spanish embassy in Washington D.C. The Japanese ambassador in Madrid was then given all this data and he, in turn, forwarded it to Tokyo in the PURPLE crypt system which U.S. cryptanalysts routinely intercepted and read. The original intention was to send at least twenty Spanish agents into the U.S., but it appears that only about eight of them actually were deployed.

The Spanish effort never really got off the ground and it ended in 1943. No doubt it was originally anticipated that the Spanish agents would work with the resident Japanese nets on the West Coast, providing a communications outlet through the Spanish embassy for their intelligence. But by the time the Spanish agents in the U.S. were organized and in place, all West Coast Japanese had been evacuated and whatever information gathering nets had been established were no longer in existence. They had been wiped out by the evacuation.

In Latin America MAGIC revealed Japan's desperate attempts to recruit spies and send them into the United States. Although Japan did succeed in dispatching a few spies recruited in South America into the United States it was a doomed effort. By February 1942 every country in Latin America except Argentina had either broken relations with or declared war on Japan, thereby depriving the Japanese of a base from which to operate.

DECLASSIFICATION

The wholesale declassification of World War II COMINT came hard to many of the old hands at the National Security Agency (NSA), the organization which is now responsible for the nation's communications intelligence and its communications security. OP-20-G and SIS (or their successor organizations) are still in existence but they are now under the operational and technical control of NSA where computer driven analysis and satellite collection devices make World War II SIGINT seem like child's play.

As a general rule COMINT is the most tightly held information in the intelligence world. The reason is simple. A country's broken codes and ciphers can reveal to its opponents authoritative, timely, and highly secret information on a daily basis. Plans, strategies, and even intentions can be derived from COMINT. Just a few messages can reveal an entire course of action, particularly when fused with other more traditional kinds of intelligence. Whole intelligence infrastructures have been built on the data gleaned from a single broken crypt system.

All of this can collapse like a house of cards if your opponent learns of your success against his communications. Overnight the source can dry up. New codes and perhaps different communications procedures will replace the old ones. In some cases, years of painstaking analysis will have gone for naught. Worse, you may never regain exploitability or it may take years to reestablish it. Is it any wonder that cryptanalysts object to even forty-five year old cryptanalytic successes being revealed? It's not the intelligence they care about; it is the technical considerations which concern them. If nothing else, it shows less sophisticated countries what can be accomplished, and it draws the attention of all nations to the security of their own communications.

It wasn't too long ago that even the term COMINT was classified. For years NSA wasn't even in the phone book, and road signs giving the location of the agency were forbidden. It was a wonder that anybody ever found the place to apply for a job. NSA's standard designator in the media was, and still is, "The nation's super secret intelligence agency." When NSA finally got into the phone book and signs were allowed on the Baltimore-Washington Parkway pointing out the agency's location at Fort George G. Meade, Maryland, some wags suggested that the phone listing and the road signs should read, "The Nation's Super Secret Intelligence Agency." This made a certain amount of sense because almost everyone had heard or read of that, but hardly anybody had heard of the National Security Agency. If we had done that it would have solved another problem. A good share of the traffic on the parkway is composed of people trying to sort out the difference between NSA and NASA (National Aeronautics and Space Administration) which is located just a few miles down the parkway from NSA.

For years it has been the government's policy to squash anything hinting of COMINT successes or techniques no matter how many years ago it may have happened. Nonetheless, there have been three major outpourings of COMINT triumphs since 1931. The first was Yardley's revelations in his book, *The American Black Chamber*. The second mass release of COMINT data occurred just a few months after the Pacific War ended in August 1945. This release was authorized by President Truman in order to facilitate the work of the Joint Committee on the Investigation of the Pearl Harbor Attack. This congressional committee was the eighth official investigation of Pearl Harbor, each one seeking to understand how this disaster could have happened and who was to blame.

In the first seven investigations MAGIC was allowed to be introduced, but only on a highly classified basis. No MAGIC could be released. Consequently, insofar as the public was concerned, and even to some of those people involved in the hearings, the findings of these seven investigations were far from satisfactory because the MAGIC evidence needed to support many of the conclusions could not be discussed.

The Joint Committee's work was by far the most thorough of all the investigations. It had the advantage of all the information developed by the previous hearings plus its own exhaustive examination. The committee labored for months. It read all the pertinent documents and interviewed everybody who could shed some light on what actually happened. The hearings are contained in thirty-nine volumes, and the single most discussed subject in the entire investigation is MAGIC.

On the first day of the hearings, November 15, 1945, Chief Counsel Mitchell opened the proceedings with two sensational revelations: he introduced Exhibit No. 1, "Intercepted Diplomatic Messages sent by the Japanese Government between July 1 and December 8, 1941" and Exhibit No 2., "Japanese Messages Concerning U.S. Military Installations, Ship Movements, and Other Matters." Thus, the American people learned for the first time of the incredible accomplishments of U.S. cryptanalysts during the war. Before it was finished the Joint Committee would introduce 183 exhibits, but it was numbers 1 and 2 that absorbed most of the attention during the investigation. Unfortunately, the committee had a start date of July 1, 1941 for evidence related to its investigation. Thus, Exhibit 2 contained MAGIC messages sending national defense information from the U.S. to Tokyo, but did not include the messages sent in the first half of 1941 which established and organized the West Coast espionage nets.

Exhibits 1 and 2 were selected from a highly classified study by U.S. intelligence organizations which was started in 1944 but wasn't completed until 1946. This study was concerned with U.S.-Japanese diplomatic negotiations and with Japanese espionage in the Western Hemisphere during 1941 as revealed in MAGIC messages. Only those messages which had some possible relationship to the Pearl Harbor attack were released from the study to the Joint Congressional Committee. That left all the rest of MAGIC still classified. Since MAGIC was a global system and the compilation covered all of 1941, only a fraction of the messages in the special study was released. In testimony given during the hearings, however, a great deal of additional information about both MAGIC and ULTRA was revealed.

In any event, the cat was now out of the bag, and from 1945 to 1972 there was a steady trickle of information about what had been the nation's most guarded secret. During the 1960s the books of three prominent historians, all of whom had done their homework very well, were published: Roberta Wohlstetter's, *Pearl Harbor, Warning and Decision*, 1962, Ladislas Farago's, *The Broken Seal*, 1967, and David Kahn's monumental work, *The Codebreakers*, 1967.

They largely captured the whole story. In 1972 practically all restraints on World War II intelligence were removed. Pursuant to President Nixon's Executive Order No. 11652 (later E.O. 12065) the Department of Defense directed NSA to declassify all World War II Japanese and German COMINT unless there were security reasons to keep some or all of certain messages classified. A questionable policy decision was made not to release the COMINT of their allies.

As part of this wholesale declassification a decision was made by NSA that it was in the public interest to update the 1946 study which had provided MAGIC messages for the Joint Congressional Committee's hearings. This was done, and the eight volume study was published by the Department of Defense in 1977 under the name, *The "MAGIC" Background of Pearl Harbor*.[4] Only in a few other instances have messages sent to the National Archives been assembled by subject matter, and none on this scale. The study contains over 5,000 intercepted Japanese messages related to the attack on Pearl Harbor of which more than half are intelligence or espionage related messages. Japanese army and navy messages are not included in the study.

All this was available to the Commission on Wartime Relocation and Internment of Civilians when it was compiling its report, *Personal Justice Denied*. Contained in the DOD study of MAGIC messages are a good many of the reasons why Executive Order 9066 was signed, and solid refutation of the flawed history that Congress has legislated into law.

---

[4]   Department of Defense, *The Magic Background of Pearl Harbor*, 8 vols. (Washington D.C.: GPO, 1977).

CHAPTER 4

THE COMMISSION

The end of the war brought a whole new era for people of Japanese ancestry in the United States. With peace and thousands of GIs serving in the Land of the Rising Sun came a new awareness and appreciation of Japan, its people, and its culture. The unflattering wartime caricatures of the Japanese enemy, which had unfairly tainted the public perception of the Issei and Nisei[1], completely disappeared. In its place arose the image of an industrious, friendly, law-abiding, and even a genteel people.

Because of the evacuation of resident Japanese from the West Coast, it had not been necessary to have a series of ugly sedition trials of the Issei and Nisei named in the MAGIC messages and the FBI and Office of Naval Intelligence reports as being involved in traitorous activities along the West Coast.

In later years this provided the opportunity for the carefully worded claim to be made by the Commission on Wartime Relocation and Internment of Civilians that "no documented acts of espionage, sabotage or fifth column activity were shown to have been committed by any identifiable American citizen of Japanese ancestry or resident Japanese alien on the West Coast."[2]

---

[1] Issei—Japanese-born, first generation emigrants to the U.S; Nisei—children of Issei born in the U.S.

[2] *Personal Justice Denied*, 2 vols. (Washington D.C.: GPO, 1982-83; reprint, The Civil Liberties Public Education Fund and the University of Washington Press, 1997) p. 457. All references to *Personal Justice Denied* in this book refer to the 1997 edition.

Several cases of a more serious nature occurred, but they were not on the West Coast. There were, for example, the convictions of Tomoya Kawakita, a Japanese-American who was sentenced to death for his brutal treatment of American prisoners of war, and Iva Toguri, another Japanese-American, known as Tokyo Rose, who was convicted of treason.

Nonetheless, public perception gradually made an 180 degree turn, and within a few years after the war Japanese residents were generally considered to have remained loyal to the U.S., as indeed the majority of them had. The composition of the Japanese community in the U.S. was itself also undergoing a transformation. As time moved on, the Issei were passing away and the Nisei, now a much more sophisticated group, were rapidly becoming the dominant force. They were assimilating into the mainstream of American society in a way that their parents never did. Passage of the American-Japanese Evacuation Claims Act in 1948 had eased the economic losses brought about by the evacuation, and, all in all, the future appeared to present new opportunities for a far better relationship between the ethnic Japanese in the United States and their fellow Americans than had ever been true in the past.

But under the surface all was not well within the Japanese community. Deep down there was seething resentment and a sense of shame. They had been labeled untrustworthy by their own country. For years afterwards they lived under this cloud of disloyalty. Evacuation for security reasons was considered to have been a terrible stain on their record as Americans, and the Japanese community was determined at all costs to erase this dishonor. Particularly galling were the Supreme Court cases in 1943 and 1944 which had upheld the legality of the U.S. government's actions as a legitimate and even a necessary wartime measure.

In 1975 the Japanese American Citizens League (JACL), at their convention in Salt Lake City, Utah announced for the first time that the organization was going to campaign for financial redress for the evacuation experience. Neither the membership nor the chapters took part in the decision to demand redress. It was simply announced by the JACL officers at the Salt Lake City convention.

Spurred on by younger Japanese-Americans, many of whom hadn't even been born until after the war, Washington lobbyists were set in motion, and a campaign for what was labeled "Redress and Reparations" was launched with an intensity and organizational skill never before matched by any ethnic group in the U.S. Their efforts bore fruit in 1980 when the U.S. government was persuaded to reopen the whole evacuation issue.

The U.S. House of Representatives, under pressure from the JACL, the American Civil Liberties Union (ACLU), and various civil rights groups, passed a bill on July 21, 1980 creating the Commission on Wartime Relocation and Internment of Civilians (CWRIC). Congress' charge to the CWRIC was clear cut and to the point. It was:

1. Review the facts and circumstances surrounding Executive Order Numbered 9066, issued February 19, 1942, and the impact of such Executive Order on American citizens and permanent resident aliens;

2. Review directives of United States military forces requiring the relocation and, in some cases, detention in internment camps of American citizens, including Aleut civilians, and permanent resident aliens of the Aleutian and Pribilof Islands; and

3. Recommend appropriate remedies.

The reference to the Aleuts had to do with their evacuation to the mainland during the war for their own safety. They too, while the war raged, lived in government camps which were claimed to be substandard, and in the view of some, their civil rights had also been violated.

President Carter appointed three members of the Commission, and the House and Senate each appointed three. By any criterion it was an impressive group, numbering among its members a former Supreme Court justice, several ex-senators and congressmen, religious leaders, and prominent civil rights advocates.

All selectees were informally approved by the JACL. It was a stacked deck from the very beginning. There was no doubt in anyone's mind what the outcome would be. Even so, the militant National Council for Japanese American Redress (NCJAR) which was founded in May 1979 for the sole purpose of obtaining redress, felt that the Commission was a waste of time. It wanted to go directly for a bill authorizing $4 billion in reparations without going through the formality of a study. In 1979 the NCJAR actually succeeded in persuading Seattle Congressman Mike Lowry to introduce a bill providing $25,000 to each evacuee or their heirs without going through the formality of a study. Twenty other congressmen endorsed the bill.

But the JACL was convinced that a reparations bill without a study which marshaled popular support by the American people behind it would have little chance of success.

With a great deal of fanfare the Commission began its investigation. Most of the Japanese community rallied around it as their champion. No one seemed concerned that the Commission might uncover information that the government had acted with legitimate reasons on the evacuation issue.

Apparently, there was no awareness or even suspicion of the intelligence bombshells which were lurking in the background.

Three of the nine commissioners, Arthur Goldberg, "a horrendous thing," Joan Bernstein, "a blot on the history of the U.S.," and Hugh Mitchell, "a great wrong," had already gone on record as to where they stood before the Commission had even started its investigation. Two of the others, William Marutani[3] and Ishmael Gromoff, were themselves evacuees and entitled to reparations. Congressman Daniel Lungren, the only sitting member of Congress on the Commission, was from a Southern California district with a huge Japanese constituency. Arthur Flemming, former chairman of the Civil Rights Commission, and ex-Senator Edward Brooke were well known liberals on civil rights matters and there was little doubt where they stood. The last of the nine, former congressman Father Robert Drinan, arrived with the question, "How much are we going to give them?"

Thirty-three people were hired to do the research, keep track of the hearings, and to compile the final report. Forty percent of them had Japanese surnames, and one of them testified as a witness. As a final mix, several militant civil rights activists who had already written and spoken out strongly on behalf of reparations were added to the Commission staff as advisers.

There was no recognized World War II historian on the staff nor was there a knowledgeable intelligence specialist, and none were called before the Commission as witnesses. If there had been, MAGIC surely would have surfaced while the Commission was compiling its report. Even the most casual knowledge about World War II intelligence should have brought MAGIC into consideration. For example, John Costello's excellent history, *The Pacific War*, was published in 1981 while the Commission was doing its "investigating." In his book he states, "The rising current of fear on the West Coast, and the evidence from the MAGIC intercepts the previous year of espionage organizations had been important factors in the President's decision to sign Executive Order 9066."

Also readily available to the Commission's researchers were two basic publications about MAGIC: *Hearings Before the Joint Committee on the Investigation of the Pearl Harbor Attack* (23 Vols), 1946, and the Department of Defense eight-volume study, *The "MAGIC" Background of Pearl Harbor*, published in 1977. Both of these multi-volume studies contain extensive data on West Coast espionage as revealed in the MAGIC messages. There are other books, studies, and documents containing similar information which could easily have been consulted.

---

[3]   Commissioner William M. Marutani later formally renounced any personal monetary recompense.

For more than two years the Commission and its large staff roamed the country interviewing people, reading various documents, investigating the "facts," and holding hearings. Before they were finished the Commission took testimony from more than 700 people, mostly evacuees. Oaths were not required by the witnesses. The hearings were not noted for their objectivity.

The one man who even the Commission itself acknowledged could shed the most light on the evacuation was John J. McCloy. He was Assistant Secretary of War at the time and the person within the War Department upon whom Secretary Stimson relied to keep an eye on the evacuation and the relocation centers. After the war McCloy served as High Commissioner of Germany, coordinator of U.S. disarmament activities, and President of the World Bank.

This distinguished American in a July 20, 1983 letter to Senator Charles Grassley had the following to say about his appearance before the Commission:

> Only as this Commission was about to close its hearings was I called upon to appear before it. By that time, a great head of steam had been built up by the news accounts of the hearings largely inspired by the lobbyists. From my personal appearance, at the hearings of the Commission, I believe its conduct was a horrendous affront to our tradition for fair and objective hearings.... Whenever I sought in the slightest degree to justify the action of the United States which was ordered by President Roosevelt, my testimony was met with hisses and boos [from the spectators] such as I have never, over an experience extending back to World War I, been heretofore subjected to. Others had similar experiences... it became clear from the outset of my testimony that the Commission was not at all disposed to conduct an objective investigation.... No current officials of the government, so far as I have heard, were ever called upon to produce evidence in support of the action which the President and his advisers took in their good judgment.... Nor were any called to produce any information from the records of the government as to the motivation for the order.... It would have been quite simple for an objective examiner of the Commission to have dug up again the so-called MAGIC revelations.... The truth is really that this Commission simply does not know whether there were any acts of sabotage or frustrated acts of sabotage committed on the West Coast.[4]

---

4   See page 343 for the McCloy letter.

Besides McCloy, there was one other person still living who played a major role in the relocation. This was Karl R. Bendetsen who was the military man in actual charge of the evacuation. When he testified before the Commission he was booed and hissed to such an extent that he was unable to make some of his points because "I knew it would be fruitless. Every commissioner had made up his mind before he was appointed."

If such prominent people as McCloy and Bendetsen, who even the Commission had to acknowledge "were the two witnesses before the Commission who were most involved in the evacuation decision," were unable to make their points, it is not difficult to imagine why some anti-reparations people were reluctant to give testimony.

On the other hand, some witnesses who wanted to testify on behalf of the government complained that they were ignored. The few who did manage to obtain some time before the Commission to testify for the government complained that they were cut short, humiliated, and sometimes lectured to by members of the Commission. Other pro-government witnesses who submitted written materials often found that their submissions were filed away and completely forgotten even though they had been assured that the documents would be given careful consideration.

It is well nigh impossible to find any statements in the Commission's final report suggesting in any way that there might have been some legitimacy to the government's actions. Former Senator S.I. Hayakawa from California, possibly the most outstanding Japanese-American in the country, testified against reparations but none of his testimony can be found in the Commission's report. Completely frustrated in making his views known, Hayakawa sent a letter to the White House pointing out one of the major considerations which went into the evacuation decision:[5]

> The Japanese and Japanese-Americans in the Western States were relocated during World War II for their own safety and protection at a time when the U.S. and Japan were at war. The relocation was in no way punitive. It was to remove the Japanese from the coastal areas for fear of what might happen to them if a hostile Japanese invasion force was to land on our shores.
>
> The puzzling thing about the demand for "Redress" is that the JACL now wants financial compensation as a result of the relocation. The assumption seems to be that the relocation was in some way punitive

---

5   Letter from S. I. Hayakawa to Howard H. Baker, White House Chief of Staff, April 21, 1988.

rather than protective, and that they ought to be given financial "redress" for the protection and safety they enjoyed for the duration of the war.

Henry Stimson in his autobiography gave a similar protective argument for the evacuation saying, "anti-Japanese feeling on the West Coast had reached a level which endangered the lives of all such individuals; incidents of extra-legal violence were increasingly frequent."[6] Stimson could not, of course, mention MAGIC as another reason because it had not yet been declassified.

Although it dismissed these considerations out of hand, the Commission did at least acknowledge Stimson's statement, but it ignored Hayakawa's viewpoint altogether.

Because of his outspoken comments on the evacuation issue, the former world-renowned semanticist, university president, and U.S. senator is anathema to the pro-reparations Japanese who contemptuously refer to him as a banana: yellow on the outside, and white on the inside. He, on the other hand, says "my flesh crawls with shame and embarrassment" to see this unconscionable raid on the U.S. treasury by "a wolf-pack of dissident young Japanese-Americans who weren't even born during WW II."[7]

Since the primary charge of the Commission was to investigate the circumstances surrounding Executive Order 9066, and the Executive Order's stated and sole purpose was to protect against espionage and sabotage, one would suppose that the Commission's investigation would be filled with all the pertinent intelligence on this subject. But it is not.

It turns out that the Commission didn't even know what constituted the intelligence community in 1941, let alone what it was producing. Consequently, it misrepresented the prevailing intelligence opinion at the time, and was unaware of, or deliberately concealed, the most important and authoritative intelligence on the subject which it was charged to investigate.

In its 500 page report, *Personal Justice Denied*, the Commission has a ten-page section labeled "Intelligence."[8] This contains some of the most curious statements ever to appear in an official document. According to the Commission, when Executive Order 9066 was signed, the sum total of all U.S.

---

6 Henry L. Stimson and McGeorge Bundy, *On Active Service In Peace and War* (Harper and Brothers: New York, 1947) p. 406.

7 Congress, Senate, Committee on the Judiciary, Japanese-American *Evacuation Redress: Hearing before the Subcommittee on Administrative Practice and Procedure*, 98th Cong., 1st Sess., July 27, 1983 (Washington D.C.: GPO) p. 422.

8 See page 347 for the Commission's section on intelligence.

intelligence available to the government on the issues of espionage and sabotage by, and the loyalty of, Japanese residents on the West Coast consisted of a handful of memos from three different sources: (1) certain fence straddling statements by J. Edgar Hoover, largely contradicted by his own West Coast field offices; (2) a non-official, personal statement by the deputy intelligence officer for the Eleventh Naval District (Los Angeles), Lieutenant Commander K. D. Ringle, which was promptly disavowed by the ONI as representing its position: (3) several reports from a newspaperman named John F. Carter who forwarded information to the President which he received from Curtis B. Munson, "a well-to-do businessman who gathered information for Carter under the guise of being a government official."

As absurd as it sounds, especially considering the magnitude of this entire episode and its many ramifications, it is on these three sources that the Commission based its contention that there was no evidence of espionage, that the intelligence community felt the situation was well in hand, and that there was no need for mass evacuation. With amazing perception (and surely with tongue in cheek) the Commission does, however, concede that none of these three sources "operated with the thoroughness of, say, the modern CIA, but they were the best and calmest eyes and ears the government had." Incredible!

By virtue of his official position alone, some credence must be given to Hoover's views even though on this issue they are heavily tinted with political considerations. It should also be noted that at this time the Office of Naval Intelligence and not the FBI was exercising primary responsibility for developing West Coast espionage intelligence. In his February 2, 1942 memorandum to the Attorney General in which he gives his views on mass evacuation Hoover equivocates. His carefully worded answer doesn't address the question head-on. Instead, he discusses the pros and the cons of mass evacuation, and although he seems to come down in favor of voting against mass evacuation, there is no concluding statement in his reply to this effect. And, to make certain that his flanks were covered, he uncharacteristically included in his memo to the Attorney General, the views of his West Coast field offices. Seattle and San Diego were vehemently in favor of mass evacuation. Los Angeles and Portland leaned heavily in that direction. San Francisco was dismissive. It was a take-your-pick memo. Whatever the decision, if something went wrong, Hoover was in the clear.

Ringle's position prior to the signing of Executive Order 9066 on February 19, 1942 is also far from clear-cut. His suggestion in his personal assessment of January 26, 1942 that only selective evacuation was necessary is considerably diminished by his assessment in the same report that up to 25 percent, or 20,000 Japanese-Americans (and presumably an even higher percentage of

Issei),[9] on the mainland were of doubtful loyalty, and that the government could expect about 3,500 individuals in the U.S. Japanese community who might act as spies and saboteurs, and that upwards of 1,500 Kibei[10] should be placed in custodial detention regardless of their U.S. citizenship.[11]

Less than two weeks later, on February 7, 1942, Ringle assessed the situation on Terminal Island in the middle of Los Angeles Harbor on which resided one of the largest concentration of Japanese residents on the West Coast. He observed that "espionage has been going forward for a great many years," and warned that:

> As long as this colony, which contains known alien sympathizers, even though of American citizenship, is allowed to exist in the heart of every activity in the Los Angeles Harbor, it must be assumed that items such as the above [arrival and departure of convoys, including size, strength of escort, and bulk of cargo; troop movements; arrival and departure of major units of the fleet; progress of shipbuilding, including launching and commissioning of men-of-war, as well as merchant marine; progress of construction of Naval Operating Base, including the new dry dock and the channel approaches thereto; delivery of new aircraft; the strength or lack of strength of the aerial defenses of the Naval Air Station and Naval Operating Base; and similar matters] are known, observed, and transmitted to the enemy quickly and easily.[12]

It is important to note that neither Hoover nor Ringle took the position that Japanese residents were not a security threat. In fact, they made it quite clear that there was a serious problem in this respect. Their argument, considerably hedged, was that the threat could be handled by means other than total evacuation, an opinion not shared by the key decision makers. It is also worth pointing out that at this stage neither Hoover nor Ringle was cleared for MAGIC, nor, of course, was Munson. Not a single person who had access to the full story on MAGIC objected to mass evacuation of Japanese residents.

It is difficult to take the Commission seriously on Munson, although in its report it does seem to rely on him even more than Ringle and Hoover to

---

[9] Japanese citizens who became enemy aliens after Presidential Proclamation 2525 on December 7, 1941.

[10] American-born individuals educated in Japan.

[11] See the January 26, 1942 Ringle personal assessment on page 315. Ref. on pages 316-317.

[12] See February 7, 1942 Ringle official assessment on page 325.

present its view that the West Coast Japanese did not constitute any kind of credible threat. While he was gathering his information for Carter on the West Coast situation, Munson interviewed Richard B. Hood, the FBI agent in charge of the Los Angeles office. Hood later testified at the 1985 Hirabayashi hearings in Seattle that Munson was naive and uninformed. Even the Commission admitted that he was an amateur, but still insisted that he was a primary source of intelligence for the U.S. government. An extract from a Munson report to Carter dated October 22, 1941 illustrates his degree of "professionalism."

> In the first place there are not so many people of Japanese descent in the U.S. that in an emergency they could not all be thrown into a concentration camp in 48 hours. Of course you might get a few Chinamen too because they sort of look alike. But the looks are a great aid to rounding them up and in keeping them away from sabotage and other troublesome pastimes.

As war became reality the play-at-intelligence boys, Carter and Munson, faded away and were not heard from again.[13]

In *Personal Justice Denied* pages are devoted to Munson's "views," but the people and organizations actually charged with producing and evaluating U.S. intelligence are almost entirely missing. Completely brushed aside is the Army's Military Intelligence Division and its chief, General Sherman Miles, who doesn't even rate a footnote. Admiral Wilkinson, Director of the Office of Naval Intelligence, does better. He is mentioned once as someone in attendance at a meeting, but Admiral Turner, charged with evaluating U.S. Naval Intelligence, is missing, as is Commander Davis, head of counterintelligence in the ONI. The Army's Signal Intelligence Service and the Navy's OP-20-G, the organizations responsible for the nation's greatest intelligence coup, MAGIC and ULTRA, are nonexistent in the report.

Not a single official intelligence report released prior to the evacuation decision from the FBI, the Office of Naval Intelligence, or the Military Intelligence Division regarding their conclusions on the status of Japanese espionage on the West Coast is cited by the Commission in its report let alone discussed. This was despite the fact that all three of these organizations repeatedly issued reports warning over and over again that large subversive

---

[13]   Within three days after Pearl Harbor, according to a letter from FBI SAC R. B. Hood of Los Angeles to Director Hoover, dated December 10, 1941, Munson was complaining to Carter in Washington who passed it on that the FBI was doing only half the job it should by apprehending aliens. The other half of the job, he felt, was the apprehension of disloyal citizens who constituted a large group of possible troublemakers.

nets utilizing Issei and Nisei, controlled by the Japanese government, were organized and operating up and down the entire West Coast. Added to these glaring omissions was the admission by the Commission that it was totally unaware of MAGIC and what it had revealed about espionage along the West Coast. In other words, the Commission either ignored or was ignorant of the most authoritative intelligence the nation possessed related to Executive Order 9066.

When he testified before the House subcommittee holding hearings on the reparations bill, Dr. David Trask, the Chief Army Historian, not an unfriendly witness to the Commission, characterized the Commission's report as follows:

> The report strikes me as essentially in the form of a legal brief rather than a history. Historical information in this brief serves a specific purpose—to present the case against the Government in the most favorable light. Such an approach means that factual information is selected to serve the interests of the client. It means also that facts are ordered and interpreted so as to provide the best support for the client.... Facts and arguments which might tend to support a contrary conclusion are either excluded or rejected.[14]

This is a charitable interpretation. It could also be claimed that the Commission's report represents a fraud on the U.S. Congress and the American public and a violation of the trust accorded to the Commission that it would produce an objective and fair investigation on its charge.

There are numerous instances where the Commission (probably not the commissioners but certain staff members and advisers) deliberately ignored vital intelligence on the subject of its investigation which would undercut its predetermined conclusions. In other cases carefully crafted statements or quotes about intelligence items have been made in such a manner as to purposely mislead the reader.

For example, when it became clear on February 11, 1942 that the President would support evacuation if the military situation warranted it, Stimson asked McCloy to make a final check on the current situation. On February 12 McCloy contacted General Mark Clark, Deputy Chief of Staff, and asked for an update. Clark immediately responded with the latest Army assessment (which included Navy input) on Japanese espionage, "Information Bulletin

---

[14] Congress, House, Committee on the Judiciary, *Japanese-American and Aleutian Wartime Relocation: Hearings before the Subcommittee on Administrative Law and Governmental Relations*, 98th Cong. 2nd Sess., June 20, 21, 27 and September 12, 1984 (Washington D.C.: GPO) p. 79.

Number 6," dated January 21, 1942, which concluded, "Their espionage net containing Japanese aliens, first and second generation Japanese and other nationals is now thoroughly organized and working underground."[15]

Stimson and McCloy had this report in hand when the evacuation decision was made and it may well have been quoted to the President because of his insistence on a military necessity. A complete copy of this particular intelligence report is included in the Army's 1964 historical study of its role in the evacuation, a document which is cited by the Commission as one of its major references. The history is relatively short. It is impossible to believe that this intelligence bulletin did not catch the attention of the staffers researching the Army's study.

Much is made by the Commission of Ringle's January 26, 1942 informal report to Admiral Stark, Chief of Naval Operations, in which he suggests that mass evacuation might not be necessary. But no mention is made of the fact that when his report was released by ONI the cover memo specifically stated that this report "does not represent the final and official opinion of the Office of Naval Intelligence on this subject."[16]

Also carefully concealed is Ringle's February 7, 1942 report quoted in some detail previously. But the Commission then had the audacity to brazenly declare in its report, "Whatever its intelligence officers thought, the Navy was intent on moving the ethnic Japanese away from its installations at Terminal Island.... Stronger political forces outside the intelligence services wanted evacuation. Intelligence opinions were disregarded or drowned out."[17]

All of the above intelligence reports in their entirety are included in Part III. They were available to the Commission, and the author has reason to believe that they were known to some of the senior advisers to the Commission. Why then were they not used? Did the Commission really believe that they were of no consequence? Not relevant? Of course not. They went straight to the heart of the question of why Executive Order 9066 was issued.

This kind of research dishonesty is prevalent throughout the Commission's report to the U.S. Congress. Additional examples of deliberately falsifying and concealing data from the courts by the Japanese American Citizens League and the National Council for Japanese American Redress and their advisers are discussed in Chapter 5. Interestingly, some of the same people involved in concealing data in the Commission's report were also guiding actions in the court cases.

---

[15]　See "Information Bulletin Number 6" on page 240. Reference on page 242.

[16]　See page 314.

[17]　*Personal Justice Denied*, p. 60.

Despite all the official information to the contrary, some of which actually named individual Issei and Nisei who were involved in subversive activities, the Commission reached the astonishing conclusion that the U.S. government had no evidence that Japanese residents on the West Coast in 1942 presented any kind of a security threat to the United States. It reported back to Congress and to the U.S. public that "there was *no knowledge or evidence* (italics added) of organized or individual Nisei spying," that "the government has conceded at every point that there was *no evidence* (italics added) of actual sabotage, espionage or fifth column activity among people of Japanese descent on the West Coast in February 1942,"[18] and that "There was *no evidence* (italics added) that any individual American citizen was actively disloyal to his country."[19]

Having thus falsely concluded that there were no security problems worth mentioning on the West Coast, no evidence of spying among Japanese residents, and that the intelligence community felt the situation was well under control, the Commission proclaimed that President Roosevelt and his key evacuation advisers were, therefore, motivated solely by "race prejudice, war hysteria and a failure of political leadership."[20] Thus, our wartime leaders, Franklin Roosevelt, Cordell Hull, Henry Stimson, John McCloy, Frank Knox, and George Marshall, some of the finest men to have ever served our nation, were all branded by the Commission and now by the U.S. Congress and the country they served as racists and political opportunists. Japanese residents along the West Coast, on the other hand, were given a clean bill of health.

Unaware of the actual intelligence background on the evacuation, a poorly informed media, the Congress, and the public accepted without question these false conclusions by the Commission as the absolute driving forces behind the signing of Executive Order 9066.

Shortly after the Commission's final report was released, I wrote a *New York Times* article that questioned the absence of MAGIC in the Commission's report. Asked by reporters why it hadn't considered MAGIC, the Commission Chairwoman, Joan J. Bernstein, the Commission Special Counsel, Angus MacBeth, and the Rev. Robert Drinan, one of the commissioners, with considerable embarrassment, all admitted that they had never heard of it. When several newspapers suggested that the Commission might have reached different conclusions if it had been aware of MAGIC, the Commission hurriedly put out a MAGIC addendum to its report.[21] Without any expertise whatsoever on the

---

18   Ibid, p. 50.

19   Ibid, p. 28.

20   Ibid, p. 16.

21   See MAGIC Addendum to *Personal Justice Denied* on page 358.

subject, the Commission's staff quickly "analyzed" MAGIC communications intelligence and reached conclusions about it in its addendum which were contrary to the opinions of every recognized authority on MAGIC for the past forty-seven years.

According to the Commission, MAGIC wasn't all that important, the messages didn't really mean what they said, and, unbelievably, "In sum, the MAGIC cables confirm the basic analysis presented by the Commission."[22]

This was too much for California's Congressman Dan Lungren, vice-chair of the Commission. In adding his views to the addendum, he wrote that the significance of MAGIC had not been grasped by the Commission and that it was inconceivable that MAGIC did not play a role in the decisions that were made. He went on to say, "For us as a Commission to deny that the decoded Japanese cables compiled in the MAGIC volumes did not influence the decisions made by America's leaders, tends to undercut the credibility of our historical pursuit."[23]

Not long after it was released the mistake-laden addendum was quietly withdrawn.

As directed in its original charge, the Commission next went on to "recommend appropriate remedies." Since it had concluded that the government had acted without cause or reason and in bad faith, it was recommended that every person of Japanese ancestry who had been evacuated or who had been registered into one of the various centers and camps for even one day should receive an official apology from the United States and be paid $20,000.

As the recommendations were laid out by the Commission, this would include the 6,000 babies born in the centers, the 4,300 young people who left to attend various colleges in the East, the 30,000 who eventually resettled to midwest and eastern states outside the West Coast exclusion areas, the nearly 10,000 adults who refused to take an unqualified loyalty oath, the more than 5,000 thousand who renounced their American citizenship and, believe it or not, the Commission's recommendations includes the 4,724 Japanese who, at their own request, were repatriated back to Japan from the camps after the war.

Altogether there are an estimated 60,000[24] people of Japanese ancestry who are still alive and eligible for the $20,000 reparations payment. The reason there

---

[22] *Personal Justice Denied*, p. 475.

[23] Ibid, p. 477.

[24] By the end of the payment program on August 10, 1998, 82,219 individuals, including enemy aliens who had been interned in Department of Justice camps as security risks to the United States, had been paid $20,000. Only twenty-nine individuals eligible for payment declined to accept it.

are so many after all these years is because the children who accompanied their parents from the exclusion areas or who were born in the centers are eligible for reparations.

Further, the Commission recommended that approximately $300 million be made available to propagandize the findings of the Commission in various ways including using its report as a textbook in schools, and "for the general welfare of the Japanese-American community."[25]

Total cost of all this to the taxpayers as spelled out by the Commission came to $1.5 billion.[26]

Shortly after issuing its MAGIC Addendum in July 1983 the Commission phased out, leaving a small unofficial cadre to cooperate with the Japanese American Citizens League and the American Civil Liberties Union in fighting its rear guard actions and to testify on behalf of the Commission in the courts and before various congressional subcommittees.

During its 1988 session the U.S. Congress voted, with a few modifications, to accept the findings and recommendations of the Commission. On August 10, 1988, in a complete turnaround, President Reagan, against the advice of the Department of Justice, signed the bill into law.

Thus, this hodgepodge of dishonest research and shocking misinformation in the Commission's report became official history. It is difficult to understand the Commission's stonewalling on some of its key points in the face of overwhelming evidence to the contrary. On three separate occasions I offered to make all my files and research available to the Commission: once to Special Counsel MacBeth, to Senator Matsunaga, and to Commissioner Arthur Flemming. In each instance my offer was refused or ignored. In the years to come, after all the emotionalism and politics have been removed from the issue, historians will take a hard, objective look at the Commission's report and modifications will be made.

Unfortunately, in the meantime, the report has been accepted by Congress and is already being used as the foundation for a five-year exhibition at the Smithsonian Institution in Washington D.C.[27] The project is funded jointly by the U.S. Congress and certain sponsors within Japan itself whose motives are

---

25   Congress allowed $5 million for this purpose. The $300 million figure was an estimate at the time based on the difference between the $1.5 billion recommended by the Commission and the estimated $1.2 billion that would be paid to 60,000 eligible individuals. In the event, as was noted earlier, over 82,219 individuals received payment.

26   The total cost was over $1.64 billion.

27   The exhibit entitled, "A More Perfect Union: Japanese Americans and the U.S. Constitution" has become a permanent exhibit in the Museum of American History.

unclear,[28] but which just happen to mesh with several recent attempts by the government of Japan to rewrite the history of World War II. Each week thousands of Americans are exposed to the Commission's "findings" through this exhibit. None of the official U.S. intelligence, which more than any other reason brought about the evacuation, is mentioned in the exhibit. Instead, only dishonorable reasons and acts by the United States are displayed as the motivation behind the evacuation.

In the not too distant future *Personal Justice Denied* will be sent to schools around the country as a textbook so children can learn this new history and how "shamefully" their government acted toward its resident Japanese population in the months following the surprise attack on the United States by the Japanese Empire.

---

[28] For example, a plaque at the exhibit credits the Japan Shipbuilding Industry Foundation with the audio-visual support.

CHAPTER 5

THE COURTS

Notwithstanding all the cries of unlawful actions and violations of constitutional rights, two Supreme Court cases decided during World War II upheld the legality of the government's evacuation actions. These cases have never been overturned and remain the law of the land, albeit there is a great deal of controversy within the legal fraternity about the cases.

The most vocal of those opposing the decisions reached in these two cases claim that the U.S. government deliberately and knowingly concealed and withheld information produced by the U.S. intelligence community from the Supreme Court which proved that the resident Japanese community on the West Coast did not constitute any kind of a threat to U.S. security. Charges have been made that there was a "conspiracy" within the government to hide certain intelligence reports and memos from the High Court which would have changed the Court's decisions if it had been aware of this concealed information. Besides the suppression of intelligence reports stating that there was no evidence of espionage by Japanese residents, the claim is made that those U.S. officials responsible for the evacuation knew their actions were in direct contradiction to authoritative intelligence.

Nothing could be farther from the truth. This chapter will deal specifically with these intelligence matters, and will demonstrate how the pro-reparations lobby and its attorneys have themselves deliberately misquoted certain intelligence reports in order to mislead the courts; have concealed intelligence findings which contradict their claims; have falsified the distribution of key reports; and have physically altered evidence which they have presented to the courts.

Before proceeding directly with this matter, however, it will first be necessary to review briefly the two landmark Supreme Court cases decided in 1943 and 1944.

The first case questioning the legality of the government's actions to come before the Supreme Court was *Hirabayashi v. United States*[1]. Gordon Kiyoshi Hirabayashi was a senior at the University of Washington in Seattle in the spring of 1942. A curfew had been imposed on all Japanese residents in the designated military area in which he lived, and he made a calculated decision to challenge its constitutionality. Accompanied by his lawyer, he turned himself into the local FBI office as an admitted lawbreaker. In subsequent proceedings he was duly indicted for violating the curfew law and for failure to report to a civil control station to register for evacuation.

As a result of his conviction Hirabayashi spent ninety days in a prison camp. He spent an additional year in jail because he also violated the country's draft evasion laws.

In a unanimous decision, the Supreme Court held in 1943 that the curfew was a legitimate exercise of the government's wartime powers. The Court did not give an opinion on registering for evacuation or the constitutionality of the evacuation itself. That was left to *Korematsu v. United States*.[2]

Fred Toyosaburo Korematsu was arrested in San Leandro, California on May 30, 1942. When questioned by the police he produced a draft registration card that identified him as "Clyde Sarah." He claimed to have been born in Las Vegas and to be of Spanish-Hawaiian origin. But his story soon fell apart. He spoke no Spanish and his draft card had obviously been clumsily altered.

The San Leandro police turned him over to the FBI. Korematsu, it then developed, was an unemployed welder from Oakland, California who had undergone plastic surgery on his face to conceal his Japanese ancestry. His reasons for defying the evacuation law had nothing whatsoever to do with any philosophical beliefs; he simply wanted to be with his Caucasian girlfriend, Ida Boitano. He wasn't fighting the evacuation; he was trying to avoid it. At his trial, Korematsu was found guilty of violating the exclusion order. He was given a suspended sentence and put on probation for five years.

Of course, Korematsu wasn't the only person apprehended for not complying with the exclusion order. At this time there were more than a dozen others

---

[1]   320 U.S. 81, 1943

[2]   323 U.S. 214-248: Oct. Term 1944.

in the central California area alone. Almost as quickly as they were arrested the violators were visited by Earnest Besig, the lawyer in charge of the American Civil Liberty Union's San Francisco office who was looking for a test case volunteer. So far everyone whom he interviewed had turned him down. But Korematsu was willing and even eager for the publicity which Besig promised would be forthcoming. Fred Korematsu was not exactly what the ACLU had in mind, but he was all they had, and they decided to go with him.

In due course, the case reached the Supreme Court and a decision was handed down in October 1944. Speaking for the 6-3 majority, Justice Hugo Black found that Executive Order 9066 was "nothing more than an exclusion order." The opinion stated that "neither in fact or by law were evacuees required to go to a relocation center and many did not." Further, the court held that Korematsu had been excluded from the military area not because of hostility to him or his race. He was excluded "because we are at war with the Japanese Empire, ... because [the Army] decided that the military urgency of the situation demanded that all citizens of Japanese ancestry be segregated from the West Coast temporarily." The Court went on to hold that the evacuation was a reasonable measure taken to defend the nation against espionage and sabotage saying, "There was evidence of disloyalty on the part of some, the military authorities considered that the need for action was great, and time was short."

There has been much talk in recent years that the High Court acted under wartime pressure, but Justice Black on September 26, 1971 stated in a *New York Times* article that: "I would do precisely the same thing today, in any part of this country. I would probably issue the same order were I President."

Neither *Korematsu* nor *Hirabayashi* have been overturned by the Supreme Court. However, on a seldom used writ of error or *coram nobis*, which asks the court to correct an alleged fundamental injustice in the original trial, the two cases were reviewed by district federal courts in 1983 and 1985 respectively. In both cases the petitioners claimed that because of newly discovered evidence it could now be proved that the U.S. government had lied to the Supreme Court and withheld key intelligence information.

The lower court in San Francisco at the Korematsu hearings accepted this so-called "newly discovered evidence" ploy. Operating on the theory that the Supreme Court would not have arrived at its 1944 decision if this evidence had been available, the federal judge in San Francisco vacated Korematsu's conviction.

None of the official intelligence reports in Part III issued by the U.S. intelligence community, nor any MAGIC was introduced by the government during the hearings. Korematsu's attorneys, who were now aware of MAGIC, seized this opportunity to request that a statement be written into the decision that there was no credible evidence that resident Japanese were involved in espionage. Having no information to the contrary, Judge Patel agreed with the request. While this was being done the U.S. Department of Justice attorney sat silently in the court room with a briefcase filled with MAGIC and U.S. intelligence reports which were absolute refutation of what the court was about to include in its decision. No attempt was made to introduce any of this data because it was the government's policy at that time not to contest this case.

In the Hirabayashi *coram nobis* hearings in Seattle, the Department of Justice decided that it would defend the government's actions, although it also offered to vacate the charges against Hirabayashi made by the district court against Hirabayashi in 1942.

Over the strenuous objections of the petitioner, Judge Voorhees allowed some MAGIC and intelligence reports to be introduced, but intelligence information's impact was severely held in check, the judge saying:

> I have some question about the relevance of the MAGIC documents.
> ...What we are here to decide, really, is whether the prosecution of
> this Petitioner was fair; whether he was denied due process in the
> prosecution, and we really are not concerned with the rightness or
> wrongness of the decisions made back in those days. But it is the
> prosecution, how it was carried on.

The government's case was crippled at the outset when the judge refused to allow a great mass of pro-government information to be used as evidence in the hearings because the proper groundwork had not been laid for its introduction.

Upon the conclusion of the testimony, Voorhees vacated Hirabayashi's conviction for disobeying the registration for evacuation. His decision was based entirely on his disagreement with a document titled, *Final Report: Japanese Evacuation from the West Coast, 1942*,[3] issued by the Commander of the Western Defense Command, General John L. DeWitt. *Final Report* was supposed to portray the military necessity behind the evacuation.

Since the report was to be made public at the time of its publication it could not discuss MAGIC in any shape or form because of security considerations. This left DeWitt largely with social and ethnic issues which weren't very

---

[3]   U.S. Army, Western Defense Command and Fourth Army, *Final Report: Japanese Evacuation from the West Coast, 1942* (Washington D.C.: GPO, 1943).

convincing in 1942 and were even less so in 1985. What little intelligence DeWitt managed to put into the report was clumsily done and highly vulnerable to attack in later years. Nor was DeWitt very diplomatic in his approach. According to him, the press of war did not allow for individual decisions on suspected espionage cases. And anyway, as he put it, the loyalty of Japanese residents couldn't be determined because "The Japanese race is an enemy race and while many second and third generation Japanese born on United States soil, possessed of United States citizenship have become 'Americanized,' the racial strains are undiluted,"[4] thereby, completely prejudicing his case. Hirabayashi's lawyers relentlessly attacked the report during the hearings.[5]

Judge Voorhees, without getting into the intelligence arena, disagreed with some of the basic conclusions in DeWitt's *Final Report*. But he did let stand Hirabayashi's curfew conviction as a reasonable wartime measure. Significantly, because MAGIC had been allowed to surface during the hearings, none of the wild accusations of lying and deliberate suppression of evidence by the U.S. government were in the decision, nor was the absurd statement that there was no evidence of espionage by Japanese residents.

Of course, the district court's decision on the curfew was appealed and, as expected, the appellate court overturned Judge Voorhees. Nonetheless, the Seattle hearings marked the first time the powerful Japanese-American juggernaut had received any kind of a setback on its relentless march through the Congress and the courts. It was also the first time that MAGIC, however slightly, had appeared in the court room.

The remaining part of this chapter will be devoted to demonstrating the blatant falsity of the outrageous accusations that some kind of a conspiracy existed within the U.S. government to deliberately mislead the courts on intelligence matters. Instead, proof will be offered which will, in fact, show that the Japanese-American lobby and their attorneys are themselves guilty of what they accuse the U.S. government of doing: lying to the court and withholding and concealing vital evidence.

These charges will be illustrated through a recent case which in the past six years has been before a federal district court, two federal appeals courts, the

---

4   *Final Report*, p. 34.

5   *Final Report* was a classic example of a cover story. It provided a plausible explanation for an operation (the evacuation) which was based on information that could not be revealed. Since then, all efforts have been directed at discrediting the cover story while at the same time denying the existence of information regarding the real basis of the evacuation.

Ironically, the often criticized racial overtones in *Final Report*, intentionally inserted or not, may have added to its plausibility since racially motivated operational decisions were common and well understood in the Japanese Empire.

Supreme Court once, and on October 31, 1988 was refused a second hearing by the Supreme Court.

Hohri v. United States is the case in question, and it involves the greatest amount of money for damages ever sought before a United States court. The real plaintiff and the force behind the lawsuit was the militant National Council for Japanese American Redress (NCJAR) which was founded in May 1979 for the sole purpose of obtaining monetary redress. The NCJAR selected twenty-five persons, living and dead, to represent the class of 125,000 plaintiffs. William Minoru Hohri is the chairman of the NCJAR. He spent much of the war in a relocation center where he refused to sign a loyalty oath to the United States. "I said no government deserved unqualified allegiance, and certainly not the United States Government." He is an unabashed admirer of Iva Toguri (Tokyo Rose), a Japanese-American who was convicted of treason. "She became my friend and one of my heroines of Japanese-American history."

In his book, *Repairing America: an account of the movement for Japanese-American redress*,[6] Hohri minces no words that it is money he is after:

> We seek the maximum compensation allowed for our causes of action. We are suing the United States of America for an unambiguously adversarial sum of twenty-seven billion dollars.
>
> ...the magnitude of our prayer for relief results from the multiplication of the class of 125,000 victims by twenty-two causes of action. We seek compensation of at least $10,000 for each cause of action. Twenty-two of them yield $220,000 per victim. Given the nature of the injuries, the individual claim is modest. This claim multiplied by 125,000 victims [or their heirs] yields 27.5 billion dollars.
>
> ... My own inclination is to demand one thousand dollars a day. That would come to around one hundred billion.

The *Hohri* case was the culmination of more than two years of legal preparation. It was filed by the NCJAR as client in March 1983, well beyond the six-year statute of limitations, but the NCJAR, joined by the JACL, claimed that the statute should not have started to run until 1980 when the Commission on Wartime Relocation and Internment of Civilians was established, and it became known through the Commission's research that:

---

[6]   William Minoru Hohri, *Repairing America: an account of the movement for Japanese-American redress* (Pullman: Washington State University Press, 1988).

United States officials knew their actions were in direct contradiction to authoritative intelligence reports already in defendant's possession.

... Newly discovered evidence further establishes that defendant has engaged in a long-standing conspiracy to deprive the plaintiff class of judicial redress for defendant's unlawful actions, by intentionally misrepresenting and suppressing information in defendant's possession which attested to plaintiff's loyalty to the United States.

The NCJAR contended that for these reasons the statute of limitations should have been postponed while the government was supposedly engaged in these "affirmative acts of concealment and fraud." Moreover, says the NCJAR, the Supreme Court in *Hirabayashi* and *Korematsu* would have arrived at a different decision if the government had not suppressed and misrepresented pertinent information.

To support all these claims the seventy-two page NCJAR complaint stated what this "newly discovered" intelligence was supposed to be, what was concealed, what was misrepresented, and what was ignored.

Of course, nothing is mentioned in the complaint about what it "overlooked," namely, all the MAGIC messages in Part II, and, with one exception, which it deliberately misquotes, all the official intelligence reports dealing with espionage in Part III.

Let us now examine the actual documents and see who is deceiving whom.

The first incidence of deception and of deliberately falsifying evidence with which we will deal is on page 31 of the NCJAR complaint which states that the War Department's own intelligence office issued confidential intelligence reports throughout the war stating:

Japan's knowledge of the United States military defenses and status was gained not through post-Pearl Harbor activities of Japanese-Americans, but through pre-war activities of accredited diplomatic, military, and naval attaches.

This doctored quotation is derived from a series of Western Defense Command weekly intelligence reports issued after Pearl Harbor.[7] The complete statement which the Western Defense Command used over and over again is:

---

7 See Western Defense Command G-2 Periodic Report, February 28, 1942 on page 244 for an example of one of these reports. Reference on page 246.

The enemy's probable knowledge of our situation has not been gained by observation or reconnaissance but by information learned during peace by the activities of accredited diplomatic, military, and naval attaches and their agents. *Efforts to deny this information to the enemy include surveillance of enemy aliens, internment of alien leaders and suspected spies and agents, seizure of contraband in possession of enemy aliens, adoption of stringent censorship measures, and transfer of many other Japanese, including second generation members of our military forces, from this theater. All Persons of Japanese ancestry, including military Personnel, will be removed eventually from this theater of operation.* (Italics added)

Note that the complaint has inserted its own words into the Western Defense Command statement, saying that Japanese-Americans did not provide any post-Pearl Harbor military information. There is outright tampering involved here. This is not what the Western Defense Command reported. Moreover, only the first part of the quotation is cited. The remainder of the quotation which spells out who these "agents" were who provided military information to Japan's accredited representatives is completely omitted. It is obvious from the full statement that the "agents" referred to here were resident Japanese and that the Western Defense Command believed the espionage problem would be largely solved by removing them from the West Coast.

By altering the first part of Western Defense Command's conclusion, and leaving out the last part of the quote, the NCJAR made a calculated decision to mislead the court into thinking that the Western Defense Command, which was responsible for the defense of the West Coast, reported that Japan's diplomatic and military representatives, but no resident Japanese, were involved in gathering information about U.S. military facilities.

To cover up their deliberate deception of the courts, the NCJAR and its attorneys failed to attach the Western Defense Command report it was citing to its complaint because if it had done so the full quotation would have been revealed to the court. Western Defense Command's complete statement is a description of how Japan's espionage organization functioned along the West Coast for the year preceding Pearl Harbor, utilizing Japanese residents, exactly as spelled out in MAGIC communications.

The reason that the Western Defense Command was able to make such an all-embracing intelligence conclusion was because after Pearl Harbor, when the MAGIC distribution system was overhauled and knowledge about MAGIC was widened to include the commands, the Western Defense Command was brought into the full MAGIC picture. Some of the concerns expressed in the full statement can be traced to specific MAGIC messages. For example, the May 1941 intercepted Japanese messages from Seattle and Los Angeles to Tokyo reported that Japanese-Americans in the armed forces had been recruited to provide intelligence.[8] This was probably the reason that the Western Defense Command was suddenly so anxious to move Japanese-Americans in the armed forces out of its command.

The second instance of deception by the NCJAR, and others, concerns certain subversive activities by Japanese residents alleged by the commander of the Western Defense Command, General DeWitt, in his *Final Report* on the West Coast situation. The *Final Report* was intended to describe to the U.S. public the military necessity behind the evacuation. Some reasons had to be given to the American people why the government felt that such drastic actions were necessary. DeWitt's report attempted to do that, and it has been a contentious document since the day it was first written with charges that there were four different versions; that it was rewritten to take out some of the racist statements made in the document; that it was deliberately withheld; and that even the Department of Justice lawyers who were defending the government's evacuation actions in the *Korematsu* and *Hirabayashi* cases knew that the intelligence information in the report was false.

Admittedly, it is a poor document, but most of the hullabaloo over DeWitt's report is meaningless because the most important reason for the evacuation, MAGIC, couldn't be put into the report. DeWitt couldn't very well describe how we were reading Japanese government messages derived from broken Japanese codes and ciphers and what those messages had revealed about espionage by resident Japanese on the West Coast. As a result, he reached out too far to justify some of his conclusions, and ever since both he and the government have been relentlessly attacked on some of the statements about the military necessity for the evacuation.

What is and what is not a racist statement is beyond the scope of this book, as is the handling of *Final Report*. For those who wish to pursue these subjects further the most complete discussion of them can be found in the 1985 hearings in Seattle on *Hirabayashi v. United States*.[9]

Be all that as it may, this book is about intelligence and only that part of DeWitt's document concerned with intelligence will be examined here.

Basically, *Final Report* discusses two types of subversive activities by Japanese residents. The first was a series of highly publicized raids by the FBI on the homes and business establishments of Japanese aliens. By May 1942 these searches had produced 2,592 guns of various kinds, 199,000 rounds of

---

8   See message #067, May 9, 1941, p. 147 and message #45, May 11, 1941, p. 148.

9   627 F. Supp. 1445 W.D. Wash. 1986.

ammunition, 1,652 sticks of dynamite, 1,458 radio receivers, 2,014 cameras and numerous other contraband items which alien Japanese had been ordered to surrender in January.[10] The importance of this has been debated over and over again, and will probably never be resolved. A little arithmetic, however, brings out a sobering statistic. Even if the FBI had confiscated every single contraband gun, which it certainly didn't, that meant there was roughly one gun for every four adult male Japanese enemy aliens on the West Coast long after they had been ordered to give up all their weapons. One of the valid reasons given for possession of all this contraband armament was self-protection. There had been a large number of unprovoked attacks, including murder and arson, particularly by Filipinos, on Japanese residents, and there were rumors of vigilante groups being formed. Protection of Japanese residents was, in fact, one of the ancillary reasons behind the evacuation, and many evacuees were grateful to the government for the safety provided in the relocation centers.

DeWitt's second subversive charge attracted more attention. He reported that there were numerous cases of illicit signaling from shore to Japanese submarines off the coast. Hundreds of cases of blinking lights and other visual signals were reported. It was asserted that numerous unauthorized radio communications from coastal areas had been intercepted, and "for a period of several weeks following December 7, substantially every ship leaving a West Coast port was attacked by an enemy submarine." The inference was that the Japanese navy was alerted by illicit transmitters. Several instances of Japanese submarines attacking shore facilities on the West Coast were also cited. It was pointed out in *Final Report* that the submarine approaches to the coast had been made in each instance in such a way as to avoid detection devices and to be just out of range of shore batteries, the inference once again being that they were guided by illegal signaling from shore.

Unauthorized radio transmissions were the business of the Federal Communications Commission (FCC), which in cooperation with the FBI and the military, undertook to locate and stamp out these illicit radio communications. Many hundreds of suspect transmissions had to be checked. Those that couldn't be identified by monitoring stations were searched out by mobile direction finding units.

All of this took time and it was months after Pearl Harbor before it was determined that illicit radio transmissions were not the problem that they were once thought to be. Both the NCJAR's complaint and the Commission

---

[10] Such items were forbidden under the authority of Presidential Proclamation 2525, December 7, 1941.

on Wartime Relocation and Internment of Civilians in its report make a great deal of these conclusions citing several Attorney General, FCC, and FBI memoranda, all written in 1944, concluding that there had been no illicit radio transmissions. The most damaging of these is an FCC memo dated April 4, 1944 which flatly denies that there were ever any illicit radio signals to Japanese warships. The FCC memo is incorporated into the NCJAR complaint as exhibit "E."

But the point is that all this was not known when the evacuation decision was made. In fact, at that time the prevailing intelligence opinion was exactly the opposite. The government had to make its decision based on the intelligence which was available at that time. And what was in the hands of the administration and General DeWitt when the evacuation decision was made in February 1942 was a J. Edgar Hoover assessment, backed by military intelligence, which said that illicit signaling by shore radios to offshore Japanese naval units was rampant in Hawaii. This report was highly important and is the one that really mattered because it was the intelligence reported to General DeWitt on the signaling problem when *Final Report* was drafted. Something written in 1944, while interesting, has no relevance to *Final Report*.

What DeWitt actually knew at the time was this: On January 14, 1942, J. Edgar Hoover, Director of the FBI, Rear Admiral Wilkinson, Director of the Office of Naval Intelligence, and Colonel Bissell of the Military Intelligence Division met to discuss shore-to-ship signaling. The three organizations represented were the most powerful and influential elements of the 1942 U.S. intelligence community. All of them, along with the FCC, were presently engaged in trying to track down and suppress suspected signaling from the West Coast, but a comparable effort did not exist in Hawaii, and this was a matter of concern to them. As a result of this meeting Hoover sent a personal letter on January 16, 1942 to James L. Fly, chairman of the FCC:

> In regard to present conditions in the Hawaiian Islands, it is apparent that illicit short-wave radio transmissions are being sent from clandestine stations operating in the islands themselves, in communication with mobile units of the Japanese Navy, through which intelligence information is being reported to the enemy. It is extremely important that these clandestine stations be located and eliminated from operation and that the individuals concerned with their operation be dealt with appropriately as rapidly as possible.
>
> On the occasion of this conference Rear Admiral Wilkinson [ONI] and Colonel Bissell [MID] expressed the desire that I call your attention to

the situation by letter and impress upon you the vital importance and necessity for establishing immediately an exhaustive coverage on these radio activities.[11]

In other words, the FBI, the ONI, and the MID believed that there was all kinds of radio signaling going on in early 1942 when DeWitt's *Final Report* was first written. But this letter was withheld from the court. It is one thing to make the best case possible for one's cause, but quite another to deliberately mislead the U.S. Courts and the U.S. Congress by omitting key information, and then have the audacity to accuse, falsely and knowingly, the other side with lying and fraud in connection with these same events.

The third and possibly most flagrant instance of deception concerns a January 26, 1942 memo to Admiral Stark, Chief of Naval Operations, from Lieutenant Commander K. D. Ringle, deputy intelligence officer for the Eleventh Naval District (Los Angeles). This was the personal memo discussed in Chapter 4 and fully reproduced in Part III,[12] which states that as many as 3,500 resident Japanese on the mainland might possibly act as spies and saboteurs; that as many as 25 percent of all Japanese-Americans were of doubtful loyalty; and that many Japanese-Americans educated in Japan (Kibei) should immediately be incarcerated without regard to the Bill of Rights. The Commission in its report and the NCJAR in its complaint ignore this part of Ringle's memo.

Understandably, they focus in on that part of the memo which suggests that the Japanese question had been magnified out of proportion, and that the decision to evacuate resident Japanese should be on an individual basis, regardless of citizenship, rather than mass evacuation.

Although the Ringle memo to Stark is somewhat self-contradictory, its individual points are reasonably straightforward. It is the interpretation, distribution, and status of the memo which have been grossly misrepresented.

The Commission and NCJAR version of the Ringle memo and its history begins with Edward J. Ennis who testified and wrote extensively in favor of reparations. At the present time Ennis is an official with the ACLU, but during the war he was the director of the Alien Enemy Control Unit of the Justice Department which was concerned with all activities involving enemy aliens during World War II.[13]

---

[11]   See Hoover letter to Fly, January 16, 1942 on page 226.

[12]   See Ringle memo, January 26, 1942 on page 315.

[13]   Ennis has since died.

When the *Hirabayashi* and *Korematsu* cases came to the Supreme Court during World War II it was the role of the Department of Justice to defend the War Department's actions in court. Ennis was a part of this Department of Justice team. It is his contention today (along with the NCJAR and the JACL) that if the War Department had not concealed from the High Court the handling of DeWitt's *Final Report*, and its alleged racist statements and lies about shore-to-ship signaling, and other acts by the government including the conceal- ment of the January 26, 1942 Ringle report, the Supreme Court would have ruled differently in both of those cases.

Exhibit "J" in the NCJAR complaint is a April 30, 1943 memo from Ennis to the Solicitor General of the Department of Justice who was in charge of the government's defense in the wartime *Hirabayashi* and *Korematsu* cases. In this memo, most of which is sheer fantasy, Ennis describes to the Solicitor General how he happened to read an article titled, "The Japanese in America, The Problem and Solution" which appeared in *Harper's Magazine* in October 1942. The article concluded that the evacuation of resident Japanese should have been handled on an individual basis rather than a racial one. The author of the article was anonymous, but Ennis said he did some sleuthing and discovered that it was written by Lieutenant Commander Ringle. According to Ennis he was able to verify this after obtaining the January 26, 1942 Ringle memo from the War Relocation Authority and comparing it with the *Harper's Magazine* article. Further checking, he went on, disclosed that Ringle's memo in fact represented the position of the ONI; moreover, he said it was his understand- ing that the Army had agreed before the war to permit the Navy to do all its Japanese intelligence for it, and thus it followed that the Army was now bound by the Navy's viewpoint; therefore, Ennis concluded, the Ringle memo represented the opinion of the entire military intelligence establishment on the evacuation issue, and should be so regarded.

In light of all this, Ennis wrote in his April 30, 1943 memo to the Solicitor General, DeWitt and the War Department had acted contrary to "the only intelligence agency responsible" for advising them. Ennis strongly recom- mended that the Supreme Court be advised of the Ringle memo, and he was attaching the "Department's only copy of this memorandum" which he said he had managed to obtain from the civilian-run War Relocation Authority. Not to notify the courts of this memo, he felt, would be a suppression of evi- dence.

The Solicitor General dismissed Ennis' recommendation to show the Ringle memo to the Court. Perhaps it was because he knew its official status was exactly zero within the military commands and that it had been specifically rejected by ONI. Understandably, he was reluctant to introduce a document to the Supreme Court written by an obscure naval officer named Ringle, which the Navy would not endorse and which Ringle himself contradicted two weeks later.

Ennis' incredible document and the rejection of the Ringle report by the Solicitor General was red meat for the NCJAR complaint: "Defendant, in bad faith, excluded from the record of pending court actions the evidence contradicting the so-called 'military necessity' for mass imprisonment of plaintiffs." The complaint went on to accuse the government of being fully aware that its actions were in direct contradiction to "authoritative intelligence reports."

The Ringle report is attached to the NCJAR's complaint as exhibit "D." Outrageously and fraudulently missing from the complaint is the ONI cover memo dated February 14, 1942 which was attached to Ringle's report forwarding it for information to the Department of Justice Special Defense Unit, the Department of Justice's Federal Bureau of Investigation, the Department of Justice's Alien Enemy Control Unit of which Ennis was the chief, and the Army's Military Intelligence Division. Thus, it was distributed to three different organizations within the Department of Justice including Ennis' own unit. This was the document which is now claimed to have been concealed.

The statement in the Ennis memo to the Solicitor General that the Army agreed to let the Navy conduct its Japanese intelligence for it would have come as a shock to the Army Signal Intelligence Service units intercepting and decoding MAGIC, and to General Sherman Miles, MID's chief who testified to the Joint Congressional Committee that he considered counterintelligence to be one of his most important responsibilities.

As to the Ennis claim he had learned that the Ringle memo represented the position of the Office of Naval Intelligence, he had only to look within his own office at the February 14, 1942 cover memo from the ONI which had forwarded Ringle's study to him a year before he "discovered" it in *Harper's Magazine*. The cover memo states most clearly that the Ringle memorandum *"does not represent the final and official opinion of the Office of Naval Intelligence on this subject."*[14] (Italics added)

Thus, the Ringle memo so heavily relied upon by the Commission and the NCJAR, was an unofficial document having no status whatsoever; was not concealed, but on the contrary was given wide distribution; did not represent the stated position of the ONI nor anyone else of any status in the military; and finally was in direct conflict with an official ONI intelligence report authored by Lieutenant Commander Ringle himself less than two weeks later.

---

[14]   See ONI cover memo February 14, 1942 on page 314.

On February 7, 1942 Ringle concluded that "As long as this colony, which contains known alien sympathizers even though of American citizenship is allowed to exist in the heart of every activity in the Los Angeles Harbor, it must be assumed that [vital military intelligence will be] known, observed, and transmitted to the enemy quickly and easily."[15] This official ONI report, authored by Ringle, with its conclusion that evacuation of the Terminal Island colony was the only way to prevent espionage and possible sabotage, was almost entirely directed toward Japanese-Americans on the island because practically all Issei males had already been removed from the island.

Ennis testified at length before congressional subcommittees, the Commission, and the courts on his version of the Ringle report and how it was suppressed. His April 30, 1943 memo to the Solicitor General is constantly quoted. Being a respected lawyer and someone who was on the scene in 1942, his testimony and his memo carried considerable weight, and made the task of documenting the true historical role played by U.S. intelligence in the evacuation decision far more difficult.

All the above issues and memos about them are involved in the so-called "newly discovered evidence" which researchers supposedly brought to light when the Commission began its investigation, and which the NCJAR said in its complaint should toll the statute of limitations.

Insofar as intelligence is concerned the "new evidence" is a myth. Most of it is nothing more than a composite of misinformation, concealment of contradictory information, and the deliberate manipulation of intelligence reports.

NCJAR's lawsuit, containing all the misinformation previously discussed, was filed on March 16, 1983 before the United States District Court for the District of Columbia, Judge Oberdorfer presiding. Two months later, on May 16, 1983 the Department of Justice filed a motion to dismiss. The U.S. presented three defenses: (1) the statute of limitations; (2) the American-Japanese Evacuation Claims Act of 1948; and (3) sovereign immunity.

In making its defense the government did not bring up MAGIC. It wasn't until May 22, 1983 in a *New York Times* article that the public (and apparently the Department of Justice) first learned of MAGIC's relationship to the reparations case. Additionally, the Department of Justice had no knowledge of how the intelligence in the plaintiff's complaint had been manipulated. Even at this late date some of the documents in Parts II and III of this book will come as a surprise to the Department of Justice.

---

15 See ONI report, February 7, 1942, on page 325. Reference on page 328.

Judge Oberdorfer's decision was handed down on May 17, 1984. His decision rebuffed NCJAR'S attempt to extend private property to constitutional rights but he found that there had been some "unjust takings" by the government during the war. Accordingly, the court reduced plaintiff's cause of actions from twenty-two to one, leaving only the "unjust taking" cause, and that, he said, was barred by the six-year statute of limitations.

Not having been given any information to the contrary, the judge accepted the plaintiff's claim that the government had lied and suppressed certain intelligence data relating to the findings of the FCC, the FBI, and the ONI. But, he wrote, "the standard by which fraudulent concealment must be judged is not one of full disclosure, but rather one of sufficient disclosure to allow the plaintiffs through due diligence, to state a claim." In other words, by inference, the court said the government had so badly bungled its attempts to conceal some of the original FCC, FBI, and ONI documents, that the plaintiff with due diligence should have been able to discover these reports in the late 1940s as well as the U.S. government's dishonesty in this matter.

This, said the court, is when the statute of limitations should have started to run. Judge Oberdorfer then granted the government's motion to dismiss.

The case was immediately appealed to the U.S. Court of Appeals for the District of Columbia by the NCJAR and on January 21, 1986 that court, in a 2-1 decision, reversed Oberdorfer's decision on the statute of limitations and remanded the lawsuit to trial. However, the appellate court partially upheld the lower court when it allowed only the "unjust taking" cause of action to remain, agreeing with the lower court on the constitutional questions.

This was clearly unsatisfactory to the NCJAR because this meant that with damages still limited to only the "unjust taking" cause there was no chance for the huge monetary award sought by the NCJAR. Moreover, NCJAR and the JACL wanted to get to the Supreme Court because only there could the mass evacuation constitutional issue be tested with the opportunity to overturn the *Hirabayashi* and *Korematsu* decisions. Only the Supreme Court itself can overturn a Supreme Court decision.

Therefore, on August 26, 1986 the NCJAR filed a petition for a *writ of certiorari*, the formal designator asking for review by the Supreme Court. The case was accepted by the High Court, and arguments before it were heard during April 1987.

It was not the U.S. government's finest hour. A trial strategy was adopted which reversed the government's previous position and ignored all the MAGIC intelligence and the reports of the 1942 intelligence community, most of which by now were in the possession of the Department of Justice. Initially, the Department of Justice lawyers felt certain that with these materials they could prove that President Roosevelt's administration acted on the evacuation in good faith based on the intelligence which was available to it.

However, even before the trial, this position began to backfire when the Department of Justice found itself up against the highly organized Japanese-American lobby and an antagonistic media, Congress, and public which came down on the side of what was perceived to be the innocent victims of a rough-shod, freewheeling, wartime government. Rather than fight all that sympathy for the "underdog" and under what must have been tremendous pressure from the Japanese-American lobby and its supporters, the Department of Justice hastily formulated a new strategy.

Wearing a straight face, Solicitor General Charles Fried proceeded to tell the Supreme Court that, regretfully, the U.S. government's actions to evacuate Japanese residents from the West Coast in 1942 were "political... shameful ... not based on intelligence or military considerations," and was "implemented by racists."

Having gotten all that baggage out of the way, Fried concentrated on jurisdiction, that the wrong court of appeals had heard the case.

In an anti-climatic decision the Supreme Court unanimously accepted Fried's jurisdictional argument and ruled on June 1, 1987 that the case should have been tried in the U.S. Court of Appeals for the Federal Circuit instead of the U.S. Court of Appeals for the District of Columbia.

Undaunted, and still driven by the possibilities of a mind-boggling $27 billion award, the NCJAR tenaciously filed its case in the U.S. Court of Appeals for the Federal Circuit. But, in a major setback, on May 11, 1988 that court handed down its 2-1 decision upholding Judge Oberdorfer's original findings in 1983.

Gathering all the support they could muster, the NCJAR and the JACL maneuvered toward what they hoped would be their final court action. They appealed the findings of the U.S. Court of Appeals for the Federal Circuit to the Supreme Court. A final opportunity and one more chance for complete triumph appeared close at hand.

But it was not to be. In a crushing blow to the NCJAR and the JACL the Supreme Court justices on October 31, 1988, without comment, let stand the findings of the appellate court. This decision effectively put an end to court actions for additional money, and left the *Korematsu* and *Hirabayashi* cases in place.

Even though they did not gain their objectives in the court system for a staggering amount of money and the overturning of the *Korematsu* and *Hirabayashi* cases, NCJAR and the JACL must find some satisfaction in the results. Their claim that the U.S. government deliberately lied to the wartime

Supreme Court and maliciously suppressed evidence from the intelligence community has gone unchallenged and remains on the court records. At no stage in the *Hohri* case was MAGIC or the crucial intelligence documents based on MAGIC and other intelligence introduced to counter the charges made in the *Hohri* complaint. Moreover, such evidence will probably never be used in any future court case by the U.S. government because it is now contrary to the position taken by the Department of Justice before the Supreme Court on this issue.

Thus, NCJAR and the JACL lost their case not on the substantive issues, but on a legal technicality, the statute of limitations.

CHAPTER 6

THE CONGRESS

Almost immediately after the Commission on Wartime Relocation and Internment of Civilians submitted its report, *Personal Justice Denied*, to the U.S. Congress in February 1983, bills were introduced to accept the findings and the recommendations of the Commission. The first of these bills was S. 1520 jointly sponsored by Senator Cranston of California and Senator Kennedy of Massachusetts. Hearings were held on July 27, 1983 by a subcommittee of the Senate Committee on the Judiciary, chaired by Senator Charles Grassley, a Republican from Iowa.

The hearings on S. 1520 lasted only one day and were concerned only with the evacuation of Japanese residents. Nothing was submitted on the Aleut question. Several senators and congressmen testified on behalf of the bill. A few evacuees told their story and Joan Bernstein, chairwoman of the Commission, testified.

There were several pro-government witnesses who testified that the circumstances surrounding the evacuation and the relocation centers were often considerably different from what was portrayed in the Commission's report. In particular, Lillian Baker of California, a research writer of note, submitted a large number of documents for the record which sharply contradicted many of the findings in *Personal Justice Denied*. Included in these submissions by Baker were several spinoff newspaper items from the May 22, 1983 *New York Times* article in which I had raised the question why MAGIC had not been considered in the Commission's report.

Although everything on the surface appeared to be calm during the Grassley hearings on the reparations bill, both the JACL and the Commission had crash programs underway to find out what this thing called MAGIC was that had suddenly emerged as a major factor. Apparently, the *Times* article and the spinoffs from it published in other newspapers around the country had created absolute havoc within the Commission. At Congressman Lungren's insistence Special Counsel Angus MacBeth telephoned me in Honolulu. It was a friendly conversation. MacBeth asked a number of questions about MAGIC. At the conclusion of the conversation, and at his request, MacBeth was given a list of references on MAGIC. As diplomatically as possible under the circumstances, I volunteered my documents and my time to work with the Commission staff to assist in straightening out the intelligence part of the report. MacBeth said he appreciated the offer, but nothing came of it. I was not contacted again by the Commission.

By the time the Grassley hearings started on July 27, 1983 the Commission, without any expertise whatsoever on the subject, managed to rush into print a MAGIC addendum[1] to its report, presumably using the list of references which I had provided MacBeth. Additionally, the Japanese American Citizens League (JACL), of all people, submitted to Grassley's subcommittee a paper titled, "Analysis of Tokyo Cablegram Story"[2] which said the MAGIC cables had no relevance to the Commission's conclusions, and that the 1942 U.S. intelligence community had refuted the cablegrams. There was no one at the hearings to counter these absurd claims or to explain MAGIC or to answer questions on it except the Commission and the JACL, both of which admitted that they had only heard of MAGIC when they read the *New York Times* article a few weeks earlier. I was not invited to testify and no historian or intelligence specialist on MAGIC was consulted.

This was not entirely the fault of the subcommittee. Time did not permit an orderly submission of materials and major testimony on a completely new topic about which the subcommittee knew little or nothing. Without a moment to spare the Commission and the JACL had managed to get their denials of MAGIC into the hearings, but the subcommittee was caught unawares, and the MAGIC issue ended up simply pasted onto the hearings with no one to speak authoritatively on the issue. By default, MAGIC remained something of an enigma, and as a result, it was a non-issue in the Grassley hearings.

---

[1]   See *MAGIC Addendum to Personal Justice Denied* on page 358.

[2]   Congress, Senate, *Japanese-American Evacuation Redress*, (Washington D.C.: GPO) pp. 412-413.

Far and away the most extensive congressional hearings on the reparations issue was by a subcommittee of the House Judiciary Committee chaired by Sam Hall, a Democrat from Texas. Approximately one year after the Grassley episode Sam Hall held hearings in the Rayburn building on June 20, 21, 27, and then jumped to September 12, 1984 for the last day. Three separate bills to accept the findings and recommendations of the Commission had been introduced into the House: H.R. 3387, H.R. 4322, and H.R. 4110, the last introduced by the Speaker of the House, Jim Wright.

MAGIC dominated the entire proceedings. Although I wasn't scheduled to testify before the subcommittee until June 27, Chairman Hall, realizing the importance MAGIC would have on the hearings, studied the intercepts and related data submitted by me prior to the hearings. From the very first day it was apparent that Hall was determined to get to the root of this matter. John J. McCloy, in response to Hall's questions, testified that MAGIC was the most important intelligence the President and his advisers possessed. He himself had been let in on the tight circle of people cleared for MAGIC by Secretary Stimson. According to McCloy, MAGIC was avidly read by the President and his wartime advisers, and was a major factor in the evacuation decision.[3]

Karl Bendetsen testified that General DeWitt regularly received sanitized MAGIC and that MAGIC was the basis for DeWitt's recommendation.[4]

Considering that McCloy and Bendetsen both played key roles in the evacuation drama, their testimony alone should have been enough to trigger changes in the Commission's report. No other living persons had the intimate and detailed knowledge of these two on the circumstances surrounding Executive Order 9066. It is true that McCloy and Bendetsen should have brought up these intelligence issues when they testified before the Commission, but both men were well advanced in years and their memories needed jogging. Instead of working gently with them and drawing out what they knew, they were driven from the witness stand by boos, whistles, foot stamping, and shouted remarks from a hostile audience. Later, when they had time to reflect on it, and had the opportunity to see the actual intelligence, some of which, in the case of McCloy, was actually addressed to him, they were able to put together many of the details.

The only other witness whose personal knowledge of what happened came close to McCloy and Bendetsen was Edward Ennis. When Hall asked him about MAGIC Ennis stoutly maintained that MAGIC had nothing to do with the evacuation, that it was nothing but a red herring. Although he admitted

---

3 Congress, House, *Japanese-American and Aleutian Wartime Relocation*, p. 117.

4 Ibid, p. 68.

that he knew nothing about MAGIC, he continued to insist that Japanese residents on the West Coast were not a security risk no matter what the Japanese government said in the MAGIC messages. One of the giants in the JACL, Mike Masaoka, took the same position at the hearings. He hadn't "seen the MAGIC code" but he was certain that there weren't any spies among the Japanese residents.

Joan Bernstein, chairperson of the Commission, and one of the commissioners, Dr. Flemming, testified before the Hall subcommittee, but when the questions on MAGIC started to come from Hall they turned the microphone over to Angus MacBeth, the Commission Counsel. He testified that MAGIC could not have played a major role in the evacuation decision because the Commission failed to discover any evidence whatsoever about MAGIC, and therefore it could not have been all that important. Additionally, he took the position that even though MAGIC had not surfaced during the Commission's investigation, the Commission was now aware of it, and after studying it had decided that MAGIC did not warrant making any changes in the Commission's findings. In response to Hall's questions MacBeth admitted, "yes," that the Commission's report was put out before it learned of MAGIC, but he said it was taken into account before the Commission made its recommendations.[5]

The chronology of events does not support MacBeth's contention. The Commission's report was published in December 1982, and submitted to Congress in February 1983. The Commission's recommendations were released on June 22, 1983 and the "MAGIC Addendum" (*Addendum to Personal Justice Denied*)[6] to the Commission's report was given to the press on June 28, six days after the recommendations. The *New York Times* article which broke the MAGIC story was dated May 22, 1983.

At a theoretical best this would have given the Commission only a few weeks to assemble all the data, analyze its significance, and then relate it to the issue of West Coast Japanese residents. Given the poor level of competence about intelligence on the Commission staff, this would seem an impossibility. Moreover, Congressman Lungren, vice-chairman of the Commission, testified, "The Commission, I must tell you, quite honestly was unable to focus attention on the decoded Japanese cables compiled in the MAGIC volumes due to time constraints."[7]

---

5   Ibid, p. 68.

6   See MAGIC Addendum to *Personal Justice Denied* on page 358.

7   Congress, House, *Japanese-American and Aleutian Wartime Relocation*, p. 91.

Hall's questions had laid bare the Commission's confusion about MAGIC and its bungling of the intelligence picture. But it was left to me on June 27, 1984 to put everything in perspective. The nature, history, importance, and distribution of MAGIC was addressed. Its relevance to the evacuation matter was discussed in detail. A number of MAGIC messages were incorporated into the record along with intelligence reports from the Office of Naval Intelligence, Military Intelligence Division, and FBI. My testimony, fully footnoted and referenced, and every major point documented, was made a matter of record by the subcommittee.[8]

Throughout my testimony I stressed that my objective in all this was not to try and prove disloyalty on the part of Japanese residents on the West Coast, but to present an accurate historical record of the intelligence which was available to key decision makers in the government and the role it played in this tragic event, something which the Commission was supposed to have done but completely failed to do. I also made the point that an objective study of this intelligence, its distribution, and its evaluation by the U.S. intelligence community would clear the good names of those key people in the wartime U.S. government who received this critical intelligence and acted on it in a responsible manner, but who were now accused by the Commission of having acted dishonorably and illegally.

When my oral testimony before the subcommittee was finished there were a number of questions, all very friendly, and I was thanked by several members of the subcommittee for making my documents, research, and findings available. There was no rebuttal from any source at this time. Within the hearing chamber there was only stunned silence from the JACL, NCJAR, ACLU, and the Commission representatives who were present in the audience. But this was only a temporary lull as the reparations lobby quickly regrouped and brought up its heavy artillery. The stakes were enormous and MAGIC was rapidly becoming a major threat to congressional acceptance of the Commission's findings and recommendations.

The two people chosen to discredit MAGIC and the reports of the intelligence community were both Caucasians to avoid the appearance of pitting one race against another. The first was retired Army Lieutenant Colonel John Herzig. He had spent some time in counterintelligence after the war and was married to a Japanese-American who was one of the principal researchers on the Commission staff. Herzig himself had done considerable research for the Commission. The second was Peter Irons, a college professor who had written a highly one-sided book on the legal aspects of the evacuation. Irons was a

---

8   Ibid, p. 441.

senior adviser to the Commission staff. Neither had heard of MAGIC until they read about it in the newspapers, but the two of them would spend a great deal of time over the coming months trying to discredit both MAGIC and the person who had the impudence to point out its omission in the Commission's report.

While the Hall subcommittee was waiting to complete its last day of hearings on September 12, 1984, a Senate subcommittee chaired by Republican Ted Stevens of Alaska held one day of hearings in Los Angeles on August 16, 1984. Only the West Coast evacuation was considered. The new Senate bill was titled S. 2116, and there were twenty co-sponsoring senators.

Only Senator Stevens was there from the Senate subcommittee, and he asked few questions. The witnesses were each permitted only a brief statement, but were allowed to turn in all their written materials to be made a matter of record. Since the subcommittee never published anything on the hearings, this turned out to be a dubious privilege. There was an assortment of congressional representatives from California testifying on behalf of the bill, various Japanese-American organizations, several evacuees, and a fair representation of pro-government people including former Senator S. I. Hayakawa. Frederick Bernays Wiener, a distinguished attorney and scholar with impressive credentials, made a scathing attack on the Commission's legal shortcomings and procedures.

I made my presentation, which was a shortened version of what had been given at the Hall hearings on June 27. Lt. Col. Herzig was the next to last witness at the hearings. It was late in the afternoon and most of the audience had gone home. They missed Herzig's opening barrage. In consultation with a variety of pro-reparations organizations and people, he had spent the last two months preparing a forty page attack on MAGIC and on me which he handed over to the subcommittee. As in the MAGIC Addendum to the Commission's report there was no attempt to reconcile MAGIC and the reports of the U.S. intelligence community with what had happened in 1942. There was an out and out denial that MAGIC played any role in the evacuation decision. The intelligence reports which Herzig chose to acknowledge were misquoted and misinterpreted. The remainder were simply ignored as were the evaluations of MAGIC made by intelligence officials and others in 1941 and 1942.

Instead, Herzig named witness after witness who had testified before the Commission and had not mentioned MAGIC, and, therefore, Herzig argued, MAGIC could not have played a role since none of these people were aware of it. This basic ignorance of communications intelligence (COMINT) and the 1942 U.S. intelligence structure and its reporting was the problem with the Commission's report in the first place. Herzig's testimony illustrated vividly as nothing else could have that the Commission did not ask the right people the right questions. Nevertheless, its report *Personal Justice Denied* continued to be held up as the final word on the subject. It was as if a blind man was constantly quoted as the ultimate witness on the details of a traffic accident which happened two blocks down the road.

In direct contradiction to every authority involved with MAGIC and every World War II historian who looked at the messages in question, Herzig insisted that the MAGIC messages really didn't mean what they said, and, in any event, were not all that important. These unique interpretations were repeated over and over again. But it wasn't possible to deny the existence of the MAGIC messages and the intelligence reports and what they actually said, so Herzig's attack shifted to the person who had brought all this information to the forefront, me. My motives and research were questioned. Words were put into my mouth which I never uttered, and then I was viciously attacked on these statements, all designed, of course, to discredit what I actually had said, and to shed doubt on the very documents themselves. Whereas my often stated purpose was to provide an historically correct record of the role intelligence played in the evacuation, and to provide authoritative data that the U.S. government did not act as charged, without evidence or cause, became distorted to accusations that my real motives were to prove disloyalty by Japanese residents and that MAGIC fully justified the evacuation decision. The accusations by Herzig actually became so fanciful and so wild as to charge me with trying to prove that Japanese-Americans were responsible for the present imbalance of trade between Japan and the United States, and trying to revive the "Yellow Peril" fears of bygone years.

After his written testimony was submitted to the Stevens' subcommittee, Herzig then forwarded it immediately to the Hall subcommittee in time for its last day of hearings on September 12, 1984.[9] At the same time Lt. Col. Herzig introduced a paper written by his former co-adviser to the Commission staff, Peter Irons. This fourteen page document tried to make the point that the MAGIC messages were nothing but an "illusion." Using different words Irons echoed the charges and claims made by Herzig, and once again "stonewalled" the Commission's defensive position that the MAGIC messages and intelligence reports had no bearing on the evacuation issue, did not constitute evidence of spying by resident Japanese, and certainly were not a factor in the government's decision on whether or not West Coast resident Japanese were engaged in subversive activities. [10]

---

9   Ibid, p. 819.

10   Ibid, p. 922.

While Irons was serving as an adviser to the Commission he was busy writing his own book on certain legal aspects of the evacuation. Some of what he had written in his book was carried directly over into the Commission report almost word for word. A glaring exception to this borrowing from his book was his description of a March 1941 break-in of the Japanese consulate in Los Angeles conducted by the ONI and the FBI which produced in Irons' own words, "lists of agents who had gathered intelligence in the form of maps, lists of army and navy installations, data on defense factories and harbors, and the locations of power stations and dams." Also omitted in the Commission report was the findings in Irons' book that papers seized from Lt. Cmdr. Itaru Tachibana, Japan's chief undercover naval spy on the West Coast who was arrested in June and deported in July 1941, incriminated many Japanese residents of spying for him. Professor Irons' exact words were, "There was no question that Tachibana headed an espionage ring on the West Coast that enlisted a number of Japanese-Americans, both aliens and citizens, nor that the government knew the identities of its members."[11]

It is apparent that Irons deliberately suppressed or ignored his own previous research in order to support the position of the Commission that there was no evidence of disloyalty, or spying, or subversive activities by any permanent residents of Japanese ancestry along the West Coast. This kind of research dishonesty was to continue unabated by both Herzig and Irons.

Anyone reading the original intelligence documents could easily establish for himself what they actually said. But few people have the opportunity of reading original intelligence documents, and so during the congressional hearings at Sam Hall's request, I undertook a point by point reply to the charges made by the two spokesmen for the Commission. My rebuttal was placed immediately following Herzig's testimony in the published House hearings. It ended with the following statement:

> Mr. Chairman, I have answered all the specific charges in Lieutenant Colonel Herzig's statement to your subcommittee. Very probably neither I nor anyone else can silence the wild and unsubstantiated accusations stated above so long as I continue to take a position that there was evidence of first and second generation Japanese spying. I have tried to stay away as much as possible from the highly emotional issues. I have carefully refrained from giving an opinion on whether MAGIC justified evacuation, leaving that for others to debate. And I have ventured no opinion whatsoever on reparations.

---

[11]   Peter Irons, *Justice at War* (University of California Press, 1983, 1993) pp. 22-23.

My only role in this matter has been to call attention to intelligence available to the President which would indicate that he did have legitimate cause for concern about the loyalty of large numbers of Japanese living on the West Coast in 1942, information which was not provided by the Commission which was charged to investigate this issue.

The Commission's problem is not with me, but with the materials which I have brought to the attention of the U.S. Congress. The Commission (and its spokesmen) would be well advised to accept the realities of the intelligence it "overlooked" and amend its report accordingly rather than to attack those private citizens who have called attention to this oversight.

In the final analysis, the MAGIC messages and their evaluation by the Joint Congressional Committee and key government officials of that era, and the army and navy intelligence reports produced at that time, all speak for themselves.[12]

There is no doubt that if Representative Sam Hall had remained chairman of the subcommittee handling Japanese reparations, H.R. 442[13] would never have reached the floor of the House. But he was appointed to a federal judgeship, and Barney Frank, a liberal Democrat from Massachusetts, became the chairman.

One of his first priorities was to move on H.R. 442. Even so it took him awhile. Under Barney Frank the subcommittee held hearings on April 28, 1986 on the Japanese matter and July 23, 1986 on the Aleutian side of the bill. The April hearings moved rapidly. I submitted some additional ONI and FBI reports I had recovered, but basically the hearings produced little new information. Most of what everybody wanted to say had already been said when Hall was the chairman, and reams of material had already been made a matter of record.

Frank's attempts to move H.R. 442 along produced some heavy infighting in the subcommittee, but after a few compromises and several changes in the wording, Barney Frank managed to get H.R. 442 to the House floor for a vote. On September 17, 1987 the House of Representatives voted, with some changes, to accept the basic findings and recommendations of the Commission

---

12   Congress, House, *Japanese-American and Aleutian Wartime Relocation*, p. 880.

13   The final House bill on redress was numbered H.R. 442 in honor of the 442nd Regimental Combat Team.

on Wartime Relocation and Internment of Civilians. The vote was 243-141 in favor, which indicated that there were probably not enough votes to override a veto. The consensus of opinion at that time was that President Reagan, while sympathetic to an apology to those Japanese residents evacuated, relocated, or interned, was opposed to the staggering cost of the legislation.

Senator Matsunaga, Democrat from Hawaii, was the sponsor of S. 1009 which was the Senate equivalent of H.R. 442. He already was assured of more than enough votes in the Senate to pass his S. 1009, and probably enough to override any veto, but he was concerned. It only took 145 votes in the House to sustain an expected veto. Senate action on a veto was not absolutely certain and there was an outside chance that it would uphold the President.

The Department of Justice at this time was strongly recommending to President Reagan that he veto the bill if it reached his desk. Its reasoning on the legislation had been quietly circulated to key members of the Senate. Essentially it was: (1) that the 1948 Claims Act had already compensated for all losses associated with the evacuation; (2) that President Ford had formally revoked Executive Order 9066 in 1975, had admitted that the evacuation was a mistake, and the nation had already apologized; (3) that "We oppose spending hundreds of millions of dollars to 'educate' the American people to accept this official interpretation of our history;" (4) that the section of the bill charging the Attorney General to investigate all criminal convictions associated with the evacuation laws, and then to take appropriate actions for a presidential pardon, was far too broad; (5) that all monies expended by the Attorney General to locate and administer the reparations bill had to be funded from the Attorney General's budget and could not be charged to the $1.25 billion to be appropriated for reparations; (6) that "It must be recognized that conclusions and subjective determinations which necessarily are an integral part of the report are subject to debate. Indeed, in June 1983, the Commission released an addendum to its report discussing the multi-volume Department of Defense publication entitled, *The "MAGIC" Background of Pearl Harbor,* because it had not discussed this important source of wartime intelligence in its report;" (7) the bill would establish an ill-conceived precedent that would encourage other politically well-organized groups to seek similar private relief legislation.

In view of the Department of Justice's position and the general impression that the President would veto the bill in its present form, Senator Matsunaga held back any Senate action on his bill, S. 1009. For the next seven months, while Senator Matsunaga kept the bill in committee, the Japanese ethnic press and the JACL urged Japanese-Americans to write to the White House in support of the reparations legislation. And they did by the thousands.

Lest anyone doubt the political clout being brought to bear, consider what happened to Congressman Dan Lungren during this seven month period. As vice-chairman of the Commission he had voted with the other commissioners in approving the Commission's report, *Personal Justice Denied*, despite some troublesome reservations in his mind because of MAGIC. He could not, however, agree with the Commission's recommendation to pay each evacuee or internee $20,000. He felt that this would set a precedent which would cause all kinds of problems down the road. In the fall of 1987 California Governor George Deukmejian named Lungren to fill the vacant state treasurer's post. The Japanese-American community rose up as one to oppose Lungren and to punish him for his vote on reparations. With only seven percent of the state's population, but disproportionate numbers of college students, scientists, engineers, and successful businessmen, the pressure was so intense that the nomination was blocked. "In the future I don't think politicians are going to take the Asian-American community as lightly as Lungren did," said a Japanese-American leader.

The write-in program and what had happened to Congressman Lungren did not go unnoticed by the Republicans. A presidential election was coming up and California was a key state. Straining for votes, both of the candidates, Governor Dukakis and Vice President Bush, told the JACL that they would sign the reparations bill. But as it turned out it wasn't necessary to wait until after the election. President Reagan, with one eye on the early polls which indicated a tight race, and the other focused on the Japanese-American political power in the key state of California, sent out word that he would sign the reparations bill.

With the assurance of a presidential signature, Senator Matsunaga's bill, S. 1009, to adopt the findings and recommendations of the Commission on Wartime Relocation and Internment of Civilians, was brought to the Senate floor on April 19, 1988. It was co-sponsored by seventy-three senators.

The bill differed slightly from the Commission recommendations because in June 1987 in Senator Pryor's subcommittee (he had succeeded Senator Stevens as chairman of the subcommittee) several senators got together in a closed session for what passed as a hearing, and made a few minor changes in the bill. The principal witnesses appeared to be Senators Matsunaga and Inouye from Hawaii. Nothing was published, but for the record the bill had had a hearing, and with the subcommittee's favorable recommendation the bill was forwarded to the full Senate.

On the opening day of debate on the floor of the Senate, Senator Matsunaga made a speech in which he said that the Office of Naval Intelligence informed President Roosevelt that evacuation of Japanese residents was unnecessary because there was absolutely no evidence of any espionage by Japanese-

Americans or their parents, before, during, or after the attack on Pearl Harbor. This was pure rubbish. No such ONI report existed, and certainly nothing of the kind was shown to the President by the ONI. Moreover, the senator knew that his statement was untrue.

On the next day, April 20, 1988, a number of senators arose and made speeches in favor of the bill, most of them quoting from the Commission's report. A handful of senators spoke against the bill because they thought the monetary award for various reasons was wrong. Every single senator who spoke on the Senate floor, however, said the evacuation was a mistake. Some allowed that it was an honest mistake, and objected to the Commission's conclusion that the decision was based entirely on racial and political considerations.

But only Jesse Helms from North Carolina spelled it out. Drawing on materials made available by me, Senator Helms cited ONI reports of December 4, 1941,[14] December 24, 1941,[15] and February 7, 1942;[16] Lieutenant Commander K. D. Ringle's personal assessment of January 26, 1942,[17] and a January 3, 1942 MID report,[18] all warning of large-scale ongoing espionage by persons of Japanese ancestry residing on the West Coast and pointing out that a major security situation existed on the West Coast. Helms read several MAGIC messages sent by the Japanese government describing their use of resident Japanese on the West Coast. He quoted John J. McCloy that this kind of intelligence was the reason President Roosevelt signed the evacuation order.

In addition to all this official U.S. intelligence, the Department of Justice's recommendation to the President describing its objections to the bill was incorporated into the floor discussion. Vice-chairman of the Commission Lungren's remarks on why he voted against the money award were incorporated along with his statements that the Commission hadn't given MAGIC sufficient consideration.

If all this changed any votes it wasn't apparent. Everyone had already made up his mind how he was going to vote. Supposedly, all the factual differences had been resolved in committee. The floor debate was merely a stage to say things that would look good to the people back home. But it didn't happen that way. Senators Matsunaga and Helms stood up on the floor of the Senate and gave absolutely opposite data to their colleagues pertaining to the

---

14   See page 251.

15   See page 277.

16   See page 325.

17   See page 315.

18   See page 236.

U.S. intelligence community and its views on the security risk posed by Japanese residents on the West Coast of the United States in late 1941 and early 1942. These differences in "facts," whether or not the administration had data from the intelligence services concluding that resident Japanese on the coast were a security hazard to the U.S. and whether or not the government then acted on this information in good faith, were the absolute crux of the matter about to be voted on. This was the whole thrust behind Executive Order 9066, and was the very reason that Congress was assembled on that day.

But no one stood up and said, "Hold on here. Who is correct? Let's get to the bottom of this because it's critical to the issue we are deciding." Of course, this is exactly what the committee system was supposed to have already done in order to prevent contradicting data from arising on the floor, but it didn't work that way on this day. In this instance conflicting statements and documents were a nuisance to be ignored and to be swept under the rug. A blue-ribbon commission had investigated the matter, made its findings, and that was the end of it.

During the floor debate Senator Helms offered an amendment to the bill "To require the Government of Japan to compensate the families of the men and women killed as a result of the Japanese bombing of Pearl Harbor on December 7, 1941 before any awards are paid under the Act." This clumsy attempt to equate Japanese residents in the U.S. with the Japanese government's bombing of Pearl Harbor got nowhere. A far more interesting amendment would have been to deny reparations to those thousands of Japanese-Americans who renounced their U.S. citizenship and asked to be expatriated to Japan, or to the almost 10,000 who refused a statement of unqualified loyalty to the United States. Such an amendment would have caused some real voting problems to the seventy-three co-sponsors of S. 1009.

Senator Helms did manage to get an amendment passed that said this Act was not to be a precedent for Mexico or any other country or Indian tribe to make similar claims against the U.S.

As it finally turned out the Senate voted 69-27 on April 20, 1988 to adopt the House of Representative's bill, H.R. 442, with certain amendments to the House bill. Because of these amendments it was necessary to set up a joint committee to resolve the differences between the two legislative bodies. This was accomplished after some squabbling over exactly who would be eligible for reparations and the period of time during which the monetary awards would be made. All of this reconciliation of the bills took time and it wasn't until late July that complete agreement was reached in the joint committee. These agreements were embodied in a document called the Conference Report which was published on July 27, 1988 and attached to H.R. 442. The two documents then became fused together and moved as a package.

Under prodding by Senator Matsunaga the Senate wasted no time in giving its approval to the compromises worked out by the joint committee. On July 27, the same day the Conference Report became available, the Senate "unanimously" approved the whole package. This unanimity, according to Senator Helms' office, turned out to be six senators voting in a late evening session. In a moment of conscience Senate Majority Leader Robert Byrd moved "to reconsider the vote by which the Conference Report was agreed to." Senator Dole, however, succeeded in having the motion tabled.

There is no question that the Conference Report would have been accepted by the full Senate, but the strategy was to avoid further picking at the bill just in case something really became unraveled.

The House voted its approval, 257-156, on August 4, 1988 and H.R. 442 along with the Conference Report were forwarded to the White House. On August 10, 1988 President Reagan, against the advice of the Department of Justice and the Office of Management and Budget, signed them into Public Law 100-383, titled the "Civil Liberties Act of 1988." Although some of the most outlandish findings and recommendations had been modified, essentially the Civil Liberties Act accepts the report of the Commission on Wartime Relocation and Internment of Civilians, *Personal Justice Denied*, with all its misinformation, misconceptions, and distortions of U.S. intelligence produced on this issue throughout 1941 and early 1942.

The stated purpose of the Civil Liberties Act of 1988 is to acknowledge the fundamental injustice of the evacuation, relocation, and internment of U.S. citizens and permanent resident aliens of Japanese ancestry during World War II. Note that the Act does not include resident aliens of Italian and German descent even though thousands of them were also arrested and detained for security reasons, exactly like those aliens of Japanese ancestry. Whatever human suffering the Japanese experienced, was equally borne by thousands of Germans and Italians who were also evacuated, held in custody, or interned, but, lacking the highly organized and disciplined political clout of the Japanese, they will receive nothing. This apparent disparity between racial groups would appear to raise serious constitutional questions.[19]

Other stated purposes of the Act are to apologize and to make restitution to those of Japanese ancestry who were evacuated or interned, and to provide

---

[19] A class action suit brought by an American citizen of German ancestry who was interned during the war and who sought redress equal to that given Japanese citizens who were in the same camp was opposed by Japanese-Americans.

funds to educate the U.S. public on this issue and to provide for the general welfare of the U.S. Japanese community.

The Act also provides for the Aleut residents who were evacuated from the Pribilof and Aleutian Islands for military reasons and who then suffered economic losses and lived in what was considered to be substandard quarters during the war. The 450 of them affected will receive $12,000 each.

The Act authorized $1.25 billion to be appropriated. To hold down the impact on the budget, payments were extended over a ten-year period, and not more than $500 million was to be appropriated in any one fiscal year. The first increment was in the 1989 budget. It was estimated that there were 60,000 people eligible for the $20,000 tax-free payment which would cost the taxpayer $1.2 billion.[20] The remaining $50 million was to be placed in a trust fund to promote the findings of the Commission in the schools, libraries, and for special exhibits, and for the general welfare of ethnic Japanese people in the United States.

The total cost was by no means $1.25 billion. The Attorney General was charged to administer the program and to seek out those individuals who were eligible for the money, but was specifically admonished not to spend any of the fund's money for these tasks. That money is to come out of the Department of Justice budget.

The Attorney General was also required by the legislation to review the convictions of anyone of Japanese ancestry who violated any of the laws of the U.S. pertaining to the evacuation, relocation and internment, and then, based on certain factors, to recommend pardons to the President. Earlier, the Attorney General had objected to this provision as being too broad and because it could be interpreted to cover any crime, "such as murder, extortion, kidnaping, theft, counterfeiting, and other offenses which may have been committed on a government reservation by [people of Japanese ancestry]."

Eligibility for the monetary award was defined by the Act as anyone of Japanese ancestry who was living on the date of the enactment of the Act (August 10, 1988), was a citizen of the United States or a permanent resident alien,[21] and was evacuated, relocated, or interned as a result of Executive Order 9066 or similar directives or laws between December 7, 1941 and June 30, 1946.

If an eligible person died after August 10, 1988 his spouse, children, or parents in that order would receive the money. The heirs of those who died

---

[20] The estimated number eligible for payment was off by a third. At the conclusion of the payment program on August 10, 1998 82,219 had been paid.

[21] "Permanent resident alien" refers to those Japanese citizens classified as "enemy aliens" by Presidential Proclamation No. 2525, December 7, 1941, many of whom were individually classified as security risks by review boards.

prior to August 10, 1988 will not receive his award. There was nothing in the Act to prevent a person from receiving more than one award. For example, it's possible for someone born in a camp, and therefore eligible, to also receive the share of his deceased mother and father if they passed away after the Act was signed into law. In that case he would receive $60,000.

Since Executive Order 9066 wasn't signed until February 19, 1942, and the Act awards compensation for actions dating from December 7, 1941, this means that all the suspected disloyal Japanese alien residents and citizens arrested by the FBI immediately after Pearl Harbor are eligible for payment. Most of them would have become eligible in any event under other provisions of the Act, but it's interesting to speculate on why eligibility for enemy aliens suspected of disloyalty began more than two months before it was decided to evacuate Japanese residents from the West Coast.

The Act did tighten up the Commission's recommendations in one important respect. It precluded from payment any Japanese resident who, by whatever means, returned to Japan during the war.

Exactly how many of the more than 20,000 who had requested repatriation or expatriation actually got to Japan in exchange for Americans held by the Japanese government is not clear. On the other hand, it left eligible the nearly 5,000 Japanese who didn't make it to Japan during the war but returned to Japan at their request immediately after the war. By the terms of the Act the Attorney General was required to seek out these people or their heirs in Japan and pay them $20,000.

Congress tightened up the Commission's recommendations in one other respect. Inserted into the Act was a provision that anyone accepting the $20,000 agreed that such payment would be in full satisfaction of all claims arising out of the evacuation, relocation, and internment. The purpose of this was to prevent a person who received payment from Congress also to share in damages received from the *Hohri* case which was still pending when the Act was signed into law. Until the Supreme Court refused on October 31, 1988 to hear the *Hohri* case on appeal from the circuit court, this caused a lively discussion in the ethnic press. It placed an eligible individual in the position of gambling a sure $20,000 against a possible $220,000. Old hands in the JACL advised taking the $20,000, and then seeking some way around the Act's prohibition in the event the *Hohri* case was won. After all, the 1948 American-Japanese Claims Act had similar wording concerning full satisfaction and the Congress had neatly slipped around that, saying that the payments in 1948 were for economic losses whereas payment under the 1988 Civil Liberties Act was for human suffering.

The Act went along with the Commission's recommendations that permitted eligibility for the 6,000 babies born in the relocation centers, the 4,300 young people who went to colleges and schools in the East, those who left the centers to work and live east of the West Coast states, and those who of their own volition left the West Coast after Pearl Harbor but before E.O. 9066 was signed on February 19, 1942, those who volunteered to serve in the armed forces, the thousands who refused to swear allegiance to the United States, and the 5,600 who renounced their U.S. citizenship during the war.

The Act also required payment to several hundred Japanese who during the war were sent from Latin America to the U.S. because they were considered to be security risks.[22] Once in the U.S. they were interned. After the war, for various reasons, they remained in the U.S. In 1949 they were given the status of "permanent legally admitted immigrants." Since the Act does not specify a date on which this status had to be achieved, these people are eligible for the $20,000 payment.[23]

In the Act there is a section titled, "Statement of the Congress" which contains the nation's apology for its actions. The statement also contains words which undercut the most fundamental premises of the Commission's findings, and provide a defense for congressional actions against that inevitable day when scholars will look at the Commission's report and proclaim it worthless insofar as it purports to be a thorough and objective investigation of the facts and circumstances surrounding the signing of Executive Order 9066.

The statement reads as follows: (all italics added) "These actions [evacuation, relocation, internment] were carried out without *adequate* security reasons and without any acts of espionage or sabotage *documented by the Commission*, and were motivated *largely* by racial prejudice, wartime hysteria, and a failure of political leadership."

The Commission certainly never used the term "adequate." Insofar as it was concerned there were no security reasons behind the evacuation whatsoever, never mind that some of the reasons might have been less than "adequate." Next, note the careful wording in the Act on espionage. It doesn't claim that there was no espionage, only that the Commission "did not document" any acts of espionage. That's true enough. The Commission was unaware of (or ignored) all the official intelligence on the subject it was investigating, and

---

[22] See MAGIC message #153, January 23, 1942, page 206 for an indication of espionage efforts in Latin America.

[23] These Latin Americans of Japanese ancestry were given $5,000 and an apology. However, as of July 2000 efforts were underway in Congress by the Congressional Hispanic Caucus to secure the full $20,000 for them.

so it couldn't very well document it, and that, of course, is one of the fatal flaws in its report. Finally, and most significantly, although the Commission had charged that the government was motivated solely by racial and political considerations and war hysteria, Congress has inserted into its statement in the Act the all-important qualifier "largely." What the other reasons were for the government's actions are left blank because to have specified that it was intelligence data would have torn the heart out of the Commission's report. Nonetheless, this change was a clear admission at long last that the United States intelligence community had produced and provided to key U.S. officials information which concluded that Japanese residents on the West Coast, citizens and aliens alike, were involved in subversive activities and were considered to be a major security risk, and that this information was a factor in the President's evacuation decision.

Even though Congress did bring some degree of sanity into the Commission's recommendations and findings, *Personal Justice Denied* has not been amended. Present plans are for the National Archives to mount a special display of the Commission's report and its supporting documents for the public. When this happens, it is essential that the testimony of McCloy, Bendetsen, Weiner, Hayakawa, Baker, myself and others who testified and submitted documents pointing out the many errors of fact, misconceptions, and extreme bias of *Personal Justice Denied* also be made available to the public.[24]

Appropriate authorities should also make absolutely certain that the report's MAGIC Addendum (including the vice-chairman's remarks) is attached to it wherever the report is displayed or utilized. The Commission's own words illustrate as nothing else could the ineptness of its handling of MAGIC. The Commission's analysis raises more questions than it answers, and is obviously shallow, contradictory, confused, and highly defensive to even the most casual reader. Historians and those familiar with World War II intelligence will immediately recognize the many fallacies in the Addendum. Nonetheless, it is an integral part of the Commission's report and must be included with it.[25]

The Civil Liberties Act of 1988 is now the law of the land, but the report upon which it is based, *Personal Justice Denied*, should be recognized for what it is, a blatant attempt to rewrite history.

---

[24] This was not done. Indeed, educational material published by the National Archives makes no mention of either intelligence information or MAGIC as it pertained to evacuation or to objections raised during the Commission's investigation or congressional hearings.

[25] See page 358 for the MAGIC Addendum.

PART II
THE MAGIC MESSAGES

All the messages in Part II are filed in the National Archives. Most of the ones displayed, however, have been culled from the multi-volume Department of Defense (DOD) publication, *The "MAGIC" Background of Pearl Harbor*. Released in 1977, this comprehensive collection contains over 5,000 MAGIC messages, about one-half of which are related to espionage-type activities. This DOD publication by no means encompasses the entire collection of MAGIC messages. It contains only those intercepted Japanese messages relating in some way to the attack on Pearl Harbor. Omitted from the study are those worldwide communications between the Japanese foreign ministry and its representatives around the globe which have no bearing on what happened at Pearl Harbor.

As of August 1988, over 160,927 pages comprising 126,869 MAGIC messages have been declassified by the National Security Agency and forwarded to the National Archives where they are filed under Record Group 457. For ease in reading, DOD retyped all the messages in its study. Original translations were heavily footnoted with cross references, identifying data, translator notes, and in some cases cryptanalytic remarks, all of which have been deleted. Otherwise, original style and format were preserved as much as possible. In general, names of private U.S. citizens have been deleted to respect their rights. Occasionally in the message text a series of dashes will occur. These blank spaces indicate that a portion of the original encrypted text was not intercepted, was garbled, or for some reason could not be decrypted.

In the upper right-hand corner is the date when the message was transmitted. The exact hour and minute of transmission have been omitted. Time of intercept by the U.S. is, of course, the same as the transmission date. Just below this date is the message number assigned by the originator. References to specific messages in this book will use this number. In the lower right-hand corner is the date when the message was translated by the U.S. The time difference between when the message was intercepted and when it was actually translated, and then available to key people in the government, occurs because of operational and technical considerations. These time differences are particularly significant in the Honolulu messages.

In the lower left-hand corner are translator remarks and references to other messages using the numbering system employed within *The "MAGIC" Background of Pearl Harbor*.

One hundred MAGIC messages have been selected, and they are displayed in eight different categories, each of which is a separate chapter in Part II. One message, because of its wide-ranging nature and significance, #44, has been used in three different categories. All other messages are used only once although a number of them contain important information beyond the arbitrary category into which they have been placed. The original intercepts are no longer available; therefore, it is not possible to recheck the decrypts or translations. The messages herein are exactly as shown to our wartime leaders.

CHAPTER 7

JAPAN ORGANIZES FOR INTELLIGENCE

In late 1940 Japan set forth on two parallel courses of action: the first was an all-out effort to resolve her differences with the United States through diplomacy; the second was to prepare for war in the event diplomatic negotiations failed. Failure, of course, would be measured by the Japanese themselves, and would be based upon how completely Japan was able to achieve her objectives.

An integral part of the Japanese war option was the establishment of an ongoing, broad-based intelligence effort. Pre-war intelligence operations against the United States were almost entirely the responsibility of the Japanese navy in cooperation with the foreign ministry. Besides providing a cover for covert operations, the diplomatic posts also provided a recognized and accepted communications channel for sending and receiving enciphered messages through commercial cable companies.

Captain Kanji Ogawa, the career intelligence officer who served as principal assistant to Admiral Minoru Maeda who headed the Third Bureau (Intelligence Bureau), was personally briefed by Admiral Yamamoto on "Operation Z," the Pearl Harbor plan, as early as February 1941 while the plan was still in the formative stage. If there was to be war, Yamamoto wanted to give Ogawa time to establish his espionage nets in the U.S. and its territories so they could support the Pearl Harbor attack and provide follow-on intelligence operations.

The Japanese foreign ministry with its people stationed around the world was an experienced intelligence collector in its own right. For the crucial period ahead, however, the foreign ministry accepted navy control and increased collection responsibilities without argument. Although it was to be a dual effort, the Japanese foreign minister was given no details on "Operation Z." The foreign ministry was in a position to help, cooperate, and work with the Third Bureau, but there was no doubt about who was running the show.

Although both diplomatic and intelligence activities were already ongoing efforts, each received new impetus in January 1941 with the appointment of a new Japanese ambassador, Admiral Nomura, and concurrent instructions from Tokyo to all diplomatic posts in the U.S. to start emphasizing intelligence. Orders from Tokyo directed that espionage nets were to be established as soon as possible and were to be organized in such a way as to be able to function in the event of war with the United States.[1]

To accomplish these new high priority intelligence objectives Japan pursued two different approaches. The first was to activate fully the already-in-place Japanese military agents previously placed in the U.S. by the Third Bureau. These consisted, for the most part, of a number of Japanese naval officers, primarily on the West Coast, who had over the previous years already established the framework of operative intelligence nets. Their cover was that they were language students, and their espionage nets in the U.S. included patriotic and militaristic Japanese organizations, Japanese business fronts, clubs, and a number of individuals, both Japanese and non-Japanese. Normally, these undercover military agents operated independently of the consulate offices, but in the case of the West Coast they functioned as a team, forming a tri-cornered net composed of consular officials, undercover naval officers, and resident Issei and Nisei.

The second approach used the Japanese foreign ministry which from this time forward regarded intelligence gathering as the primary mission of its American consulates. Carefully located throughout the United States wherever there were large numbers of Japanese residents, the Japanese consulates were in an excellent position to carry out their espionage responsibilities. For many years they had been serving as a sort of "father-confessor" to the Japanese living in their area. The consulates were the tie to back home. They were the channel for financial, legal, and educational contacts with the motherland. They took care of registering the newly-born as Japanese citizens and provided arrangements for children to be educated in Japan. They saw to it that local Japanese schools and newspapers were properly supported, sometimes

---

1   See MAGIC message #043, January 30, 1941, p. 128 and #44, January 30, 1941, p. 129.

providing teachers from Japan and funds for Japanese newspapers and a variety of organizations and societies.

From this position of trust and authority it was easy for the consulates to recruit local Japanese to keep tabs on movements of ships, aircraft, and military supplies, particularly by those who lived in close proximity to military bases. For the more militant Japanese residents in the U.S. there were more complex espionage tasks within the interlocking organizational complex established by the consulates for espionage purposes all up and down the West Coast.

Intercepted Japanese messages in January and early February ordering the installation of these espionage nets set off alarm bells within the U.S. Office of Naval Intelligence. On February 12, 1941 the Director of ONI forwarded a memorandum to the Chief of Naval Operations urging him to bring the information in these early organizational messages to the immediate attention of the President of the United States.[2]

Japanese attempts to bring their intelligence nets up to full operational effectiveness along the U.S. West Coast proceeded as quickly as possible, but the program suffered a severe setback in June when the U.S. broke the back of the military agent system by arresting and deporting Lieutenant Commander Itaru Tachibana, Japan's chief undercover spy on the West Coast. Tachibana was tripped up when he tried to recruit a former U.S. Navy man who turned him in to the FBI. His arrest led to the apprehension of other undercover Japanese naval officers who also operated intelligence nets on the West Coast. Documents discovered on these officers and in their apartments provided U.S. authorities with a great deal of data on Japanese residents and various organizations which were working closely with these Japanese agents.[3]

Within hours after this catastrophe to the Japanese espionage effort, the consuls on the West Coast were notified by the Japanese embassy in Washington, D.C. that in addition to the intelligence nets they were already running to meet their own intelligence requirements, they would now have to pick up the spy functions of the arrested undercover agents, particularly on U.S. Navy intelligence.[4]

All of this, of course, placed a great deal of added responsibilities onto the consulates. Not only did they have to establish and run their own intelligence

---

[2]   See Office of Naval Intelligence memo, February 12, 1941, on page 249.

[3]   See Office of Naval Intelligence report, December 4, 1941, on page 251. Reference at p. 274.

[4]   See MAGIC message #386, June 10, 1941 on page 158. This amazing message demonstrates the effectiveness of the espionage operation as well as its flexibility and extent. Clearly it shows that the Japanese intelligence operation was not destroyed by the arrest of Tachibana and others.

nets, but now they had to manage and maintain the nets formerly controlled by the Japanese undercover naval officers. These added responsibilities created a great deal of additional pressure on the consulates. The necessity to recruit more agents must have mounted significantly. The U.S. Department of Justice wanted to prosecute the Japanese naval spies, but the Department of State, still hoping for a diplomatic solution, didn't want to antagonize the Japanese government any more than was absolutely necessary. It felt that relations with Japan, already strained, might be damaged beyond repair if there were a sensational trial revealing the extent of Japanese espionage along the West Coast. State Department's views prevailed and the Japanese spies were quietly deported in July 1941. Tachibana returned to Japan where his American expertise was put to good use by assigning him to the Third Bureau.

In the event of war, Japanese plans called for the flow of intelligence and overall control of espionage in the U.S. to move to Mexico or to Central or South America if Mexico didn't work out for them. During World War I relations between the U.S. and Mexico were anything but friendly, and Japan counted on that happening once again; but in this regard she could not have been more wrong. Mexico broke relations with Japan the day after Pearl Harbor and declared war on May 22, 1942. Other Central and South American countries quickly followed suit. Having almost no bases on the American continents from which to operate, coupled with the unforeseen mass evacuation of all residents of Japanese ancestry from the West Coast, completely wrecked Japan's espionage network in the United States.

MESSAGE SUMMARIES

#763   December 17, 1940—Lists Japanese organizations in the U.S. to be used for propaganda and intelligence information gathering.

#043   January 30, 1941—De-emphasize propaganda and emphasize intelligence. Prepare for the worst. We are conferring with the intelligence bureau [The Third Bureau].

#44   January 30, 1941—In the event of U.S. participation in the war, our intelligence setup will be moved to Mexico, making that country the nerve center of our intelligence. Recruit agents for spying.

#056   February 5, 1941—Have the intelligence reports of various representatives sent through diplomatic channels for secrecy.

#239   February 5, 1941—Plan to have a fallback position for intelligence in Central and South America for espionage directed against the U.S. Organize Japanese residents in these countries for espionage. Maintain contact with the German and Italian intelligence organizations. Be careful.

#126   March 17, 1941—Put Terasaki in charge of intelligence and propaganda in the U.S. Provide him with all possible assistance. (Terasaki was the second secretary in the Japanese embassy.)

#180   April 24, 1941—Tokyo wants to know the status of the intelligence nets in the U.S. as directed by three previous messages: (1) emphasize intelligence and prepare for the worst [#043]; (2) recruit agents for spying [#44]; (3) intelligence requirements for economic, political, and military information [#073].

#287   June 11, 1941—Investigate the possibilities of using Negroes for subversive purposes.

#349   July 10, 1941—Tokyo warns its embassy in Washington D.C. that the German and Italian intelligence nets in the U.S. were broken when the U.S. closed their consulates. To guard against the "day of evil" when the Japanese diplomatic posts will be closed, Terasaki is to visit Mexico and the West Coast in order to make plans for keeping in contact with Japanese intelligence nets in the U.S. from Mexico. Routes are to be prepared for contacts and exchanges on the border. Laredo, Ciudad Juarez, and Mexicali are to be the crossover routes from the United States into Mexico.

FROM: New York (Iguchi)   December 17, 1940
TO: Tokyo (Gaimudaijin)   # 763.

(2 parts—completed.)

Re your msg. to Wash. # 591[a].

As propaganda and enlightenment organs here, we have the Japan Institute, the Tourist Bureau, and the silk office of the Ministry of Commerce and Communication. Other groups whose importance we cannot ignore for collecting information are the financial adviser, the Army and Navy Inspection Offices, Representatives of Domei, ASAHI, NITINITI, AND YOMIURI, the Bank of Japan, the Specie Bank, Mitsui, Mitsubishi, N.Y.K., O.S.K., the Manchurian R.R. and OKURA Co.

In order to obtain the fullest cooperation from the above it is well to establish an information committee centering around the press attaché.

----
[a]See I, No. 112.

Trans. 1-9-41

FROM: Tokyo (Matsuoka)   January 30, 1941
TO: Washington (Koshi)   # 043.

Foreign Office secret.

Heretofore, we have placed emphasis on publicity and propaganda work in the United States. In view of the critical situation in the recent relations between the two countries, and for the purpose of being prepared for the worst, we have decided to alter this policy. Taking into consideration the small amount of funds we have at our disposal, we have decided to de-emphasize propaganda for the time being, and instead, to strengthen our intelligence work.

Though we must give the matter of intelligence work our further study—in this connection we are at present conferring with the intelligence bureau—we have mapped out a fundamental program, the outline of which is contained in my supplementary cable No. 44[a].

Please, therefore, reorganize your intelligence set-up and put this new program into effect as soon as possible.

Cable copies of this message, as "Minister's orders" to Canada, Mexico, (a copy to be relayed from Mexico to Mexicali), San Francisco, (copies from San Francisco to Honolulu, Los Angeles, Portland, Seattle, and Vancouver), New York, New Orleans, and Chicago.

----
[a]See I, 119.

Trans. 2-7-41

FROM: Tokyo (Matsuoka)   January 30, 1941
TO: Washington (Koshi)   # 44.

(In two parts—complete).

(Foreign Office secret).

(1) Establish an intelligence organ in the Embassy which will maintain liaison with private and semi-official intelligence organs (see my message to Washington #591*a* and #732*b* from New York to Tokyo, both of last year's series).

With regard to this, we are holding discussions with the various circles involved at the present time.

(2) The focal point of our investigations shall be the determination of the total strength of the U.S. Our investigations shall be divided into three general classifications: political, economic, and military, and definite course of action shall be mapped out.

(3) Make a survey of all persons or organizations which either openly or secretly oppose participation in the war.

(4) Make investigations of all anti-Semitism, communism, movements of Negroes, and labor movements.

(5) Utilization of U.S. citizens of foreign extraction (other than Japanese), aliens (other than Japanese), communists, Negroes, labor union members, and anti-Semites, in carrying out the investigations described in the preceding paragraph would undoubtedly bear the best results.

These men, moreover, should have access to governmental establishments, (laboratories?), governmental organizations of various characters, factories, and transportation facilities.

(6) Utilization of our "Second Generations" and our resident nationals. (In view of the fact that if there is any slip in this phase, our people in the U.S. will be subjected to considerable persecution, and the utmost caution must be exercised).

(7) In the event of U.S. participation in the war, our intelligence set-up will be moved to Mexico, making that country the nerve center of our intelligence net. Therefore, will you bear this in mind and in anticipation of such an eventuality, set up facilities for a U.S.-Mexico international intelligence route. This net which will cover Brazil, Argentina, Chile, and Peru will also be centered in Mexico.

(8) We shall cooperate with the German and Italian intelligence organs in the U.S. This phase has been discussed with the Germans and Italians in Tokyo, and it has been approved.

Please get the details from Secretary Terasaki upon his assuming his duties there.

Please send copies to those offices which were on the distribution list of No. 43*c*.

---

*a*See I, 112.
*b*Has no bearing on this subject. #732 probably an error.
c(See No. 4)—See I, 118.

Trans. 2-7-41

FROM: Tokyo (Matsuoka)   February 5, 1941
TO: Washington (Koshi)   # 056.

Re my #591*.

In connection with New York to Tokyo message #763,[b] the business men (including Sumi-tomo's representatives) and representatives of newspapers were invited to call here. One of my men discussed the following points with them:

(1) To have the various representatives of business firms engage in collecting intelligence material.

(2) To have all such representatives abroad (in the United States) cable their opinions and manipulations in so far as they are related to politics, through diplomatic channels so as to maintain secrecy.

We were able to obtain their agreement to cooperate with us in this respect, so please proceed with this program.

We have the perfect understanding and agreement of the Army and Navy in this connection. They promise to give us whatever aid they can.

---

*See I, 112. "With the appointment of Ambassador Nomura we wish to formulate a definite plan for our propaganda and information gathering work by seeking cooperation of Japanese bank and business officials in the U.S."

[b]Refers to above message and lists 18 Japanese organs in New York as potential sources of information.

Trans. 2–11–41

FROM: Tokyo (Matsuoka)   February 5, 1941
TO: Mexico City (Koshi)   # 239.

(Circular) (In 2 parts—complete).

In view of the critical times we wish to revise our information policy of our offices in South and Central America, along the following lines:

(1) Investigate the general national strength of the United States.

(2) Investigate the United States policy towards South and Central America.

(3) Investigate the extent of South and Central America's participation in the policy of the United States.

(4) Investigate the extent of competition between Germany, Italy and the United States in South and Central America.

1. Appoint persons to direct these investigations and report their names.

2. Consider plans to use South and Central America for obtaining information regarding the United States in the event that that country is drawn into war, and have an information gathering machinery ready for operation when that situation occurs.

3. Keep a close contact with the German and Italian organs (of information).

4. To organize Japanese residents, including newspaper men and business firms for the purpose of gathering information. Care should be taken not to give cause for suspicion of espionage activities.

5. To formulate a suitable plan for dispatching information obtained under any condition.

Relay to Chile, Peru, Panama, Argentina (?), Venezuela (?), and Brazil and retransmit by code to Santos and Ribeiro Preto.

Trans. 2–14–41

FROM: Tokyo   March 17, 1941
TO: Washington   # 126.

Regarding my # 43[a].

(1) Please put Secretary Terazaki[b] in full charge of directing information and propaganda in the United States.

(2) Please have him maintain close contact with all our offices for the purpose of coordinating information gathered through these channels.

Also please have him convene or visit officials concerned whenever he deems it necessary.

(3) Please allow him to travel to South and Central America, whenever he feels it necessary to contact our information officials in these countries.

(4) Bearing in mind that sufficient funds have been provided to give him a reasonable amount of freedom of action in pursuing his work, please offer him every assistance at your disposal.

---

[a]We have decided to de-emphasize our propaganda work and strengthen our intelligence work in the U.S. See I, 118.

See I, 119. Outline of major points of investigation in connection with setting up of intelligence operations in the U.S.

Cooperation of Jap bank and business officials in U.S. will be sought in connection with propaganda and intelligence work in U.S. See I, 112.

[b]Terazaki was formerly a secretary at the Legation in Peking; was ordered to Washington on 20 December, 1940.

Trans. 3–18–41

FROM: Tokyo   April 24, 1941
TO: Washington   # 180.

I would like to be informed of the intelligence organization in your office and of its recent activity relative to my # 43[a], # 44[b], and # 73. Please transmit this request as coming from the Foreign Office, from Washington to Mexico City (?) and from that city to Mexicali.

---

[a]Regarding the de-emphasizing of propaganda in the United States and the strengthening of intelligence work.

[b]Regarding the establishment of an intelligence organ in the Embassy which will maintain liaison with intelligence organs from New York to Tokyo; also, the removal of the intelligence set-up to Mexico should the United States become involved in the war.

Trans. 8–18–41

FROM: Tokyo (Matsuoka)   June 11, 1941
TO: Washington   # 287.

With reference to propaganda among Negroes as a scheme against the United States, your immediate reply in regard to the following points is requested:

1. Training of Negroes as (fifth columnists ?).

2. The way to utilize them in order to begin the movement ?).

3. The method of contacting the agitators and leaders among the Negroes, as well as both right and left wings. Also, the amount of expenses involved.

The Minister requests that the above message be forwarded to New York, New Orleans, San Francisco and Los Angeles.

Trans. 5–27–42

FROM: Tokyo   July 10, 1941
TO: Washington   # 349.

Secret outside the Department.

(To be handled in Government Code.)

Re # 18ª from New Orleans and # 244 (?)ᵇ from Mexico to this Foreign Minister.

We wish Consul ITO to go to Mexico City. Lately the offices housing the German and Italian Consulates were closed and their intelligence net broken. Intelligence activities in the Americas and suitable liaison are now essential, so we wish Secretary TERAZAKI also to go to Mexico to confer with our Minister there, in order to realize our plans in a concrete fashion based on the policy described in previous messages. We want Secretary TERAZAKI, and him only, to stop off at Quito, Los Angeles, San Francisco, etc. In this connection the points which we would like to bring to your attention are as follows:

1. We will have three routes to Mexico from the United States, consisting of Laredo, Ciudad Juarez and Mexicali. Mexicali in particular is a convenient point for us on the west coast. In case we need more personnel, we can get them from our Ministry in Mexico.

2. We will establish a Chile route from Mexico to Manzanillo and a Brazil route by way of Vera Cruz.

3. Various officials in the United States and Mexico will work out all the details of their own espionage nets, correlate them, and develop a concrete plan for making contacts and exchanges on the border.

4. In order to succeed in the objective, ways and means for keeping in contact through telegraphy, telephones, memoranda, and word of mouth will be decided upon and put into effect.

5. These routes are to be established against the day of evil and, while all is calm, nothing must be done which would jeopardize their security; therefore, at present investigate only the feasibility of circulating over them.

6. The expenses are to be paid by the several offices.

Because of its geographical position, Mexico is the main point for intelligence work in Brazil, Argentina and Chile, as well as in the United States. Therefore, before we think of relying too much upon Brazil, Argentina and Chile, let us concentrate on Mexico. However, the other three bases are different. In case the United States joins the war, they would inevitably come under her control, but so long as Mexico does not officially join the war, we can continue our intelligence schemes there. Paralleling these plans of ours, if you can also work out a plan for establishing a liaison net with Brazil, Argentina and Chile, it would be excellent groundwork for the establishment presently of an intelligence net. Please transmit this to Mexico City and take with you to New Orleans.

ªNot available.
ᵇNot available.

Trans. 7-25-41

CHAPTER 8

JAPANESE INTELLIGENCE REQUIREMENTS

Japan, like Germany, believed in total intelligence. Her requirements included the usual military and war material information, but also reached out for economic, political, financial, and even sociological data.

Since the pre-war intelligence effort against the U.S. was almost entirely the responsibility of the Japanese navy, it followed that most of the requirements were originated by the navy. Although the foreign ministry was specifically ordered to collect military intelligence for the Japanese navy, its own requirements, simply by being a part of the collection effort, were also given high priority.

How well the Japanese navy kept the army informed is not clear. However, in both the Philippines and the Canal Zone, MAGIC messages going back to Tokyo carried some information which appeared to be of primary interest to the Japanese army. Even though there was a fierce rivalry between the Japanese navy and army, it is highly probable that most of the information which was of concern to the Japanese army was passed on to it by the Third Bureau.

Almost all the intelligence requirements issued by the Third Bureau (Intelligence Bureau) were for raw data. In-depth analysis was performed by its large professional staff in Tokyo. Information requirements covered the gamut from tactical to strategic and were both short-range and long-range.

An exception to this centralization of intelligence analysis was the research on and the attempt to utilize what Tokyo considered to be dissident groups in the U.S. This was left for agents in the U.S. to develop. But the project never got off the ground because Japan never understood the diversity that characterized the United States. Being a racially homogeneous society whose actions, goals, and even thoughts were centrally controlled, Japan could never reconcile American reality with what she regarded as a badly divided society which lacked a determined, cohesive war effort. Labor unions in the United States went on strikes and caused production problems; therefore, reasoned the Japanese, they could be used to Japan's advantage. This same kind of thinking was applied to such widely divergent groups as the Communist Party, the Silver Shirts, and various ethnic minorities. Thus, along with traditional intelligence requirements, there was a steady flow of directives to investigate these groups to see if they could somehow be used for subversive activities or to frustrate the aims of the U.S.

Japan's nearly complete lack of success against U.S. codes and ciphers forced her to rely almost exclusively on agents to meet her intelligence requirements. The Japanese navy's communications intelligence (COMINT) efforts began as early as 1925 when the Tokumu Han (Special Section) was created. Encouraged by some early successes against Chinese communications, the Tokumu Han enthusiastically geared up for the war against the United States, and managed to collect a great deal of U.S. traffic, but it all ended right there. No medium or high-grade U.S. crypt systems were ever broken by analytic means alone. Tokumu Han's cryptanalysts were able to read the U.S. State Department's BROWN code just prior to the war, and during the war they read a complex Allied merchant ship super-enciphered code named BAMS. Their ability to read the BROWN code, however, stemmed from a carefully executed break-in of the American consulate in Kobe during which the BROWN code was photographed. Their other big "success" was primarily due to the fact that Germans had supplied the Tokumu Han with the basic code book for the BAMS system which the German raider Atlantis had earlier captured from an Allied ship.

Although the Japanese army achieved good results for a short while on Filipino guerrilla traffic, its overall COMINT effort was summed up in a single sentence after the war by Lieutenant General Seizo Arisue, Chief of Army Intelligence: "We couldn't break your codes at all."

MESSAGE SUMMARIES

#44   January 30, 1941—The focal point of our investigations shall be the determination of the total strength of the U.S. Our investigations will be economic, political, and military. Survey all organizations opposed to war. Make investigations of all groups opposed to war. Check out anti-Semitic organizations and the Negro and labor movements. If war comes Mexico will be our intelligence nerve center.

#073   February 15, 1941—Tokyo said it particularly needed information from the U.S. and Canada on military preparations, ship and plane movements, data on merchant vessels, arms production, troop movements, airplane production, training of military personnel, and alterations to airports.

#154   April 1, 1941—Tokyo wants information on U.S. labor unions on the theory that "In the event of war we think that the Labor Unions will become a major political factor in hindering unity in the United States."

#263   September 4, 1941—In addition to general intelligence requirements the Japanese had spot requirements. This message wants information on the possibility that the U.S. might be transferring bomber aircraft to Siberia.

#2187   October 4, 1941—This spot requirement was sent just a few weeks before the Japanese fleet began assembling in the Kurile Islands for its strike across the Pacific against Pearl Harbor. Tokyo wanted priority reporting on warship movements by the U.S. or its allies. Of particular interest was the inauguration of any sea or air patrols.

FROM: Tokyo (Matsuoka)   January 30, 1941
TO: Washington (Koshi)   # 44.

   (In two parts—complete).

   (Foreign Office secret).

(1) Establish an intelligence organ in the Embassy which will maintain liaison with private and semi-official intelligence organs (see my message to Washington #591[a] and #732[b] from New York to Tokyo, both of last year's series).

   With regard to this, we are holding discussions with the various circles involved at the present time.

(2) The focal point of our investigations shall be the determination of the total strength of the U.S. Our investigations shall be divided into three general classifications: political, economic, and military, and definite course of action shall be mapped out.

(3) Make a survey of all persons or organizations which either openly or secretly oppose participation in the war.

(4) Make investigations of all anti-Semitism, communism, movements of Negroes, and labor movements.

(5) Utilization of U.S. citizens of foreign extraction (other than Japanese), aliens (other than Japanese), communists, Negroes, labor union members, and anti-Semites, in carrying out the investigations described in the preceding paragraph would undoubtedly bear the best results.

   These men, moreover, should have access to governmental establishments, (laboratories?), governmental organizations of various characters, factories, and transportation facilities.

(6) Utilization of our "Second Generations" and our resident nationals. (In view of the fact that if there is any slip in this phase, our people in the U.S. will be subjected to considerable persecution, and the utmost caution must be exercised).

(7) In the event of U.S. participation in the war, our intelligence set-up will be moved to Mexico, making that country the nerve center of our intelligence net. Therefore, will you bear this in mind and in anticipation of such an eventuality, set up facilities for a U.S.-Mexico international intelligence route. This net which will cover Brazil, Argentina, Chile, and Peru will also be centered in Mexico.

(8) We shall cooperate with the German and Italian intelligence organs in the U.S. This phase has been discussed with the Germans and Italians in Tokyo, and it has been approved.

   Please get the details from Secretary Terasaki upon his assuming his duties there.

   Please send copies to those offices which were on the distribution list of No. 43[c].

---

[a]See I, 112.
[b]Has no bearing on this subject. #732 probably an error.
[c](See No. 4)—See I, 118.

                                                              Trans. 2–7–41

FROM: Tokyo (Matsuoka)   February 15, 1941
TO: Washington (Koshi)   #073.

(2 parts—complete)

Re my #43[a].

The information we particularly desire with regard to intelligence involving U.S. and Canada, are the following:

1. Strengthening or supplementing of military preparations on the Pacific Coast and the Hawaii area; amount and type of stores and supplies; alterations to air ports (also carefully note the clipper traffic).

2. Ship and plane movements (particularly of the large bombers and sea planes).

3. Whether or not merchant vessels are being requisitioned by the government (also note any deviations from regular schedules), and whether any remodelling is being done to them.

4. Calling up of army and navy personnel, their training, (outlook on maneuvers) and movements.

5. Words and acts of minor army and navy personnel.

6. Outlook of drafting men from the view-point of race. Particularly, whether Negroes are being drafted, and if so, under what conditions.

7. Personnel being graduated and enrolled in the army and navy and aviation service schools.

8. Whether or not any troops are being dispatched to the South Pacific by transports; if there are such instances, give description.

9. Outlook of the developments in the expansion of arms and the production set-up; the capacity of airplane production; increase in the ranks of labor.

10. General outlooks on Alaska and the Aleutian Islands, with particular stress on items involving plane movements and shipment of military supplies to those localities.

11. Outlook on U.S. defense set-ups.

12. Contacts (including plane connections) with Central and South America and the South Pacific area. Also outlook on shipment of military supplies to those areas.

Please forward copies of this message as a "Minister's Instruction" to New York, San Francisco, Los Angeles, Seattle, Portland, (Chicago or New Orleans ?) Vancouver, Ottawa, and Honolulu. Also to Mexico City and Panama as reference material.

———————

[a] "We have decided to de-emphasize our propaganda work and strengthen out intelligence work in the U.S." See I, 118.

Trans. 2-20-41

FROM: Tokyo   April 1, 1941
TO: Washington   # 154.

(2 parts—complete).

Secret.

It has been reported that recently strikes have broken out in (Chicago ?) After you have made a very thorough investigation, please wire me your findings along the following lines:

1. The political motivating forces behind these strikes and their expected development.

2. The extent to which these strikes interfere with national defense organization.

3. The relation between C.I.O's anti-ROOSEVELT policies since the elections last year and the current strikes.

4. To what extent is the LEWIS-MURRAY faction using their criticism of the (Cabinet ?) and President ROOSEVELT's foreign policy?

5. Recent A.F. of L. attitude.

6. The attitude of the Communist Party to these strikes.

7. In the event of a breakdown of strike mediation, what are the anticipated Government measures and what is the C.I.O's attitude toward this? In the event of war we think that the Labor Unions will become a major political factor in hindering unity in the United States. In the future arrange to get in touch with the leaders of labor unions, the Communist Party, the Socialist Party, and other anti-ROOSEVELT movements. At the same time, I would like to have you study the possibility of using such a person as (IKU ?) O OYAMA[a].

Furthermore, with regard to German and Italian Fifth Column activities, I gave you instructions in my #546[b] of mid-November last year, but at this time particularly I would like to have you give the subject your careful attention.

On the authorization of the Foreign Minister, please transmit this message to all of our officials in the United States with the exception of -----. Please communicate the foregoing to Canada, ----- and Mexico for their information.

-----

[a]A self-exiled Japanese Socialist now in residence at Northwestern University in Evanston, Illinois.

[b]Investigations requested on (1) activities of German and Italian Americans in present election; (2) attitude of Communist Party toward election; (3) extent of Fifth Column activities by German and Italian Americans in case of America's entry into the war.

Trans. 9-9-41

FROM: Washington (Nomura)   September 4, 1941
TO: San Francisco, Los Angeles, Seattle   # 263.

Message to Tokyo # 780.

Strictly secret.

Possibly the United States is preparing now for the eventuality when a considerable bombing force will have to be transferred to the (Siberian ?) area. Please secure intelligences on this matter.

1. Please investigate the state of affairs and the possibility of the Russian Military Commission, now in the United States, flying American planes via Alaska when they return home. (They have given their greatest consideration to large size Consolidated military planes and amphibions.)

Trans. 9-29-41

FROM: Tokyo (Toyoda)   October 16, 1941
TO: Seattle   # 2187 (Circular).

Henceforth, I would like to have you refer in your reports to the movement of warships as follows.

1. As long as there are no great changes in the movement and basing of warships, report on them at least once every ten days. In the event of priority intelligence, report such on each occasion.

a. The arrival or departure of American flagships of the fleet or scouting force.

b. Should more than ten vessels of any type arrive or depart from port at one time.

c. The arrival or departure of warships of countries other than the United States (give as detailed a report as possible on the class of -----).

2. Should patrolling be inaugurated by naval planes, report it at once.

Trans. 10-29-41

CHAPTER 9

ISSEI AND NISEI

According to the thinking of pre-war Japan, anyone born of Japanese parents anywhere in the world was not only a citizen of Japan by law, but was also inherently Japanese and owed allegiance to the Emperor. It was difficult for the Japanese war lords to conceive that all those Japanese living abroad were anything but loyal to the homeland, and would not do whatever was asked of them when the time came to defend and support the Emperor and to further Japan's destiny. And, indeed, this was exactly what happened in every country conquered by the Japanese armed forces. In the MAGIC messages people of Japanese ancestry living in the United States were referred to as "our second generation," and "our nationals," and "our people in the U.S." Militaristic Japan regarded all overseas Japanese as extensions of the Empire and as a resource to be utilized at the appropriate time. With that kind of thinking it should have come as no surprise to U.S. authorities that Japan turned to its Doho[1] when it needed help in establishing its intelligence nets along the West Coast of the United States.

When the resident Japanese population was evacuated from the West Coast, the Japanese government was outraged. It was as if their own countrymen were being discriminated against by some foreign power. Foreign Minister Tani made a speech in the Japanese Diet in which he angrily denounced the United States for its actions and threatened to sue the

---

[1]   "Compatriots," the term used in Japan to describe overseas Japanese.

141

American government for reparations on behalf of the evacuees after the war was over. Of course, all this was presuming that Japan won the war. It did not; but the U.S. Congress took care of that detail in 1988 by awarding each evacuee $20,000 of taxpayers' money.[2]

The Japanese government recognized the extreme sensitivity of using permanent resident aliens and Japanese-Americans in the U.S. for subversive activities, and warned its representatives to use the greatest caution in recruiting and using them.

Messages intercepted during the formative period of the intelligence nets and then the operational period during the last six months of 1941 were sufficient to give U.S. intelligence specialists a reasonably clear picture of the scope, direction, nature, and success of Japanese espionage activities in the U.S., and how local Japanese were being absorbed into the operation. Particularly revealing were the two messages intercepted in May from the consulates in Los Angeles and Seattle.[3] All Japanese diplomatic posts had been ordered in April to forward a progress report on their espionage efforts. Only the replies from Seattle, Los Angeles, and Washington D.C. were intercepted. If one were to take the two West Coast messages as representative of what was also happening in Portland, San Francisco, and San Diego there certainly was legitimate cause for alarm at what appeared to be the formation of large espionage nets operating along the entire West Coast of the United States under the control of the Japanese government and largely manned by local Issei and Nisei.

The two May messages from Los Angeles and Seattle with their detailed information on recruiting local Japanese for espionage were probably the reason for a June 2, 1941 message from Tokyo warning its representatives to keep sensitive information, even though it was encoded, off the airwaves whenever possible.[4] Presumably, the other consulates had forwarded their progress reports by diplomatic pouch since the material was not urgently required.

---

[2]   A UPI piece in the March 5, 1942 *San Francisco News* reported that Japanese radio called plans for the evacuation "diabolic savagery" and contrasted the "viciousness" with the treatment given civilians in lands conquered by Japan. The criticism specifically mentioned American citizens and did not mention alien Japanese. Since it was tailored to address the fairness of actions taken against U.S. citizens, and thereby appeal to the inherent sense of fairness of the American people, it is tempting to speculate whether such statements from Tokyo were a last-ditch effort to prevent an evacuation that would wipe out their well planned intelligence program. American-born Japanese were known to hold important positions in the Imperial government.

[3]   See MAGIC messages #067, May 9, 1941, p. 147 and #45, May 11, 1941, p. 148.

[4]   See MAGIC message #1166, June 2, 1941, p. 158. This critical message effectively stopped the flow of intelligence regarding Japanese espionage organizations.

This would also explain why U.S. intercept sites failed to intercept the replies from the other consulates.

All intelligence services zealously guard the names and locations of their agents, and Japan was no exception. Secure codes or not, the policy was to not put the names of agents in messages sent out by radio; but occasionally that rule was violated. When that did happen, and the U.S. intercepted the message, the agent's names were routinely passed on to the appropriate U.S. intelligence organization. Accordingly, all of the Issei and Nisei named in the following messages can also be found with amplifying data in FBI or ONI intelligence reports in Part III.

MESSAGE SUMMARIES

#44   January 30, 1941—In order to acquire the vast amount of intelligence Tokyo wanted, its diplomatic posts were instructed to recruit agents into its intelligence nets. This was to include "our Second Generations [Nisei] and our resident nationals [Issei]." Caution in this endeavor was advised lest "our people in the U.S." be subjected to persecution.

#067   May 9, 1941—In response to a request from Tokyo wanting to know the status of the intelligence nets which it had ordered, Los Angeles replied, "We are doing everything in our power to establish outside contacts in connection with our efforts to gather intelligence material." Further, Los Angeles reported that contacts have already been established with "absolutely reliable Japanese in the San Pedro and San Diego areas who will keep close watch on shipments of war material and airplanes." Shipments of war material across the Mexican border are being watched. In other areas Los Angeles went on to say "Connections will be maintained with the Japanese Chamber of Commerce and Japanese newspapers. We also have connections for intelligence purposes with second generation Japanese who are in the armed forces and who are working in airplane factories." Nakazawa, a resident Japanese, is compiling data on military movements and other matters. Contacts have been established with influential Negroes for subversive purposes.

Plans are underway to have certain Japanese organizations keep close watch on U.S. military installations.

#45 May 11, 1941—In its response to Tokyo's request for an intelligence status report Seattle reported progress in the political and economic areas. Second generation Japanese are discussed with regard to contacts in the economic area but the message is garbled here and how they are involved is not clear. As to contacts to gather military information Seattle reported that information was being gathered on the Bremerton Navy Yard, mercantile shipping, airplane manufacturing, and military movements. Men (presumably resident Japanese) are being sent out into the field to gather intelligence. They will report to Lieutenant Commander Okada (a Japanese undercover naval officer deported along with Tachibana by the U.S. in July for espionage activities). Additionally, Seattle reported arrangements have been made with second generation Japanese draftees to provide military intelligence; a first generation Japanese is providing labor union information; a second generation Japanese, Okamura, is in charge of gathering information on labor unions and the Socialist Party; a second generation lawyer, Kenji-Ito, is gathering intelligence on anti-war organizations.

#319 May 19, 1941—This message is from the Japanese embassy in Washington D.C. in response to Tokyo's request for a status report on its intelligence operations. The embassy discusses some of the problems in establishing an intelligence network, but reports that personal contacts are being made "on every hand." Some high level contacts are mentioned and the embassy concludes that if Tokyo expects to recruit nationals and foreigners a great deal more money will be required, and requests $500,000 be sent for this year alone.

#93 June 2, 1941—In discussing intelligence expenses and intelligence plans for a fall back position to Mexico in case of war with the U.S., Tokyo assures Mexico that "... in case the United States joins the war, we will endeavor to use our nationals there to our best possible advantage...."

#36   June 10, 1941—Before the U.S. Department of State intervened and stopped the Department of Justice from prosecuting Lieutenant Commander Tachibana and several other Japanese naval officers for espionage on the West Coast, the Japanese government was busily attempting to minimize the damage such a trial would cause to its intelligence network. Any such trial was also bound to create a sensation when it became known that the Japanese government was utilizing U.S. residents for espionage. One of Tachibana's primary go-betweens was a resident Japanese named Toraichi Kono who used to be Charlie Chaplin's chauffeur. This message recommends that Kono be paid a $25,000 bribe to keep him from testifying on Tachibana's contacts and his various subversive activities. Immediately after Pearl Harbor was attacked Kono was arrested and interned. For a discussion of some of the Japanese organizations and individuals with whom Tachibana had been working see ONI report December 4, 1941 pages 14 and 15.[5]

#62   June 12, 1941—There was a series of messages which discussed the Silver Shirt[6] movement in the U.S. and the role of a resident Japanese named Iwasaki who was recruited by the Japanese government to work with the Silver Shirts for subversive purposes.

#1265   December 5, 1941—The Japanese were obsessed with the idea of using Negroes for subversive activities within the U.S. This message is one of several which discuss the Negro movement and a Japanese resident, Hikida, who was the primary Japanese contact point with various Negro groups. It was Japan's notion that America's war efforts would enable Negroes to advance into war industry jobs not previously available to them and they could then be recruited for espionage and sabotage. Hikida's contacts were considered to be so valuable by the Japanese embassy that it recommended he be invited to Japan to carry on his work. His usefulness in the U.S. had been seriously handicapped because of increased surveillance by the FBI which had been alerted to his activities through the MAGIC messages.

---

5   See ONI report December 4, 1941 on page 251. Reference on pages 264-265.

6   Silver Shirts was the popular name for The Silver Legion of America, a fascist and anti-Semitic organization modeled on the German Nazi Party.

FROM: Tokyo (Matsuoka)   January 30, 1941
TO: Washington (Koshi)   # 44.

(In two parts—complete).

(Foreign Office secret).

(1) Establish an intelligence organ in the Embassy which will maintain liaison with private and semi-official intelligence organs (see my message to Washington #591[a] and #732[b] from New York to Tokyo, both of last year's series).

With regard to this, we are holding discussions with the various circles involved at the present time.

(2) The focal point of our investigations shall be the determination of the total strength of the U.S. Our investigations shall be divided into three general classifications: political, economic, and military, and definite course of action shall be mapped out.

(3) Make a survey of all persons or organizations which either openly or secretly oppose participation in the war.

(4) Make investigations of all anti-Semitism, communism, movements of Negroes, and labor movements.

(5) Utilization of U.S. citizens of foreign extraction (other than Japanese), aliens (other than Japanese), communists, Negroes, labor union members, and anti-Semites, in carrying out the investigations described in the preceding paragraph would undoubtedly bear the best results.

These men, moreover, should have access to governmental establishments, (laboratories?), governmental organizations of various characters, factories, and transportation facilities.

(6) Utilization of our "Second Generations" and our resident nationals. (In view of the fact that if there is any slip in this phase, our people in the U.S. will be subjected to considerable persecution, and the utmost caution must be exercised).

(7) In the event of U.S. participation in the war, our intelligence set-up will be moved to Mexico, making that country the nerve center of our intelligence net. Therefore, will you bear this in mind and in anticipation of such an eventuality, set up facilities for a U.S.-Mexico international intelligence route. This net which will cover Brazil, Argentina, Chile, and Peru will also be centered in Mexico.

(8) We shall cooperate with the German and Italian intelligence organs in the U.S. This phase has been discussed with the Germans and Italians in Tokyo, and it has been approved.

Please get the details from Secretary Terasaki upon his assuming his duties there.

Please send copies to those offices which were on the distribution list of No. 43[c].

---

[a]See I, 112.
[b]Has no bearing on this subject. #732 probably an error.
[c](See No. 4)—See I, 118.

Trans. 2–7–41

FROM: Los Angeles (Nakauchi)
TO: Tokyo (Gaimudaijin)

May 9, 1941
067.

(In 2 parts—complete).

Strictly Secret.

Re your message # 180 to Washington.[a]

We are doing everything in our power to establish outside contacts in connection with our efforts to gather intelligence material. In this regard, we have decided to make use of white persons and Negroes, through Japanese persons whom we can't trust completely. (It not only would be very difficult to hire U.S. (military ?) experts for this work at the present time, but the expenses would be exceedingly high.) We shall, furthermore, maintain close connections with the Japanese Association, the Chamber of Commerce, and the newspapers.

With regard to airplane manufacturing plants and other military establishments in other parts, we plan to establish very close relations with various organizations and in strict secrecy have them keep these military establishments under close surveillance. Through such means, we hope to be able to obtain accurate and detailed intelligence reports. We have already established contacts with absolutely reliable Japanese in the San Pedro and San Diego area, who will keep a close watch on all shipments of airplanes and other war materials, and report the amounts and destinations of such shipments. The same steps have been taken with regard to traffic across the U.S.-Mexico border.

We shall maintain connection with our second generations who are at present in the (U.S.) Army, to keep us informed of various developments in the Army. We also have connections with our second generations working in airplane plants for intelligence purposes.

With regard to the Navy, we are cooperating with our Naval Attaché's office, and are submitting reports as accurately and as speedily as possible.

We are having Nakazawa investigate and summarize information gathered through first hand and newspaper reports, with regard to military movements, labor disputes, communistic activities and other similar matters. With regard to anti-Jewish movements, we are having investigations made by both prominent Americans and Japanese who are connected with the movie industry which is centered in this area. We have already established connections with very influential Negroes to keep us informed with regard to the Negro movement.

---

[a]See I, 165. It is routed as Foreign Minister's instructions to: Ottawa, Mexico, San Francisco, New York, New Orleans. San Francisco to relay to Honolulu, Los Angeles, Seattle, Portland, Vancouver.

Trans. 5-19-41

FROM: Seattle (Sato)   May 11, 1941
TO: Tokyo   # 45.

(3 parts—complete).

Re your # 180 to Washington.

1. *Political Contacts.*

We are collecting intelligences revolving around political questions, and also the question of American participation in the war which has to do with the whole country and this local area.

2. *Economic Contacts.*

We are using foreign company employees, as well as employees in our own companies here, for the collection of intelligences having to do with economics along the lines of the construction of ships, the number of airplanes produced and their various types, the production of copper, zinc and aluminum, the yield of tin for cans, and lumber. We are now exerting our best efforts toward the acquisition of such intelligences through competent Americans. From an American, whom we contacted recently, we have received a private report on machinists of German origin who are Communists and members of the labor organizations in the Bremerton Naval Yard and Boeing airplane factory. Second generation Japanese ----- ----- -----.

3. *Military Contacts.*

We are securing intelligences concerning the concentration of warships within the Bremerton Naval Yard, information with regard to mercantile shipping and airplane manufacturer, movements of military forces, as well as that which concerns troop maneuvers.

With this as a basis, men are sent out into the field who will contact Lt. Comdr. OKADA, and such intelligences will be wired to you in accordance with past practice. KANEKO is in charge of this. Recently we have on two occasions made investigations on the spot of various military establishments and concentration points in various areas. For the future we have made arrangements to collect intelligences from second generation Japanese draftees on matters dealing with the troops, as well as troop speech and behavior. ----- ----- -----.

4. *Contacts With Labor Unions.*

The local labor unions A.F. of L. and C.I.O. have considerable influence. The (Socialist ?) Party maintains an office here (its political sphere of influence extends over twelve zones.) The C.I.O., especially, has been very active here. We have had a first generation Japanese, who is a member of the labor movement and a committee chairman, contact the organizer, and we have received a report, though it is but a resume, on the use of American members of the (Socialist ?) Party. ----- OKAMARU is in charge of this.

5. In order to contact Americans of foreign extraction and foreigners, in addition to third parties, for the collection of intelligences with regard to anti-participation organizations and the anti-Jewish movement, we are making use of a second generation Japanese lawyer.

This intelligence ----- ----- -----.

Trans. 6-9-41

FROM: Washington   May 19, 1941
TO: Tokyo   #319.

Re your #45*ᵃ* and #180*ᵇ*.

I have had Terazaki*ᶜ* of Intelligence make an official trip to New York for the purpose of keeping in touch with the Consul-General*ᵈ* there, and we have come to the following conclusions.

1. We are of the opinion that Roosevelt's dictatorial attitude is becoming more pronounced and the government is leaning toward all-out war. Therefore, we desire that you remit immediately as large an amount as possible so that we may have funds with which to carry on intelligence work in the emergency created by America's entry into the war. For this purpose we assume that Japanese-American relations will continue as at the present.

2. The duties of an intelligence office are becoming increasingly difficult. Because of the existence of the Dies Committee and of the application of the regulations regarding Americans in foreign employ and regarding foreigners resident in America the gathering of accurate secret information is far from easy. This is only one example and there are many other "delicate" problems, so please understand the delay in my answering telegraphic (requests for information).

3. We wish to make Washington and New York one unit and have a unified policy for it. Therefore we wish to get your approval before Terazaki starts for his post. We wish to have Consul Inagaki come here to serve. We feel that we should have here at least one-third of the personnel that they have in Shanghai for intelligence. Therefore, we are looking for temporary employees, (non-career clerks). Furthermore, we wish to have the officer in charge of intelligence visit New York about the 10th of every month.

4. The title of the officer in charge of intelligence will be that of "press attaché". His duties will be as decided in the business conference on March 4th, Article 61 (1), as follows:

    A. Ordinary investigations and,

    B. The development of intelligence.

"A" will of course include the investigation and gathering of secret information on the division in American public opinion regarding the rapprochement in Japanese-American relations based on the peace movement. But we wish to preclude such policies as the strategy being employed in the present negotiations.

5. A summary of the present state of the policy is as follows:

We are making personal contacts on every hand. However, at this place and in New York we are continuing the existing formal contacts and gathering secret information. In addition, to this, the officer in charge of intelligence has contacts with:

(A) J, and W, who are in close touch with the President and his wife.

The President is cultivating power through the "relief workers" and the "W.P.A." and other agencies. In addition to this, since his third term anyone who opposes him becomes the target of his attacks and his dictatorial tendencies are becoming more marked, therefore it is natural that we should pay special attention to those in close touch with him.

One or two items regarding Roosevelt's position: Evidence was brought out in the Senate to the effect that the former Ambassador to England, Kennedy, had not paid his 1932 income tax, but the President maintained silence. According to other secret information, Willkie had a secret understanding with Roosevelt and attacked him in his public speeches more than was necessary as a Presidential candidate and enjoyed scandalizing public opinion, however, had he by any chance become President he would have become a mere puppet of Roosevelt. Again, ----- told Terazaki that originally he was an isolationist, but that now in view of the opposition he was keeping silent. Six months from now if he said he were an isolationist he would not be able to go about in safety.

(B) W of the State Department.

When Terazaki was a student at Brown University he became well acquainted with W.

(C) G of the Senate.

When Terazaki was in Brown University he was greatly helped by this G.

(D) The relationship of the "America First Committee" to Lindberg and W.

Every time Lindberg makes a speech the German newspapers approve and American newspaper reporters in Germany write it up and American newspapers make a big thing of it so that the impression is conveyed that Lindberg is an agent of Germany. Because of this, Lindberg and the Committee are very perplexed and according to W, Lindberg has been cautioned by the German Embassy. Since then he has been in touch with W.

(E) D, an Irish American.

D told our intelligence officer that a Jewish American Justice of the Supreme Court, Frankfurter, was packing the key posts of the government with Jewish Americans. But that American antipathy toward Jews is increasing to such an extent that eventually anti-Jewish influence would prevail.

(F) Persons with religious affiliations. (1) Catholic. (2) Protestant. (3) Undecided.

The Catholics are the ones who are concerned in the present negotiations.

(G) The Brown University Club.

This meets regularly once a month and at other times at which times he (Terazaki) is present.

6. Concerning the salary for employing nationals and foreigners. The future is another matter; however, judging from the past unless our general funds are increased it will be impossible to move. We wish to have you cognizant of the actual situation and when the opportune time comes we wish to take decisive action.

7. Looking at the funds for general intelligence, of the $30,000 income, only about $3,900 a year is available for actual development of intelligence and about $1,800 a year for entertainment and receptions. However, in the decision of the committee held on March 4th of this year regarding intelligence business, and the stipulations of the policy regarding propagation of intelligence, it was variously affirmed that of course the utmost effort would be put forth and that we would need no small sum for expenses. According to the present allotment we will need for the present year the sum of $500,000 for the development of intelligence. We respectfully request this.

---

[a]"In view of our decision to deemphasize propaganda and concentrate on Intelligence, as directed in my dispatch #44, please make recommendations for ensuing propaganda allotments.

[b]Not available

[c]Especially assigned to U.S. for intelligence and propaganda work.

[d]Morishima; he had long experience in intelligence work in Manchuria and China; Counselor of Embassy, Washington, until March 1941.

Trans. 5-21-41

FROM: Tokyo (Matsuoka)   June 2, 1941
TO: Mexico   # 93.

We have appropriated 100,000 yen for your intelligence and enlightenment expenses during the current fiscal year, and I am hereby sending you the first installment of 25,000 yen. This money is to be used as follows:

1. If worse comes to worst, we consider Mexico City, along with Rio de Janeiro, Buenos Aires, and Santiago as most important bases for intelligence concerning the United States. From a geographical standpoint it is most natural that we should endeavor to set up in Mexico City an establishment where we can carry on routine business in the matter of collecting intelligence concerning the United States. This point I stressed particularly in the outline in the first paragraph of my secret ____ # 62*a* with reference to propaganda activities.

2. Though the funds are in the main to be used in intelligence concerning the United States, what is left should be used in gathering intelligence in Mexico. Bear in mind that in putting this policy into effect our principal aim is to collect every possible bit of intelligence concerning the United States and, with this in view, I want you to contact and work out a cooperative policy with our officials in Los Angeles, Houston, New Orleans and New York. Furthermore, in this connection, Mexicali might well be used.

3. Please also plan to use RAFAEL MUNAS for purposes of interception.

4. Concerning propaganda and enlightment, in case the United States joins the war, we will endeavor to use our nationals there to our best possible advantage and we will do our very best to use Rightist and Leftist Labor organizations and promote their anti-American revolutionary influence. Please use your best efforts to achieve this.

Secret outside the Department.

---

*a*Not available.

Trans. 7-1-41

FROM: Hollywood (Nakauchi)   June 10, 1941
TO: Washington   # 36.

Secret.

To the Naval Attaché from TERAI.

1. Our lawyer is of the opinion that KONO*a* should be (kept in the country for thirty days ?) in view of the danger that he might give evidence unsatisfactory to TACHIBANA*b*. It would be wise to subsidize him. Furthermore, as KONO has no funds, the lawyer has suggested that the Navy be responsible for paying this man a subsidy of $25,000 and all court costs. In order that the Navy be kept out of the picture, some of KONO's friends should be selected to appear to be supporting him. We are in the process of making these arrangements. Should you have any objection to this manner of procedure, please advise us.

Furthermore, in view of the fact that ----- is a good friend of the Intelligence Chief and in cahoots with the investigating authorities, it would be wise for the Navy to have little to do with the matter.

2. Though our lawyer would not predict the outcome of this incident, as the hearings will be complicated, at the very earliest it will be tomorrow, the 11th, before counter-schemes can be developed.

It is going to be necessary for TACHIBANA to have frequent communication with the lawyer; therefore, we believe that it would be ill-advised for TACHIBANA to go to Washington at the present time.

---

*TACHIBANA's chauffeur.

'Japanese Naval Language Official who has been held on charges of espionage.

Trans. 6-25-41

FROM: Tokyo (Matsuoka)   June 12, 1941
TO: San Francisco   # 62.

Secret outside the Department.

Will you have Consul INAGAKI go to ----- and find out from TOTARO IWASAKI (YOZEN) in strict secrecy and, if necessary, from some American concerned, the ----- and the present condition of the Silver Shirts Movement. Then wire me information concerning the necessary travelling expense, date of sailing and other expenses in connection with preparations for IWASAKI to come to Japan inasmuch as we would like to use him under our direction in connection with the Silver Shirts Movement if you find that his personality and training (judged not on the basis of his reputation) are suitable for this purpose. What I would like to do, in carrying out our political policy toward the United States, is not to depend on mere pecuniary connections, but also to direct the aforementioned movement in order to establish justice in the United States. Will you, therefore, send me detailed information regarding the world views which form the basis of the movement, the personality and intellectual capacity of those carrying on the movement and, also, such other information that might be of interest to me?

Trans. 7-7-41

FROM: Washington   December 5, 1941
TO: Tokyo   # 1265.

New York to Tokyo # 532.

From New York # 532.

Deniti Hikida—an authority on the Negro problem in the United States we have been utilizing in propaganda work among the Negroes, gathering general intelligence, investigations, and in various other capacities—expresses his desire to return on the Tatsuta Maru.

Recently, he is being subjected to strict surveillance by the authorities of this country, and for this reason, we feel that it is to our interest to have him return home. In view of his excellent record of cooperation with this office in the past, will you please give consideration to our advancing him his passage for his return voyage. (We are paying him his discharge allowance from our secret intelligence fund.) Because the time of departure is fast approaching, please advise us immediately.

Will you give consideration to employing this man upon his return home in our offices there. We feel his specialized knowledge will be of value to us.

Trans. 12-6-41

CHAPTER 10

SPECIAL INTEREST MESSAGES

The messages in this chapter represent a variety of high-interest, intelligence related activities by the Japanese government which do not fit neatly into any of the categories chosen to illustrate MAGIC intelligence. Messages in this section range from starting a revolution in Guatemala to how the Japanese government intends to handle its own enemy alien problem, that is, American or Allied citizens who were residing in Japan or its conquered territories, or who simply happened to be there when the war commenced.

MESSAGE SUMMARIES

#40   April 1, 1941—Directions given to all consulates in the U.S. to send specific data on first and second generation Japanese in each consulate area to Tokyo. For security reasons, the information was to be sent in code. The purpose of the information is not given, but the message was handled by the U.S. in the intelligence category.

#12   April 19, 1941—Chicago's reply to the above message lists the documents upon which it relied to accumulate the requested

information. Obviously, the consulates were maintaining
extensive records on all people of Japanese ancestry living in
their area of responsibility, American citizen or not.

#1166   June 2, 1941—This message from Tokyo warns all diplomatic
posts to send sensitive information by diplomatic courier rather
than in code over the airwaves because of greater security.
Espionage information, of course, was some of the most
sensitive data sent from the U.S. to Tokyo. After this instruction
from Tokyo, almost all the espionage data intercepted by the
U.S. flowing between Japanese diplomatic posts in the U.S. and
Tokyo, was time-sensitive information such as airplane and ship
movements. There were no longer any detailed intelligence
status reports or in-depth messages of what the Japanese were
up to in the U.S.   All that now went by courier. Fortunately,
enough messages had been intercepted during the formative
stage of Japan's intelligence network to allow the U.S.
intelligence community to maintain a continuing insight into the
modus operandi of these nets for the remainder of 1941.

#386   June 10, 1941—The Japanese embassy in Washington D.C. tells
its West Coast consulates that they will have to pick up the
espionage load of the Japanese undercover naval officers on the
West Coast who had just been arrested for espionage. These
arrests meant that Japan lost its two most important military spy
masters, Tachibana, whose special area was Los Angeles, and
Okada, who operated out of Seattle. The net result of this
round-up was to put more pressure on the already harassed
consulates which now had to manage and to keep intact
Tachibana's and Okada's networks, and to recruit even more
local Japanese to meet the additional intelligence requirements
levied on them.

#247   July 4, 1941—In an attempt to disrupt the "Good Neighbor"
policy of the U.S. the Japanese ambassador to Mexico proposes
in this message that Japan bring about and finance a revolution
in Guatemala. He explains that even if the revolution is only
partially successful, it will cause the U.S. problems.

#278   July 19, 1941—This startling message from the Japanese ambassador to Mexico reports to Tokyo that he has met with representatives of all the Japanese nationals living in Mexico and that they have agreed to follow the directions of the Japanese embassy. For purposes of relaying instructions to the Japanese population, the country has been divided into nine districts with a liaison officer in each area responsible for passing on directions to the Japanese living in each section. In 1941 there were approximately 6,000 ethnic Japanese living in Mexico. No similar message was intercepted pertaining to the resident Japanese population living in the United States or Canada, but the possibility that such an arrangement existed, at least to some degree, could not be totally discounted.

#500   August 9, 1941—Looking toward the possibility of war with the United States, the Japanese consul general in Manila, as early as August, wants plans drawn up to have ships available for the evacuation of ethnic Japanese in the Philippines. This is to be done as a safety measure for the protection of resident Japanese.

#875   September 30, 1941—Apparently following the same line of thinking as in the Philippines, the Japanese ambassador in the U.S. is concerned about evacuating Japanese people from the United States. But, the message states, "It will be impossible to get accommodations for all Japanese and Nisei in this country to return to Japan." It is difficult to believe that the ambassador was really contemplating that the entire Japanese population would leave if shipping were available. He probably meant all the Japanese who desired to leave. Nonetheless, these kinds of statements by high Japanese officials were bound to be disconcerting to U.S. authorities.

#1245, #896, #1262   December 3-5, 1941—In this series of messages Hidenari Terasaki, second secretary at the embassy, and in charge of all intelligence in the Western Hemisphere, is ordered by Tokyo to leave Washington several days prior to the Pearl Harbor attack. The Japanese ambassador asks that Terasaki be allowed to remain a few days longer. The request is denied and the ambassador then asks that Terasaki remain as a personal favor to the ambassador. By this time it was too late, and Japan's spy master for the Western Hemisphere never got to South America to run the espionage nets so laboriously established by him for just this eventuality. Message #896 along with a handwritten note explaining Terasaki's role was one of many MAGIC espionage messages routed directly to President Roosevelt.

#2493   December 7, 1941—This interesting message sets forth the Japanese policy toward enemy nationals residing in Japan. Apart from diplomatic personnel, all males between the ages of 18 and 45, as well as certain other categories were to be immediately arrested. The message goes on to say, "However, in view of the fact that we have a very large number of subjects residing in enemy territory, we will exercise caution so that there be nothing of the nature of ill treatment occasioned for them." In other words, enemy nationals will not be ill treated, not because of internationally recognized rules of behavior, but because large numbers of Japanese were living in enemy territory. There was no such problem with Japanese citizens of Caucasian descent because Americans of Caucasian descent were not allowed to become Japanese citizens even if they wanted to, which was highly unlikely. In view of the barbaric treatment of POWs by Japan, one cannot help but wonder at the fate of enemy nationals in Japan if there had not been a large number of Japanese residing in the United States and in Allied countries.

Japanese who held dual citizenship and were caught in Japan at the outset of the war could legally be drafted into the Japanese armed forces, and many were. Others, such as Tokyo Rose, served in other capacities. In any event, and no matter what their loyalties were, it must have been an extremely difficult time for the many Issei and Nisei who were visiting or studying in Japan when Pearl Harbor was attacked and had to remain in Japan throughout the entire war. For those who were truly loyal to the United States and were forced by circumstances to become a part of the Japanese war effort it was particularly agonizing.

FROM: Tokyo (Konoe)   April 19, 1941
TO: San Francisco   # 40.

Please wire immediately of the information you have based on the figures in your office taken at the time of the census in October of last year on the following points:

1. Number of first generation and second generation Japanese (listing male and female separately).

2. List second generation Japanese maintaining only one nationality, and those having dual citizenship.

3. List also those who are dependent and those who are independent.

Forward by mail in code form to Los Angeles, Portland, and Seattle. Relay information from New York to Chicago and New Orleans.

Trans. 4-25-41

FROM: Chicago (Omori)   April 30, 1941
TO: Tokyo   # 12.

Regarding the census of Japanese citizens, the following figures have been ascertained:

1. First generation men _____ 336
   First generation women _____ 100
   Second generation men _____ 177
   Second generation women _____ 384
2. Those of one nationality _____ 337
   Those claiming dual nationality _____ 239
3. Those in independent business _____ 552
   Those not working independently _____ 5
Total Japanese residents _____ 977

The large part of these figures was taken from the annual Japanese occupational report. A large number was also taken from the 1936 Japanese census, the yearly status report and the record of the movement of Japanese nationals. There are other not included in this report, but a separate report concerning the (Japanese) population will be forthcoming in the near future.

Trans. 5-8-41

FROM: Tokyo (Matsuoka)   June 2, 1941
TO: Rome, Washington, Berlin, Moscow, Berne and Rio   Circular # 1166.

(Urgent)

(3 parts—complete) (Washington Circular # 126)

In various countries the science of cryptography and cryptanalysis is being practiced more and more. To tell the truth, no absolute confidence can be placed in the secrecy of a code. We, ourselves, in this office are worrying about drawing up a set of new codes, so we would like for you to give us some suggestions from time to time as to suitable procedures. Please pay the strictest attention always during the transfer and tenure of codes and heed the following points on the maintenance of the security of codes, independent of reliance on safes alone.

1. Needless to say, courier mail is a more secure method of transmitting information than by reliance upon codes, so when there is some secret matter which might arouse a given nation, please send the message by courier mail or some other method equally as safe.

2. I am having an official in charge of this work keep the various offices informed. Each time you get a list, keep one copy of it only and burn the preceding list immediately.

3. Hereafter, as a matter of principle, code messages in ----- are not to be sent anywhere except to this office. As a matter of fact, all other code messages, except those to this office, save in cases of necessity, are to be stopped.

Please see to it that there is no misunderstanding to the effect that after abolishing this sort of dispatches it is not our intention to increase the difficulties of those in charge of tele-graphic work through the necessity of safeguarding dispatches, or the sudden complication of our codes, but that I am merely trying to make our dispatches in general more safe and facile.

Trans. 6-10-41

FROM: Washington   June 10, 1941
TO: Tokyo   # 386.

(To San Francisco, Los Angeles, & Seattle, Cir. # 121)

Secret.

Because of the suppression exercised against our Naval representatives (Language Officers) by the United States authorities in a series of recent incidents, our Navy has, for the time being, stopped stationing these officials by limiting the personnel. Inasmuch as in the light of the relations at present prevailing between Japan and the United States, observation of the movements of the American Navy is one of the most important matters, will you observe the movements of ships and gather other information that may be of interest to our Navy and wire us the required information as it comes to you?

Trans. 6-25-41

FROM: Mexico (Miura)   July 4, 1941
TO: Tokyo   # 247.

Strictly Secret.

To be handled in Government Code.

(Part 1 of 2)[a].

Re your #93[b] and my #244[c].

1. Need I tell you that I will try my very best to knit closely and strengthen our American intelligence net (please consider the question of the route in an entirely different category) and to foster the anti-American and anti-war atmosphere in Mexico? But, still I feel I may say fairly conclusively that, in the light of existing conditions in this country, we cannot expect to achieve very much along these lines.

2. I mean to say that the political and foreign policy of Mexico is directed by President CAMACHO and his cabinet, which is with him body and soul. It is not too much to say that they will brook absolutely no interference or even suggestions. Not only that, but every one of these gentlemen is strongly pro-American and it would be absolutely impossible, I think, to procure any information which would stand our glorious Empire in good stead. Since CAMACHO seized control here, particularly in recent times, there has been a fierce and relentless campaign to control or stamp out labor, Communist, Nationalist and anti-American groups. I am sorry to say that I cannot see any chance at all of our succeeding here with any of our schemes.

3. Well, the first and foremost aim or our schemes is to ruin the position of leadership which the United States has with regard to the other nations of the hemisphere, to break up its so-called "Good Neighbor Policy" and thereby destroy any possibility of future coordination among these nations. Granted that this is our main objective, if we are to succeed, I should think it would be a better policy to turn our eyes elsewhere, rather than to pin our hopes upon a fruitless nation like this. I do not think it would be amiss to try some relatively simpler plan.

---

[a]Part 2 of 2, See II, 414.

[b]In which MATSUOKA says 100,000 yen have been appropriated for intelligence and enlightenment expenses during the current fiscal year and gives instructions as to its use. See II, 384.

[c]Not available.

Trans. 7-9-41

FROM: Mexico (Miura)   July 4, 1941
TO: Tokyo   #247.

(Part 2 of 2)*.

Secret outside the Department.

Military Attache NISI, attached to this office, has a great deal of confidence in the possibility of planning a rebellion in Guatemala. Although he had submitted his suggestion about three months ago to the military authorities in Tokyo, he was advised to wait and watch developments while maintaining liaison with those interested, because at that time our relations with the United States were delicate. On the other hand, is it not also a good plan to get Marshall URUTAADO of Nicaragua, concerning whom I made reference in my secret message #62*, to lead a rebellion, since he is not only a very influential man but a greatly respected person?

5. Such a plot might not necessarily be a success in every respect; however, even if it fails, if it's carried out to a certain extent, it would have to be quieted by the United States using its armed forces. In such a case, it would cast a shadow on the so-called "Good Neighbor Policy" of the United States and cause a cleavage among the countries on the American continent. It would also endanger considerably the fundamental policy on which the United States attaches the greatest importance, a policy which envisages placing within her influence the regions extending to Panama. If it succeeds to an extent, it would at least upset at once the political balance among the countries as far as Panama. It would seem to me that there is considerable likelihood of its turning that region into an arena of political confusion.

6. Therefore, I wish to request that you give this matter your careful consideration in the light of our national policy. Furthermore, even if we provide the funds necessary for this plot, it is plain that the plans would not be carried out immediately on the following day, and so it seems to me that we should provide funds sufficient to commence preparations for the rebellion in accordance with the contingencies that may arise.

7. In case the above plot is carried out, I am of the intention of placing the entire leadership in the hands of a military official who has had the greatest amount of training and experience as a specialist in plotting. May I have a reply as soon as possible?

---

*See II, 413.
*Not available.

Trans. 7-8-41

FROM: Mexico City
TO: Tokyo

July 19, 1941
#278.

Re your message #144ᵃ to Brazil.

In accordance with the contents of my message #251ᵇ, I summoned the more influential people in Mexico City and representatives from the various areas in Mexico, to my office. I relayed to them your instructions with regard to our giving guidance to our nationals residing in Mexico. Following this up, I warned them of the things they as Japanese should be prepared to face, and asked them to consider ways and means of making the best of them.

The various points listed below were decided upon as being the best way of meeting the present situation. All those present assured me that our nationals would understand them, and would do everything in their power to adhere to our decisions.

1. In view of the times, it is of the utmost importance that there be an efficient system of liaison with this office so that we may act in unity. We decided that we could best accomplish this by, first of all, strengthening the Federation of Japanese Associations. At the same time, we divided the country into nine areas, taking into consideration its geography, transportation facilities, and the distribution of the population of our nationals. In each area a liaison officer will be installed who will offer guidance to our nationals residing in his area as well as to report, at suitable intervals, the general conditions of his area. He will, also, relay in the most effective manner instructions issued by this office to the Japanese population in his area.

2. As a means of protecting our nationals in the event of unfavorable developments in the future, we shall endeavor to at all times promote better feeling toward the Japanese people among the Mexicans. Towards this end, we should urge the members of the Japanese Associations and more particularly influential Japanese persons, to make an even greater effort than heretofore. When and if worse comes to worst, each area will put into effect the most appropriate means of protecting the people therein. Funds to be used in such an emergency will be collected within the areas themselves.

3. Means of protecting Japanese businesses in the event of unfavorable developments as well as steps which shall be taken if there are indications that Japanese assets in Mexico will be frozen, were decided upon along the lines contained in my message #174ᶜ.

ᵃNot available.

ᵇSee II, 421. Mexico City wires Tokyo that a great majority of Japanese residents will probably remain in the U.S. in the event of a break with the U.S. That Mexico would probably not permit Japanese from U.S. to enter that country. A conference of Japanese representatives from various parts of Mexico will meet shortly in Mexico City to formulate plans for mutual help among Japanese districts.

ᶜNot available.

Trans. 7-22-41

FROM: Manila (Nihro)   August 9, 1941
TO: Tokyo   #500 (?).

(Abstract)

From the Manila office of the N.Y.K. the Consul General learns of the suspension of overseas shipping. He is concerned about the safety of Japanese in the Philippine Islands in case of war with the United States, especially in view of the inadequacy of the police system. Consequently he urges that ships for the evacuation of Japanese be kept available for prompt use.

Trans. 9–16–41

FROM: Washington (Nomura)   September 30, 1941
TO: Tokyo   #875.

Re my #864[a].

URGENT.

The opinion of my legal advisor (formerly legal advisor at the State Department) is as stated in separate message #876[b], but I believe that in the case of private lines application may be made to ship baggage ahead of time and that the authorities cannot do anything to stop this.

Regarding your message #610[a], since the United States Government attaches a great deal of importance to the matter of allowing Americans in Japan to leave, please consider from the very beginning determining the number of persons (according to ADAMS there are still about 140 or 150 applicants for first and second class passage) and grant them permission to embark. (In any case it will be impossible to get accommodations for all Japanese and Nisei in this country to return to Japan.)

Relayed to all Consuls in the United States, Ottawa and Honolulu.

---

[a] Not available.

[b] Ambassador NOMURA discusses the question whether or not in an Admiralty Court of the United States a private merchant ship could be attached or libeled for the purpose of obtaining compensation.

Trans. 10–13–41

FROM: Washington   December 3, 1941
TO: Tokyo   # 1245.

Terasaki now in the midst of----- intelligence work at a most important time, would like to have him stay over a while and go by the sailing on the 19th. Takagi busy on Tatsuta Maru business. (Negotiating with State Department for securing space) ----- air plane.

(*Note:* Many gaps in this message.)

Trans. 12-4-41

FROM: Tokyo   December 5, 1941
TO: Washington   # 896.

Re your # 1245ᵃ.

Will you please have Terasaki, Takagi, Ando, Yamamoto and others leave by plane within the next couple of days.

ᵃSee IV, 442.

Trans. 12-6-41

FROM: Washington   December 5, 1941
TO: Tokyo   # 1262.

Re your # 896ᵃ.

From Kurusu to Secretary Tasiro.

I feel confident that you are fully aware of the importance of the intelligence set-up, in view of the present condition of the Japanese-U.S. negotiations. I would like very much to have Terasaki, who would be exceedingly difficult to suddenly replace, because of certain circumstances, remain here until we are definitely enlightened as to the end of the negotiations. I beg of you, as a personal favor to me, to make an effort along these lines. I shall have him assume his post as soon as his work here is disposed of.

ᵃSee IV, 457.

Trans. 12-6-41

FROM: Tokyo   December 7, 1941
TO: Net   Circular # 2493.

In 2 parts complete.

Secret.

Separate Message.

Policies:

In regard to our handling of enemy subjects and enemy property in Japan, we will approach this matter in the magnanimity of a great nation, complying with international law as far as possible, and exercising care not to give the enemy nations or other third party nations any occasion for taking retaliatory measures, or for making unfavorable propaganda.

Main points:

(1) Diplomatic officials of enemy countries:

(a) Evacuation. The evacuation of enemy diplomatic officials will be carried out on the basis of exchanges for our diplomatic and consular officials resident in enemy countries.

(b) Handling of the above until their evacuation. The inviolable rights pertaining to diplomatic officials of enemy countries, whose duties come to an end simultaneously with the beginning of war, will be respected as a general rule. However, telephones will be cut off, and the use of wave radios and wireless transmitters will be seized. Members of the staffs of embassies and legations, for the present, as a general rule will be allowed to live in the embassy or legation compounds, and no inconvenience will be caused in the matter of daily living.

(2) Consular officials.

(a) Evacuation. As far as possible consular officials will be handled under the same heading with diplomatic officials.

(b) The handling of the same until the time of their evacuation: The offices will be closed and sealed. Short wave radio and wireless equipment will be seized. Members of consulate staffs for the time being will be allowed to live at their present places of abode and as far as conditions warrant may use their official residences, with no restrictions upon their daily living.

(3) Enemy subjects residing in Japan: In addition to such police surveillance and protection as is necessary, individuals regarding whom there is ample ground for suspicion will be rounded up; and all military men, seamen, or aviation personnel as well as those qualified for these services, persons of special technical skill, persons suspected of being foreign spies, and all males between 18 and 45 will for the present be placed under arrest. However, in view of the fact that we have a very large number of subjects residing in enemy territory, we will exercise caution so that there may be nothing of the nature of ill-treatment occasioned for them.

(4) Publicly owned enemy property: Such public property, aside from embassy, legation and consular buildings, which can be used either directly or indirectly for military purposes will, if necessary, be confiscated.

(5) Privately owned enemy property: Privately owned property will not be seized or confiscated except in the event of general requisitioning.

(6) While no special restrictions will be placed upon the diplomatic and consular officials of neutral countries resident in Japan, those of quasi enemy countries (such as Panama, Iran, Norway, Belgium, Egypt, Greece, etc.) will be denied the use of codes.

The evacuation of the enemy diplomatic and consular officials who are in Manchukuo and China will be handled in the same manner as the above.

Trans. 12-9-41

CHAPTER 11

WEST COAST

During the latter half of 1941 the U.S. intercepted hundreds of messages sent to Tokyo from the United States, Panama, Hawaii, and the Philippines containing national defense information. Although requirements for this kind of information had been levied upon the consulates as early as January, it was not until early June that this information began to be forwarded to Tokyo. This was about three weeks after the consulates had reported that they had successfully recruited local Japanese and were beginning to move ahead operationally with their nets.

Espionage messages sent by the consulates to the Third Bureau (Intelligence Bureau) were usually addressed simply to Tokyo although occasionally, as a matter of form, the foreign minister's name might appear on the cable even though he himself probably never saw the message. Purely diplomatic messages, of course, remained within the foreign ministry. When the consulates sent out their cables it was customary to show the consul general as the originator, and he most likely did read most of these messages since espionage during 1941 was his primary responsibility. Message summaries have been eliminated from this chapter and the remaining three chapters of Part II because the messages are largely to the point, short, and self-explanatory.

FROM: Hollywood (Los Angeles)   June 2, 1941
TO: Washington   # 7.

(Circular)

Message to Tokyo # 83.

On the 20th, the Saratoga, and on the 24th, the Chester (?), Louisville, the 12th Destroyer Squadron and Destroyers # 364, 405, 411, 412, and 413 entered San Diego, and all of them left on the 31st.

Trans. 6–20–41

FROM: San Francisco (Muto)   June 5, 1941
TO: Washington   # 022.

Action Tokyo as # 092. *(Abstract)*

Report to Washington and Tokyo on announcement on the 4th by the Maritime Commission that 28 ships are to be pressed into service for the Army and Navy (7 to Army, 21 to Navy), etc.

Trans. 6–19–41

FROM: Seattle (Sato)   June 23, 1941
TO: Tokyo (Gaimudaijin)   # 056.

(1) Ships at anchor on the 22nd/23rd (?):
(Observations having been made from a distance, ship types could not be determined in most cases.)
    1. Port of Bremerton:
     1 battleship (Maryland type)
     2 aircraft tenders (one ship completed and has letter "E" on its funnel).
    2. Port of -----:
     1 destroyer
     11 coast guard cutters
     (Ships under repair):
     1 destroyer
     11 (appear to be) minesweepers
    3. Sand Point:
     2 newly constructed hangars
    4. Boeing:
     New construction work on newly built factory building # 2. Expansion work on all factory buildings.

Trans. 7–14–41

FROM: Hollywood (Nakuchi)
TO: Tokyo

August 16, 1941
156.

Re my message # 151ª.

1. The St. Claire took on a cargo of 95,000 barrels of aviation gasoline and left port for Vladivostok on the afternoon of (date). The Fitzsimmons is in the process of taking on a similar cargo of 75,000 barrles at Erusegundoᵇ. Aside from these two, three other ships are scheduled to leave port carrying similar cargoes. All of them, it is understood, are under charter with the Maritime Commission.

2. All of the above mentioned ships are to rendezvous at some point in the Pacific. It is understood that a number of United States destroyers are on maneuvers at the present time. Rumor has it that they are bound for Vladivostok.

3. The crew of the St. Claire, mentioned above, ----- ----- -----.

Relayed to Washington and San Francisco.

ª Not available.
ᵇ Kana spelling.

Trans. 8–22–41

FROM: Seattle (Sato)
TO: Tokyo

August 16, 1941
91.

(Secret outside the office)

According to a spy report, the English warship *Warspite* entered Bremerton two or three days ago.

Trans. 10–4–41

FROM: Seattle (Sato)
TO: Tokyo

August 21, 1941
93.

The Russian ship *Vladimar Mayskovsky* arrived one or two days ago and entered dry dock for repairs which will require a week or more. The present movements of the ship are ----- -----, but as soon as it is repaired, it is going to California to load on freight for Vladivostok. The *Minsk* has left harbor as previously stated. The *Patrovsuky* is still in dry dock.

Trans. 8–25–41

FROM: Los Angeles (Nakauchi)   September 16, 1941
TO: Tokyo   # 184.

Strictly Secret.

(Part 1 of 2.)

An outline of airplane production in the various factories of Southern California (up to date):
a. Orders placed with each company (40 % of total orders in the Los Angeles area and 10 %
centers around San Diego).

Company	Amt. of Orders	Employees	Monthly Salaries
Lockheed	$371,000,000	32,791	$5,287,000
Vega	120,000,000	7,364	1,201,000
Douglas	491,000,000	31,818	4,749,000

(for subsequent data on orders placed in the various factories of Santa Monica, El Segundo
and Long Beach, see my # 147ª)

Company	Amt. of Orders	Employees	Monthly Salaries
North American	$385,000,000	11,443	$1,976,000
Vulte	86,000,000	9,720	1,579,000
Northrop	49,000,000	2,549	461,000
Consolidated	540,000	2,000	--------

ªNot available.

Trans. 9-24-41

FROM: Los Angeles (Nakauchi)   September 16, 1941
TO: Tokyo   No number.

(Part 2 of 2.)

b. Types of craft on order in the various companies:

Company	For Britain	For American Army
Lockheed	Hudson bombers	P–38 Interceptor pursuit planes
Vega	Vega "Ventura" bombers	B–39–E heavy bombers
Douglas	Bombers	DC–3 transport planes. B–39–E and B----- heavy bombers A–20 bombers
North American	B–medium bombers Mustang pursuit planes	(Same as for Britain)
Vulte		"Valiant" primary pursuit planes "Vengeance" high-speed bombers
Consolidated	B-type heavy bomber(?)	B-type heavy bombers(?)

Relayed to Washington.

Trans. 9-24-41

FROM: Seattle (Sato)   September 4, 1941
TO: Tokyo   # 105.

(Part 2 of 2)

3. The 39th Bombardment Group (44 planes), the 89th Observation Squadron (15 planes), and the 310th Signal Company, all of Spokane, left August *23 (?)* to take part in the September maneuvers in Louisiana.

4. The planes (number unknown) which the 54th Bombardment Group at *(?)* near Everett are to get are *Republics (?)* or twin-motored *Lockheeds (?)*.

5. The Naval Air Base at Dutch Harbor was opened on the 2nd. W. N. Updegraff has been named Commandant *as has been previously reported (?)*. The Naval supply base at Port *Andrews* (?) was opened on the 4th, according to reports.

6. The *steering apparatus (?) (diameter 8 inches, double cylinders (?), gear ratio 410 to 1 (?)* for the 312 10,000 ton freighters to be leased to England are to be manufactured in two factories, one in Everett and one in *New York (?)*.

Trans. 9–10–41

FROM: San Francisco (Muto)   September 18, 1941
TO: Tokyo   # 218.

According to a spy report, the English warship *Warspite* arrived here from Bremerton on the ----- and is at present moored near the (naval arsenal at Mare Island?). It has been determined that it requires two more months for repairs at Liverpool (my message # 187[a]).

Relayed to -----, Los Angeles and Seattle.

---

[a]See II, 771.

Trans. 9–25–41

FROM: Seattle (Sato)   September 20, 1941
TO: Tokyo   # 123.

1. The following warships are now at Bremerton:
The Warspite (repair work continuing. The upper part of the bridge and the port side of the bow spotted here and there with red paint).
Maryland class—one ship (the bridge, turrets and other main armaments have been painted red. Also, they seem to be constructing mountings on the foreward main deck for ten anti-aircraft guns).
Saratoga class air-craft carrier, 1 ship (tied up alongside the pier).
One ship which appears to be a cruiser (it has two smoke stacks but we were unable to distinguish anything else).
One other ship just arrived for repair.
2. The New Mexico class ship mentioned in message # 101[a] has departed.

---

[a]See II, 855.

Trans. 9–27–41

FROM: San Francisco (Muto)   October 2, 1941
TO: Washington   # 222.

   Message to Tokyo as # 230.

   1. One Oklahoma class battleship has arrived in port and is moored in front of the Bethle-
hem ship-building yard. No reconstruction work is going on on the outside but a great deal of
repair work appears to be in progress within the ship.
   2. It has been announced by the local headquarters of Naval District # (?) that the Hunters
Point shipyard, which was bought last year and which has been undergoing repairs, will be
taken over formally in the near future in advance of expectations. (Refer to confidential letter
216[a] of last year.)
   Relayed to Washington, Los Angeles, Seattle and Honolulu.

-----

   [a] See II, 745.

                                                  Trans. 10–17–41

FROM: San Francisco   October 16, 1941
TO: Tokyo   # 243.

   Re my # 217[a].

   The Russian freighter, MEJINSKI, is now in the process of docking. The IGARKA is three
days out of New York, the NANTES 7 days from Vladivostok, and the MICHULIN 10 or 12 days
from Vladivostok.
   The NANTES is loaded with a large quantity of wheat, 20,000 barrels of fuel oil, and also
some machine guns, tanks, etc.
   Relayed to Washington, Los Angeles, Seattle, Portland.

-----

   [a] See II, 29.

                                                  Trans. 10–23–41

FROM: Hollywood (Nakauchi)   October 12, 1941
TO: Washington   # 48.

   Message to Tokyo # 202.

   Re my # 185[a].

   The Russian ship, Kiev, now in port here, will take on its load of war materials as soon as
repairs are completed and proceed to Vladivostok when orders are received. For this purpose,
it is equipped with a 500 watt radio for the reception of orders and war news from Moscow.
   Relayed to -----, Seattle.

-----

   [a] Not available.

                                                  Trans. 10–22–41

FROM: Seattle (Sato)　　　　　　　　　　　October 28, 1941
TO:　　Tokyo　　　　　　　　　　　　　　# 150.

(Priority.)

In commemoration of Navy Day, the 27th, fifteen Coast Guard vessels sailed through the harbor here in single file. Their names were as follows: The *Kane, Giruma*[a], the *Brooks,* the *Fox* (the above listed vessels have had their four-inch guns replaced by five-inch guns; all of these were brand-new ones), the Frigate *Bird,* the *Crow,* the *Pintail,* the *Eagle 57, Batukei*[a], the *Butternut,* the *Amber,* the *YP 83, 87, 89,* and *90.*

———————

[a] Kana spelling.

Trans. 11–19–41

FROM: Tokyo　　　　　　　　　　　　　November 29, 1941
TO:　　San Francisco　　　　　　　　　　Circular # 2431.

Make full report beginning December 1st on the following.

Ship's nationality, ship's name, port from which it departed, (or at which it arrived), and port of destination, (or from where it started), date of departure, etc., in detail, of all foreign commercial and war ships now in the Pacific, Indian Ocean, and South China Sea.

Trans. 12–4–41

FROM: Seattle　　　　　　　　　　　　　December 6, 1941
TO:　　Tokyo　　　　　　　　　　　　　# 184.

Urgent intelligence.

1. The ships at anchor in Bremerton on the 5th were the Warspite (came out of the dock and at present is tied up at a pier) and the Colorado.

2. The Saratoga sailed the same day.

Trans. 12–8–41

CHAPTER 12

Panama

Being responsible for intelligence on the Panama Canal Zone as well as several Central American countries, the Japanese minister to Panama was a busy man indeed. In June 1941 his main problem was to find a safe means to get the secret charts of the Canal Zone administration back to Tokyo. These charts showed the location of equipment, fortifications, and other military data about the Canal Zone. Somehow the Italian minister had obtained the charts and made them available to the Japanese minister.[1]

This wasn't as alarming as it sounds because over the months MAGIC messages out of Panama from the very active Japanese diplomatic post there made it painfully apparent that the Japanese already knew practically all the military details on the Panama Canal that were of interest. Intercepted MAGIC messages revealed that the minister had obtained this information from a broad network of Japanese residents who served as canal watchers.

The Joint Congressional Committee investigating the attack on Pearl Harbor after the war had this to say in its report about MAGIC and the Canal Zone:

> While no instructions from Tokyo to Panama are available subsequent to August 2, 1941 the reports to Tokyo contain detailed information

---

[1] Secretary of War Henry L. Stimson believed that the Panama Canal would have been a better target than Pearl Harbor for the initial Japanese attack because of its strategic location and difficulty to repair. See *On Active Service*, p. 407.

concerning the location of airfields, air strength, ammunition, location and camouflage of petroleum supply tanks, location and strength of artillery patrols, radar detectors and their range, map procurement and other matters which would be of interest only if an attack on the Panama Canal were contemplated.

One would think with this kind of input, Akiyama, the minister of the legation in Panama, would be a favorite of the foreign ministry and the Third Bureau. If so, one would never know it from his September 20, 1941 message to Tokyo wherein he apologizes for his extravagance in spending $550.00 a month to maintain a whole network of spies and informers throughout Panama and other Central American countries. Unfortunately, neither SIS nor OP-20-G intercepted Tokyo's reaction to this "outrageous" expenditure of yen.

FROM: Panama (Izawa)   June 17, 1941
TO: Washington (Koshi)   # 19.

(Part 1 of 2)

Action Tokyo as ≠ 62.

The Italian Minister showed me many secret charts made by the Canal Zone Administration, showing the locations of equipment, guns and other military establishments in the Canal Zone.

I glanced through them, and found them to be extremely detailed. In considering the process by which these charts were obtained, I feel that it would be absolutely impossible to obtain them in the future. Accordingly, I approached the Italian Minister regarding them. It appears that he has no objections to our making copies of them, provided that this is done in Tokyo, after we have delivered them to the Italian Embassy there. However, as all ports here are being very closely watched, there is no other way of taking these charts out except by plane.

I wonder if it would not be possible to have some Japanese merchant in South America, who is either returning to Japan, or is being transferred to some other country, take these charts out; or to have one of our office-staff deliver them to a designated place? At present, all the places where recent defense operations are being carried out are being marked on these charts. This work is estimated to take about one week to finish.

The Italian Minister stated that if *(handling)* of this in Japan caused too much delay, there is no other way than to take them by plane from ----- to *Washington (?)*. In this case, he stated that he would want to have it *(copied ?)* at *(Washington ?)*. Please send instructions without fail.

Secret.

Note: Translation doubtful. Part 2 of 2 unavailable.

Trans. 6-25-41

FROM: Tokyo (Foreign Minister)   June 23, 1941
TO: Mexico (Koshi)   # 106.

Regarding the plans for procuring maps of the Panama Canal and vicinity, please have career attaché, Kihara, make an official trip to Panama. It might be well to have secretary Yoshimizu accompany him.

Have the maps taken out by plane, and then have Sato, the Naval attaché, bring them to Tokyo with him when he returns.

Furthermore, since the Panama Legation, in their report # 62[a] of 17 June from Panama to me, mentioned the question of a trip, get in touch with them regarding date and time of arrival. (American surveillance will unquestionably be vigilant. There are also some suspicions that they read some of our codes. Therefore, we wish to exercise the utmost caution in accomplishing this mission. Also, any telegrams exchanged between you and Panama should be very short for security, or be in innocuous plain language.)

---

[a]See II, 227.

Trans. 6-24-41

FROM: Panama (Akiyama)   August 18, 1941
TO: Tokyo   # 120.

Report on observations:
1. Ships moving through the Panama Canal toward the Atlantic:
August 15th   Four U.S. submarines (number -----)
August 16th   Two U.S. freighters
August 17th   One U.S. freighter

  2. Moving toward Pacific:
August 15th   One U.S. freighter
                  One DeGaullist Government
                  destroyer (Triomphant) (now
                  anchored at Balboa)
  3.
August 17th   One U.S. destroyer anchored
                  at Balboa.
                  One warship which appeared to
                  be a cruiser was seen to arrive.
Recently five large-size destroyers have been in port (taking on fuel, rations and other supplies).

                                                                  Trans. 9-29-41

FROM: Panama (Akiyama)   September 20, 1941
TO: Tokyo   # 169.

(Part 1 of 2.)

Since taking office, I have made a special study of the attitude of the United States and also of the nature of the people and topography of this section; and as a result have made the following estimate of the amount of money needed for enlightenment and propaganda purposes. This amount is necessary in making contacts for intelligence purposes, and already some expenditures have been made. I know that this will be "hard to take," but beg of you that you will consider the matter carefully and wire me the result (all per month expenses):

1. (a) Bonuses for officials or spies residing at some distance from the Canal who go at night to observe the movement of warships --$ 70.00
(b) For those who from time to time give warning ----------------------------- 150.00
2. Money to supplement the activities of the Kyōwa Company in this country -------$100.00
(Part 2 of 2.)
3. Running expenses of our broadcasting office ---------------------------------- 50.00
4. Money for special spies -- 50.00
5. To follow the principle of paying well those who try as well as those who accomplish results --- 100.00
6. For maintaining contacts with newspaper reporters and other agents ------------ 130.00
7. Costs of making arrangements -- 30.00
8. Money for spying in other countries to which I am accredited ------------------ 50.00
The above are for the current fiscal year.

                                                                  Trans. 10-3-41

FROM: Panama (Akiyama)
TO: Washington

September 30, 1941
Circular #51.

Message to Tokyo #188.

On the (29th ?) two (French ?) warships left port bound for the Pacific. One vessel of the Omaha class left port on the night of ----- for an unknown destination. In spite of the rumor that the raider is in the neighborhood of the Galapagos, rumors are circulating that it is in water adjacent to the Canal.

Trans. 10-10-41

FROM: Panama (Akiyama)
TO: Tokyo

October 2, 1941
#191.

Between the 30th and the 2nd, three American freighters and one English hospital ship transited the canal to the Pacific, and nine American freighters and one American liner transited the canal to the Atlantic.

Trans. 10-18-41

FROM: Panama (Akiyama)
TO: Tokyo

October 2, 1941
#190.

(2 parts—complete)

1. Since the recent shift in military aviation efforts to the Pacific Area the "Panama Air Depot" located at France Field was transferred to Curundu Heights (immediately adjacent to Albrook Field).

2. Rear Admiral SADLER, Commander of the 15th Naval District, since the extensive activities on the Pacific end of the Canal, made public on the 1st a statement to the effect that because of the increase of naval supplies a four-story warehouse built on pier 18 (it will be completed the middle of November), the ammunition unloading pier (west of pier 18) consisting of 32 buildings, and the existing buildings in the neighborhood of the Balboa dry dock would all be taken over as warehouses. Furthermore, the petroleum supply tanks at Boca on the Pacific side and at Mt. Hope (the railroad junction from which the line branches to Colon and Ft. Randolph) on the Atlantic side (recently it is believed that these tanks have been camouflaged) have been taken over.

3. There are intelligences at hand concerning the construction of a good storage depot at Corozal which would contain sufficient foodstuffs to supply the Canal Zone for a six-month period, even though shipping routes between this point and the United States are severed.

Trans. 10-20-41

FROM: Panama (Akiyama)   October 4, 1941
TO: Tokyo   # 194.

Re my message # 193ª.

One vessel left for the Pacific at 11:00 A.M. on the 3rd.

From the 3rd until the morning of the 4th, three American freighters and one French steam-
er moved out into the Pacific. During the same interval, seven American freighters, the "Union
tanker", one destroyer and two British freighters went through the Canal in the direction of the
Atlantic (one of the two British freighters was of the 10,000 ton class). All of the vessels bound
for the Atlantic went through the Canal successively. The two cruisers, which I mentioned in
my caption message, accompanied these vessels as far as Balboa. Therefore, it would seem
indicated that their entire cargoes were made up of military supplies.

Relayed to Washington.

_____

ª Not available.

Trans. 10–18–41

FROM: Panama (Akiyama)   October 28, 1941
TO: Tokyo   # 231.

According to intelligences coming from Costa Rica, I have learned the following:

1. It is understood that the American air force has decided to take over bases in the Golfo
Dulce off Costa Rica and the Gulf of Fonseca which faces on the territory of (Honduras ?).

2. It is understood that the Government of the United States has admonished the various
nations of Central and South America to watch rigorously residents of Axis affiliation.

3. The Government of the United States is now preparing to construct destroyer, submarine,
and air bases in the (Gulf/Bay?) of Keyatamuª in the southeastern area of the Island of Cocos
off the coast of Puntarenas.

_____

ª Kana spelling.

Trans. 11–19–41

FROM: Panama (Akiyama)   October 28, 1941
TO: Tokyo   # 232.

1. On the 27th, a warship of the Omaha class left this port for the Pacific.

2. On the same day, two single-funnel destroyers, one light cruiser, and one 10,000 ton class
transport were anchored in Balboa harbor.

3. On the 26th, one American destroyer and two submarines were anchored in the harbor at
Christobal.

4. From the 22nd until the 27th, four American and four British merchant vessels passed
through the Canal bound for the Pacific (one of the British vessels was of the 14,000 ton class).
Six American merchant vessels, one American tanker, and one Netherlands cargo ship
passed through the Canal in the direction of the Atlantic.

Trans. 11–19–41

FROM: Panama (Akiyama)
TO: Tokyo

November 11,(?)
1941
273.

Ships passed through Panama on 11th and 12th.

To Pacific:
Freighters: 1 American, 2 British, (one 10,000 ton with tower looked like warship).
To Atlantic:
Freighters: 3 American, 3 British, (one with 2 guns, two with 1 gun).

Trans. 11–25–41

FROM: Panama (Akiyama)
TO: Tokyo

November 12, 1941
282.

1. On the night of the 11th, a British light cruiser went through the Canal in the direction of the Atlantic. This cruiser is understood to have undergone repairs in San Francisco and seems to have been the *Liverpool*.
2. On the 12th, a British military transport of approximately 27,000 tons, of the Union Castle class, passed through the Canal on its way from the Pacific, filled to capacity with military personnel.
3. Early in November, 12 Douglass two-motored bombers and six Airacobra pursuit planes, flew here to increase the Canal air force.

Trans. 12–3–41

FROM: Panama (Akiyama)
TO: Tokyo

November 13, 1941
285.

Panama shipping report.

(1) A commercial ship of Union Castle type passed through towards the Atlantic, with about 1000 of what seemed like evacuees (women and children) and a few wounded, aboard, on the 13th.
(2) The heavy cruiser which passed through on the 11th is believed to be passing through to make up a convoy on the Atlantic, and looks as though it had accompanied # 1 (Union Castle type commercial ship) from the Pacific. The German reports say it is a Liverpool class cruiser, but not the Liverpool.
(3) The Omaha type ship has the bow painted black and the stern painted white and at a glance looks like a destroyer.

Trans. 11–24–41

FROM: Washington
TO: Panama

December 1, 1941
040.

Report passage through the Canal of the U.S.S. MISSISSIPPI, NORTH CAROLINA, WASHINGTON, WASP.

Trans. 12–10–41

CHAPTER 13

MANILA

The Philippines occupied a unique pre-war position in the U.S. military's cryptanalytic structure. OP-20-G maintained a cryptanalytic organization at Cavite, just outside Manila, cover named CAST, which was the only COMINT unit outside Washington D.C. authorized to work MAGIC. Not only was CAST in a superb geographic position to intercept certain high priority international links, but it also had one of the few PURPLE machines in existence and thus had the capability to decipher Japan's vaunted machine cipher system. Daily changing PURPLE key settings and other technical support were forwarded to CAST from OP-20-G in Washington over the secure COPEK communications system. In addition to MAGIC, CAST also intercepted and processed the Japanese navy's main operational crypt system, JN-25.

When it became apparent in early 1942 that the Philippines was going to fall, extraordinary actions were taken to evacuate the Navy CAST unit. Japanese interrogation methods were well known and had any of the CAST personnel been captured, given their knowledge of both MAGIC and JN-25, the whole course of the war could have been changed.

A complex plan was worked out whereby the CAST personnel were evacuated by submarine in three increments of approximately twenty-five men each. The first left in February, the next in March, and the third on April 9, 1942 the day Bataan surrendered. Included in each group was a mixture of linguists, cryptanalysts, and radio men, carefully selected so that COMINT operations could continue without interruption during the evacuation.

The Japanese had two consulates in the Philippines, one in Manila and the other in Davao. During 1941 CAST intercepted and processed MAGIC espionage messages passing between these two consulates and Tokyo. Post-war analysis of the messages sent from the Japanese consulates to Tokyo show a very high degree of accuracy on the espionage data forwarded. All messages of the type displayed in this chapter were reported on to appropriate U.S. authorities in the Philippines and in addition were relayed back to Washington, D.C.

FROM: Manila   September 15, 1941
TO: Tokyo   # 604.

Re my # 601ᵃ.

According to secret information received, it is the ST. LOUIS, with three other vessels (names unknown), said to be starting for Singapore. Bow waves of indicating speeds of 24 to 25 knots were observed. Also, apparently ammunition is being handled (red flags are hoisted).

ᵃSee III, 342.

                                                        Trans. 9-18-41

FROM: Manila (Nihro)   September 16, 1941
TO: Tokyo   # 605.

Re my # 604ᵃ.

They left the harbor early on the 16th loaded with food supplies. On the stern three seaplanes (single wing) were observed. Designation is as stated in my previous message. It is also reported that they (arrived here?) by way of Australia but whether this is true or not I don't know.

ᵃSee III, 346—I have secret information that the ST. LOUIS and three other ships are leaving for Singapore and that they apparently have ammunition on board.

                                                        Trans. 9-25-41

FROM: Manila (Nihro)   October 3, 1941
TO: Tokyo   # 654.

Message to Singapore # 8 on the 2nd.

The American Cruisers, ST. LOUIS and PHOENIX recently docked here and sailed on the 16th and 22nd respectively. Now, I have received a spy report that their destination was Singapore. What I want to know for sure is if they have arrived there or not, also I am very much interested in checking on the accuracy of this spy report. Please investigate and wire me back immediately.

                                                        Trans. 10-7-41

FROM: Tokyo (Toyoda)   October 4, 1941
TO: Manila   # 318.

I want you to make a reconnaissance of the new defense works along the east, west and southern coasts of the Island of Luzon, reporting on their progress, strength, etc. Also, please investigate anything else which may seem of interest.

                                                        Trans. 10-8-41

FROM: Manila (Nihro)   October 14, 1941
TO: Tokyo   # 685.

On the afternoon of the 13th, the HOUSTON, the MARBLEHEAD, the HOH[a], five destroyers, and two mine layers left port. Their destination is unknown.

The following ships are tied up in this harbor at the present time: The BLACK HAWK, the
PAS[a], four destroyers, 10 submarines (the submarines are of classes 170 and 190), and the
GOLD STAR (all of the above-mentioned submarines are tied up on either side of the GOLD
STAR and are taking on supplies).

---

[a]Kana spelling.

Trans. 10-21-41

FROM: Manila   October 17, 1941
TO: Tokyo   # 691.

Reports of reliability A.

On the afternoon of the 17th the
TON
MADDO
HON
4 destroyers
5 submarines (140 class)
BERU
1 minelayer and
oiler TRINITY
entered harbor.

In addition to the above ships in port at present on the 18th are as follows:
A. Manila.
   The same as my # 685[a].
B.   Cavite.
   REI
   2 minelayers
   ----- (4 groups missing)

3. Large scale barracks are being constructed at NUEBA ESIHA between Cabanatuan and
Laur (about 131 kilometers from Manila).

4. It is said that mechanized maneuvers are being carried out between Laur and Aguilla.

---

[a]See III, 353.

Trans. 10-22-41

FROM: Manila (Nihro) October 20, 1941
TO: Tokyo # 693.

Primary intelligence. The Houston, the Marblehead, eight destroyers, ten submarines (of the 170 and 190 class) and one mine layer left port on the morning of the 20th. Their destination is unknown.

Trans. 10–24–41

FROM: Davao (Kihara) October 21, 1941
TO: Tokyo # 156.

Regarding My # 124ᵃ.

As an air base for central Mindanao district, 300 men are being managed by Americans, and the ground is now being leveled.

An underground hangar and underground oil tanks are planned; however, the material for this is delayed so that building on this is not progressing as planned.

Already several times a week planes are flying here, and it seems they are expecting large heavy bomber planes too, very soon.

_____

ᵃ Not available.

Trans. 12–1–41

FROM: Manila (Nihro) October 22, 1941
TO: Tokyo # 701.

The American ship *American Leader* which arrived in port on the 20th is unloading more than ten tanks, each tank equipped with a gun having a barrel about six feet long.

Trans. 10–25–41

FROM: Manila (Nihro)   October 25, 1941
TO: Tokyo   # 711.

1. The REI[a] and one destroyer left during the morning of the 25th. Destination is not known.
2. Ships in port are the following:
a. Manila.
TON[a]
MADDO[a]
CHESTER
BUKKU[a]
BERU[a]
ROYGXOMU (?)
HON[a]
5 destroyers
11 large submarines
5 small submarines
b. Cavite.
PASU[a] (under repair)
2 destroyers
3. There are indications that all of the vessels are to be repainted into an ash color (almost a grey). The TON[a] and one destroyer have already been repainted.

---

[a] Possible equivalents for these abbreviations are:

REI	— Langley
TON	— Houston
MADDO	— Marblehead
BUKKO	— Black Hawk
BERU	— Isabel
HON	— Heron
PASU	— Canopus

Trans. 10–29–41

FROM: Manila (Nihro)   November 1, 1941
TO: Tokyo   # 722.

1. The TON^a, MADDO^a, HON^a, 7 destroyers, 8 submarines and 3 minesweepers entered port on the 31st. But the TON^a left again on the morning of the 1st, destination unknown.

2. On the morning of the 2st the President Cleveland and President Madison left port loaded with American soldiers whose time was up, (number uncertain).

3. According to reports received from what we believe are reliable sources the number of American military and naval planes in the Philippine Islands is as follows:

(a) Military planes.
Large bombers, 29.
Scout planes, 324.
The same, B type, 62.
Fighters, 317.
The same, B type, 131.
Pursuit planes, 302.
The same, D type, 69.
Training planes, 49.
Total, 1283.
(b) Naval planes.
Large flying boats, 26.

4. Ships in port on the 1st: MADDO^a, BAKKU^a, PISU^a, HON^a, BERU^a, 9 destroyers, 3 submarines, WOHOTOSU, 3 minelayers. In Cavite: REI^a, PASU^a, 2 Z.

5. According to a report from the De La Rama steamship company two of their ships, the Dona Estaban (1616 tons), and the MADBUKARU (191 tons), had been requisitioned by the local American Army.

---

^{a}Possible equivalents for these abbreviations are: TON (Houston); MADDO (Marblehead); HON (Heron); BUKKU (Black Hawk); PISU (Canopus); BERU (Isabel); REI (Langley); PASU (Canopus).

Trans. 11–8–41

FROM: Manila   November 15, 1941
TO: Tokyo   # 767.

The following is from a report of a Japanese resident in Cebu.

1. At present there are about 300 American and 2500 Filipino soldiers stationed there. (There are four barracks each with a capacity of about 500 or 600 soldiers.)

2. The airport has an area of about 196 acres but is being enlarged (by use of convict labor). About 12 planes (of medium size) used by the Philippine Army, have been transported to Java by air, and 12 or 13 American Army planes, (monoplanes—whether they were scout planes or pursuit planes was not clear), are now stationed there. In addition to these there is one large bomber in the hangar (double type, capacity 40 planes).

3. The headquarters of the former patrol force are being used as the commisariat store-house and all sorts of provisions are being stored there.

4. On the 22nd of September, about 20 American warships anchored on the northwest coast of the Sulu Archipelago. Around the middle of October two destroyers and one cruiser entered Cebu Harbor and early this month, one oil supply ship of the 20,000 ton class, and a camou-flaged cruiser of the 10,000 ton class, entered port and anchored for two or three days. It has been recognized that occasionally two or three American ships anchor around the south of Mactan, Bacol, and Panglao.

5. There is an open drydock at MAKUGAA (operated by Chinese) capable of handling ships up to 10,000 tons.

Trans. 11-18-41

FROM: Manila (Nihro)   November 12, 1941
TO: Tokyo   # 754.

According to a report handed on to me by a Japanese who has lived in the Province of Ilocos Norte for some fourteen or fifteen years, the following has been ascertained.

1. At the present time there are approximately 400 Philippine soldiers and seven or eight officers stationed in Laoag[a]. It is being rumored, however, that the Philippine troops will be increased to approximately 1,700. At the present time they are constructing additional bar-racks.

2. There seems to be no indication that they plan the expansion of the present civil airport in Laoag (length, 1,200 metres; width, 850 metres) nor are they stationing any military planes at that field. Aside from a reconnaissance flight nightly (one plane) over the coastal area in the vicinity of the city, no extensive activity is in progress.

3. Though it is said that Claveria[b] and Burgos[b] are being equipped with ----- -----, the details are unknown. (I am continuing my private investigations in this connection.)

---

[a] Seaport in the Province of Ilocos Norte on the Island of Luzon, P.I.

[b] Towns on the northern shore of the Island of Luzon, P.I.

Trans. 11-21-41

FROM: Manila (Nihro)   November 12, 1941
TO: Tokyo   # 755.

A report given me by a Japanese who resides in Camarines Norte[a] is as follows:

1. In that area at the present time there does not seem to be many troops stationed. Only about 60 members of the Philippine Patrol organization, with headquarters in Daet[b], are located in that area. Every day five or six of these patrolmen are dispatched as a relief unit to Paracale[c] and Jose Panganiban[d].

2. The Civil Airport at Paracale is not being used at the present time. Insofar as the military air field at Daet is concerned, though one or two military planes landed there during February of this year, from that time to this there has not been a single military plane alight on this field. As this field is located right on the beach, should it be necessary it is said that naval planes could land in the shipping lane just off of the beach as well.

3. On the point of land, San Muricio[e], north of Jose Panganiban it is rumored that they are equipping ----- with -----, but this has not been verified. (I am continuing my secret investigations.)

4. Twelve or thirteen coastal reconnaissance planes were seen to have flown over the area within a period of three days. Toward the latter part of last year 13 American freighters are said to have entered the port of Panganiban. Since then, almost on the average of once a week, American freighters sail from Batganas[f] to Hondagua[g].

----

[a] Province near southeastern extremity of Luzon.
[b] City on southeastern extremity of the Island of Luzon.
[c] Seaport in the province of Camarines Norte.
[d] English spelling. Cannot identify.
[e] English spelling. Point of land cannot be identified.
[f] Seaport in southwestern Luzon.
[g] Seaport on Lopez Bay off Lamon Bay.

Trans. 11-24-41

FROM: Manila (Nihro)   November 29, 1941
TO: Tokyo   # 805.

Ships in port on the 29th.
1. Manila:
   Submarine tender WOTOSU and HORAN[a]
   Submarines 190 class 5
   Submarines 170 class 5
   Submarines 170 class 5
(When the 180 class entered port there were 8 but 3 departed, destination unknown)

Submarines 150 class 5
Submarines small size 4
Oilers, 2 (PISU[a] and TRINITY)
Destroyers, 2
Gunboats, 1 (BERU[a])
Minelayer, 1
2. Cavite:
TON[a]
PASU[a] (being repaired)
3. It was announced on the 27th that for a time the lights at Langley Point in Cavite, at Manila, Baguio, and on the buoys in the bay would be turned out.

---

[a] Probably HOLLAND, PECOS, ISABEL.

Trans. 12–8–41

FROM: Manila (Nihro)   December 1, 1941
TO: Tokyo   # 812.

Ships in port on the 1st.
A. Manila:
Submarine tender HOLLAND.
Submarines, small 2.
Submarines, large 6.
Oilers, 2 (PISU[a] and TRINITY).
Gunboats, 1 (KASUBERU).
The PASU[a] which was undergoing repairs at Cavite lies at anchor of –––––.
Cargo ship, 1 (4,000 tons class), taking on provisions.
The submarine tender, WOTOSU.
14 large submarines and 2 destroyers, left port this morning, destination unknown.
The American Navigation (10,000 ton class) entered port about 3 days ago. From it are being unloaded 12 objects 1 meter in diameter and about 3 meters in length. I think they are boilers. (I am making investigations.)
A former Danish ship, the Manchen Maersk (10,000 ton class), present registry Panama, present name unidentifiable (under investigation) entered port this morning, about half loaded, it appeared.
5 British freighters (6,000 ton class) are at the pier taking on cargo, details not ascertainable.
The Spencer Kelogg (American registry, 6,000 ton class), entered port about 2 days ago, unloaded crude oil and is scheduled to load castor oil.
The Don Esteban (requisitioned by the American Army) entered port this morning.
B. Cavite:
TON[a]

---

[a] Probably PECOS, CANOPUS, and HOUSTON.

Trans. 12–8–41

CHAPTER 14

HONOLULU

Although this is not a book about the attack on Pearl Harbor, and it does not bear directly on the primary subject of this book, no discussion of 1941 COMINT can be complete without some comments about the Honolulu MAGIC messages.

In March 1941 Ensign Takeo Yoshikawa arrived in Honolulu. A graduate of Japan's Annapolis, Eta Jima, he had just completed four years of intensive postgraduate study of the United States Navy. He was an expert on U.S. warships, their configuration, speed, armament, and all kinds of other relevant data about the Pacific Fleet and its base at Pearl Harbor. Insofar as the outside world was concerned, he was Vice-Consul Morimura, but his real job was to keep the Third Bureau informed on the movements and the activities of the Pacific Fleet.

He did this mostly by observing Pearl Harbor from Aiea Heights with his binoculars, then sending the information he had learned back to Tokyo in the consular crypt system, J-19, which was completely readable by the U.S. throughout 1941.[1] Message traffic between the Third Bureau and Yoshikawa was routinely intercepted by Signal Intelligence Service and OP-20-G and

---

[1]   One of his assistants was a Japanese-American named Richard Kotoshirodo who was later sent to the Topaz Relocation Center in Utah and was never charged with espionage. See Robert B. Stinnett, *Day of Deceit* (New York: The Free Press, 2000) for a detailed description of Yoshikawa's activities.

forwarded back to Washington D.C. where it was decrypted and translated, *but not forwarded to the U.S. commands in Hawaii.* All the messages were shown as being sent by Consul General Kita. Morimura's name never appeared on a message. After December 2 when the consulate was ordered to destroy its major codes and ciphers, he sent his messages to the Third Bureau in the relatively simple PA-K2 system which was the only one left to him.

Although both the FBI and the ONI had the Japanese consulate in Honolulu staked out for months, and both had telephone taps on the consulate's phones, they never tumbled to Yoshikawa. After Pearl Harbor, Yoshikawa became a part of the exchange program for diplomats. He was never questioned, and never really identified for what he was until 1953 when a Japanese newspaper interviewed him. After that he was bombarded with offers to publish his entire story. But he did not respond because he said too many people had been involved in his espionage and he did not feel free to expose them or the system under which they worked.[2]

Yoshikawa ended the war still an ensign. He never received a medal, a pat on the back, or any other recognition even though, for a short period, he held history in the palm of his hand.

All the MAGIC espionage messages from Honolulu came from Yoshikawa, with one exception. That was the long December 3, 1941 cablegram which was from a German named Fritz Kuehn, a sleeper placed on Oahu by Captain Ogawa as a backup in case the U.S. closed the Honolulu consulate. In his message Kuehn identifies himself by his code name, Ichiro Fujii. Yoshikawa forwarded Kuehn's message, but they never worked as a team. This one message was Kuehn's only contribution, and he paid dearly for it.

Kuehn claimed to be a former Gestapo official, and he had been under FBI surveillance for some time. Within hours after Pearl Harbor was attacked he was arrested. Subsequently, he was tried by a military court and sentenced to death. This was later changed to life imprisonment. After the war, his sentence was commuted so he could be deported, and he left for Buenos Aires, Argentina on December 3, 1948, never to be heard from again.

Although there were earlier messages between Yoshikawa and the Third Bureau, the first one displayed in this chapter is the September 24, 1941 Tokyo message which many people later claimed was a bombing plot scheme. Admiral Kimmel, who was the Pacific Fleet commander when Pearl Harbor was

---

2   Takeo Yoshikawa with Lieutenant Colonel Norman Stanford, U.S.M.C., wrote an article entitled, "Top Secret Assignment" which was published in the December 1960 *U.S. Naval Institute Proceedings*, pages 27-39. In the article Yoshikawa gingerly steps around the issue of help given him by local Hawaiian residents. Some information in the article was refuted in FBI reports which were declassified years later.

bombed, stated that this one message alone would have been a tip-off to the authorities in Hawaii that Pearl Harbor was the likely Japanese target. According to him, and others, this instruction put an invisible grid over Pearl Harbor which was used as an overlay for planning the kind of attack information which the Japanese pilots would need in order to perfect their bombing and torpedo runs.

When the Japanese strike force, Kido Butai, set sail for Hawaii from the Kurile Islands on November 26, 1941 the Third Bureau radioed Yoshikawa's messages to the fleet commander, Admiral Nagumo, probably using JN-25 which the U.S. was not reading at that time. Kido Butai, of course, was on radio silence. It could receive messages, but did not make any transmissions itself for fear of being detected by U.S. radio direction finding techniques.

But the U.S. had an ace in the hole, MAGIC. U.S. cryptanalysts could read all the Japanese foreign ministry communications sent in the MAGIC crypt systems. That meant they could read all of Yoshikawa's messages to the Third Bureau. Unfortunately, these messages were processed only in Washington D.C., and all the ones transmitted in the week prior to the attack were not read until several days after the Pearl Harbor disaster.

The U.S. Navy cryptanalytic group located in Pearl Harbor, HYPO, could easily have broken out these Honolulu cables, and kept Admiral Kimmel and General Short, the Army commander, informed on a timely basis on the correspondence between the Third Bureau and Yoshikawa. But HYPO had been assigned another mission, to break the Japanese navy's Flag Officers' Code. MAGIC, by definition meant foreign ministry codes, and was, therefore, "diplomatic traffic," and diplomatic traffic, as everyone knew, could only be worked in Washington. To further compound the problem, once the Honolulu cables were in Washington they were in competition for processing with worldwide MAGIC messages. The overworked, understaffed cryptanalysts and linguists had to set priorities on which MAGIC messages they were going to process first. High-interest links and high-grade crypt systems usually received top priority. The Honolulu consulate sending messages in the lowly PA-K2 system, after destroying its major codes and ciphers, in those last few days wasn't very high on the list.

Ironically, Captain Layton, who was Admiral Kimmel's intelligence chief, was an old hand at COMINT. He knew its value, how to use it, and how to interpret it. If he had been on distribution for all the MAGIC messages dealing with espionage within his area of responsibility there is little doubt how he would have reacted. Unquestionably, he would have alerted Kimmel that Pearl Harbor was a possible, if not likely, target for the Japanese. Having tutored Kimmel on COMINT over the several months before Pearl Harbor, surely Layton would have had no problem convincing him that something regarding the Pacific Fleet was afoot, and precautionary measures over and above what were taken, would have been implemented. Kimmel and Layton both testified to that before the Joint Congressional Committee. That committee, however, concluded that although the Honolulu MAGIC messages were somewhat different than those from other U.S. cities, there was nothing in the Honolulu messages to indicate that Pearl Harbor was being singled out as a target. Perhaps, but comparing the Honolulu messages with those from the West Coast, Panama, and Manila there does appear to be a significant difference in the character, tone, and subject matter of the Honolulu messages which distinguishes them from the others.

If so, it is a distinct possibility that because of poor operational control and administrative mismanagement of MAGIC that we squandered the "finest intelligence in our history." Of the three essential components of successful intelligence: collection, evaluation, and dissemination, we had only collection.

Not one of the following messages, all intercepted before the Pearl Harbor disaster, was sent to either the U.S. Navy or the U.S. Army in Hawaii. None. Not a single one. Fourteen of them didn't even get translated until after December 7, 1941.

FROM: Tokyo (Toyoda)   September 24, 1941
TO: Honolulu   # 83.

Strictly Secret.

Henceforth, we would like to have you make reports concerning vessels along the following lines insofar as possible:

1. The waters (of Pearl Harbor) are to be divided roughly into five sub-areas. (We have no objections to your abbreviating as much as you like.)

Area A. Waters between Ford Island and the Arsenal.

Area B. Waters adjacent to the Island south and west of Ford Island. (This area is on the opposite side of the Island from Area A.)

Area C. East Loch.

Area D. Middle Loch.

Area E. West Loch and the communicating water routes.

2. With regard to warships and aircraft carriers, we would like to have you report on those at anchor, (these are not so important) tied up at wharves, bouys and in docks. (Designate types and classes briefly. If possible we would like to have you make mention of the fact when there are two or more vessels along side the same wharf.)

Trans. 10-9-41

FROM: Honolulu (Kita)   September 29, 1941
TO: Washington   Circular # 041.

Honolulu to Tokyo # 178.

Re your Tokyo's # 083ᵃ.

(Strictly secret)

The following codes will be used hereafter to designate the location of vessels:

1. Repair dock in Navy Yard (the repair basin referred to in my message to Washington # 48ᵇ); KS.

2. Navy dock in the Navy Yard (the Ten Ten Pier); KT.

3. Moorings in the vicinity of Ford Island: FV.

4. Alongside in Ford Island: FG (East and west sides will be differentiated by A and B respectively).

Relayed to Washington, San Francisco.

ᵃ See III, 356.

ᵇ Not available.

Trans. 10-10-41

FROM: Tokyo (Togo)   November 15, 1941
TO: Honolulu (Riyoji)   # 111.

As relations between Japan and the United States are most critical, make your "ships in harbor report" irregular, but at a rate of twice a week. Although you already are no doubt aware, please take extra care to maintain secrecy.

Trans. 12-3-41

FROM: Honolulu (Kita)   November 18, 1941
TO: Tokyo   # 222.

1. The warships at anchor in the Harbor on the 15th were as I told you in my # 219[a] on that day.
Area A[b]—A battleship of the Oklahoma class entered and one tanker left port.
Area C[c]—3 warships of the heavy cruiser class were at anchor.
2. On the 17th, the Saratoga was not in the harbor. The carrier, Enterprise, or some other vessel was in Area C. Two heavy cruisers of the Chicago class, one of the Pensacola class were tied up at docks "KS". 4 merchant vessels were at anchor in area D[d].
3. At 10:00 a.m. on the morning of the 17th, 8 destroyers were observed entering the Harbor. Their course was as follows: In a single file at a distance of 1,000 meters apart at a speed of 3 knots per hour, they moved into Pearl Harbor. From the entrance of the Harbor through Area B to the buoys in Area C, to which they were moored, they changed course 5 times each time roughly 30 degrees. The elapsed time was one hour, however, one of these destroyers entered Area A after passing the water reservoir on the Eastern side.
Relayed to —————.

---

[a] Not deciphered. Dated 14 November 1941.
[b] Waters between Ford Island and the Arsenal.
[c] East Loch.
[d] Middle Loch.

Trans. 12-6-41

FROM: Tokyo (Togo)   November 18, 1941
TO: Honolulu   # 113.

Please report on the following areas as to vessels anchored therein; Area "N" Pearl Harbor, Manila Bay, and the areas adjacent thereto. (Make your investigation with great secrecy.)

Trans. 12-5-41

FROM: Tokyo (Togo)   November 20, 1941
TO: Honolulu   #111.

Strictly secret.

Please investigate comprehensively the fleet ----- bases in the neighborhood of the Hawaiian military reservation.

Trans. 12-4-41

FROM: Honolulu (Kita)   November 24, 1941
TO: Tokyo   #234.

Part 1 of 2. Strictly secret.

Re your #114ª.

1. According to normal practice, the fleet leaves Pearl Harbor, conducts maneuvers and forthwith returns.

2. Recently, the fleet has not remained for a long period of time nor conducted maneuvers in the neighborhood of Lahaina Roads. Destroyers and submarines are the only vessels who ride at anchor there.

3. Battleships seldom, if ever, enter the ports of Hilo, Hanalei, or Kaneohe. Virtually no one has observed battleships in maneuver areas

4. The manner in which the fleet moves:

Battleships exercise in groups of three or five, accompanied by lighter craft. They conduct maneuvers for roughly one week at sea, either to the south of Maui or to the southwest. Aircraft carriers maneuver by themselves, whereas sea plane tenders operate in concert with another vessel of the same class. Airplane firing and bombing practice is conducted in the neighborhood of the southern extremity of the island of Kahoolawe.

ªNot available.

Trans. 12-16-41

FROM: Honolulu   November 24, 1941
TO: Tokyo   # 234.

   Part 2 of 2.

   The heavy cruisers in groups of six carry on their operations over a period of two to three
weeks, doubtless going to Samoa. The length of time that they remain at anchor in Pearl Harbor or tied up at docks is roughly four or five days at a stretch.

   The light cruisers in groups of five spend one to two weeks in operations. It would seem that
they carry on their maneuvers in the vicinity of Panama.

   The submarines go out on 24-hour trips Monday, Wednesdays, and Fridays.

   The destroyers, in addition to accompanying the principal units of the fleet, carry on personnel training activities in the waters adjacent to Hawaii.

   Mine layers (old-style destroyers) in groups of -----, have been known to spend more than
three weeks in operations in the Manila area.

   Furthermore, on the night of the 23rd, five mine layers conducted mine laying operations
outside Manila harbor.

                                                                   Trans. 12-16-41

FROM: Honolulu   November 28, 1941
TO: Tokyo   # 238.

   Military report:

   (1) There are eight "B-17" planes at Midway and the altitude range of their anti-aircraft
guns is (5,000 feet?).

   (2) Our observations at the Sand Island maneuvers are: number of shots—12; interval of
flight—13 seconds; interval between shots—2 minutes; direct hits—none.

   (3) 12,000 men (mostly marines) are expected to reinforce the troops in Honolulu during
December or January.

   (4) There has usually been one cruiser in the waters about (15,000 feet?) south of Pearl Harbor and one or two destroyers at the entrance to the harbor.

                                                                   Trans. 12-8-41

FROM: Tokyo (Togo)   November 28, 1941
TO: Honolulu   # 119.

Re your message # 243ª.

Secret outside the Department.

Intelligences of this kind which are of major importance, please transmit to us in the following manner:

1. When battleships move out of the harbor if we report such movement but once a week the
vessels, in that interval, could not only be in the vicinity of the Hawaiian Islands, but could
also have traveled far. Use your own judgment in deciding on reports covering such movements.

2. Report upon the entrance or departure of capital ships and the length of time they remain at anchor, from the time of entry into the port until the departure.

ª Not available.

Trans. 12-8-41

FROM: Tokyo (Togo)   November 28, 1941
TO: Honolulu   # 118.

(Priority.)

Re your # 232ª.

To be handled in government code.

Anticipating the possibility of ordinary telegraphic communication being severed when we
are about to face the worst of situations, these broadcasts are intended to serve as a means of
informing the diplomats in the country concerned of that situation without the use of the usual
telegraphic channels. Do not destroy the codes without regard to the actual situation in your
locality, but retain them as long as the situation there permits and until the final stage is
entered into.

ª Not available.

Trans. 12-7-41

FROM: Tokyo   November 29, 1941
TO: Honolulu   # 122.

We have been receiving reports from you on ship movements, but in future will you also
report even when there are no movements.

Trans. 12-5-41

FROM: Honolulu (Kita)   December 1, 1941
TO: Tokyo   # 241.

(In 2 parts complete.)

Re your # 119[a].

Report on ship maneuvers in Pearl Harbor:

1. The place where practice maneuvers are held is about 500 nautical miles southeast of here. Direction based on:

(1) The direction taken when the ships start out is usually southeast by south and ships disappear beyond the horizon in that direction.

(2) Have never seen the fleet go westward or head for the "KAIUI" straits northwards.

(3) The west sea of the Hawaiian Islands has many reefs and islands and is not suitable as an ocean maneuver practice sea.

(4) Direction of practice will avoid all merchant ship routes and official travel routes.

Distance based on:

(1) Fuel is plentiful and long distance high speed is possible.

(2) Guns cannot be heard here.

(3) In one week's time, (actually the maneuvers mentioned in my message # 231[b] were for the duration of four full days of 144 hours), a round trip to a distance of 864 nautical miles could be reached (if speed is 12 knots), or 1152 miles (if speed is 16 knots), or 1440 nautical miles (if speed is 20 knots) is possible, however, figuring on 50% of the time being used for maneuver technicalities, a guess that the point at which the maneuvers are held would be a point of about 500 miles from Pearl Harbor.

2. The usual schedule for departure and return of the battleship is: leaving on Tuesday and returning on Friday, or leaving on Friday and returning on Saturday of the following week. All ships stay in port about a period of one week.

---

[a]See IV, 287.

[b]Not available.

Trans. 12–10–41

FROM: Tokyo (Togo)   December 2, 1941
TO: Honolulu   # 123.

(Secret outside the department.)

In view of the present situation, the presence in port of warships, airplane carriers, and cruisers is of utmost importance. Hereafter, to the utmost of your ability, let me know day by day. Wire me in each case whether or not there are any observation balloons above Pearl Harbor or if there are any indications that they will be sent up. Also advise me whether or not the warships are provided with anti-mine nets.

Trans. 12–30–41

FROM: Honolulu (Kita)   December 3, 1941
TO: Tokyo   # 245.

(In 2 parts complete.)

Military secret.

From Ichiro Fujii to the Chief of # 3 Section of Military Staff Headquarters.

1. I wish to change my method of communicating by signals to the following:
a. Arrange the eight signals in three columns as follows:

Meaning		*Signal*
Battleship divisions including scouts and screen units	Preparing to sortie	1
A number of carriers	Preparing to sortie	2
Battleship divisions	All departed between 1st and 3rd.	3
Carriers	Several departed between 1st and 3rd.	4
Carriers	All departed between 1st and 3rd.	5
Battleship divisions	All departed between 4th and 6th.	6
Carriers	Several departed between 4th and 6th.	7
Carriers	All departed between 4th and 6th.	8

2. Signals.
a. Lanikai*ᵃ* Beach. House will show lights during the night as follows:

	Signal
One light between 8 and 9 p.m.	1
One light between 9 and 10 p.m.	2
One light between 10 and 11 p.m.	3
One light between 11 and 12 p.m.	4
b.	
Two lights between 12 and 1 a.m.	5
Two lights between 1 and 2 a.m.	6
Two lights between 2 and 3 a.m.	7
Two lights between 3 and 4 a.m.	8

Part 2.

c. Lanikai[a] Bay, during daylight.

If there is a "star" on the head of the sail of the Star Boat it indicates signals 1, 2, 3, or 4.

If there is a "star" and a Roman numeral III it indicates signal 5, 6, 7, or 8.

d. Lights in the attic window of Kalama House[b] will indicate the following:

Times	Signal
1900 – 2000	3
2000 – 2100	4
2100 – 2200	5
2200 – 23--	6
2300 – 2400	7
0000 – 0100	8

e. K.G.M.B.[c] Want Ads.

A. Chinese rug etc. for sale, apply P.O. box 1476 indicates signal 3 or 6.

B. CHICH..GO farm etc. apply P.O. box 1476 indicates signal 4 or 7.

C. Beauty operator wanted etc. apply P.O. box 1476 indicates signal 5 or 8.

3. If the above listed signals and wireless messages cannot be made from Oahu, then on Maui Island, 6 miles to the northward of Kula Sanatorium[d] at a point halfway between Lower Kula Road and Haleakala Road (latitude 20° 40′N, longitude 156° 19′W., visible from seaward to the southeast and southwest of Maui Island) the following signal bonfire will be made daily until your EXEX signal is received:

Time	Signal
From 7 – 8	3 or 6
From 8 – 9	4 of 7
From 9 – 10	5 or 8

---

[a] Between Waimanalo and Kailua Beaches on east coast of Oahu.

[b] A beach village on east coast of Oahu, 1 mile northwest of Lanikai.

[c] A radio broadcast station in Honolulu.

[d] At latitude 20-42-45 N., longitude 156-20-20 W.

Trans. 12-11-41

FROM:　Honolulu (Kita)　　　　　　　　　　　　　December 3, 1941
TO:　　Tokyo　　　　　　　　　　　　　　　　　　# 247.

Ship report.

2nd. Military transport (name unknown) sailed out toward mainland.

3rd. RARIN came into port from San Francisco.

Trans. 12-10-41

FROM: Honolulu (Kita)   December 3, 1941
TO: Tokyo   # 248.

    Ship report.

    December 3rd. Wyoming and 2 seaplane tenders left port. No other movement.

Trans. 12–10–41

FROM: Honolulu (Kita)   December 4, 1941
TO: Tokyo   # 249.

    On the afternoon of the 3rd, one British gunboat entered Honolulu Harbor. She left port early on the morning of the 4th. She was roughly of the 1,100 tons class. She had but one funnel and carried one 4 inch gun fore and aft. ----- -----.

    Furthermore, immediately after the vessel entered port, a sailor took some mail to the British Consular Office and received some mail in return.

Trans. 12–12–41

FROM: Honolulu (Kita)   December 5, 1941
TO: Tokyo   # 252.

    (1) During Friday morning, the 5th, the three battleships mentioned in my message # 239[a] arrived here. They had been at sea for eight days.
    (2) The Lexington and five heavy cruisers left port on the same day.
    (3) The following ships were in port on the afternoon of the 5th:
    8 battleships
    3 light cruisers
    16 destroyers
    Four ships of the Honolulu class and ----- were in dock.

---

[a] Not available.

Trans. 12–10–41

FROM: Honolulu   December 6, 1941
TO: Tokyo   # 253.

Re the last part of your # 123[a].

1. On the American continent in October the Army began training barrage balloon troops at Camp Davis, North Carolina. Not only have they ordered four or five hundred ballons, but it is understood that they are considering the use of these balloons in the defense of Hawaii and Panama. Insofar as Hawaii is concerned, though investigations have been made in the neighborhood of Pearl Harbor, they have not set up mooring equipment, nor have they selected the troops to man them. Furthermore, there is no indication that any training for the maintenance of balloons is being undertaken. At the present time there are no signs of barrage balloon equipment. In addition, it is difficult to imagine that they have actually any. However, even though they have actually made preparations, because they must control the air over the water and land runways of the airports in the vicinity of Pearl Harbor, Hickam, Ford and Ewa[b], there are limits to the balloon defense of Pearl Harbor. I imagine that in all probability there is considerable opportunity left to take advantage for a surprise attack against these places.

2. In my opinion, the battleships do not have torpedo nets. The details are not known. I will report the results of my investigation.

---

[a] See IV, 291.
[b] Kana spelling.

Trans. 12-8-41

FROM: Honolulu   December 6, 1941
TO: Tokyo   # 254.

1. On the evening of the 5th, among the battleships which entered port were ----- and one submarine tender. The following ships were observed at anchor on the 6th:

9 battleships, 3 light cruisers, 3 submarine tenders, 17 destroyers, and in addition, there were 4 light cruisers, 2 destroyers lying at docks (the heavy cruisers and airplane carriers have all left).

2. It appears that no air reconnaissance is being conducted by the fleet air arm.

Trans. 12-8-41

(ed)

SI FU 2   (All Naval Stations.)
DE
HA FU 6   (TOKYO Radio)
U TU 2111
- SU U

- -

From: YO WI ØØ   (CinC Combined Fleet.)
Action: WA KA 3   (Combined Fleet)

12/060750/I 1941   (TOI 6 December 1941 B)

Date time of release of this message: 0000, 7th.

Supplement to Combined Fleet SMS # 775.

I, the Emperor, on the occasion of ordering the expedition, leave the matter up to you, as the Commander-in-Chief of the Combined Fleet.

The responsibility of the Combined Fleet is indeed a great one as the entire rise or fall of our nation rests on its success or failure.

You, the Commander in Chief, must prove my trust by summoning all your resources acquired during the many years of training of our fleet towards advancing on the enemy to annihilate it, and to prove to the whole world the greatness of our forces.

Comment: For Combined Fleet SMS # 775, see CZ 000A Z.

SHAPE UP	
AREA	A
COMMENT	
WATCH C	

(JAPANESE)

JN 5   0004 Z   (edgs) Navy Trans 10/24/45

From: Tokyo
To: Lima
23 January 1942

Circular #153.

Regarding Rio (?) to Lima #4*.

The principle functions of the diplomatic organization in war time are political and informational, and that which particularly applies to our diplomatic organization in Latin America is the latter.

The brilliant success of our armed forces at Pearl Harbor was due, mainly, to the military information based on reports sent by our informers on the spot, whose efforts represent untold sacrifices in blood and tears.

Although we could hardly hope to effect a decisive destruction of England and the United States, the success or the failure of our efforts will depend largely on the information which your office will be able to furnish us. In view of this, the maintenance of neutral attitude by the Latin American countries has a special significance. However, bearing in mind the possibility of the breakdown of relations, please take immediate steps to extend the intelligence net set up by our Legation in Peru (in accordance with Tokyo Lima #7*), to include Argentina and Chile.

Please relay Tokyo - Lima #7* to Argentina and to Chile and also this message to Argentina, thence to Chile.

(Secret outside the Department.)

(C.O.R.)

* Not available.

28912

JD-2: 796   (A) Navy Trans. 1-29-42 (2-TT)

PART III
THE INTELLIGENCE REPORTS

The Army and Navy organizations responsible for cracking Japan's codes and ciphers, Signal Intelligence Service and OP-20-G, did not evaluate or distribute the intelligence gleaned from Japanese communications. Once the plain text was broken out by the cryptologic services and the message translated, it was turned over to Military Intelligence Division (MID) and the Office of Naval Intelligence (ONI) which were responsible for assembling intelligence from all sources. Their job was to fuse the intelligence, evaluate it, and distribute it to appropriate recipients. In addition to COMINT, their other intelligence sources consisted, for the most part, of military attaches, informers, telephone taps, undercover agents, and open literature.

In point of fact, almost all the intelligence on West Coast subversive activities by Japanese nationals and U.S. residents of Japanese ancestry was derived from COMINT. Consequently, ONI and MID intelligence reports on this subject were largely filled with information derived from COMINT. Those few high-level people in 1941 who were cleared for MAGIC were often serviced by simply showing them the translated messages. Other intelligence recipients, those not cleared for COMINT, received the same information, but in the form of sanitized reports which attributed the information to a highly reliable but unnamed source.

Reading the intelligence reports and the memos in Part III one cannot help but notice how the same information contained in the MAGIC messages is repeated over and over again by each reporting agency, literally impregnating the data into the thinking and actions of those organizations and individuals who were on distribution for these reports. In this connection, note that the memos and reports in Part III were released by and distributed to officials at the highest levels of government. Two of the documents contain recommendations that they be shown to the President of the United States who was already on direct distribution for the MAGIC messages.

While the Army and Navy intelligence organizations were busily engaged throughout 1941 and early 1942 investigating and evaluating the subversive threat to the U.S. on the West Coast, the FBI played a minor role in these operations. Prior to 1939 the FBI had no mandate to work in this area. It was primarily a highly trained federal police force with a reputation for absolute integrity which was rightfully earned during the gangster-ridden days of the 1920s and 1930s. They were the famed G-men and the nemesis of all racketeers.

Then, in 1939, President Roosevelt, in an effort to shore up the nation's defenses, widened the FBI's mission to include a partnership with the Army and Navy in dealing with espionage, sabotage, and fifth column threats against the U.S. This new responsibility was expanded still further in 1940 when the President decreed that the FBI would play the leading role in combating internal subversion. Thus, the FBI became not only a crime fighting organization, but also, at least to a limited degree, an intelligence agency. The military services, while retaining their foreign intelligence operations, were to phase back to being responsible only for counterintelligence matters affecting the security of their own organizations.

However, wily bureaucrat that he was, J. Edgar Hoover wasn't about to be placed in a position where he would be the key figure for this sensitive undertaking until he had the resources and know-how to cope with the rapidly accelerating problems in this area. He well remembered how the FBI's predecessor, the Bureau of Investigation, with its 219 agents failed miserably to prevent sabotage during World War I. The clever espionage and sabotage nets established by German Ambassador Johann von Bernstorff made fools of the Bureau when his saboteurs were able to bring about such outrages as the infamous "Black Tom" explosion in the New York harbor which destroyed the United States' greatest arsenal. This success was followed by a series of attacks using explosives on a number of defense plants.

Hoover notified his Honolulu office in December 1940 to hold off in assuming supervisory responsibility for all subversive investigations in Hawaii. Following this, he declared in 1941 that the FBI was not yet prepared to assume these duties on the mainland. Consequently, it was agreed that ONI and MID would continue to operate as they had in the past until the FBI was ready to assume the role of senior partner in anti-subversive matters within the U.S. As the war progressed and the FBI gained experience it gradually assumed a leadership role. Hundreds of new agents were acquired. When the war began the FBI had 2602 agents. Two years later it had 5072 and most of the new ones were assigned to counterintelligence work.

During the critical time period of 1941 and early 1942 the Office of Naval Intelligence was far and away the dominant authority on Japanese espionage in Hawaii and on the West Coast, producing a wide range of information and in-depth analysis on what was happening. The Army played an important but lesser role. During the Pearl Harbor hearings Sherman Miles, Chief of Military Intelligence Division, testified that he considered counterintelligence to be one of MID's most important functions. Nonetheless, MID's efforts trailed those of ONI by a considerable margin. The FBI's intelligence reports on the internal threat to the U.S. from Japanese subversive activities consisted almost entirely of what the ONI told them. The combination of being new in the counterintelligence world and not having access to MAGIC operations automatically relegated the FBI to the status of a very junior partner. At this stage its performance was almost entirely concerned with police-type activities, arresting suspected spies, searching for illegal transmitters, and making raids on enemy aliens' homes to confiscate contraband materials.

The reports in Part III reflect the above distribution of effort. ONI's reports were by far the most comprehensive and authoritative produced by the U.S. on the concerns expressed in Executive Order 9066.

The intelligence reports and the memos in Part III are by no means all of the documents on the subject of espionage on the West Coast; but they are the most important ones from the intelligence standpoint. All the reports have been reproduced in their entirety with two exceptions. The thirty-six page FBI report dated June 27, 1941 has been drastically cut back because of its length and because the intelligence in it parallels information already reported by ONI and MID. Additionally, the appendix to the September 26, 1941 FBI report has been eliminated. It consists entirely of suspected Japanese spies along with their addresses and short biographical sketches. On the list are American citizens of Caucasian, Negro, and Japanese ancestry as well as a number of Japanese nationals. No useful purpose would be served by publishing this list. On the other hand, names of suspected Japanese agents have been retained in several ONI reports because they are intertwined with the report itself.

Sections in the reports which have been blotted out contain information which was not declassified. Other marks on some of the documents are declassification stamps, analyst's remarks, distribution, reliability evaluation, and on a few documents federal court admission stamps used during the

Hirabayashi hearing in Seattle where that particular document was allowed as evidence.

All of the reports and memos are copies, some of them copies of copies made before reproduction techniques were as sophisticated as they are today. As a result, readability is not always as clear as one would wish, but, all things considered, the documents are surprisingly legible. As with the MAGIC messages, none of the official intelligence reports in Part III were mentioned by the Commission On Wartime Relocation and Internment of Civilians. It cited only selected parts of the unofficial January 26, 1942 Ringle to Stark memo which was later disavowed by the ONI as representing its position.

All of the documents in Part III are now declassified and available from the originating organization through the Freedom of Information Act.

CHAPTER 15

THE FEDERAL BUREAU OF INVESTIGATION

DOCUMENT SUMMARIES

reference is made to the recruitment of "reliable Japanese in the San Pedro and San Diego areas" and the placement of "second-generation Japanese" (U.S. citizens) in airplane plants and "contact with second-generation Japanese who are now in the United States Army."

Page 217   June 27, 1941—Cover letter from FBI Director, J. Edgar Hoover to Major General Edwin Watson, Secretary to the President, forwarding a memo entitled, "Subversive Activities by Consular and Diplomatic Services of the Japanese Government in the United States," suggesting that the memo may be of interest to the President. Much of the information is referenced to the Office of Naval Intelligence. Only brief excerpts are provided because the 37 page memo is primarily repetition of information in other reports.

Page 221   September 26, 1941—Cover memo from Harry Kimball, FBI, to D. M. Ladd, FBI, transmitting a "brief resume of information known to the Bureau concerning Japanese espionage activity in the United States." The appendix to the report which lists suspected Japanese spies, their addresses and short biographical sketches is omitted. On the list are American citizens of Caucasian, Negro and Japanese ancestry as well as a number of Japanese nationals.

Page 224   December 22, 1941—Memo from Director John Edgar Hoover to senior FBI officers reviewing the situation two weeks after Pearl Harbor. Of particular interest is the second paragraph on page two in which Hoover quotes Pieper, Special Agent in Charge, San Francisco, as saying, "the problem now is citizens." Hoover states that the Attorney General, Francis Biddle, will not prosecute citizens under the sedition laws, that he (Hoover) was not sympathetic to the policy and "felt you had to teach some of those fellows a lesson."

PERSONAL A
CONFIDENTIAL

March 12, 1941 CONFIDENTIAL

DECLASSIFICATION ON 5/1/85
BY 1628KEP/AG
HS DC 83-122

MEMORANDUM FOR MR. HOOVER

HOOVER	DRAYTON	FATTERSON
TOLSON	EGAN	PENNINGTON
CLEGG	GLAVIN	RENNEBERGER
FOXWORTH	HARBO	ROSEN
LADD	HENDON	TAMM, Q.
TAMM, E. A.	HINCE	TRACY
CARSON	LAUGHLIN, R. H.	
COFFEY	NICHOLS	

RE: JAPANESE ESPIONAGE ORGANIZATION
IN THE UNITED STATES.

ALL INFORMATION CONTAINED
HEREIN IS UNCLASSIFIED EXCEPT
WHERE SHOWN OTHERWISE.

Dear Sir:

    Naval authorities have advised that information has
been received from what is described as "highly confidential
and reliable sources" to the effect that the Japanese Nation
has decided to strengthen its intelligence network in the
United States.

    According to naval authorities, Japanese Diplomatic
and Consular representatives have been instructed to reorganize
and strengthen their intelligence networks in this country.

    According to available information, Hidenari Terasaki,
Secretary of the Japanese Embassy, Washington, D. C., will be
the guiding influence in intelligence work and will establish
an intelligence unit which will maintain liaison with private and
semiofficial organizations.

    Available information indicates that the main objective
of all Japanese espionage is to be the determination of the total
strength of the United States. Investigations allegedly will be
divided into political, economic, and military classifications,
and a definite course of action is to be mapped out. Naval
authorities advised "the intelligence net will make a survey of
all persons and organizations which either openly or secretly

FEDERAL BUREAU OF INVESTIGATION
U. S. DEPARTMENT OF JUSTICE

CONFIDENTIAL

- 2 -

CONFIDENTIAL

oppose the United States participation in the present war, and will make a survey of all anti-Jewish, Communistic, Negro, and labor movements.

It is reported that citizens of foreign extraction, Communists, Negroes, labor union members, anti-Semites, and men having access to government departments, experimental laboratories, factories, transportation facilities, and governmental organizations of various characters will be utilized. While second generation Japanese and Japanese resident nationals are also to be employed, the Japanese authorities have allegedly indicated that any Japanese individual who might be caught will be subject to considerable persecution.

Naval authorities report that Japanese representatives in this country have been cautioned to bear in mind that war between Japan and the United States is an eventuality, in which case the Japanese intelligence setup will be moved to Mexico, making that country the nerve center of the intelligence net in the western hemisphere. In further anticipation of such an eventuality, the United States - Mexico international intelligence route will be established. It is stated that the Japanese intelligence net covering Argentina, Brazil, Chile, and Peru will be centered in Mexico. Japanese representatives allegedly have been instructed to cooperate with German and Italian organizations which move has reportedly been approved in Tokyo by representatives of the Axis Alliance.

It has been stated by Naval authorities that Los Angeles, San Francisco, Seattle, New Orleans, Chicago, New York, and Washington will be the espionage centers in the United States, with all instructions emanating from Washington; whereas Mexicali, Sonora, and Vancouver, B. C. will also be centers in proximity to the United States boundary.

Very truly yours,

J. E. Hoover

John Edgar Hoover
Director

May 22, 1941

THP:AB

MEMORANDUM FOR THE ATTORNEY GENERAL

      The Office of Naval Intelligence, Washington, D. C., has advised this Bureau that a considerable amount of general information concerning Japanese Intelligence activities in the United States has been received from a source which is described as "thoroughly reliable and highly confidential."

      With reference to their intelligence activities in Southern California, it is stated that Japanese authorities are making every effort to establish useful contacts and in this connection they are endeavoring to make use of white persons and negroes, as well as Japanese associations, Japanese chambers of commerce and Japanese newspapers. It is stated that they have already established contacts with reliable Japanese in the San Pedro and San Diego areas who will observe closely all shipments of airplanes and other war materials and who will report the amounts and destinations of such shipments. It is indicated that they have also taken steps to have the traffic of war materials across the Mexican border closely watched.

      It is further stated that Japanese authorities plan to establish close relations with appropriate individuals and organizations in order to keep airplane manufacturing plants, as well as military and naval establishments under close surveillance. In this connection, it is stated that a number of second-generation Japanese have been placed in airplane plants for intelligence purposes and it is stated that Japanese authorities maintain contact with the second-generation Japanese who are now in the United States Army, in order that the Japanese authorities may be currently informed of developments in that branch of the service.

      It appears that Japanese authorities are interested in negro movements and anti-Semitic movements in this country. It is stated that they have established contacts with influential negroes for the purpose of being informed with reference to negro movements. They are reported to have employed prominent Americans and Japanese connected with the motion picture industry to investigate anti-Semitic movements, particularly on the West Coast.

Respectfully,

John Edgar Hoover
Director

ENT:KVP   June 27, 1941

Major General Edwin M. Watson
Secretary to the President
The White House
Washington, D. C.

Dear General Watson:

        As of possible interest to the President and you,
I am transmitting herewith a memorandum containing information with respect to sympathies expressed by persons acting
for the Japanese Government.

        It should be borne in mind that the informant is
not in possession of complete details, but in view of the
importance of this matter it is considered advisable to bring
these data to your attention.

                    With assurances of my highest regards,

                                        Sincerely,

                                        J. Edgar Hoover

DECLASSIFICATION CH 5/14/85
BY

Enclosure

Mr. Tolson
Mr. E. A. Tamm
Mr. Clegg
Mr. Foxworth
Mr. Glavin
Mr. Ladd
Mr. Nichols
Mr. Rosen
Mr. Carson
Mr. Quinn Tamm
Mr. Hendon
Mr. Tracy
Miss Gandy

— Note: Only brief excerpts are provided. —

SECRET   Strictly ~~Confidential~~

SECRET

MEMORANDUM

SUBVERSIVE ACTIVITIES BY CONSULAR

AND DIPLOMATIC SERVICES OF THE

JAPANESE GOVERNMENT IN THE

UNITED STATES

June 27, 1941

CLASSIFIED BY
DECLASSIFY ON:
C A 83-122

COPIES DESTROYED
9 08 JUN 22 1961

Mr. Tolson
Mr. E. A. Tamm
Mr. Clegg
Mr. Foxworth
Mr. Glavin
Mr. Ladd
Mr. Nichols
Mr. Rosen
Mr. Carson
Mr. Drayton
Mr. Quinn Tamm
Mr. Nease
Mr. Tracy
Miss Gandy

FEDERAL BUREAU OF INVESTIGATION

7   JUL 2 941

U. S. DEPARTMENT OF JUSTICE

<u>MEMORANDUM</u>

FEDERAL BUREAU OF INVESTIGATION

(

THE FBI

June 27, 1941

<u>JAPANESE DIPLOMATIC AND</u>
<u>CONSULAR SERVICE - GENERAL</u>

SECRET

Information from sources currently available to the Federal Bureau of Investigation, the Office of Naval Intelligence and the Military Intelligence Division, as well as information furnished by the Office of Naval Intelligence which it is stated is based upon years of observation of Japanese intelligence activities, has indicated that such activities are organized and regulated by Japanese diplomatic and consular officials in this country.

All instructions relating to intelligence matters reportedly emanate from Washington, D. C., where ~~the~~ ~~secretary~~ of the Japanese Embassy, is the official charged with the responsibility of directing Japanese information and propaganda organizations. The funds at Terasaki's disposal are sufficient to permit him to contact personally Japanese officials in this country and also in South and Central American countries who are engaged in intelligence work. (Source: ONI, file 100-14925-2.)

Inasmuch as the intelligence problem of the Japanese Government in the United States is largely concerned with naval matters, the Naval Attache of the Japanese Embassy is a person of prime importance in Japanese intelligence matters. While, in general, the Naval Attache refrains from directly gathering information of an intelligence character, it is known that he has a special fund for payment for intelligence information. There are associated with his office a number of officers of the Japanese Navy, known as Language Officers, who engage in espionage activities under his supervision. Detailed information concerning the activities of officers in this category will be set forth elsewhere in this memorandum. (Source: ONI, memorandum attached to memo from E. A. Humphrey to E. A. Tamm, January 3, 1941, not recorded.)

It is known that the facilities of the Japanese Embassy and the various consulates are available to the military and naval attaches for transmission of intelligence information. Messages transmitted to Japan by various Japanese consulates furnishing intelligence information gathered by agents in the United States and in Hawaii have been intercepted by the United States Navy. In addition, the commercial counselors and attaches maintain close liaison with the naval and military attaches, as well as with the Japanese naval inspectors' office and the Japanese Army ordnance inspectors' office in New York City, and furnish the military and naval authorities with commercial information deemed to be of value with intelligence matters. (Source: ONI, file 61-10556-191. ONI, memo attached to memo from E. A. Humphrey to E. A. Tamm, January 3, 1941, not recorded.)

SECRET

MEMORANDUM

SUBVERSIVE ACTIVITIES BY CONSULAR

AND DIPLOMATIC SERVICES OF THE

JAPANESE GOVERNMENT IN THE

UNITED STATES

SECRET

June 27, 1941

FEDERAL BUREAU OF INVESTIGAT

7   JUL 2 941

U.S. DEPARTMENT OF JUSTICE

They are planning to establish close relations with individuals and various organisations in order to keep airplane manufacturing plants and military and naval establishments under close surveillance. They have already established contacts with reliable Japanese in the San Pedro and San Diego areas who will keep a close watch on all shipments of airplanes, and other war materials and report the amounts and destinations of such shipments. They have already taken steps to watch closely the traffic of war materials across the United States-Mexican border.

They are maintaining relations with second generation Japanese who are now in the United States Army so that the Japanese authorities can be kept informed of the various developments in that branch of the service.

The influence of the Japanese Consul in Portland is said to reach into every Japanese organisation in Oregon. This includes youth groups, sport clubs, language schools, nationalistic organisations, and various Japanese societies. These groups have been used in the past for the dissemination of Japanese propaganda and for obtaining intelligence information. It is indicated that the Consul's advice and direction is often resented by older Japanese who dominate the aforementioned organisations inasmuch as they feel they have a better grip on local affairs than the Consul. It is believed, however, that although this fact may preclude actual control by the Consul over the operations of these organisations, the policy of these groups is definitely influenced by the consular representatives. (Source:

HMK:ECR   September 26, 1941

                    MR. D. M. LADD

        There is attached hereto a brief resume of infor-
mation known to the Bureau concerning Japanese espionage
activity in the United States including a general summari-
zation regarding the more important individuals connected
therewith, as well as contemplated investigation concerning
each.

        It is to be noted that most of the suggestions
for investigative activity mentioned in the attached memorandum have already been referred to the field for attention.
The additional suggestions promulgated as a result of this
review are being furnished to the field at once for prompt
action.

                        Respectfully,

                        Harry M. Kimball

Attachment

JAPANESE ESPIONAGE

Available information indicates that Japanese espionage activities in the United States are participated in, controlled and directed by representatives of the Japanese Embassy and Consulates. It is known that the facilities of these offices are available for the transmission to Tokyo of information of an intelligence character. Further, it has been alleged that the Consulates have a secret fund in cash for the purchase of intelligence data.

It is also asserted that instructions have been issued to the various Consulates to employ Japanese Military and Naval Officers under the guise of ordinary civilian clerks in order that their activities would not be limited by reason of their official connections. In addition, the offices of the Naval and Military Attaches have been staffed with extra personnel and there is a rather constant flow of visiting Japanese Naval and Military Officers into this country, giving rise to the belief that these men are being used as couriers by their Government. Because the intelligence problem of the Japanese Government in the United States is essentially concerned for the most part with Naval matters, the office of the Naval Attache is particularly active in the espionage field, and it is known that this office has a special fund for the payment of intelligence information.

Investigation has disclosed that a number of language officers have been associated with the Office of the Naval Attache. These men are representatives of the Japanese Navy ostensibly in the United States for the purpose of studying the English language. Some of them have been definitely known to engage in espionage activities, chiefly in regard to the movements of the United States fleets and occurrences at the various shipyards.

In addition to the Japanese Consulate and Diplomatic Officers, Japanese banks, business organizations, clubs and newspaper representatives are considered to be a part of the Japanese espionage service. Investigations have indicated that activities in this field are centered in Washington, D. C., Los Angeles, San Francisco, Seattle, Honolulu and New York City. They show that the focal point of Japanese interests apparently is the determination of the total strength of the United States. Their inquiries towards this end have disclosed particular interest in information of a political, economic and military character.   RESTRICTED

Our investigations have also revealed that the Japanese Government is anxious to secure reports regarding the movements of all ships, especially movements of fleet units, progress of the manufacture of war equipment and any other matters pertaining to the Army and Navy. Furthermore the sailings of merchant ships, mobilization of reserve officers and men, the launching of Class "B" cruisers since January, 1941, data regarding preparations for fleet maneuvers, the progress of shipbuilding in Navy and civilian plants, number of men-of-war in the various oceans except the vicinity of Honolulu and the Far East, and the method of training youths for Navy aviation and large size Army planes, particularly training in bad weather conditions on sea and over land, are items in which the Japanese agents have manifested a definite interest in the past.

It has been reported that the Japanese will make a survey of all persons and organizations which openly or secretly oppose the United States' participation in the present war, possibly for the intention of approaching such parties for information of an intelligence nature. Further, it has been averred that the Japanese contemplate using citizens of foreign extraction, communists, negro labor union members, anti-Semites and men having access to Government Departments, experimental laboratories, factories, transportation facilities and Governmental organizations of various characters, in their activities in this field.

In this connection, as recent as September 8, 1941, MID has advised that a report from a reliable source indicates that a large number of manufacturing firms in and around Chicago have been contacted by Japanese agents for the purpose of obtaining information and the latest improvement methods of manufacturing and other pertinent data dealing with general production methods. Also, the Japanese business men in Chicago are generally engaged in attempting to secure the services of Americans familiar with the latest manufacturing processes.

The services of second generation Japanese (known as Nesei Japanese) and Japanese resident nationals are to be enlisted in this field, but utilization of such persons is to be handled most cautiously because of the belief that any such individual who might be caught would be subject to considerable persecution.

The possibility of war between Japan and the United States has been given consideration and it has been decided that in such an eventuality the Japanese Intelligence network would be moved to Mexico, which would make that country the nerve center of their intelligence unit in the western hemisphere. Closer cooperation between Germany and Italy, through Tokyo, is also being given attention.

There are attached hereto a brief resume of what are believed to be the outstanding suspected Japanese espionage agents presently operating in the United States.

— Note: List of suspects omitted. —

COPY/aw

JEH:JRB   December 22, 1941

3:56 PM

MEMORANDUM FOR MR. TOLSON
                     MR. GLAVIN
                     MR. LADD

          At this time I called SAC Pieper in San Francisco
relative to a conversation I had just had with the Attorney
General. I told him that the Attorney General advised me that
General DeWitt, commanding the Army Ninth Corp Area, had communicated with the War Department relative to using local police
to keep certain groups of aliens under surveillance. I told
Pieper that the Attorney General had been pretty vague about
the details of this matter, so that the material I would give
him might not check completely when he checked into the matter.

          I told Mr. Pieper that the substance of the comm-
unication was that General DeWitt wants to use the police at
the direction of the Army to keep certain groups of aliens
under surveillance. I told Mr. Pieper that the Attorney General
had been in consultation with a Mr. Bundy, a civilian assistant
to the Secretary of War and it had been agreed here at Washington
that if the Army wants anything dealing with police or the civilian character, that should be taken up with the FBI; that the
police and all civilian agencies are mobilized under us and that
therefore if there is any surveillance of aliens that the Army
thinks should be done, the matter should be taken up with the
appropriate SAC of the FBI who could then evaluate it and decide
exactly what he thinks should be done and if it is then decided
that we should use police on the surveillance the orders and
instructions will be given by the FBI to the police. I told Mr.
Pieper that a man who the Attorney General believed was General
Langley, an assistant to General DeWitt was behind this and that
I wanted him, Pieper, to find out who and where this General
Langley was, that of course if he were at Los Angeles, I would
call Mr. Hood on this matter.

          I instructed Mr. Pieper to take this matter up in a
tactful manner with General Langley, or if need be, General DeWitt,
and explain that these police and civilian agencies were looking
to the FBI for necessary direction and orders, that we are in
direct touch with them and have them well lined up, and therefore
any projects that the Army may have that it could be simplified
by taking it up directly with him, Pieper, who is authorized to
handle these matters. I also warned Pieper not to be stampeded
into agreeing to anything, to keep his feet on the ground. I
told him confidentially that the feeling here was that DeWitt
might be a bit excited about things that he ought not be; that the
idea about arresting Harry Bridges was probably not a bad idea,

-2-

but it was something that should not be done just yet. I told
Pieper that it would be well if he could get over that until such
time as martial law might be declared, it would simplify things
if at such times as the Army wants things done by the local authorities, to have them take it up with him or any other SAC on the
West Coast. I also told Mr. Pieper to suggest that if General
DeWitt wanted anything through any of our other Coast offices, all
he would have to do would be to have his aide contact Pieper who
would see that the matter is handled in the other districts. Such
a procedure would eliminate having Generals up and down the Coast
running in and out.

I remarked to Mr. Pieper that it did not seem necessary
to me to grab a lot of aliens at the present time, that we have
the so-called 'bad' aliens locked up. Mr. Pieper then remarked
that the problem now was citizens. I told him that was an entirely
different problem and that the Attorney General would not authorize
anything to be done against citizens; that he didn't believe in
any prosecution under the Sedition Laws. I told him that they
had a good case built up in Los Angeles and it had been dismissed
by the Attorney General. Pieper said that he believed there would
be some newspaper comment on that. I told him that I did not
sympathize with that policy at all as I felt that you had to teach
some of those fellows a lesson; that on the other hand in regard
to the Army wanting local authorities to do this, that and the
other thing, it might be necessary and if so should be cleared
with him. I told Mr. Pieper to keep in very close touch with
either Mr. Tamm or myself so that we could get clearance on policy
as there are a lot of things that he, Tamm and I might want to do
but would be prevented from doing so by higher ups here.

I instructed Mr. Pieper to have very cordial relations with
General DeWitt on this matter. Mr. Pieper stated that he had
always got along very well with the General, that the General in
his conversation yesterday stated that he realized Pieper could not
make any recommendations but had just wanted to talk with him. He
said that while talking with the General he had tried not to be
critical of anyone but tried to just state positions. I told him
certain policies whether we believed in them or not. Mr. Pieper
stated that he felt that was what the General's view was. He stated
that the General felt he might be able to get some action out there
where we couldn't. I remarked that maybe he could because in due
time there might be things happening that would require action. Mr.
Pieper stated that DeWitt felt very keenly about the Bridges matter
and had stated that it would create quite a stir in Washington, but
he felt we weren't getting the action we desired and that he was
going to see what he could do. I remarked that DeWitt was the
Commanding General of that Area and was free to do as he wished.

Pieper stated that he would keep in very close touch with
General DeWitt and would call me as soon as he got the latest
developments.

Very truly yours,

John Edgar Hoover
Director

January 16, 1942

62-40185-322

Honorable James Lawrence Fly
Chairman
Federal Communications Commission
Washington, D. C.

Dear Mr. Fly:

In regard to present conditions in the Hawaiian Islands, it is apparent that illicit short-wave radio transmissions are being sent from clandestine stations operating in the islands themselves, in communication with mobile units of the Japanese Navy, through which intelligence information is being reported to the enemy. It is extremely important that these clandestine stations be located and eliminated from operation and that the individuals concerned with their operation be dealt with appropriately as rapidly as possible. It is also highly important that bearings be obtained on radio transmissions from Japanese naval craft which may be operating in the vicinity of the Hawaiian Islands in order that their location and direction of travel may be determined and appropriate action taken by our armed forces.

The question of monitoring the transmissions of the illicit radio stations in the Hawaiian Islands and vicinity was discussed with Rear Admiral Wilkinson, Director of the Office of Naval Intelligence, and Colonel Bissell of the Military Intelligence Division on January 14, 1942, and it was agreed that the problem presented is most serious and is one which should be given early attention. We were all of the same opinion, that radio monitoring activities in Honolulu, Hawaii, and throughout the islands are the primary responsibility of the Federal Communications Commission. On the occasion of this conference Rear Admiral Wilkinson and Colonel Bissell expressed the desire that I call your attention to the situation by letter and impress upon you the vital importance and necessity for establishing immediately an exhaustive coverage on these radio activities.

In order that this situation in the Hawaiian Islands may be clarified with the least possible delay, it is urged that monitoring activities on the part of the Federal Communications Commission in the islands be intensified to the highest possible degree and that information developed and problems arising in connection with these activities be promptly worked out in collaboration with the military and naval authorities and with the office of the Federal Bureau of Investigation at Honolulu.

Sincerely yours,

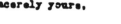

John Edgar Hoover
Director

JCH:ESK

February 9, 1942

ALL INFORMATION CONTAINED
HEREIN IS UNCLASSIFIED
DATE 5/14/85 BY 1678RRP/AV

RECORDED 62-65880-25X1

MEMORANDUM FOR THE ATTORNEY GENERAL

Re: ENEMY ALIEN PROGRAM IN THE
WESTERN DEFENSE COMMAND

With reference to the above-entitled program, I wish to
advise you of the results of a series of searches and apprehensions
made by the Portland, Seattle, and Los Angeles Field Divisions on
the afternoon and evening of February 7, 1942.

The Portland Field Division searched eighty-one premises
and interviewed the one hundred fifty-one aliens who were found to
be occupying these premises. Four arrests were made in connection
with the seizing of twenty-one sticks of dynamite, sixty-two dynamite
caps, and one hundred forty feet of fuse. These searches were conducted at Hood River, Oregon, in the vicinity of Bonneville Dam.
The vicinity in which these searches were conducted is considered
to be the most vital military area in the Portland Field Division.

The Seattle Field Division conducted searches of the premises
and residences occupied by twenty-eight German and Japanese aliens
who reside on Vashon Island, near Bainbridge Island, on which a
Naval radio station is located. Two Japanese aliens and one German
alien were found to be in possession of prohibited articles and are
being held for custodial detention. During these searches one revolver, two cameras, one shortwave radio set, approximately twenty
feet of fuse, approximately one hundred dynamite blasting caps, and
one-half box of dynamite were found.

On the same date the Los Angeles Field Division conducted
searches of forty-six homes which were occupied by enemy aliens and
as a result of interviews with the occupants and the location of
prohibited articles, seventeen enemy aliens were apprehended. In
connection with these arrests, the following material was seized:
seven radio sets capable of receiving shortwave, one radio oscillator,
four boxes of assorted radio equipment, two cameras, twenty-three
flashlights, four large searchlights, three telegraphers' keys,

-2-

one small radio transmitting set, one microphone, one .38
caliber revolver, fifty cartridges, one .22 caliber rifle,
four blasting caps, three pounds of black powder, three
feet of fuse, and two reels of 8 millimeter film containing
photographs of battleships and fortifications. Further
investigation is being conducted regarding the aforementioned
film. The searches by the Los Angeles Field Division were
conducted in the Palos Verdes Hills area which adjoins Fort
MacArthur.

Respectfully,

J. Edgar Hoover

John Edgar Hoover
Director

CHAPTER 16

THE ARMY MILITARY INTELLIGENCE DIVISION

DOCUMENT SUMMARIES

Page 231   February 12, 1941—Memo from Chief, Intelligence Branch to
            Chief, Counter Intelligence Branch outlining Japanese plan for
            intelligence operations in the United States. Information
            attributed to "a highly reliable source," clearly MAGIC. Under
            normal circumstances the information in the memo would
            have gone from the Counter Intelligence Branch, which is
            charged with gathering this sort of information, to the
            Intelligence Branch which had a much wider interest.

Page 233   May 21, 1941—Memo from Chief, Intelligence Branch to Chief,
            Counter Intelligence Branch outlining specifics of Japanese
            intelligence plan.

Page 234   June 9, 1941—Memo from Chief, Intelligence Branch to Chief,
            Counter Intelligence Branch giving specific information on
            individuals involved in collecting information for the Japanese.

Page 236   January 3, 1942—Military Intelligence Report, "Japanese
             Activities and Intelligence Machine in the Western
             Hemisphere." Discusses operations in Latin America and Peru
             in particular.

Page 239   February 12, 1942—Cover memo from Brigadier General Mark
             Clark to Assistant Secretary of War, John J. McCloy, "Enemy
             Aliens on the West Coast," transmitting "Information Bulletin
             No. 6, Japanese Espionage" dated January 21, 1942. This was
             the final information given to the Secretary of War before the
             signing of Executive Order 9066. Page 3, paragraph 6b
             concludes "Their espionage net containing Japanese aliens, first
             and second generation Japanese and other nationals is now
             thoroughly organized and working underground."

Page 243   January 25, 1942—Letter from Secretary of War Stimson to
             Attorney General Biddle urging the Attorney General to
             prescribe restricted areas in California as requested by the
             Commander, Western Defense Command.

Page 244   February 28, 1942—G-2 Periodic Report, Western Defense
             Command and Fourth Army. Note wording in paragraph 3f
             regarding sources of information used by the Japanese.

DECLASSIFIED -277-
AND 746052
By ___ NARS. Date 5/1/65

CONFID

WAR DEPARTMENT
WAR DEPARTMENT GENERAL STAFF
MILITARY INTELLIGENCE DIVISION G-2
WASHINGTON

G-2
RSB

WAR DEP

February 12, 1941

MEMORANDUM FOR THE CHIEF, COUNTER INTELLIGENCE BRANCH:

Subject: Reorganization of Japanese Intelligence
Service in the United States.

1.   This Branch has information from a highly reliable source
to the effect that the Japanese intelligence service in the United
States is being reorganized and enlarged and is cooperating with
German and Italian services.

2.   The salient points of the directive sent to the Embassy
in Washington are as follows:

"1. Establish an intelligence organ in the
Embassy which will maintain liaison with private and
semi-official intelligence organs.

"2. The objective of investigations is to determine the total strength of the United States. Investigations will cover the political, economic and
military fields.

"3. Surveys to be prepared of all persons or
organizations which either openly or secretly oppose
participation in the war.

"4. Investigation to be made of all anti-
Semitism, communism, Negro movements, and labor movements.

"5. Utilization to be made of citizens of
foreign extraction (other than Japanese), aliens (other
than Japanese), communists, Negroes, labor union
members, and anti-Semites, in carrying out investigations, to get best results. These agents should have
access to governmental establishments, laboratories,
governmental organizations of various sorts, factories,
transportation facilities, etc.

CONFIDENTIAL

CONFIDENTIAL

"6. Utilization of second generation Japanese to be made with utmost caution as a slip in this phase would subject Japanese in America to considerable persecution.

"7. Plans to be made to move the Japanese intelligence net to Mexico in the event the United States enters the war.

"8. The net covering Brazil, Argentina, Chile. and Peru to be centered in Mexico.

"9. Close cooperation to be had with German and Italian intelligence organs in the United States."

C. H. MASON,
Colonel of Infantry, G.S.C.,
Chief, Intelligence Branch.

fk

CONFIDENTIAL

R DEPARTMENT
ARTMENT GENERAL STAFF
Y INTELLIGENCE DIVISION G-2
WASHINGTON

May 21, 1941

MEMORANDUM FOR CHIEF, COUNTER INTELLIGENCE BRANCH:

Subject: Espionage Activities of
Japanese Consul in Los
Angeles.

1. This Branch has information from a highly reliable
source to the effect that the Japanese Consulate in Los Angeles
is the Japanese espionage headquarters for that region. Their
plans include the following:

a. Use of white agents and Negroes through trusted
Japanese residents.

b. Close contact with the Japanese Association,
Chamber of Commerce and the press.

c. Close surveillance of airplane factories and
other plants producing military equipment.

d. Intelligence on shipments of aircraft.

e. Close contact with second generation Japanese at
present in the U.S. army or working in aircraft factories.

f. Close cooperation with the office of the Japanese
Naval Attache.

g. Gathering intelligence on military movements,
labor disputes and communist activities.

h. Connection with influential Negroes to secure
data on the "Negro movement."

C. H. MASON,
Colonel of Infantry, G.S.C.,
Chief, Intelligence Branch.

CONFIDENTIAL

A-23a

D

CONFIDENTIAL

June 9, 1941

MEMORANDUM FOR THE CHIEF, COUNTER INTELLIGENCE BRANCH:

Subject: Japanese Espionage.

This branch has information from a highly reliable source to the effect that the Japanese intelligence and espionage unit centering in the Seattle Consulate has made the following "contacts":

.a.   Political.

John Sylvester, Speaker of the State Lower House.
Ralph Horr, Chairman local committee, Republican Party,
Daniel Trefethen, local Republican Party official.

From these men the Japanese collect information on political questions and on the degree of America's participation in the war.

b.   Economic.

Employees in American and Japanese companies.

These men furnish information as to our war effort, construction of ships, number of planes produced, copper, zinc and aluminum production, the yield of tin for cans, lumber, etc. One such person (name unknown) recently gave the Japanese a report on machinists of German origin who are communists and members of the labor organizations in the Bremerton Naval Yard and the Boeing Aircraft Factory.

c.   Military.

One Kaneko is in charge of men sent out into the field to get information concerning movement of naval craft, mercantile shipping, airplane manufacture, troop movements

1628 REP/AE   5/14/85

and maneuvers. ~~These~~ ~~men~~ contact a ~~Major~~ *Lt Comdr* Okada (not listed in The Diplomatic List) who ~~wires his reports to Tokyo.~~

~~Second generation Japanese selectees report on the military service, morale, discipline, etc.~~

d. <u>Labor Unions</u>.

One <u>Okamura</u>, a first-generation Japanese and a member of the C.I.O. reports on labor disorders, etc.

A second-generation Japanese lawyer named <u>Ito</u> collects information on anti-war-participation organizations.

C. H. MASON,
Colonel of Infantry, G.S.C.,
Chief, Intelligence Branch.

~~CONFIDENTIAL~~

DECLASSIFIED
F... ..... Sec. ?3
255004
FPLJY) ... Dec. 2/27/65

<u>January 3, 1942.</u>
(Date)

Subject: Japanese Activities and Intelligence Machine in the
Western Hemisphere.

Summary of Information:

     a. <u>Recent Japanese Activities in Latin America</u>. Recent
reports have been received of suspicious movements of Japanese in
various parts of Latin America, particularly Mexico. Approximately
5,000 Japanese are congregating at some undetermined point in strategic Baja California. In this connection, 100 of a Japanese population of 600 in and around Ensenada, recently left the region in
a ship anchored off the coast.

     The Japanese practice of cloaking subversive operations
with "legitimate business fronts" exists in Mexico as well as in
the United States. The Japanese have placed Colonel Tadafumi Waki,
I.J.A., in an important position within their Intelligence Network
in Mexico. Reports believed reliable indicate that Colonel Waki
has in his possession maps of strategic areas in the Hawaiian Islands.

     In Peru it is reported that the 30,000 or more Japanese
living there are highly organized and that, following anti-Japanese
riots, they distributed rifles to all their establishments. In the
United States there is a possible infiltration of Japanese espionage
agents through Cuban and Florida ports. A similar danger exists on
the Pacific Coast and Mexican border.

     Since the outbreak of hostilities, Spanish Consuls in the
United States have taken over all official business for the Japanese
Consulates. Japanese and Spanish Fascist collaboration is carried
on extensively in Mexico and the Philippines through the following
organizations: Las Misiones Jesuite del Japon, Sociedad Nipo-
Espanola, Falange Exterior Espanola, and Liga Anti-Comintern Espanola.

     b. <u>Japanese Intelligence Machine in Western Hemisphere</u>. In
December, 1940, it became apparent that the Japanese were going to
effect a reorganization of their Intelligence Network in this hemisphe.

Previous Distribution: Evaluation
FBI   State Dept.   —of source——————of informa
MID   Sp.Def.Unit D.J.   ~~——— A ———~~
                                            ~~——— B ———~~ Credible
Distribution: ———— C ———— Questionable
1st C.A.   2nd C.A.   ———————— Undetermined
3rd C.A.   4th C.A.
5th C.A.   6th C.A.
7th C.A.   8th C.A.   ~~CONFIDENTIAL~~

10—17897-1

CONFIDENTIAL.

by intensifying the espionage activities of non-political agencies here.

In streamlining their Intelligence Machine the Japanese have been guided by two major considerations--that of a system of "total intelligence" such as the Germans have developed; and establishment of a completely integrated intelligence organisation which in time of war and the breaking off of official relations would be able to take over intelligence operations on a major scale.

The focal point of the Japanese espionage effort has been the determination of the total strength of the United States. In anticipation of possible open conflict with this country, Japan vigorously utilised every available agency to secure military, naval, and commercial information, paying particular attention to West Coast, Panama Canal, and Hawaii. Surveys were made of persons and organisations opposing United States' intervention in the European War, and close attention was paid to all anti-Jewish, Communist, Negro, and Labor Movements.

Although never fully developed, this new espionage organisation was characterised by a high degree of decentralization. The general pattern included individuals, small groups, and commercial organisations functioning separately yet directly controlled by Imperial Japanese Government through Embassy and Consulate.

The new program provided for the utilisation of citizens of foreign extraction, aliens, Communists, Negroes, Labor union members, anti-Semites, and individuals having access to Government Departments, experimental laboratories, factories, transportation facilities and governmental organisations of various kinds. Nisei and Japanese aliens were not overlooked.

In event of open hostilities, Mexico was to be the Japanese intelligence nerve center in the Western Hemisphere, and in anticipation of war, U.S.-Latin American intelligence routes were established, involving extensive cooperation among Japanese, German and Italian intelligence organisations.

In this connection there should be kept in mind the proximity of San Diego to Tiajuana and of El Centro to Mexicali, along with Yuma, Nogales, El Paso, Laredo, and Brownsville, are well known Japanese "post offices" and espionage centers.

Outstanding among the Japanese espionage projects was their comprehensive surveys of the entire western coast of North America.

Japanese Propaganda in the United States has for the most.

~~CONFIDENTIAL~~

part been under direction of a special division of the Japanese Foreign Office in Tokyo. Local control was administered through the Embassy in Washington, as well as the Consulates in key cities and Consular Agents in Japanese communities.

    2. The Tokyo Club Syndicate. This is an excellent illustration of the extremely complicated interlockings which characterize Japanese groups.

    Until recently the Tokyo Club of Los Angeles, with chief subsidiaries, the Nishibei Kogyo Kaisha of Los Angeles and the Tokyo Club of Seattle, constituted the nucleus of a system of gambling clubs from Alaska to Mexico. A widespread decentralized system of Japanese "clubs," labor organizations, and legitimate business groups has been converted into an important unit of the central Japanese Intelligence Network. There can be no doubt that most of the leaders have been and still continue to function as key operatives for the Japanese Government along the West Coast.

    It is reported that the Tokyo Club is no longer in existence but it may be that the former leaders have retired behind new "fronts."

    3. Japanese Canneries, Alaska and West Coast. Whether floating or shore-based, American- or foreign-owned, the Alaskan canneries employ a considerable amount of Japanese capital and labor. American leaders in the fishing-canning industry stress the fact that the Japanese involved are scattered in definitely strategic places throughout Alaska, and that there exists the possibility that some of these Japanese may have military or naval connections.

mh

~~CONFIDENTIAL~~

GENERAL HEADQUARTERS, U. S. ARMY

ARMY WAR COLLEGE

WASHINGTON, D. C.

REPLY REFER TO:
1 DC of 8

February 12, 1942

MEMORANDUM FOR MR J J McCLOY, ASS'T SECRETARY OF WAR,
      ROOM 2046 MUNITIONS BLDG, WASHINGTON, DC.

    Subject: <u>Enemy Aliens on the West Coast.</u>

        Confirming our telephone conversation this date on the
above subject, there is attached hereto an information bulletin
published by this headquarters on the subject of Japanese
Espionage.

        Some of the information contained therein may be of
assistance to you in settling this question.

        I am sure that the G-2 of the Western Defense Command
has all this information for practically all of it was obtained
from War Department G-2 sources and from the Office of Naval
Intelligence.

                  MARK J. CLARK,
            Brigadier General, G. S. C.,
              Deputy Chief of Staff

MTC-KM
Inclosure:
    Info Bul No. 6,
    G-2 GHQ, 1-21-42.

DECLASSIFIED
DOD Dir. 5200.9, Sept. 27, 1958
by   date 3-18-71

ALIENS

~~CONFIDENTIAL~~

INFORMATION BULLETIN)
                      :
NUMBER...........6)

G-2 SECTION
GENERAL HEADQUARTERS, U.S. ARMY,
Army War College,
Washington, D. C.,
January 21, 1942.

JAPANESE ESPIONAGE

1. Underline{General}. - The alien Japanese organize for every conceivable purpose,
a characteristic brought from Japan. Japanese societies existed in the Hawaiian Islands from the earliest migration. Every alien Japanese in Hawaii belongs
to one or more organizations. These organizations exist in the United States,
and are inimical to our best interests.

Japanese organization flows in specific and distinct channels, interlocked through the duplication of activity and the plurality of positions held
by individual Japanese. Each of these channels is at least strongly influenced,
if not directly controlled, by groups of similar type and purpose in Japan and
under Japanese governmental supervision.

2. Diplomatic and Consular Organization. - a. Japanese espionage activities in the United States were participated in, directed and controlled by representatives of the Imperial Japanese Government through the officials of its
Embassy and Consulates. The Secretary of the Embassy was charged with the responsibility of coordinating and directing Japanese Intelligence activities in
this country. He was instructed to visit Japanese officials in North, South
and Central American countries. During July, 1941, he traveled over 20,000
miles in Mexico, Central America, Peru, Ecuador and other South American countries. Further, his travels in the United States substantiated his position as
the director of Japanese espionage in this country. The facilities of the Embassy and the Consulates were available to the Military and Naval Attaches for
transmission of intelligence, and the Consulates maintained secret funds in
cash for the purchase of information.

b. Naval Attache. - The Naval Attache, attached to the Japanese
Embassy was particularly active. He was generally a Naval captain, with pre-
vious experience in the United States or England in the capacity of Assistant
Attache or language officer, and was an experienced Intelligence officer.
Working with the Attache were several assistants, one of whom was generally a
Naval aviator with Intelligence experience. In addition, several experienced
Navy men were employed as clerks. There were always a number of Naval officers
in the United States on temporary visitors visas. The Office of Naval Intelligence pointed out that over one hundred Naval officers visited the United State
last year.

c. Naval Inspector. - A counterpart of the Naval Attache's office
was the Naval Inspector's Office at New York City, with a branch in Los Angeles
California. Aircraft parts, radio, electrical equipment, tools and accessories
were purchased almost daily, apparently for examination. Japanese Naval officers connected with the Naval Inspector's Office cooperated with German agents
by accepting confidential data for transmission to Germany via Japan.

- 1 -

~~CONFIDENTIAL~~

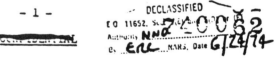

d. **Military Attache**. - The office of the Military Attache in Washington, D.C., was also active. During the early part of 1941, the Chief of the American Section of the Japanese Army made an extensive tour of the United States to ascertain the attitude of the people toward present conditions and to gather maps. During his brief visit to Cuba, he conferred with various Japanese colonists there.

e. **Ordnance Inspector**. - A complement of the Military Attache's Office, the Japanese Ordnance Inspector's Office, was maintained in New York for some time, and was similar to the Naval Inspector's Office.

3. **Religious Organizations**. - The Buddhist and Shinto sects acted as Japanese propaganda agencies with the Japanese communities, holding services in Japanese. The Priests, held in deep respect, are in an excellent position to disseminate propaganda. Many of the Buddhist and Shinto priests entered the Hawaiian Islands as non-quota aliens and resided there only a short time.

4. **Educational Organization**. - Japanese espionage recognized the strategic position of the Japanese Language Schools in molding the beliefs and ideals of Japanese students and the effect on their behavior and loyalty to the United States.

5. **Commercial and Civic Organizations**. - a. **Commercial**. - The value of representatives of Japanese business organizations, banks, and newspapers has not been overlooked. In Japan, several of the large business firms must be considered semi-official in nature.

b. **Civic**. - The Overseas Japanese Central Society is a liaison agency for all Japanese residing in countries foreign to Japan. It is connected with all Japanese organizations in the United States, such as:

(1) **Japanese Association of America**. - National headquarters at 1619 Laguna St., San Francisco, Calif. Estimated membership of 100,000, with 10,000 active members. The purpose of this organization is to protect the rights of alien Japanese residents residing in America and to assist them in coping with social and economic problems.

(2) **Japanese American Citizens League**. - This organization of approximately 10,000 members is composed of persons of Japanese descent born in America. Headquarters are located at 1623 Webster St., San Francisco, Calif. In recent months, the league conducted a vigorous campaign to abolish dual citizenship and prove that the members are loyal to this country.

(3) **Sokoku Kai (Ancestral Country Society) Seattle, Wash**. - Sokoku Kai is reported to have connection with the Silver Shirts in that state. It published a magazine devoting itself to building up pride in the superiority of the Japanese race.

(4) **Japanese Association of Utah**. - This is comprised of native born Japanese with the purpose of building closer relations between Americans and Japanese. One function is to register births with the Japanese Consul at San Francisco to insure dual citizenship.

CONFIDENTIAL

        (5)   Intermountain Japanese Association. — This organization is a farmers cooperative concern, located at Ogden, Utah. It registers births with the Japanese Consul to insure dual citizenship and arranges passports and re-entry permits for its members. In August, 1941, it completed a survey of Japanese property holdings and a census of Japanese for the Consul. It received literature propagandizing Japanese justification in the Far East and directed the activities of the Japanese language schools in Utah.

        6.   Conclusions. — a.   It may be expected that Japanese diplomatic and consular communications will be replaced now by using the diplomatic and consular organization of an allegedly neutral power identified with the Axis. They may also use officials of other neutral countries whom they have subverted.

        b.   Their espionage net containing Japanese aliens, first and second generation Japanese and other nationals is now thoroughly organized and working underground.

        c.   In addition to their communications net through neutral diplomats, they may be expected to have their own underground communication net.

        d.   Extensive use of Occidentals, such as Axis nationals, neutral nationals, and subverted Americans, is to be expected.

P. M. ROBINETT,
Lieut. Colonel, G.S.C.,
Ass't Chief of Staff, G-2.

Not to be disseminated
lower than division.

CONFIDENTIAL

SECRET

WAR DEPARTMENT

WASHINGTON

January 25, 1942.

CAUSE C83-122V

~~DEFENDANT~~ *Respondent*

EXHIBIT
NO. A-2

ADMITTED _____

The Honorable,

    The Attorney General.

Dear Mr. Attorney General:

    There are transmitted herewith a letter dated January 21, 1942, from Lieutenant General J. L. DeWitt, Commanding General, Western Defense Command and Fourth Army, Presidio of San Francisco, California, and two inclosures thereto. Those inclosures are a description of areas proposed to be restricted under the provision of paragraph nine of the President's proclamation of December 7, 1941, and incorporated by reference into the proclamation of December 8, 1941, and a book of maps which outline graphically these areas.

    In recent conferences with General DeWitt, he has expressed great apprehension because of the presence on the Pacific coast of many thousand alien enemies. As late as yesterday, January 24, he stated over the telephone that shore to ship and ship to shore radio communications, undoubtedly coordinated by intelligent enemy control were continually operating. A few days ago it was reported by military observers on the Pacific coast that not a single ship had sailed from our Pacific ports without being subsequently attacked. General DeWitt's apprehensions have been confirmed by recent visits of military observers from the War Department to the Pacific coast.

    The alarming and dangerous situation just described, in my opinion, calls for immediate and stringent action.

    I urge that, under the provisions of paragraph nine of each of the President's proclamations hereinbefore referred to, you prescribe the restricted areas in the state of California as recommended by General DeWitt.

    This recommendation is limited at this time to the state of California only because General DeWitt has not yet had time to make recommendations with reference to other Pacific states within his jurisdiction. As California is the principal danger spot, the prescription of restricted areas within that state ought not be delayed pending receipt of further recommendations with reference to the other states. Those recommendations will follow.

                         Sincerely yours,

                         Henry L. Stimson

3 Inclosures
  Incl. 1-Ltr. to Atty.Gen. fr.
      Gen. DeWitt 1-21-42.
  Incl. 2-Descr. of proposed restr. areas.
  Incl. 3-Book of Maps

                    Secretary of War.

SECRET

G-2 PERIODIC REPORT

From: 12:00 Noon 21 February 1942 GMT
To : 12:00 Noon 28 February 1942 GMT

Headquarters Western Defense Command and Fourth Army
Presidio of San Francisco, California
12:00 Noon 28 February 1942 GMT

No. 9

Maps: See sketch.

1. ENEMY SITUATION AT END OF PERIOD.

a. Troops of the Western Defense Command and Fourth Army are not in contact
with hostile ground forces. The following operations were reported occurring
offshore:

(1) A hostile submarine was reported about 17 miles southeast of
CHERNOFSKI, UNALASKA 20 February (not reported in G-2 Periodic Report
No. 8) but result of subsequent search was negative. At least eight
radio fixes have been established in the area 200 to 600 miles off
VANCOUVER ISLAND since 14 February, the last three being registered at
the closer distance. This may be further indication of presence of a
hostile standing patrol which is observing our northwest Pacific water
lanes. Other fixes were established as shown on attached sketch.

(2) A hostile submarine stood off the shore near ELLWOOD, CALIFORNIA
about 7:00 PM 23 February and fired 25 rounds at oil installations of
that area. Only minor damage was caused to an oil derrick and no
casualties were reported. Five or 20% of the total rounds fired were
duds. From the duds obtained, the following data was determined. The
diameter of the projectile is 5.5" and is 21" long with fuse unattached.
The fuse is attached to the nose and there is provision for a booster.
The rotating band is 1.75" wide and the bursting charge resembles our
"Explosive D". The submarine was tentatively identified as one of the
I type, probably the larger classification numbered from 5 to 8. This
class is capable of carrying an airplane. Contact with this sub has not
been regained.

(3) Early 25 February LOS ANGELES was blacked out because of report of
unidentified planes over the city. The AA defenses opened fire but no
known hits were registered. Verification of reports of eye witnesses,
apparently reliable persons, indicated that from one to five planes were
overhead. No bombs were dropped. No Army or Navy planes were in the air
at this time and possibility exists that these planes were commercial type
based on interior valley points in CALIFORNIA or elsewhere. The theory
that these planes may have been planes carried by a hostile submarine is

to have been in this vicinity, is largely discounted because of the heig
at which planes were estimated to be flying - 9000 to 18,000 feet.

(4) It is probable that there is at least one, possibly two, hostile
submarines off the southern CALIFORNIA coast. Indications of subs have
been reported but definite proof of presence is lacking. No friendly
ships have been attacked by torpedoes or shells.

(5) No hostile ground units are believed to be nearer than the enemy
forces in the JALUIT - WOTJE area of the eastern MANDATED ISLANDS, about
2000 miles west by south of the HAWAIIAN ISLANDS.

b. Hostile naval forces which may operate in the waters of the PACIFIC off
the west coast could be reinforced by special task forces, locations not
definitely known, or by elements of the enemy FIRST and FOURTH FLEETS
estimated to be in the MANDATED ISLANDS. It is possible for elements of
these units, including carriers to elude our naval defense and air patro
in the vast expanse of the PACIFIC especially to the northwest. Ground
troops for raids or attack in force of the PACIFIC COAST including ALASK
or our island possessions in the eastern Pacific are available in JAPAN,
FORMOSA, and possibly in the MANDATED ISLANDS.

2. ENEMY OPERATIONS DURING PERIOD

No hostile operations were conducted within this theatre of operations.

3. MISCELLANEOUS

a. Enemy Casualties

None.

b. Morale

The hostile morale undoubtedly remains high because of his successes
so far. In a country where press, radio and public opinion are controll
entirely by the Government as in Japan, no hint of lowering of national
morale is likely to reach the outside world. It is equally certain that
reverses and losses will not be truthfully reported to the public.

c. Supply and equipment

The supply and equipment of the enemy is believed to be adequate for the
campaign he is waging outside of this theatre. It is probable that he w
be equally well supplied and equipped in the event he operates in this
theatre for sometime in the future, at least as far as quality of weapon
and equipment is concerned.

d. Terrain not under our control:

(1) Mexico

(a) Probable change General Cardenas Headquarters.

The headquarters of General Lazaro CARDENAS, commander of the
Military Region of the Pacific, now at ENSENADA, Lower California,

-2-

will be moved to MAZATLAN about 1 March, 1942 according to the Mexican press. The Liaison Officer of this headquarters questioned the Mexican Chief of Staff in General CARDENAS' absence, who stated that no decision had been made by the General. He stated that this decision would be communicated to our Liaison Officer if and when made.

(b) U. S. Submarine Maneuvers

The 11th Naval District on 17 February notified General CARDENAS' headquarters of plans to conduct submarine maneuvers in the vicinity of CORONADO ISLANDS outside of the 3-mile limit and asked if there were any objections to these maneuvers by the Mexican authorities. The reply of the Mexican Chief of Staff on 19 February is quoted:

> "The Headquarters of the Military Region of the Pacific has no objections to these maneuvers in the vicinity of the Islas Coronado, and considers the possibility that they may enter the Mexican nine mile limit as unintentional."

(c) German and Italian Prisoners

German and Italian prisoners interned at GUADALAJARA, Mexico have been active in spreading propaganda in that city, according to a confidential report, which hinted that the Mexican Government had done nothing to halt these activities. Restrictions on their movements are reported as not strict.

(2) Pacific Ocean

The waters of the Pacific Ocean, particularly to the north, northwest and west are so vast as to be considered not completely under our control.

e. <u>Weather and visibility, including meterological conditions, in enemy territory.</u>

Unknown.

f. <u>Enemy's probable knowledge of our situation.</u>

The enemy's probably knowledge of our situation has not been gained by observation or reconnaissance but by information learned during peace by the activities of accredited diplomatic military and naval attaches and their agents. Efforts to deny this information to the enemy include general surveillance of enemy aliens, internment of alien leaders and suspected spies and agents, seizure of contraband in possession of enemy aliens, and adoption of stringent censorship measures, and transfer of many other Japanese, including second generation Japanese members of our military forces, from this theatre. All persons of Japanese ancestry, including military personnel, will be removed eventually from this theatre of operations.

CHAPTER 17

THE OFFICE OF NAVAL INTELLIGENCE

DOCUMENT SUMMARIES

Page 249   February 12, 1941—Memo from the Acting Director of Naval
            Intelligence to the Chief of Naval Operations recommending
            that the enclosed information concerning Japanese espionage
            be brought to the attention of the Secretary of the Navy and the
            President.

Page 251   December 4, 1941—ONI report, "Japanese Intelligence and
            Propaganda in the United States During 1941," a 26 page,
            comprehensive assessment of Japanese operations provides a
            broad overview of what was known at the time of Pearl
            Harbor. The report discusses objectives, plans and intelligence
            relationships with various organizations and foreign govern-
            ments. Pages 10-12 of the report cover the West Coast.

Page 277   December 24, 1941—ONI report, "Japanese Tokyo Club
            Syndicate, with Interlocking Affiliations." This report discusses
            post-Pearl Harbor Japanese intelligence operations in the

Western Hemisphere. Its main emphasis is on the Tokyo Club and it provides a number of case histories and schematics to illustrate the interlocking affiliations of seemingly disparate organizations. Organizations are described and names are named.

Page 312   January 26, 1942—Report by Fourteenth Naval District Intelligence Officer, Captain Mayfield, concerning an incident that took place after the attack on Pearl Harbor in which a downed Japanese flyer was assisted in taking control of a small island by an American of Japanese ancestry.

Page 314   February 14, 1942—ONI cover memo transmitting the personal assessment of Lieutenant Commander K. D. Ringle on the "Japanese Question" made for the Chief of Naval Operations to Mr. Tamm of the FBI for information. The memo clearly points out that the report does not "represent the final and official opinion of the Office of Naval Intelligence." The distribution notation at the bottom of the memo indicates that Ringle's report was also sent to the Military Intelligence Division; Alien Enemy Control Unit, Department of Justice; and the Special Defense Unit, Department of Justice.

Page 315   January 26, 1942—Personal assessment of Lieutenant Commander K. D. Ringle, USN for the Chief of Naval Operations on the "Japanese Question." This is the report, parts of which received so much attention by the Commission on Wartime Relocation and Internment of Civilians, the courts and Congress.

Page 325   February 7, 1942—Official report, "Japanese Menace on Terminal Island, San Pedro, California," prepared by Lieutenant Commander K. D. Ringle, USN. Paragraph IV, 2, a is a clear statement of the reasons for evacuating Terminal Island.

NAVY DEPARTMENT
Office of the Chief of Naval Operations
OFFICE OF NAVAL INTELLIGENCE
WASHINGTON

In reply refer to No.

Op-16-B

February 12, 1941

MEMORANDUM for the Chief of Naval Operations

Subject: Japanese Espionage Organization in the United States

1. It is recommended that the following be brought to
the attention of the President and the Secretary of the Navy.
This information has been compiled from highly confidential and
reliable sources by the Domestic Intelligence Branch of the
Office of Naval Intelligence from documentary evidence in its
possession.

"In view of the critical situation existing between the United
States and Japan, the latter has decided to strengthen its
intelligence network in the United States upon the arrival of
Admiral Kichisaburo NOMURA, the new Japanese Ambassador.

"Japanese Diplomatic and Consular representatives have been
instructed to reorganize and strengthen their intelligence nets
in this country. A fairly accurate portrayal of Japan's espionage
organization is as follows:

1. Hidenari TERASAKI, Secretary of the Japanese Embassy, Washington,
will be the guiding influence. He will establish an intelligence
unit which will maintain liaison with private and semi-official
intelligence organizations.
2. Focal point of all Japanese investigations shall be the
determination of the total strength of the U.S.   Investigations
will be divided into political, economic and military classifications,
and a definite course of action shall be mapped out.
3. Intelligence net will make a survey of all persons and organization
which either openly or secretly oppose U.S. participation in the
present war.
4. The net will make a survey of all anti-Jewish, Communistic,
Negro and labor movements.
5. Citizens of foreign extraction except Japanese, aliens except
Japanese, Communists, Negroes, labor union members and anti-Semites
and men having access to government departments, experimental
laboratories, factories, transportation facilities and governmental
organizations of various characters will be utilized.

- 2 -

6. Nisei Japanese and Japanese resident nationals are
to be employed but if there is any 'slip' in this phase,
the Japanese Government thinks these nationals in the
United States will be subject to considerable persecution;
therefore, extreme caution should be exercised.
7. Japanese representatives in this country are cautioned
to bear in mind that war between Japan and the United States
is an eventuality. In such a case, the Japanese intelligence
setup will be moved to Mexico, making that country the nerve
center of the intelligence net in the western hemisphere.
In further anticipation of such an eventuality, the United
States - Mexico international intelligence route will be
established. The Japanese intelligence net covering Argentina,
Brazil, Chile and Peru will be centered in Mexico.

"The Japanese shall cooperate with the German and Italian
intelligence organizations. This phase has been discussed
in Tokyo with German and Italian representatives and has been
approved.

Los Angeles, San Francisco, Seattle, New Orleans, Chicago,
New York and Washington will be the espionage centers in the
United States, all instructions emanating from Washington.
Mexicali, Sonora and Vancouver, B. C. will also be centers
along our boundary."

   2.   This information has been transmitted to the
Military Intelligence Division of the Army and the Federal
Bureau of Investigation.

                              Jules James
                              Captain, U.S. Navy
                              Acting Director of Naval Intelligence

NAVY DEPARTMENT
Office of Naval Intelligence
Washington, D. C.

~~CONFIDENTIAL~~

December 4, 1941

Subject: JAPANESE INTELLIGENCE AND PROPAGANDA IN THE UNITED STATES
DURING 1941.

Note   :   Prepared by the Counter Subversion Section, Office of Naval
Intelligence, from information received from various sources.

INTRODUCTION

The Kurusu mission to Washington represents the culmination of a
year of intense activity which has streamlined Japanese espionage pat-
terns, conditioned programs of sabotage and determined the character
and extent of their propaganda launched throughout this hemisphere.

As Ambassador to Berlin, Kurusu signed the Tripartite Pact of September 1940, but it is said that he did so with no great enthusiasm. A
top-flight diplomat, he has also been Japanese Consul in New York,
Chicago, and Honolulu, as well as Consul General in Manila. In 1929 he
was Minister to Chile and for seven years thereafter served in Tokyo as
a director of the Commercial Bureau of the Foreign Office.

Methods of Operation and Points of Attack

With tension growing between the United States and Japan, the Japanese Government decided its system for securing information was inade-
quate to meet a situation involving war. As early as February, 1941 and
coincident with the arrival of the new ambassador Admiral Kichisaburo
Nomura, diplomatic and consular representatives were instructed to reorganize and strengthen the intelligence network in this country and to
relax the former policy of "cultural propaganda and enlightenment".

Designed to continue in operation, even in the event diplomatic
and commercial relations between the two countries were severed, an
intelligence machine geared for war was put into operation. As a pre-
liminary measure, Japanese representatives in the United States were
instructed to maintain constant watch over American politics, as well
as over the economic and social activities of representatives of the
U.S.S.R. in this country, particularly as they affect Latin America.
For this work, the Japanese planned not only to hire Americans but also
to send competent "researchers" from Japan. A decision was also made

~~CONFIDENTIAL~~

DECLASSIFIED
755004
By ___/SB   NARS, Date 9/5/83

to spread as much political propaganda as possible throughout the United States by means of personal contacts with members of the press and persons influential in American politics and business.

The focal point of the Japanese Espionage effort is the determination of the total strength of the United States. In anticipation of possible open conflict with this country, Japan is vigorously utilizing every available agency to secure military, naval and commercial information, paying particular attention to the West Coast, the Panama Canal and the Territory of Hawaii. To this end, surveys are being made of persons and organizations opposing U. S. intervention in the present European War, and close attention is being paid to all anti-Jewish, Communist, Negro and Labor Movements.

Although not yet fully developed, this new Espionage organization is characterized by a high degree of decentralization. The activity of the Military and Naval section, which is divided into a number of different groups, is supplemented by the work of independent agents, and the general pattern includes individuals, small groups and commercial organizations functioning separately and energetically. In the background lies the Imperial Japanese Government exercising direct control over individuals and organizations through the Embassy and the Consulates.

The new program envisages the use of citizens of foreign extraction, aliens, communists, negroes, labor union members, anti-semites, and individuals having access to Government departments, experimental laboratories, factories, transportation facilities, and governmental organizations of various kinds. Nisei (second generation) Japanese and alien Japanese residents have not been overlooked. Realizing, however, that its nationals in this country would be subject to prosecution "in the event of a slip," the Japanese Government has advised extreme caution in their employment.

In the event of open hostilities, Mexico will probably be the Japanese Intelligence nerve center in the Western Hemisphere, and in anticipation of war, U. S. - Mexican Intelligence routes are being established. This network, covering Argentina, Brazil, Chile, Peru and the Central American countries, will come together in Mexico City, and Japanese cooperation with the German and Italian Intelligence organizations is expected. Such co-operation has been discussed in Tokyo with representatives of the Axis powers and the plan is said to have been approved by them.

At the present time, the District of Columbia, New York City, New Orleans, Los Angeles, San Francisco and Seattle are the espionage centers in the United States with Mexicali, Baja California and Vancouver, British Columbia important boundary outposts.

GERMAN-JAPANESE COLLABORATION

As an incident of the treaty with the Axis powers, all possible avenues by which mutual benefit could be achieved began to be explored. Instructions were sent to all diplomatic and consular missions to maintain close contact with officials of Germany and Italy for purposes of exchanging information and to encourage friendships between citizens of the three nations who were living abroad.

A recent investigation conducted in New York City disclosed that Takeo Ezima and Kanegoro Koike, Japanese Naval Officers attached to the Naval Inspector's Office, were co-operating with German espionage agents by accepting confidential data for transmittal to Germany by way of Japan.

On October 19, 1940, instructions were issued from Germany by short-wave radio for a German agent in the United States to contact E. Sato at the NIPPON CLUB in New York City. He made unsuccessful attempts to comply with these instructions until October 31, 1940 when another radio message was received from Germany directing that these efforts be discontinued.

Germany radioed again on May 18, 1941 asking whether its agent in the United States was prepared to turn over material, inscribed "Sato from Staemer", on May 22, 1941, to E. Sato in the Miyako Restaurant, 20 East 56th Street, New York City. The message also indicated that further meetings should be agreed upon and that this method of transmitting material was safe.

Shortly thereafter, two German agents in the United States complied with these instructions and established contact with an individual who gave his name as Kato. After identifying themselves, they were taken by him to a Japanese restaurant at 41 East 19th Street, New York City, where they occupied a private room. Kato there identified himself as Lt. Commander Takeo Ezima, I.J.N. and took from them a number of items for transmittal to Germany by way of Japan. These items consisted of information developed through the activities of the German Espionage system in the United States, some of which had been microfilmed. However, the original physical articles such as ammunition, a drawing of a hydraulic unit with pressure switch A-5 of the Sperry Gyroscope and an original drawing from the Lawrence Engineering and Research Corporation of a soundproofing installation were also turned over to Ezima on this occasion.

Immediately following a meeting on June 24, 1941, when Ezima received a number of microphotographs of material obtained by German espionage agents, he contacted Kanegoro Koike, Paymaster Commander of the Japanese Imperial Navy, assigned to the Office of the Japanese Naval Inspector in New York City. At the request of the State Department, Ezima was not prosecuted. However, he sailed for Japan on July 5, 1941, and Kanegoro Koike followed on August 14, 1941.

-3-

Reports from the middle west indicate that German and Japanese nationals are carrying on espionage activities through their control of re-insurance companies who underwrite insurance carried by National Defense Industries. Although they appear to be owned and operated by Americans, the largest re-insurance companies in the world are German owned.

In the summer of this year, the German Consul Fritz Wiedemann was said to have been considerably perturbed because Japanese steamship lines were not co-operating with him in evacuating German nationals from the United States. He was particularly incensed over the refusal of the NYK Steamship Company to grant accommodations to Karl Anton Bayer and claimed that the failure of the Japanese Consul General to override the Captain of the boat gave the Germans grounds for suspicion that the Japanese were working against them. Additional reports of friction were received from Shanghai where it was stated that the Japanese were generally hated by the Germans. However, German war vessels are known to have been over-hauled in the ports of Nagasaki and Kobe and there has been a certain amount of trade in metals between the Germans living in Mexico and Japan.

German-Japanese conferences were scheduled to take place in Havana early in September, and it was reported that they would be attended by such important Germans as Wiedemann, Vonspiegel and Arthur Dietrich.

RELATIONS WITH THE NEGROES

As early as May 1941, the Office of Naval Intelligence became aware that the Japanese Government was establishing connections with influential Negroes in this country for the purpose of studying the negro movement. A short time later it became apparent that representatives of the Japanese Government in the United States were attempting to organize the Negroes for the purpose of retarding National Defense efforts and to commit sabotage. In furtherance of this project, the Japanese expect to take advantage of the political strength of such organizations as the NEGRO CONGRESS, THE NEGRO ALLIANCE, and the NATIONAL ASSOCIATION FOR THE ADVANCEMENT OF COLORED PEOPLE.

The Japanese decision to utilize this minority group for their own advantage was first manifest in the latter part of 1940 when the government in Tokyo financed the opening of a news service for negro newspapers by a negro literary critic named Utley. According to reliable reports, Utley has had relatively good results in stimulating subversive activities among the negroes.

A Japanese by the name of Hikida (probably K. Hikida of 257 W. 85th Street, New York City) is the most intimate contact with negro groups and their leaders. Reported to be a well-to-do research worker and writer, he led a round-table discussion on the Negro problem in the office of the

Japanese Naval Inspector in New York City in December 1938. Since then, he is reported to have received grants of money from the Consul General in New York City to carry on propaganda among the Negroes in an effort to organize them.

The District of Columbia is the focal point of this particular branch of the Japanese Espionage system because nearly all Negro organizations have their headquarters in this city. However, Hikida's organization in New York will receive strong support for the purpose of encouraging its rapid expansion, and when organizations in both cities are working satisfactorily, attention will be turned to Chicago, Los Angeles, and New Orleans.

Japanese authorities are watching closely the Negroes who are employed in defense production plants, naval stations, and other military establishments, particularly in the naval bases at Norfolk, Va., Philadelphia, Pa., and Brooklyn, N.Y. They plan to organize skilled and unskilled workmen in these cities to secure military and naval information for the Japanese Government.

In the summer of 1941, a closer association between young Japanese and young Negroes in the San Francisco Bay area was observed. Meetings have been held at the Mikado Grill, 1699 Post Street, San Francisco, Calif. but no definite connections between these mixed groups and Japanese Government representatives have been established. Such mixed parties are known to have gone to Oakland, Calif., to attend meetings of the Nisei Young Democratic Club.

In propagandizing the Negroes, the Japanese are utilizing the services of J. H. Smythe and Walker Matteson. Because of his success in arousing negro opinion, Smythe has been put in charge of the column "Behind the Headlines" for negro publications and both men will be used for editorializing.

FALANGE

Suppression of Axis organizations has caused a shift of totalitarian support to nationalist Latin American groups and these are employed to create unrest with the ultimate object of destroying Pan-American solidarity.

For years it has been a well established fact that Nazi, Fascist, and Falange agents are co-operating extensively in their espionage activities, and it now appears that the Japanese as well as the Germans and Italians are making increasing use of members of Falange organizations because of the limitations on their own connections and activities throughout the Americas.

The present organization of the Falange Party dates from April 18, 1937 when General Franco was chosen as its leader. One day later, he announced that the Falange would be the one and only official party in Spain. In direct opposition to Pan-Americanism and the Monroe Doctrine, the basic aim of this group is the restoration of the Spanish Empire of the days before the defeat of the Spanish Armada. This group, together with Nazi and Fascist organizations, is believed to subsidize financially the Union Nacional de Sinarquistas, generally known as "Sinarquistas", which was organized in Mexico in 1936. Drawing its membership and support from the Peons and lower middle-class Mexicans, it is opposed by the Mexican Federal Authorities as well as by labor unions in that country.

According to the terms of an agreement signed by Berlin, Madrid, and Tokyo, the Philippine Falange is coupled with that in Japan and instead of being a German, its chief is Japanese. The Spanish Board for the Philippines is subordinate to the Spanish Embassy at Tokyo and also has a Japanese Councillor.

SILVER SHIRTS MOVEMENT

In the summer of 1941, it became apparent that the Japanese Government was interested in the Silver Shirts Movement in the United States. Kazuyoshi Inagaki, attached to the office of the Japanese Consul General in San Francisco has been mentioned as a Government contact man in the west coast area, and Totaro Iwasaki, an alien Japanese, is also reported as having made inquiries about the status of this group. The Japanese Government appears to be interested in acquiring detailed information about the movement with particular emphasis on its world views and the personal and intellectual capacities of its members.

It appears that Tokyo wishes to use this political group as a means of establishing "Justice" in the United States. If, after a thorough investigation, it is found that Iwasaki has the proper background and training, he will be sent to Japan at Government expense in connection with the movement.

LABOR UNIONS

In the spring of 1941, the Japanese Government indicated that in the event of war with the U.S., labor unions would become a major political factor in obstructing the unification of this country. With that in mind, Japanese officials here were instructed to contact leaders of labor unions, the Communist party, Socialist groups and other anti-Roosevelt movements. In this connection, the Japanese are studying the possibility of using a self-exiled Japanese socialist now living at Northwestern University in Evanston, Illinois. His name is believed to be Oyama (C. Oyama or Iku Oyama).

-6-

CONFIDENTIAL

ESPIONAGE AND PROPAGANDA

For many years, the Japanese have maintained an extensive organization in the United States to gather intelligence information and to disseminate propaganda. Information of a commercial and political nature has normally been collected by the various consulates which also carry on propaganda under the direction of the Embassy in Washington. Numerous agents have been employed at various times to supplement this work and military and naval information has been gathered by groups of Army and Navy officers and technical experts attached to the Office of the Japanese Army Ordnance Inspector and the Japanese Naval Inspector's Office in New York City. Regular military and naval attaches have also contributed to the pool of information, as have the personnel of Japanese business organizations located throughout the United States. In general, although much information of a military and naval character has been obtained, the system as a whole has been effective only in producing data of a general nature and in disseminating propaganda favorable to the Japanese point of view.

Organization

The military and naval espionage system is organized into more than one independent de-centralized machine. Information sought may be classified as professional, commercial, domestic, and political, and while the duty of each section is practically the same, the detection and destruction of one group will in no way lead to the destruction of the remaining ones.

In addition to the organized machines operating under their respective chiefs, there are many individual agents whose trail will never be picked up. If they are apprehended, they can never be proved to be anything but irresponsible individuals operating without pay, authority, or direction. It is also well to remember that every Japanese commercial organization is an actively functioning information unit for the Japanese Government. Their normal business activities are nationwide, as are their contacts, and the Japanese Government exercises direct control over these groups through its Embassy in Washington as well as through its many consulates.

The Second Secretary of the Japanese Embassy, Hidenari Terasaki, was reportedly charged with the responsibility of co-ordinating and directing Intelligence operations in the United States. Morita Morishima, Japanese Consul General at New York City, is the directing head of the New York unit, and there is a possibility that the Washington and New York units may be combined into one agency with the latter as the "nerve center".

New Policies

In March, 1941 a meeting was held at the Japanese Embassy to formulate new policies concerning intelligence activities. A decision was

CONFIDENTIAL

made to carry out a most vigorous and comprehensive program and the
Embassy requested an allotment of $500,000 for its development during
the year.

In reorganizing the Espionage Network and pursuing a new Propaganda
policy, Japanese officials decided to dismiss immediately all persons of
little value; to divert the most capable persons currently being used for
the dissemination of propaganda into intelligence collecting and espionage
activity; and to transfer to the JAPAN INSTITUTE the most effective groups
and persons in their employ. Because of "freezing legislation" which
brought about a shortage of funds available for distribution to civilian
personnel, salaries and expense funds were also streamlined.

Pursuant to this program, the "Culture on Wheels" Library was transferred to the JAPAN INSTITUTE which was also made responsible for the
distribution of propaganda films. Operated for several years by Helmut
Ripperger, an American citizen who registered with the Department of State
as a propaganda agent for the Japanese Government, this reference library
carried propaganda by truck to various parts of the U. S., concentrating
particularly on American colleges and universities. Until recently,
Ripperger received approximately $1,300 a month from the Consulate General
in New York City. The JAPAN INSTITUTE is an affiliate of the KOKUSAI
BUNKA SHINKOKAI (Society for Promotion of International Cultural Relations) in Tokyo, a powerful quasi-official propaganda organization, international in scope.

Early in July, it was disclosed that the Japanese were financing the
"Living Age" Magazine. At that time its backers decided to sell it and
ceased publication in September. If a purchaser is not found soon, the
organization will probably go into bankruptcy.

Publication of the "Foreign Observer" was discontinued during the
summer; the distribution of films through the Y.M.C.A. and other agencies
is to be discontinued as soon as present contracts have expired; plans
for publishing propaganda booklets in connection with the World-Over Year
Book have been scrapped; the English edition of the Japanese American
newspaper has been temporarily suspended; the Japanese subsidy of the
Globe Wireless Company has been withdrawn. In addition, in accordance
with the policy of utilizing to better advantage the services of its
propagandists, two lecturers for the JAPAN INSTITUTE, Arthur Clifford Reed
and Arthur Donald Bate, are in reality being used as espionage agents.

Approximately one year ago, Japanese Consulates on the West Coast
began to collect information about the movement of British, French and
American naval and air forces, stressing the importance of having eye
witnesses make reports. At the same time, it was suggested in Tokyo
that a naval officer be assigned to each consulate in the United States
as a "clerk" to secure information for the Naval Ministry.

CONFIDENTIAL   -8-

The officer in charge of intelligence at the Embassy in Washington, was designated "Press Attache". His duties include investigation and the gathering of secret information on the division of American public opinion about Japanese-American relations.

In accordance with instructions to pay particular attention to German and Italian fifth column activities, the Japanese studied the reactions of German and Italian Americans in the recent Presidential Election and the attitude of the Communist party at that time.

Latin America

In accordance with its new Espionage policy, the Japanese have established an organization in Latin America to evaluate U.S. public opinion as well as our military and diplomatic situation. Its function is to collect and evaluate information obtained from the offices and personnel of American ministries in Latin America; to study the effectiveness of American and Latin American printed matter and radio broadcasts; and to secure information from offices of third powers in Latin America as well as from individuals in government offices in those countries.

In this connection, it is interesting to note that the Foreign Office in Tokyo has announced the reassignment of Hidenari Terasaki to the Legation in Brazil.

Close attention is being paid to the selection of spies by all Japanese representatives in the Americas. They are particularly anxious to obtain the services of any informants who have been seamen, in order to place them in the employ of steamship companies, and are prepared to spend large sums of money for this purpose. They have advised extreme caution in making selections since they believe FBI makes a practice of trying to get its men into confidential positions in the offices of the Axis Powers. The importance of broadcasts is also stressed and a modified radio monitoring system is envisaged. Leading U.S. newspapers and magazines are carefully scrutinized and efforts are made to obtain detailed information about Panama. To this end, telegraphic sections of all offices concerned are being expanded, sources of information open to Domei News Agencies and other special correspondents tapped and indirect use of Spanish and Portugese language correspondents is being made. The Japanese plan to keep abreast of current U.S. economic conditions through their merchants.

In the event German and Italian diplomatic officers are ordered out of the country before the Japanese, Tokyo plans to take over confidential informants used by Axis representatives. These informants are not limited to Latin Americans but include those living in Spain and Portugal.

Continental United States

In June 1941, after the Tachibana Espionage Case was exposed to the public, the Japanese consulates at Los Angeles, San Francisco, and Seattle were instructed to observe the movements of American warships, to gather other information of interest to the Japanese Navy, and to cable it to Tokyo without delay. This action was taken because the activities of Japanese Naval Representatives (Language Officers) in the United States had been suppressed by the U.S. authorities in a series of "incidents", and there was a shortage of naval personnel to do this work.

In reporting progress in the U.S. shipbuilding industry to the Foreign Minister in Tokyo, an espionage agent in this country stated that "America is moving heaven and earth in her Defense Program."

West Coast

In an effort to establish an integrated intelligence organization in the Southern California area, Japanese authorities are intensifying their efforts to establish contacts. Dr. Ken Nakazawa, who is Professor of Japanese Culture and Oriental Studies at the University of Southern California at Los Angeles, is actively engaged in this work. An attache of the Los Angeles Japanese Consulate, as well as an Aide for Japanese propaganda, he is investigating and summarizing first hand information as well as newspaper reports about military movements, labor disputes, communist activities, and other matters of interest to the Government in Tokyo.

Working through white persons as well as Negroes and maintaining close relationships with Japanese Associations, Chambers of Commerce, and newspapers, this group is attempting to keep aeroplane manufacturing plants, military and naval establishments under close surveillance. Its members have already added to the ranks of this group reliable Japanese in the San Pedro and San Diego areas who will keep a close watch on all shipments of aeroplanes and other war materials, and will report the amounts and destinations of such shipments. In addition, observers have been stationed to watch traffic in war materials across the U.S. - Mexican border.

Reports of activities within the United States Army are sought from second generation Japanese in that branch of the armed services, and although the information has not yet been confirmed, there are reports which indicate second generation Japanese are working in west coast aeroplane plants for intelligence purposes.

Prominent Americans and Japanese connected with the motion picture industry have been employed by the Consular Intelligence Network to investigate anti-Jewish movements in this country, particularly on the West Coast, and influential Negroes have kept this group currently informed about the negro movement.

California-Mexican Border

Yoshiaki Miura, Japanese Minister in Mexico City, has been the head of the Japanese Intelligence Network in Mexico and Central America. In June, 1941, Kiyoshi Yamagata, travelling Japanese Ambassador, conferred with Miura about plans for organizing the Mexico City office on a wartime basis. During the same month, Yamagata held a conference with Fujio Kato, Japanese Consul at Mexicali. Kato told Yamagata that due to the predominance of American influence in that area and the fact that its many Japanese inhabitants were uneducated, personnel and funds should be supplied to operate Mexicali only as a branch intelligence center. They both agreed that in spite of the difficulty in carrying on their work in a border city with a population of only 15,000 persons, work there would prove useful providing the intelligence network in Los Angeles and vicinity was well organized and particularly if the Japanese Government found it necessary to withdraw its officials from the United States. As a result, Yamagata recommended that connections be established at once between Los Angeles and Mexicali.

Pacific Northwest

In this region also, there is considerable evidence that Japanese agents have put into operation their new policies of espionage.

Kanji Kaneko, Chancellor of the Japanese Consulate at Seattle, is in charge of Intelligence and has been collecting information from second generation Japanese draftees on matters dealing with troops and morale in the United States Army.

Labor unions and political organizations in this area appear to have been intensely utilized by the Japanese. The legal representative of the Cannery Workers and Farm Laborers Union (C.I.O. Local #7 in Seattle) is a second generation lawyer whose name is Kenji Ito. Legal Adviser to the Japanese Consulate in Seattle, he has been active in the collection of information about anti-government organizations and the anti-Jewish movement. It is worth noting that this particular union is composed of about 70% Filipinos and 30% Japanese.

Shoji ("Welly") Okamaru, an American born Japanese with dual citizenship, is head of a unit which contacts labor unions in search of Communist Party members. For the past six or seven years, he has acted as a Secretary of the Japanese Consulate at Seattle, but was promoted to Consular Assistant in June, 1940. He has as an associate an alien Japanese who is active in the labor movement as a committee chairman and organizer.

Before war broke out between Germany and Russia, communist machinists of German origin who are members of labor organizations at the Bremerton Navy Yard and Boeing Aeroplane factories, were supplying information to Japanese authorities. This is but another example of the

effort Tokyo is making to obtain information on military efforts, construction of ships, aeroplane production, production of copper, zinc,
aluminum, yield of tin from cans and labor resources through competent
Americans.

Such efforts were supplemented until July, 1941 by the activities
of Lieutenant Commander Sadatomo Okada of the Imperial Japanese Navy.
He, like Commander Itaru Tachibana, who operated from Los Angeles, was
requested by the State Department to leave the country because of his
espionage activities in the Pacific Northwest.

Information on political questions is sought by the Japanese in
this area, from John Sylvester, speaker of the lower house in the state
of Washington, Ralph Horr, chairman of the Republican Party's local committee, and Daniel Trefethen, who is a strong Catholic layman.

Alaska

Although their reliability has not been ascertained, reports have
been received which indicate that the Japanese Consulate in Vancouver,
B. C., is endeavoring to employ Canadians to visit Alaska to obtain information on land and sea-plane bases in the Yukon, the strength of military supplies and personnel in that area, the distribution, location,
and quantity of heavy oil, and progress of base construction in Fairbanks,
Seward, Anchorage, and Kodiak. Tokyo is also said to be interested in
having a description of dry-docks, data on troops and arsenals in the
vicinity of Kodiak and the number of war craft visiting Alaska during the
past year. Further, they would like to have a confirmation or denial
of the fact of U.S. troops crossing Canada from Fort Haynes to Alaska
and their construction of a military road. The Japanese are particularly
anxious to determine whether roads are being built to carry heavy oil
from Fort Nelson to Alaska.

TERRITORY OF HAWAII

Out of a total population of 423,330 in the Hawaiian Islands, there
are 157,905 Japanese, approximately one third of which are aliens. Japanese are known to organize for every conceivable purpose, and social,
civic, educational and religious societies have existed in the Hawaiian
Islands from the time of the earliest Japanese migrations. It is believed
that every Japanese resident in Hawaii belongs to one or more purely Japanese organizations. However, only the more important groups are of interest, since they are in a position to engage in espionage, sabotage and
other acts inimical to the best interests of the U. S.

A study of these organizations discloses interesting inter-relations
through duplication of activity and plurality of position held by many

-12-

individuals. For example, a Buddhist priest may be the principal of a Japanese language school as well as a consular agent or an officer or member of an organization appearing in another category.

Each of these groups is at least strongly influenced if not directly controlled by similar ones in Japan. The consular organization is obviously controlled by the Japanese Foreign Ministry, and religious sects are supervised from headquarters in Japan, which in turn are under governmental domination.

Consular Agents

The center of the consular organization, as well as of alien Japanese activity, is the Japanese Consulate General at Honolulu under the direction of Consul General Nagao Kita. For purposes of disseminating instructions or news, it is said to utilize the services of such prominent organizations as the United Japanese Society of Honolulu, the Honolulu Japanese Chamber of Commerce, the Hilo Japanese Chamber of Commerce as well as the Hilo Japanese Society and the Japanese Language Press.

By far the largest and most diversified group under the direction of the Consulate General is that of the "Consular Agents" or "Toritsuginin". Two hundred and nineteen of these agents are located geographically so as to form a comprehensive information system for the Consulate General throughout the Hawaiian Islands. These men are well educated American born and alien Japanese above average in intelligence. Many of them are non-quota aliens operating as Buddhist priests and principals or teachers in Japanese language schools. Scattered throughout the Island, these agents have denied being under the control of the Consul General, and there are none located in the City of Honolulu.

Propaganda

The Buddhist and Shinto sects, the Japanese language schools and civic and commercial societies are powerful propaganda agencies because of the nature of their work with the Japanese community and the fact that their business is carried on usually in the Japanese language.

Each community in the Hawaiian Islands where there are Japanese residents has one or more Buddhist temples or preaching places (Fukkyojo). Because of respect which the Japanese have for priests, they are readily influenced by these men who hold services in accordance with Japanese custom. In this connection, many Buddhist and Shinto priests are non-quota aliens who have lived in the Islands a comparatively short time.

Schools

The Japanese educational system in the Territory of Hawaii centers around the Hawaiian Japanese Language School Association. This is an organization composed of representatives or directors from each of fourteen districts. These districts or sub-groups all carry distinct titles and in turn are composed of teachers from the individual schools and school boards under their jurisdiction. In this connection, it should be noted that while the majority of male teachers are alien, many of the citizen teachers were also educated in Japan. Almost invariably, school principals are aliens and frequently they are Buddhist priests.

At the present time, more than 39,000 pupils attend Japanese schools in Hawaii.

Newspapers·

Of nineteen newspapers and magazines printed in the Japanese language, the NIPPU JIJI and the HAWAII HOCHI, published daily at Honolulu, are of principal importance. All of the news organs, however, carry pro-Japanese editorials and news items from time to time.

THE TACHIBANA CASE

Head of the Japanese Espionage Network on the West Coast during 1940 was Commander Itaru Tachibana, IJN, who came to the United States as a language officer. Following his arrest in 1941 for violation of the espionage statutes, he was released on $50,000 bond and finally left the country in June, 1941 at the request of the State Department.

Other Japanese Naval Officers involved in this subversive group were Lieutenant Commander Sadatomo Okada, Commander Iwao Arisaka, Lieutenant Commander Sadayoshi Nakayama and Engineer Lieutenant Wataru Yamada. Okada and Yamada, like Tachibana, were requested to leave the U. S. because their activities were considered to be inimical to the safety of this country, and Commander Arisaka and Lieutenant Commander Nakayama sailed suddenly from New York for Brazil in July, 1941.

Prominent among the organizations which were apparently furnishing information to the Japanese Government through Tachibana were the NIPPON KAIGUN KYOKAI (Japanese Navy Association), the SAKURA KAI (Cherry Association) and the SUIKO SHA (Reserve Officers Club).

The many ramifications of Tachibana's activities were disclosed by translating into English numerous Japanese papers, documents, and reports which were seized by the F.B.I. at the time of his arrest at the Olympic Hotel in Los Angeles.

Part of the material seized consisted of the records of the North American branch of the JAPANESE NAVY ASSOCIATION (Nippon Kaigun Kyokai). With headquarters in Tokyo, this organization has as its chief objectives the dissemination of information about navies of other countries and the development of Japanese Naval strength. To this end, it has established investigating agencies to study domestic and foreign navies, maritime transportation and other maritime matters. Investigation disclosed that members of the Japanese Navy Association had been working in collaboration with rank officers of the Imperial Japanese Navy stationed in Los Angeles, and it appears that Tachibana, who was collecting intelligence for the benefit of the Japanese Navy, was assisted by the investigating branch of that association.

Among Tachibana's effects was found considerable correspondence from Dr. Takishi Furusawa, director of the Los Angeles Suiko Sha, which is an organization composed of officers and reserve officers of the Imperial Japanese Navy. He and his wife, Mrs. Sachiko Furusawa, appear to be the directive force behind this organization. Both of them are exceedingly prominent in Japanese affairs.

The names of Dr. Kijima Amano, secretary of the Sakura Kai, Shunten Kumamoto, president of the Los Angeles Japanese Association and Gongoro Nakamura, president of the Central Japanese Association of California, also appear among Tachibana's papers and it is interesting to note that all of them, including the Furusawas, are on the research committee of the Sakura Kai.

During the course of investigation of the activities of Dr. Furusawa and the Japanese Navy Association, a large amount of evidentiary material was uncovered indicating a probable violation of federal statutes. As a result, the FBI is conducting a vigorous investigation of this association at the present time.

Tachibana's correspondence also included the names of representatives of a few of the important Japanese language newspapers such as the RAFU SHIMPO (Los Angeles News), KASHU MAINICHI (California Daily), and the NANKA SANGYO NIPPO (Southern California Industrial Daily News).

EXPATRIATION

Reports from Hawaii indicate that the Japanese are resorting to subterfuge to convince Americans that expatriation is reducing the number of dual citizens in that territory. Recently, the acting Japanese Consul General announced that he had asked the Foreign Office for additional employees to handle the increasing number of expatriation applications received by the Consulate in Honolulu. He stated that more than four hundred such applications are submitted each month and that a marked increase has been noted during the past eight months. It is worth noting, however, that the total number of expatriations in 1940 was only slightly higher than the figure for 1933.

Formal expatriation of Japanese citizenship, heretofore required of public school teachers as a condition precedent to their continued employment in the Territory of Hawaii, was recently relaxed in the case of American citizens of Japanese ancestry who are not registered with the Japanese Government. This action was reported to be the result of intercession on the part of the Hawaiian-Japanese Civic Association of Honolulu.

Out of a total Japanese population of 320,000 in the United States and its possessions, it is estimated that more than 127,000 have dual citizenship. This estimate is based on the fact that more than 52% of American born Japanese fall into this category. In the Territory of Hawaii alone, dual citizens constitute approximately 35% of the total Japanese population.

Recently, a petition carrying over 30,000 signatures was submitted to the Secretary of State requesting this government to negotiate a more simplified expatriation procedure with the Japanese Government. Many people who signed this petition were already expatriated and it appears that the emphasis of the campaign was on obtaining an imposing number of signatures to the petition rather than to represent the real desires of dual citizens.

Expatriation is almost universally opposed by the parents of dual citizens who claim that for the names of their children to be struck from the family register is an affront to their ancestors and an act of disloyalty to Japan.

The present Japanese Nationality Law of 1924, which liberalized the process of expatriation, was announced as a result of representations made by a group of Hawaiian Japanese who went to Japan especially for that purpose. It would seem that if the Japanese were sincere in their desire to facilitate expatriation at this time, they would follow the method previously so successfully employed. The fact that they now call upon the State Department to intervene with the Japanese Government on their behalf and surround the campaign with a fanfare of publicity, gives rise to the belief that those behind the present movement are deliberately trying to portray the dual citizens of Hawaii as the unwilling possessors of Japanese citizenship.

It is worth noting that the various expatriation campaigns have coincided with junctures in American-Japanese relations or with the development of local issues which tend to bring the Japanese racial situation sharply into focus. This recent campaign in the Territory of Hawaii is believed to have arisen from the questioning of Japanese candidates about their citizenship status during the recent Territorial elections.

Residents in the United States and Hawaii have had 18 years in which to renounce their Japanese allegiance. The fact that comparatively few have done so negates the supposition that they now desire to cast off their Japanese citizenship as an expression of their Americanism.

Recently it was brought to the attention of the Office of Naval Intelligence that out of a total of 198 postal employees in Honolulu, 51 have dual citizenship and that the foreman in the registry section, Ernest Hirokawa, is an alien Japanese. As a result of this discovery the registered mail for the fleet stationed in Hawaiian waters is now routed directly to the Pearl Harbor Navy Yard as a security measure.

MILITARY CONSCRIPTION

Japanese residents in the United States, especially dual citizens, have been urged to return to Japan to do military service with the armed forces of that country. In some cases even expatriated citizens of Japanese ancestry have been encouraged to do this while visiting Japan. All male Japanese citizens are eligible for military duty during the so-called "military age" (Tekirei Nendo) which is the year following that in which they reach their twentieth birthday.

Considerable evidence exists of such pressure being brought to bear on dual citizens and even expatriated citizens of Japanese ancestry who are in Japan as students or workers. In this connection, a certain Kazuichi Hashimoto of Terminal Island, California is reported to have taken a group of forty young Japanese to Japan, ostensibly for the purpose of teaching them fencing. However, it is suspected that these young people were taken to Japan for military duty.

Once each year, local Japanese consulates publish announcements in Japanese language newspapers concerning registration and deferment applications. Japanese males living abroad who have retained their Japanese citizenship, but who have already been excused from military duty, must nevertheless submit reports of residence. Those who wish to be deferred, upon reaching military age, must execute a "Deferment Application for Residents Abroad".

It is important to note that the categories of those eligible for military service in Japan include males with dual citizenship (Japanese born in the United States after 1924 whose birth was registered with the Japanese Consulate within fourteen days). Under Japanese law, these persons are just as liable to answer to the military authorities as are full Japanese citizens.

Toward the end of 1940, the Government in Tokyo conducted a national
and international census. All persons of Japanese ancestry were required
to fill out questionnaires, even those United States citizens of Japanese
ancestry who had expatriated themselves.

JAPANESE NAVAL COMMUNICATION AND COURIER SERVICE

A heavy traffic of telegrams, radios, and cables has been noted
between the Japanese Ministry of Marine in Tokyo, and the various Naval
Attaches and Inspectors in the United States, Canada, Mexico, and Europe.

There is strong evidence that the Naval Attache's Office in Washington
operates a short wave sending and receiving set disguised as an "Amateur
Station", and that it is linked to the numerous "Ham" stations known to
be operated by Japanese on the West Coast and in Hawaii. This fact has
yet to be proved, but the interest shown by the Naval Inspector for Radio
in New York City seems to be a bit out of the ordinary. In addition,
leads from a radio transmitting antenna enter the building of the Japanese
Embassy in Washington, and one of the Embassy clerks recently made an
unsuccessful attempt to secure an amateur radio operator's license.

In addition to radio and cable, the Naval Attache has at his disposal
the service of the diplomatic mail pouch. However, it is evident that
the Naval Attache relies on his own couriers to transmit items between
this country and Japan. It is believed that the greater part of this
service is concerned with sending to Japan samples, charts, models,
reports and other documents which are not entrusted to the usual mail and
express service.

An analysis of the itineraries of visiting officials and certain
language officers indicates a systematic and periodic movement between
strategic points throughout this country. Language officers are used
for transcontinental officer-messenger service only when there is no
"visiting officer" available. Their primary function is to collect and
distribute information to agents located in various key cities throughout the country. If no naval personnel are aboard incoming or outgoing
Japanese ships, a language officer will contact the Captain (who is a
Naval Reserve Officer) to receive and send Naval Attache mail.

Confidential mail service between the Japanese Embassy and the Naval
Attache in Ottawa, Canada appears to be indicated by the regularity of
officer travel between Washington and Buffalo. Likewise, at frequent
intervals, officers are sent from Washington to Miami, New Orleans,
Houston and return.

While in Miami, they invariably fly to Havana and return the same day. On the West Coast, a language officer from Los Angeles or Seattle. frequently travels up and down the Coast from Vancouver, B.C. to Tiajuana, Mexico for no apparent reason unless it is to contact agents to collect and distribute information. On occasion, the West Coast language officer will travel from Los Angeles to Chicago and return via Seattle, Portland, and San Francisco. On the East Coast, an officer frequently goes from Washington to Chicago via New York and Cleveland. It would appear therefore, that Chicago is the meeting place for officers stationed on the East and West Coasts.

EXPENDITURES

Secret funds in cash are maintained by the Japanese Embassy and Consulates for the purchase of intelligence information from civilian agents who report directly to consular agents and representatives.

While the Naval Inspector's Office was in operation, it was primarily interested in obtaining detailed technical information which could be used to advantage by the Japanese Navy. Disbursements of this office in New York City alone amounted to approximately $500,000 a month, but aside from fuel oil, the purchases were all nominal and varied. They covered aircraft parts, radio, electric equipment, tools and accessories which were apparently obtained for purposes of examination only.

Archer Saki Huntington reported that Fukichi Fukumoto, former New York representative of the OSAKA MAINICHI and TOKYO NICHI NICHI newspapers, paid him $2300 to obtain the drawings of an exhaust super-charger used in aeroplane engines.

Prior to the Executive Order freezing the assets of all Japanese and Chinese nationals in the United States, the Yokohama Specie Bank, Ltd. withdrew $150,000 in cash from the Guaranty Trust Company in New York City and $50,000 in cash from its account at the Chase National Bank.

In the summer of 1941 the Yokohama Specie Bank of San Francisco prepared to pack and ship a large number of Japanese bonds to Japan aboard the NYK Liner "Tatuta Maru". As a result of Federal action, Japanese bonds of various descriptions having a par value of $9,621,100 were recovered.

Through confidential sources it was learned that on July 25, 1941, cash funds amounting to $180,000 were allotted by the management of the Yokohama Specie Bank in San Francisco to its officers and employees, most of whom are Japanese nationals. These funds were distributed in

-19-

proportion to the yearly salary received by the individuals and this move appears to have been made in order to prevent total loss of funds through seizure by the U.S. Government in time of war.

Funds of Japanese nationals and corporations located in the District of Columbia, New York City, San Diego, Los Angeles, San Francisco, Seattle, Honolulu, and New Orleans are being monitored at the present time to determine the source of income and the nature of withdrawals made from accounts in various banks in these localities. Any deposits of unusual size, and likewise any withdrawals, made by individuals, Japanese owned corporations and organizations are brought to the attention of the proper Federal authorities, and serial numbers of bills in denominations of $500 and $1,000 are recorded in order to permit investigation of subsequent negotiation of such bills. In this way, it is possible to determine whether funds are being used for activities inimical to the welfare of this country.

JAPANESE LANGUAGE NEWSPAPERS

Since November, 1940 there has been a definite effort on the part of certain agencies and ministries of the Japanese Government to establish control over the Japanese language press throughout the world. Following the organization of the powerful OVERSEAS JAPANESE CENTRAL SOCIETY late in 1940, officials of the Japanese Ministries of Commerce and Industry, Foreign Affairs, Navy, War, Overseas Affairs, and other lesser agencies determined to ensure further control over Japanese living abroad through the medium of the press. They scheduled a convention to be held in Tokyo in November, 1941 and invited the most pro-Japanese publishers and editors to attend. At the conclusion of the convention, half the delegates toured China, while the others traveled through Japan Proper at government expense.

A similar tendency is revealed in a report of a meeting held in Japan during the summer of 1941 by the WORLD ECONOMIC FEDERATION (formerly the JAPANESE ECONOMIC FEDERATION) at which representatives of overseas Japanese newspapers were requested to act as an investigative unit in a study of world economic movements. Efforts of this sort on the part of Tokyo are entirely in keeping with that Government's comprehensive re-organization of intelligence and propaganda policies. Close contact between Japanese newspaper correspondents and officials of the Embassy and Consulates has been observed during 1941, and many Japanese news-papers in the U.S. are being pressed into service by the Embassy, the consulates and officials in Tokyo to assume intelligence duties previous-ly carried on by regular military and naval agents. At the same time, they are expected to function as instruments of propaganda.

As an example of this arrangement, when Fukuichi Fukumoto, the former New York representative of the Osaka Mainichi and Tokyo Nichi Nichi newspapers was ordered to return to Japan by his employers, the Embassy procured a recision of his orders and he was designated Washington representative of the Tokyo Nichi Nichi.

Most Japanese language newspapers in the U. S. appear to be conventional news organs with no more pro-Japanese bias than one would expect in view of their affiliations. Others, however, such as the NEW WORLD SUN DAILY NEWS and the JAPANESE AMERICAN NEWS, both of San Francisco, are strongly pro-Japanese, and their editorials, from time to time, severely criticize American domestic and foreign policy vis-a-vis the Japanese. Representatives of these two papers were particularly active in the Tokyo meetings mentioned above.

There is also a small category of radical Japanese newspapers published in this country, perhaps the most interesting of which is the DOHO, a communist organ in Los Angeles. The TAISHU weekly of Seattle, Washington, a one man proposition with no consistent editorial policy, would also be included in this category.

In conclusion it should be mentioned that in several instances where there have been both English and Japanese sections within a paper, two diametrically opposed points of view are expressed, that in English being either neutral or pro-American, whereas the Japanese language section is definitely pro-Japanese. The UTAH NIPPON of Salt Lake City, Utah, and the ROCKY NIPPON of Denver, Colorado, are perhaps the best examples of this dual editorial policy.

ORGANIZATIONS

Although many Japanese residents of the United States are leaving the country in anticipation of war, and many representatives and officials of Japanese commercial interests have been recalled or transferred South, the span of Japanese organizations across the United States continues to be useful in collecting intelligence and disseminating propaganda for Tokyo.

Commercial Interests

Normal business activities of Japanese commercial firms in this country are nation wide and until the advent of the National Defense Program, contacts of their employees were practically unlimited. Both the firms themselves and their directive heads are under the immediate control of the Embassy and the various consulates.

Until recent legislation forced their retrenchment or withdrawal there were sixty Japanese companies in New York City alone available for the collection of technical information as well as for the dissemination of propaganda. Chief among these were:

     Bank of Chosen (Korea)
     Bank of Taiwan (Formosa)
     Domei News Agency
     Japanese Army Ordnance Inspector's Office
     Japanese Chamber of Commerce
     Japanese Financial Commission
     Japanese Naval Inspector's Office
     Japanese Raw Silk Intelligence Bureau
     Mitsui and Co.
     Mitsubishi Shoji Kaisha, Ltd.
     Nippon Yusen Kaisha
     Okura and Co.
     Osaka Shosen Kaisha
     South Manchuria Railway Co.
     Sumitomo Bank, Ltd.
     Tokyo Commercial and Industrial Museum

Most of them, as well as other important ones not listed, maintain well staffed branch offices in other cities.

Such gigantic organizations as the Mitsui, Mitsubishi, Okura, and Sumitomo interests may be said without exaggeration to control the financial and economic life of Japan. They are all directly or indirectly subsidized by the Japanese Government and may be considered quasi-official in nature.

In connection with the intensification of Japanese Intelligence efforts in the Americas, it is worth noting that the Mitsubishi interests have been extremely active in the shipment of various metals, fuel and lubricating oils, concentrating particularly on scrap iron, heavy machinery, and machine tools. In addition, they are known to have collaborated with German interests in an attempt to corner the market on mercury at the expense of the United States.

Mitsubishi is one of the fourteen semi-official organizations specifically designated to collect and report intelligence information formerly sought by Tokyo through regular Military and Naval agents. Reports of ship and troop movements, arrangements of inspection trips for visiting Japanese officials to important American plants and military establishments and the collection of all available information about the National Defense effort are illustrations of the "extra curricula activities" carried on by this organization. The same general pattern holds true with respect to other Japanese business houses.

Since the freezing of funds in July of this year, all Japanese business houses in the United States are closing or continuing operations with a skeleton force.

Civic

By far the most important Japanese civic organization in the United States is the JAPANESE-AMERICAN CITIZENS' LEAGUE which is an outgrowth of the AMERICAN LOYALTY LEAGUE. It has a total membership of approximately 10,000 persons distributed among 51 individual chapters and grouped geographically into four regional councils which cover the Pacific Coast and extending inland as far as Arizona, Idaho, and Utah. Its alleged objective is to encourage better citizenship among Americans of Japanese ancestry. It also supports all movements designed to improve the status of the Japanese in the United States.

One section of this organization which warrants particular attention is the so-called KIBEI group. Representing approximately 6% of the total membership, these members must be considered as pro-Japanese in their ideas and affiliations. Although American born, they have been educated in Japan and ordinarily have little or no background of American culture or appreciation of our form of government.

Recent reports indicate that the JAPANESE-AMERICAN CITIZENS' LEAGUE flatly rejected an offer of subsidy from the CENTRAL JAPANESE ASSOCIATION, apparently for fear of loss of independence if it accepted financial aid from this source.

Religious

Japanese religious organizations in the U. S. embrace Buddhist and Shinto temples and Christian churches as well as affiliated social or welfare clubs and schools. The Buddhist and Shinto priests in the U. S. and Territory of Hawaii number over 350. In addition to serving as principals or teachers of Japanese Language Schools, most of them are Japanese consular agents. Inasmuch as strict supervision of religion has for centuries been a characteristic of Japanese governmental policy, it follows that both priests and teachers are to a considerable extent subject to orders from Tokyo or, what amounts to the same thing, from their religious superiors in Japan.

To appreciate fully the potentialities of these organizations as media for subversive activity, it should be noted first, that there are well over 100,000 Buddhists in the continental U. S. alone, and secondly, that every Japanese, no matter what his professed faith, is a Shintoist. Shintoism is commonly though somewhat erroneously referred to as a religion. In reality, it is defined by the Japanese Government as a patriotic code founded upon the worship of the imperial line and the mythological gods accredited with the creation of Japan.

The work of these priests involves travel along the West Coast of the U.S., throughout Hawaii and to Japan. Investigations of Japanese organizations suspected of subversive activity disclose that these priests frequently hold office in such suspect groups as the HOKUBEI ZAIGO SHOKO DAN (North American Reserve Officers Association) and the NICHIBEI KOGYO KAISHA (Nichibei Kinema Co.).

Affiliated with Buddhist and Shinto temples are Japanese Language Schools, welfare societies, young people's Buddhist societies, and Buddhist women's associations. They provide excellent resources for intelligence operations, have proved to be very receptive to Japanese propaganda, and in many cases have contributed considerable sums to the Japanese war effort.

Japanese Christian Churches are much less closely affiliated with the Japanese Government, and there is considerable evidence to indicate that their major concern outside of religious matters centers on improving Japanese-American relations and the restoration of peace in Eastern Asia. At the same time, it is true that some individuals and groups among Japanese Christians are working against the interests of this country. In this connection, the JAPANESE STUDENTS' CHRISTIAN ASSOCIATION in New York City, is reported to disseminate pro-Japanese propaganda among the Nisei in addition to carrying on its regular functions as a religious association.

Military

Of the many and varied types of Japanese organizations in the United States, by far the most active and subversive to the interests of this country are such military organizations as the NANKA TEIKOKU GUNYUDAN (Southern California War Veterans), Los Angeles, NIPPON KAIGUN KYOKAI (Japanese Naval Association), Los Angeles, SAKURA KAI (Patriotic Society), Los Angeles, HOKUBEI BUTOKU KAI (Military Virtue Society of North America), Alvarado, California, and the HOKUBEI HEIFKI GINUSHA KAI (Association of Japanese in North America Eligible for Military Duty), San Francisco.

These organizations are intensely nationalistic and until recently made heavy contributions to the Japanese War Chest. Members of the NANKA TEIKOKU GUNYUDAN, NIPPON KAIGUN KYOKAI, and SAKURA KAI are suspected of being either veterans of or reservists in the Japanese armed forces. They have co-operated closely with official Japanese Agencies in the United States and the arrest of Commander Tachibana disclosed that the last two organizations, together with the SUIKO SHA (Reserve Officers' Club) in Los Angeles, were supplying him with intelligence information to be sent to Tokyo.

-24-

Although their membership is drawn from a younger age group, such organizations as the HOKUBEI BUTOKU KAI and HOKUBEI HEIEKI GIYUSHA KAI are none the less loyal to Japanese principles, particularly to the expansionist program of the present military regime in Tokyo. In both of these organizations, internal friction has been noted and in those branches where the conservative element is dominant, there has been a tendency to de-emphasize military activities and in some cases to sever altogether affiliations with headquarters in Japan. On the other hand, where extremists have retained control, a marked increase in attendance to military sports, to local intelligence activities, and closer co-operation with the home government have been noted.

Many local branches of these organizations have changed their names during the last few months in order to avert suspicion. In the event of war between the United States and Japan, Japanese organizations of this general type are certain to be delegated important espionage and sabotage functions in the area where they now operate.

Cultural

Two of the most influential of the Japanese cultural organizations in the U. S. coming under the direct control of the Government in Tokyo are the JAPAN INSTITUTE in New York City, and the JAPANESE CULTURAL CENTER OF SOUTHERN CALIFORNIA at Los Angeles. Operating on extremely generous budgets they distribute propaganda of all kinds, sponsor lectures and demonstrations, and subsidize American and Japanese scholarship in Oriental studies. Many individuals associated with both organizations are known dangerous propagandists and espionage agents.

It is interesting to note that the JAPAN INSTITUTE is preparing to cease operations and early in December of this year began to destroy its records.

Of minor importance are such cultural groups as the FAR EASTERN INSTITUTES held every summer at different American colleges and universities, THE STUDENT INSTITUTE OF PACIFIC RELATIONS and the ZAIBEI NIPPON-JIN JISEKI HOZON KAI. The latter is a small group carrying on American historical research.

In March of 1941 the NICHIBEI KOGYO KAISHA of Los Angeles which is one of the most active propaganda - espionage organizations in the United States was reorganized under the name of the NICHIBEI KINEMA COMPANY, INC. Incorporated in December, 1937, it was originally designed as a front for the LITTLE TOKYO GAMBLING CLUB owned by Hideichi Yamatoda. At the present time, however, most of the control rests with officials of the CENTRAL JAPANESE ASSOCIATION of San Francisco, California, and the LOS ANGELES JAPANESE CHAMBER OF COMMERCE. Most of its officers are suspects and have wide affiliations with suspect organizations and firms. This organ-

-25-

ization acts as a distribution center for foreign and domestic motion
pictures and gramaphone records. It also co-operates closely with Tokyo
in arranging engagements for lecturers, theatrical troupes and musicians
along the West Coast and in Hawaii. As an indication of the importance
of its function, this organization's capital stock was increased from
$25,000 to $250,000 in March, 1940.

CONCLUSION

During the first week in December, large scale shifts in key diplomatic personnel from Canada and the United States to Mexico and Latin
America have taken place, and a mass exodus of Japanese residents is
under way. On December 1, 1941, the Consulate General on the West Coast
began to destroy its records, as did the Consulate General, the Japanese
Chamber of Commerce and the Japan Institute in New York City. Secret
codes and ciphers at the Japanese Embassy were burned on the night of
December 5, 1941.

Such organizations as the Japanese Raw Silk Intelligence Bureau,
the Silk Department of Mitsui & Co., Gunze Corporation, Asahi Corporation,
Japanese Cotton & Silk Trading Co., Hara & Co., Katakura & Co., Morimura
& Co., Arai & Co., and Shinyei & Co. closed on Saturday December 6, 1941,
and personnel of these commercial houses plan to leave this country
December 16 aboard the Tatuta Maru. The Japan Institute has announced
its closing date as December 9, 1941.

Although incomplete, the foregoing picture of Japanese intelligence
and propaganda activities during 1941 illustrates the extent of Tokyo's
effort to penetrate this Hemisphere. Current U.S.-Japanese relations
are not clearly defined. However, in anticipation of a possible crisis,
the FBI is prepared to take into custody and detain all persons whose
activities are inimical to the best interests of the United States.

To: All Naval Districts, FBI, MID, COI, State Dept.   B-7-J

NAVY DEPARTMENT
Office of Naval Intelligence
Washington, D. C.

CONFIDENTIAL

DECLASSIFIED BY *1678 RFP/AHR*   December 24, 1941
5/14/85

Subject: °JAPANESE TOKYO CLUB SYNDICATE, WITH INTERLOCKING AFFILIATIONS.

Note: Prepared by the Counter-Subversion Section, Office of Naval
Intelligence, from information received from various sources.

INTRODUCTION

Custodial Detention

With the sudden outbreak of hostilities between Japan and the
United States on December 7, 1941, a comprehensive program for the detention of enemy aliens was put into operation. Hundreds of known dangerous suspects were rounded up, official representatives of the Axis
Powers were put under surveillance or taken into custody, and Alien Enemy
Hearing Boards were appointed to inquire into the activities and loyalty
of the individuals concerned. Aided by their recommendations, the U. S.
Attorney General will decide whether an alien should be released uncon-
ditionally, paroled, or interned for the duration of the war.

Recent Japanese Activities in Latin America

Although handicapped by the detention of many of its key individuals, the Japanese Intelligence Network in this hemisphere continues
in operation. Recent reports have been received of suspicious movements
of Japanese in various parts of Latin America, particularly in Mexico.
On December 13th, one vessel of the Japanese fishing fleet, the ALERT,
which was captured off Costa Rica by a Navy Air Patrol, was found to be
carrying some 10,000 gallons of Diesel fuel oil. The ALERT, of American
registry, is partly owned and manned by Japanese. At the time of her
capture, it is believed she was headed for a rendezvous with an enemy
submarine or surface raider.

From Mexico have come numerous rumors that approximately five
thousand Japanese are congregating at some undetermined point in strategic
Baja California. In this connection, one hundred of a Japanese population
of six hundred in and around Ensenada, recently left the region in a ship
which had been anchored off the coast. Moreover, during the night of

CONFIDENTIAL

COPIES DESTROYED

8 JAN 1 6 1974

CONFIDENTIAL

December 10, 1941, all Japanese nationals living in Tijuana disappeared,
apparently because of a report that the Mexican Government was recruiting Chinese for their armed forces. Those Japanese who remain are observed
to be closely associated with Italians in the vicinity.

The Japanese practice of cloaking subversive operations with
"legitimate business fronts" exists in Mexico as well as in the United
States. Late in November, 1941, it was reported that Shuro YOSHIZAKI,
a button manufacturer of San Luis (near Mexicali) had installed short
wave radio transmitting and receiving sets in his factory and that all
of the Japanese in the surrounding district came there to listen. He is
also believed to be connected with radio station KEY in Yuma, Arizona,
and is considered potentially dangerous.

Strategically placed in Mexicali itself is one Yokoyama (or
Chokichi) TAKAHASHI, a Japanese barber who, it is reliably reported, is
a naval officer and also operates a short wave radio transmitter.

It also appears that the Japanese have placed Colonel Tadafumi
WAKI, I.J.A., in an important position within their Intelligence Network
in Mexico. Originally designated as the Assistant Military Attache of
the Japanese Embassy in Washington, Colonel WAKI landed in Mexico on
October 4, 1941, but there is no evidence that he ever came to this country. Reports believed to be reliable indicate that Colonel WAKI has in
his possession maps of strategic areas in the Hawaiian Islands. Similar
maps were reported to have been used by Japanese naval aviators in the
attack on Pearl Harbor.

Japanese activities are by no means limited to Mexico. In
Peru it is reported that the 30,000 or more Japanese living there are
highly organized and that, following anti-Japanese riots, they distributed rifles to all their establishments. Here in the United States there
has been reported a possible infiltration of Japanese espionage agents
through Cuban and Florida ports. A similar danger exists with regard to
the Pacific Coast and the Mexican border.

Since the outbreak of hostilities, Spanish Consuls in the U.S.
have taken over all official business for the Japanese Consulates. Japanese collaboration with Spanish Fascist groups has also been extensively
demonstrated in Mexico and the Philippine Islands. Among the organizations carrying on espionage and propaganda in the Philippines are LAS
MISIONES JESUITE (JESUITICAS ?) DEL JAPON, SOCIEDAD NIPO-FS ANCLA,
FALANGE EXTERIOR ESPANOLA, and LIGA ANTI-COMINTERN ESPANOLA.

Isolated as these instances may appear to be, they are actually integral parts of a comprehensive hemispheric intelligence program which the Japanese have been developing for well over a year. The
war has barely begun; undoubtedly before many more weeks elapse the
significance of the Japanese planning will be more actively and clearly
demonstrated.

CONFIDENTIAL

CONFIDENTIAL

Japanese Intelligence Machine in Western Hemisphere

Early in December, 1940, it became apparent that the Japanese were about to effect a comprehensive reorganization of their Intelligence Network in this hemisphere. At that time, soon after the arrival of Admiral Kichisaburo NOMURA as Ambassador, it was reported that the Japanese Government would intensify the espionage activities of their non-political agencies in this country, relaxing their former policy of "cultural enlightenment and propaganda."

In streamlining their Intelligence Machine the Japanese have been guided by two major considerations. In the first place, the totalitarian doctrines adopted by the Japanese military clique required as a corollary, some such system of "total intelligence" as the Germans have developed in recent years. This meant that the scope of propaganda, espionage, and sabotage activities and, in turn, the individuals and agencies responsible for that coverage had to be enlarged to include commercial, financial, industrial, and social spheres of action in addition to regular military, naval, and political operations.

Allied with this first consideration was the conviction, apparently shared by most members of the Japanese ruling clique, that Japan must act quickly to establish in the U.S. and Latin America a completely integrated intelligence organization which in time of war and the breaking off of official relations would be capable of taking over intelligence operations on a major scale.

Evidence of concrete steps taken to put this new Intelligence Machine into operation is available in numerous reports received during the Spring of 1941. From these it appears that the focal point of the Japanese espionage effort has been the determination of the total strength of the United States. In anticipation of possible open conflict with this country, Japan vigorously utilized every available agency to secure military, naval, and commercial information, paying particular attention to the West Coast, the Panama Canal, and the Territory of Hawaii. To this end, surveys were made of persons and organizations opposing U.S. intervention in the present European War, and close attention was paid to all anti-Jewish, Communist, Negro, and Labor Movements.

Although never fully developed, this new espionage organization was characterized by a high degree of decentralization. Before the outbreak of hostilities the activity of the military and naval section, which was divided into a number of different groups, was supplemented by the work of independent agents, and the general pattern included individuals, small groups, and commercial organizations functioning separately and energetically. In the background lay the Imperial Japanese Government, which until recently exercised direct control over both individuals and organizations through the Embassy and the Consulates.

-iii-

CONFIDENTIAL

CONFIDENTIAL

The new program provided for the utilization of citizens of
foreign extraction, aliens, Communists, Negroes, labor union members,
anti-Semites, and individuals having access to Government Departments,
experimental laboratories, factories, transportation facilities, and
governmental organizations of various kinds. Nisei (second generation)
Japanese and alien Japanese residents were not overlooked. Realizing,
however, that its nationals in this country would be subject to prosecution "in event of a slip," the Japanese Government advised extreme
caution in their employment.

It was also decided that, in the event of open hostilities,
Mexico would be Japanese intelligence nerve center in the Western Hem-
isphere, and in anticipation of war, U.S.-Latin American intelligence
routes were established. This network, covering Argentina, Brazil, Chile,
Peru, and the Central American countries, is designed to operate from
Mexico City and will, of necessity, involve extensive cooperation among
Japanese, German, and Italian intelligence organizations.

Outstanding among the espionage projects of the Japanese Army
and Navy were their comprehensive and systematic surveys of the entire
western coast of North America. Similar studies have been made of the
inland western mountain area. The total body of information covers
every conceivable military objective - railroads, highways, rivers, key
industries, terrain features, etc. Needless to state, military and
naval installations also received close attention.

Japanese propaganda in the U.S. has for the most part been
under the direction of a special division of the Japanese Foreign Office
in Tokyo. Local control was administered through the Embassy in Washington, D. C., as well as through the Consulates in key cities and Consular Agents in regions having Japanese communities. The media employed
ranged from radio broadcasts and printed matter to subsidized speakers
and underworld "pressure" groups. Private business firms, as well as
official and quasi-official agencies, have been particularly active in
propaganda dissemination. At the same time they rendered invaluable
service to the Japanese Army and Navy in the acquisition of technical
information.

The Tokyo Club Syndicate

It is believed that the organizations treated in this present
report offer an excellent illustration of the extremely complicated in-
terlockings which frequently characterize Japanese groups. What would
appear to be legitimate businesses and totally unrelated activities are
shown to have a definite community of interests as well as administrative
and financial connections. These inter-relationships are far too numerous
to be termed coincidental and are at the same time of a definitely subversive nature.

-iv-

CONFIDENTIAL

CONFIDENTIAL

The TOKYO CLUB of Los Angeles, with its chief subsidiaries, the NICHIBEI KOGYO KAISHA (NICHIBEI KINEMA CO.) of Los Angeles and the TOYO CLUB of Seattle, until very recently constituted the nucleus of a system of gambling clubs extending from Alaska to Tijuana and Mexicali, Mexico. Through extensive use of interlocking directorates and high-pressure methods, the sphere of control was gradually extended to numerous other individuals and organizations. Concomitantly there were developed or imposed elements of control by the Japanese Consulates and Japanese Army and Navy officials on the West Coast. The result has been to convert a widespread decentralized system of Japanese "clubs," labor organizations, and legitimate business groups into an important unit of the central Japanese Intelligence Network.

The organizations involved number six and are suspected of such diverse activities as dope smuggling, espionage, extortion, fishing, gambling, labor organization and control, murder, police bribery, propaganda, radio, and the operation of business "fronts," canneries, courier routes, and "post offices." Many of the individuals involved are classed as dangerous suspects and have interlocking affiliations among both these and other subversive organizations. There can be no doubt that most of the leaders have been and that many still continue to function as key operatives for the Japanese Government along the West Coast. Under present wartime conditions both they and their subordinates constitute a very serious threat to our internal security in the areas where they operate.

Case Histories and Schematic Diagrams

The attached case histories and diagrams provide essential detailed information with respect to both the individual organizations and their interlocking affiliations. The tabulation showing the leaders with their various activities (designated by "x" under the vertical headings) is based upon an analysis of various sources of information covering the period 1936-1941. Each mark may be interpreted as representing an affiliation of definite and durable nature; in those cases where the connection was spasmodic, of brief duration, or in any way uncertain, a question mark has been added alongside the "x".

The diagram on the TOKYO CLUB NETWORK is designed to portray the geographical distribution as well as the diversity of functions of the original TOKYO CLUB system. (Although a confidential report, dated 11/5/41, alleges that the TOKYO CLUB (sometimes called the LITTLE TOKYO SOCIAL CLUB) is no longer in existence, it is known that the TOYO CLUB in Seattle and many of the other branch clubs along the West Coast are still operating. It may be that the former leaders of the TOKYO CLUB have retired behind new "fronts" or that the TOYO CLUB has become the new headquarters.) The Los Angeles headquarters is shown in relationship to its subsidiaries in Alaska, Canada, and along the West Coast, as well as to other organizations with which it is affiliated through interlocking of officials or identity of interests.

-v-

CONFIDENTIAL

CONFIDENTIAL

   The diagram also indicates the flow of information and control though Mexico and thence to Japan and Latin America. In this connection there should be kept in mind the proximity of San Diego to Tijuana and of El Centro to Mexicali, all four places, along with Yuma, Nogales, El Paso, Laredo, and Brownsville, being well known Japanese "post offices" and local espionage centers. With the advent of hostilities it seems safe to anticipate further development and utilization of these U.S.-Latin American intelligence channels.

TOKYO CLUB
(Formerly at 317½ Jackson St.)
Los Angeles, California

Officers:

Present officers unknown.

Summary:

BACKGROUND: The TOKYO (or TOKIO) Club was first organized about 1919 by one Jitetsu YASUDA as the center of a Pacific Coast gambling syndicate. The central club, it is reported, used thugs and gunmen to "shake down" the individual clubs, but at the same time offered them no protection or other services other than financial loans. During the ensuing years of the syndicate's operation there was a succession of leaders or bosses of the TOKYO CLUB; if a boss were not killed off beforehand, he would voluntarily return to Japan at the expiration of a customary 2-3 year term. It is also reported that bosses of the CLUB were schooled for their jobs by first serving as president of the affiliated NICHIBEI KOGYO KAISHA (see case history).

KANEKICHI YAMAMOTO CASE (1937-1938): YAMAMOTO, head of the Seattle TOYO CLUB, was deported January 23, 1939, from Seattle after having spent approximately one year in the Federal (McNeil Island) Penitentiary on an income tax fraud conviction. It appears from investigation reports on the case that YAMAMOTO's guilt was suggested to Government officials by -one Hideichi YAMATODA, 1937 head of the TOKYO CLUB whose position was being threatened by YAMAMOTO. Tasaburo WAKATAKE, who had preceded YAMATODA as TOKYO CLUB president and who favored YAMAMOTO to succeed to the leadership of the syndicate, returned to Japan in February 1937; thus, when YAMAMOTO, too, was removed from the scene by his above-mentioned conviction, YAMATODA was left free to engineer a coup and assume full control of the club chain.

It was reported (March, 1938) that YAMAMOTO, for the sake of the future of the organization, had initiated efforts to patch up relations between the syndicate members, the TOKYO CLUB, and NICHIBEI KOGYO KAISHA. E. MORII of Vancouver, B. C., and S. YASUMURA of San Francisco acted as mediators, apparently motivated by the fear of what YAMAMOTO might report "to his principals in Japan."

YAMATODA KIDNAPING CONSPIRACY CASE (1938 -): Having once gained the upper hand in the TOKYO CLUB and its affiliates, Hideyoshi YAMATODA was unable to maintain the strong and widespread organization which his predecessors had ruled through the use of gangster methods. Accordingly the syndicate broke down into separate clubs, the TOKYO CLUB remaining

largest and most powerful and still controlling those clubs located at
El Centro, Guadalupe, Visalia, Lodi, and elsewhere. In addition
YAMATODA separated the JAPANESE THEATRICAL ASSOCIATION AND FILM EXCHANGE
(see NICHIBEI KOGYO KAISHA case history) from the activities of the
TOKYO CLUB. Since 1938 YAMATODA has posed as a film executive, using
the NICHIBEI KOGYO KAISHA as his headquarters and front.

In the Fall of 1938 a group of New York Japanese gamblers, headed
by one Kamenosuke YUGE, united with a group of West Coast Japanese
gamblers, led by Mitsui TAGAWA, and formed a conspiracy to oust
YAMATODA, seize control of the TOKYO CLUB and the JAPANESE THEATRICAL
ASSOCIATION AND FILM EXCHANGE, and, apparently, to rebuild the original
TOKYO CLUB and unite it with the New York gambling hook-up. They obtained
the assistance of certain Los Angeles police officers and in September,
1938, managed to have YAMATODA arrested. YAMATODA later asserted that
the police thereupon ordered him to leave Los Angeles and return to Japan
within three months.

In the meantime YUGE and his associates had united with one Richard
YOSHIDA and taken over the Japanese gambling club at El Centro, California,
ousting Ryotaro ITAHASHI, who had operated the club some 10 years "as a
lieutenant of the TOKYO CLUB." They also obtained the aid of the El Centro
police chief, one J. Sterling OSWALT, in making the attempt to reconstruct
the original gambling syndicate.

In December, 1938, there occurred a kidnaping from the El Centro
jail in which YAMATODA was the victim and YUGE, YOSHIDA, OSWALT, and
others the kidnapers. Taken eventually to Mexico, YAMATODA escaped,
gathered his friends to his aid, and returned to Los Angeles to press
charges against the kidnapers. As a result of this charge, YUGE, OSWALT,
and eight others were indicted by the Los Angeles Federal Grand Jury
(9/6/39). The trial was never completed, owing to YAMATODA's flight
to Japan in April, 1941, to avoid his prosecution for murder which was
scheduled to follow, but did result in YUGE, among others, being convicted
of conspiracy and confined to McNeil Island Penitentiary.

CONCLUSION: The present status of the TOKYO CLUB in Los Angeles
and its affiliated clubs and activities along the West Coast of the
United States and in Alaska, British Columbia, Mexico, China, and Japan,
is undetermined. However, in view of the extremely widespread and diversified nature of its operations in the past few years and, more particularly, in the light of recently intensified Japanese espionage activities, it is deemed advisable to maintain a strict watch on the chief
individuals formerly identified with subject club (inasmuch as they may
resort to new "fronts" for their operations) and to investigate further
their numerous interlocked connections with such subversive activities
as canneries, fishing, espionage, propaganda, sabotage, etc.

(See schematic diagram, copy attached.)

                     -2-

CONFIDENTIAL

Former Personnel and Members:

COUGHLIN, Ray T. - Sacramento (Calif.) attorney (White American) who reportedly managed the legal aspects of the establishment of the TOKYO CLUB syndicate.

FURUSAWA, (Mrs.) Koko - Class "A" suspect, wife of Dr. Takashi FURUSAWA who is likewise an "A" suspect. She is reported to have formerly been the wife of a Japanese naval officer (in Japan), whom she left to become a maid in a Japanese inn. Subsequently she came to the U. S. to work as a waitress in the Lil' Tokyo section of Los Angeles, and while there helped Takashi FURUSAWA through college, marrying him when he became established.

To date Mrs. FURUSAWA is the only woman member of the extremely suspect SAKURA KAI, and, with her husband, was a member of the group who founded the equally suspect KAIGUN KYOKAI. She holds office in the AIKOKU FUJIN KAI in California, a popular society for women, and is also a director of the SOUTHERN CALIFORNIA ASSOCIATION OF JAPANESE WOMEN'S CLUBS. Her widespread activities among Japanese naval and army officers warrant her being classified as an espionage and "post office" suspect.

HIRAO, Kane - Class "B" suspect, in frequent communication with Kanekichi YAMAMOTO and associated with him in the gambling syndicate from 1926 to 1938; thenceforth (after YAMAMOTO'S deportation) until 1940, he continued his affiliation in the TOKYO CLUB. Was tried and convicted for illegal shipment of arms to Shanghai in 1939-1940.

ICHIKAWA , Hakui - Class "A" suspect, chief lieutenant of Kanekichi YAMAMOTO at the TOYO CLUB in Seattle prior to the latter's deportation in 1938. In 1937 he became active head of the club. Did much traveling and had repeated contacts with suspects "George" Naokazu ISHIBASHI, Dr. Benjamin Masayoshi TANAKA, OHTA, Takeyaki SASAKI, and consular and military-naval representatives.

Some time later he became proprietor of the STAR POOL HALL (517 Jackson Street, Seattle), reputed to be another gambling place. Is believed to have been behind the gun smuggling attempt of Kane HIRAO, and in turn probably had YAMAMOTO behind him at the time.

Most recent reports on ICHIKAWA (9/5/41 and 10/22/41) indicate that he has been extremely outspoken in his criticism of the appeasement efforts of certain Japanese statesmen which have prevented Japan's southward expansion. These same reports suggest that he hoped to return to Japan in the near future, that he had sold his pool parlor and had sent considerable sums to a former TOYO CLUB leader (probably Takeyaki SASAKI) at the KUMAMOTOYA HOTEL, Yokohama.

CONFIDENTIAL

MARUYAMA, Norio - Nothing is known other than the fact that he was one of the officers who assumed control of the TOKYO CLUB syndicate when Hideyoshi YAMATODA took over its management in 1937.

MATSUMOTO, Ken (or Tai) - A lieutenant of Kanekichi YAMAMOTO in the TOYO CLUB and interested with him in the fishing-cannery business and labor contracting. May possibly be the Ken MATSUMOTO who is presently national vice president of the J.A.C.L.

MORI, Yatsuma - Closely affiliated with Kanekichi YAMAMOTO and the TOKYO CLUB chain through his position (1936) as official of the Los Angeles TOKYO CLUB, manager of LITTLE TOKYO CLUB, and director of the NICHIBEI KOGYO KAISHA (see case history of the latter).

MORII, Eitsuji - Alien, Class "A" suspect. Head of the JAPANESE CANADIAN AMUSEMENT SOCIETY, a part of the TOKYO CLUB syndicate, and reputedly leader of the Japanese in Vancouver. He was for a long time associated with Kanekichi YAMAMOTO in the TOKYO CLUB and NICHIBEI KOGYO KAISHA, does extensive traveling, and is classified as an espionage suspect.

OHTA, —— - Early in 1939 he was reported to control Japanese gambling in Imperial Valley, California, and to be endeavoring to re-open the TOKYO CLUB in Los Angeles. (OHTA was supposed to have "fixed" the police to such an extent that he had complete control of Japanese gambling throughout Southern California.)

SMALLPAGE, Lafayette - Stockton (California) attorney (White American) who participated in the organization of the TOKYO CLUB as legal adviser.

SUZUKI, Makoto - Class "B" suspect who has posed as a member of the Japanese fishing colony at Terminal Island. He is suspected of being a Japanese agent and of having recently traveled in South America.

TOMINAGA, Keisuke - Aide to Hideyoshi YAMATODA in the TOKYO CLUB (1937-) and also a contact of Kanekichi YAMAMOTO (1936). Was for some time suspected of participation in a dope smuggling ring as "delivery man" for the CLUB.

WAKATAKE, Tasaburo - Nothing known other than his early leadership in subject syndicate. Is believed to have returned to Japan.

YAMAMOTO, Kanekichi (or Kinpachi) - Head of the Seattle TOYO CLUB and one of the heads of the NICHIBEI KOGYO KAISHA (see case history) who was slated to assume leadership of the TOKYO CLUB system, under the sponsorship of WAKATAKE, as stated above in the summary. This plan

CONFIDENTIAL

-4-

CONFI~~X~~TIAL

was thwarted by the income tax case which resulted in YAMAMOTO's imprisonment and subsequent deportation in 1939. He was also interested in the fishing-cannery business and the organization of related labor unions (see case histories on the ALASKA CANNERY WORKERS UNION and the CANNERY WORKERS AND FARM LABORERS UNION). At present he is reported to be in Shanghai, probably active in the Chinese-Manchurian clubs of subject organization for which SASAKI used to be the contact.

YAMATODA, Hideyoshi (or Hideichi) - Class "A" suspect and for some time (1938-1941) the "boss" of the TOKYO CLUB syndicate and the closely affiliated NICHIBEI KOGYO KAISHA (see case history). In addition he was a member of the dangerous SAKURA KAI and maintained intimate contacts among Japanese consular and military-naval officials. It should also be noted that the TOKYO CLUB's murder trade was quite brisk during the period of YAMATODA's leadership; he himself is suspected of having committed some of the crimes (see Summary above).

Following his kidnaping and the unfinished trial which resulted from it, YAMATODA fled to Japan via Mexico and is presently being sought there by the U. S. Department of State.

YASUMURA, S. - Nothing is known save his membership in subject club.

(For further information on above individuals see schematic diagram and supplement on TOYO CLUB.)

CONFIDENTIAL

TOKYO CLUB - Supplement

TOYO CLUB

Summary:

The club which ranked second, next in importance to the TOKYO CLUB
in Los Angeles, was the TOYO CLUB of Seattle. While posing as a gambling establishment, as have the parent and other sister organizations,
this club actually carried on such "extra-curricula" activities as dope
smuggling, police "fixing," espionage, cooperation with labor unions
in fishing-cannery interests, etc.

It is reliably reported that subject club was established by a
Japanese named SASAKI (probably Takeyaki, alias Tosayama, SASAKI, see
pp. 3,5 of this report), who returned to Japan a number of years ago
to become the gambling syndicate's representative there as well as
in North China and Manchoukuo. After SASAKI's departure the club was
operated by Kanekichi YAMAMOTO, who employed Seiichi "Sam" TAKENO (since
deceased), Hakui ICHIKAWA (see p. 3), and one J. NAKATSU--all of whom
are suspects--to assist him. When YAMAMOTO left the U. S. in 1939,
after serving his prison term, his three assistants inherited the
club and its business, ICHIKAWA eventually becoming the most active
of the group. Shoichi NOJIMA, son-in-law of NAKATSU and a Class "A"
suspect, does the bookkeeping for the club.

In connection with TAKENO, who died August 17, 1941, it should be
noted that he resided with a Japanese woman known as Mrs. S. FURUMOTO
and, with her, operated the NEW CENTRAL CAFE of Seattle.

Listed under Personnel are names of a few of the Japanese who were,
at one time or another in recent years, identified with the TOYO CLUB.
ONI also has in its possession a comprehensive list of the contacts of
Kanekichi YAMAMOTO, acquired at the time of his arrest in 1937. Many
of them are Class "A" suspects.

Personnel:

ASAKURA, Makutaro - Class "A" suspect, proprietor of the STACY
STREET TAVERN (see appended list of Restaurants, Cafes, etc.). Entered
the United States illegally but has been here too long for deportation.
Was at one time connected with the TOYO CLUB as dealer both at the club
and in logging camps.

FUKAO, "Paul" Kenichi - Class "A" suspect and a henchman of
Kanekichi YAMAMOTO. In January, 1941, was reported to be employed by
the TOYO CLUB as lottery ticket salesman and driver of the car operated
by the club to transport Japanese crews back and forth between ship and
club.

CONFIDENTIAL

CONFIDENTIAL

HASHIMOTO, "Hashi" - Class "A" suspect.

IMAIZUME, Yasugi - Class "A" suspect.

KIKAGAWA, Sho (Tadashi or Masa).

KOMATSU, Ryo (Riyo) - Class "A" suspect.

KONO, Junsaku - Class "A" suspect and special henchman of Hakui ICHIKAWA. In February, 1941, was reported to be employed as a dealer at the gambling tables of the STAR POOL HALL (owned by ICHIKAWA).

MORIMIZU, "Tony" Rinta - Japanese citizen, Class "A" suspect. Was, in January, 1941, president of the PUGET SOUND VEGETABLE GROWERS ASSOCIATION and considered to be one of the three most influential Japanese in the White River Valley area. In 1938, 1939, and 1941 was president of the JAPANESE ASSOCIATION of Summer, Washington. Was also active in the KUMAMOTO PREFECTURAL ASSOCIATION in 1939 and 1940.

NAGAMATSU, Henry Heiji - (See case history on JAPANESE CANNERIES.)

NAKATSU, Jiutaro (alias Jintaro, Gintaro, etc.) - Class "A" suspect. Subject was active in the 1937 Sumo Tournament at Seattle and for some time gunman for the TOYO CLUB and private bodyguard to Y.MADA (once head of said club). In March, 1941, was still a leader in sumo groups and an adviser of the KUMAMOTO OVERSEAS ASSOCIATION. It is believed his son-in-law has returned to Japan, but NAKATSU continues to participate in the management of the TOYO CLUB.

OBATA, K. - Class "A" suspect and operator of a restaurant located at 604 Main Street, Seattle (probably the ROSE CAFE). During fishing-canning season OBATA has worked as foreman at an Alaskan Cannery. It should also be noted that it was at his residence that Kanekichi YAMAMOTO went into hiding from U. S. Treasury authorities in 1937.

OGAMI, Teiichi - Japanese citizen, Class "A" suspect. He is proprietor of the OGAMI SACK CO., which handles second hand gunny sacks and is located at 809 Maynard Avenue, Seattle. As early as 1935 and 1936, OGAMI was known to be an intimate of Kanekichi YAMAMOTO and of other Japanese suspects, Sataro MINAMI (deceased) among them. He has also been active in Japanese activities in the Seattle region. In 1938 he was one of the vice presidents of the suspect HOKUBEI BUTOKU KAI. In 1939 he was treasurer and in 1940 vice president of the OKAYAMA PREFECTURAL ASSOCIATION. Was also one of the Japanese who were honored with a wooden sake cup by the Japanese Foreign Office on the occasion of the 2600th Anniversary Celebration held in Tokyo in November, 1940.

CONFIDENTIAL

CONFIDENTIAL

This past year he has been reported as having donated money to the
SEATTLE JAPANESE CHAMBER OF COMMERCE, the HOKUBEI BUTOKU K.I, the BUDDHIST
CHURCH, and to a local kendo club.

The U. S. Immigration Service reports that he entered the United
States in 1921. Business associates state that he is of good reputation
and not outspokenly pro-Japanese.

SAITO, (Dr.) Moriya - Class "A" suspect and a dentist with office
at 670 Jackson Street, Seattle. In February, 1941, he was reported to
operate gambling tables at the NIPPON POOL HALL on Main Street, Seattle
(see appended list of Restaurants, Cafes, etc.) and to have been intimate with Kanekichi YAMAMOTO.

Subject may possibly be the "Mori SAITO" of Seattle who is listed
as a member of the suspect HINOMARU K.I.

SAKINO, Bunro (Fumiro) - Class "A" suspect, editor of "THE COAST
TIMES" newspaper of Portland, and secretary in 1940 of both the
JAPANESE ASSOCIATION of Portland and the suspect SOKOKU KAI. Is an
intimate of "George" Naoichi ISHIBASHI (see case history on JAPANESE
CANNERIES) as well as of Hakui ICHIKAWA (see above). SAKINO was one
of 17 Japanese residents in 13 ND who were honored with wooden sake
cups by the Japanese Foreign Office on the occasion of the 2600th
Anniversary Celebration held in Tokyo in November, 1940.

SAKAMOTO, Tamizo - (See case history on JAPANESE CANNERIES).

SUYETANI, "Roy" Kiyoshi - Class "A" suspect, listed in the Seattle
City Directory as a chauffeur. Was, for some time, bodyguard and gunman for Kanekichi YAMAMOTO and other leaders of the TOYO CLUB. His
wife (?) is connected with the NIPPON POOL HALL referred to above, and
he himself is presently reported to be head of subject club and "fixer"
for the local Japanese community.

TATEOKA (TAKEOKA), Hisashi· - Class "A" suspect.

CONFIDENTIAL

NICHIBEI KOGYO KAISHA (Japanese-American Theatrical Company)
NICHIBEI KINEMA CO., INC.
NICHIBEI KINEMA KAISHA
GREAT FUJI (FUJII) THEATER

Headquarters: Yokohama, Japan

U. S. Main Branch: 201 N. San Pedro Street
                    Los Angeles, California

Officers:

KUMAMOTO, Shunten (Shinsuke) – President

NARUMI, Jutaro   – Vice President

HASUIKE, George Susumu   – Vice President

UYEDA, Yaozo   – Treasurer

KIDA, Masataro   – Treasurer

TSUDA, Noboru   – Director

KIMURA, Muneo   – Managing Director

LUKAEDA, Katsuma   – Auditor

BAN, Takeshi (Rev., Dr.)   – Auditor

Summary:

Subject company was first incorporated in December, 1937, and was originally controlled as a front for the LITTLE TOKYO GAMBLING CLUB, owned by Hideichi YAMATODA. After the latter's kidnapping in 1937, however, the leader of the Japanese community advised him that they believed the operation of subject company was a matter of vital interest to the community, and through pressure brought upon him, his interest in the company was reduced to two shares of a total of fifty. The remaining shares are held chiefly by officers in the CENTRAL JAPANESE ASSOCIATION and the LOS ANGELES JAPANESE CHAMBER OF COMMERCE.

Articles of incorporation, dated April 22, 1939, show the purpose of the company to be the buying and selling, and importing and exporting of still and motion pictures, films, and musical records; the contracting of players and actors; the booking of lectures, plays, and musical acts at theatrical places.

CONFIDENTIAL

This organization has been distributing highly nationalistic Japanese films which portray Japanese expansion in Asia and the might of the Japanese Army. It is also believed to have booked lectures which praised Japanese customs as being superior to American.

On March 30, 1940, capitalization was increased from $25,000 to $250,000. Subject organization was reorganized March 5, 1941, and its name changed to NICHIBEI KINEMA COMPANY, INC. It is also known under the title JAPANESE THEATRICAL ASSOCIATION, INC., this being the name to which newsreels are consigned by the Yokohama headquarters.

Personnel:

 BAN, (Rev., Dr.) Takeshi - Japanese citizen, Class "A" suspect. In 1938 was reported to be a Doctor of Divinity, head of the JAPANESE SOCIETY OF RELIGIOUS EDUCATION, and minister of the CONGREGATIONAL CHURCH. A news article in a Los Angeles Japanese paper (September, 1938) described BAN as having been an Imperial Army Officer during the Russo-Japanese War and as having won the Seventh Order of the Rising Sun for outstanding conduct. At about the same time (i.e. September, 1938) he reportedly joined the suspect HOKUBEI HEIEKI GIMUSHA KAI. For the past several years he has been active in the leadership of the TAIHEIYO BUNKA KYOIKU KAI (Pacific Cultural Education Society) and at present is reported to be president of this organization. Recent information also shows him to hold office in the suspect NANKA TEIKOKU GUNYU-DAN.

Since 1937 and up to the present time subject has been exceedingly active as a propagandist. He has lectured and has directed the distribution of nationalistic motion picture films along the West Coast and inland as far as Colorado. (In 1939, it was reported that he received subsidies from the JAPANESE TRADE PROMOTION BUREAU of the Ministry of Commerce for his propaganda activities.) In this connection it might be noted that the automobile which he used for his travels in 1938 carried, in addition to films and projector, all the necessary equipment for taking and developing motion pictures.

Because of the nature of his activities and the wide area over which he operates he is classified by ONI as an espionage suspect.

HASUIKE, Susumu - Citizenship unknown. Class "A" suspect. In 1940 subject was reported to be owner of the THREE STAR PRODUCE COMPANY (932 Wall Street, Los Angeles, Calif.), also to be a member of the suspect SAKURA KAI, and to have donated $1,000 to the equally suspect NIPPON KAIGUN KYOKAI. In addition he has been very prominent in Japanese circles in Los Angeles and holds, or has held, office in several Japanese organizations other than those mentioned above.

CONFIDENTIAL

KIDA, Masataro - A native of Shizuoka Prefecture, and probably a Japanese citizen, Class "B" suspect, occupation restaurant owner. In addition to his affiliation with the NICHIBEI KOGYO KAISHA, in which he is also a stockholder, KIDA is president of one of the Los Angeles Buddhist kendo organizations.

KIMURA, Muneo - Native of Yamaguchi Prefecture and probably a Japanese citizen, Class "B" suspect. As business manager of the NICHIBEI KOGYO KAISHA, KIMURA has made frequent "business trips" to the Hawaiian Islands and was one of the group of Japanese, lead by Shunten KUMAMOTO, who went to Japan in 1940, ostensibly to engage a theatrical troupe for a U. S. tour. This troupe arrived in San Francisco on November 13, 1940, traveled extensively, and reportedly made numerous contacts for espionage purposes.

KIMURA has been reported as a member of both the SAKURA KAI and the NIPPON KAIGUN KYOKAI, but his affiliation with these organizations has not yet been confirmed.

KUMAMOTO, Shunten (Shinsuke) - Citizenship unknown, Class "A" suspect. During the past three years has been exceedingly active in Japanese organizations in the Los Angeles area. He is known to be auditor and director of the CULTURAL CENTER OF SOUTHERN CALIFORNIA and is also connected with the Los Angeles branch of the JAPAN TOURIST BUREAU, both of which organizations are Japanese propaganda agencies. Is an ex-president of the JAPANESE CENTRAL ASSOCIATION at Los Angeles, as well as of the LOS ANGELES JAPANESE CHAMBER OF COMMERCE, and has for some time been influential in the suspect SAKURA KAI.

His business concern, known as the S. K. PRODUCE CO., is reportedly backed by Keisuke TOMINAGA and the TOKYO CLUB (see case history on TOKYO CLUB).

In the latter part of 1940, KUMAMOTO visited Japan with Muneo KIMURA for the purpose of organizing a theatrical troupe (allegedly espionage agents) and also to participate in the 2600th Anniversary Celebration. It is believed that at this latter convention he represented the CENTRAL JAPANESE ASSOCIATION, and, furthermore, that during the six months he was abroad he made an extensive study of conditions in various sections of Japan, Reports on the convention in Tokyo indicate that KUMAMOTO had entre to the Japanese Foreign Office, probably as member of its "non-official" staff, and that he participated in round table discussions sponsored by the Ministries of Foreign Affairs and Overseas Affairs.

KUKAEDA, Katsuma - Native of Kumamoto Prefecture, Class "A" suspect. He is a prominent attorney-at-law and pro-Japanese propagandist who has, in the past, been closely associated with the Japanese Con-

CONFIDENTIAL

sulate in Los Angeles. For the past eight years he has been active in
Japanese nationalistic organizations and has, at the same time, been in
contact with Japanese Navy and Army Officers.

In reward for his services to the Japanese Empire he was recently decorated by the Emperor and honored with a letter of commendation
from the Foreign Office.

In 1933 MUKAEDA served as president of the FEDERATED JAPANESE
ASSOCIATIONS OF SOUTHERN CALIFORNIA; in 1935 was president of the CENTRAL
JAPANESE ASSOCIATION and a member of the organizing committee of the
SOCIETY FOR ORIENTAL STUDIES of Claremont, California; in 1939 he was
identified with both the SAKURA KAI and the JAPANESE CULTURAL CENTER OF
SOUTHERN CALIFORNIA. It is also known that for some years past he has
been contact man on the Pacific Coast for the JAPAN INSTITUTE (formerly
of New York City). and that he is also a supporting member of the NIPPON
KAIGUN KYOKAI. When the Japanese spy Lt. Comdr. Itaru TACHIBANA, IJN,
was arrested by the FBI in the Spring of 1941, MUKAEDA'S name was mentioned in the material seized.

While president of the CENTRAL JAPANESE ASSOCIATION, subject
established a new department with the name "JOHO-BU" (Intelligence
Bureau), the main activities of which were to procure speakers to lecture
on Japanese culture and, with the cooperation of the Los Angeles branch
of the JAPAN TOURIST BUREAU, the JAPANESE CONSULATE in Los Angeles, and
the KOKUSAI BUNKA SHINKO KAI (Society for the Promotion of International
Cultural Relations) in Tokyo, to invite prominent Japanese lecturers to
this country. Professor Ken NAKAZAWA, of the University of Southern
California, assisted in this project.

Within the last several months it has become apparent that
MUKAEDA has been cooperating with the CENTRAL JAPANESE ASSOCIATION of
Los Angeles in attempting to gain control of the JAPANESE AMERICAN
CITIZENS LEAGUE in Southern California. Fred TAYAMA, president of the
Los Angeles branch of the J.A.C.L., is reported to be heavily indebted
to MUKAEDA and to one Gongoro NAKAMURA (Class "A" suspect), which fact
puts these latter two individuals in a position to dictate the policy
and action of the local J.A.C.L. through TAYAMA.

NARUMI, Jutaro - Native of Wakayama Prefecture, and believed
to be a Japanese citizen, Class "A" suspect. For some time he has been
manager of the ASIA CO. in Los Angeles. In 1935 was treasurer of the
LOS ANGELES JAPANESE CHAMBER OF COMMERCE; for the past several years he
has been closely associated with the SAKURA KAI and has been a regular
member of the NIPPON KAIGUN KYOKAI. In 1939 he was known to be collecting donations for the Japanese war fund, and in 1940 represented the
SUMO KYOKAI in the local 2600th Anniversary Celebration of the Japanese
Empire, held in Los Angeles.

CONFIDENTIAL   -12-

CONFIDENTIAL

TSUDA, Noboru - Native of Fukushima Prefecture, and probably a Japanese citizen, Class "A" suspect. Has been a resident of the United States since 1906, but has made many trips to Japan in the interim and has five sons residing there. Serves as manager and is one of the chief stockholders of the GREAT FUJI (FUJII) THEATER. For some years past he has been very active in Japanese nationalistic organizations and, among other things, was in charge of some of the various Japanese theatrical troupes which came from Japan and toured Hawaii and the West Coast.

In addition to these activities, TSUDA is a regular member of the suspect NIPPON KAIGUN KYOKAI and is considered by ONI to be a potential Japanese agent.

UYEDA, Yaozo - Subject himself is treasurer of the NICHIBEI KOGYO KAISHA, and his wife, Yoshiye C. UYEDA, is listed as a member of the suspect NIPPON KAIGUN KYOKAI. (It is believed that subject is actually a member of the latter organization but attempts to hide the fact by having his wife pay his dues.)

Branches:

El Centro	IWABASHI, Yoshitaro	San Francisco	MISTURA, Sadakichi (Class "B" suspect) MIZUNO, Hiroshi (Class "B" suspect)
Guadalupe	ITO, Setsuji		
Lodi	YAMADA, Tomosaburo	Suisun	ISHIBASHI, Chokichi
Fismo	HAMAI, Otoichi (Class "B" suspect)	Vallejo	NAKATA, Manabu
Sacramento	SERA, Katsutaro NAKASHIMA, Kenkichi	Visalia	HAGIHARA, Yonekichi

(All branches are in California, officers as of 1938)

CONFIDENTIAL

CONFIDENTIAL

JAPANESE CANNERIES
    Alaska and West Coast

Owners and Operators:

ISHIBASHI, "George" Naoichi   - Portland, Oregon.

NAGAMATSU, "Henry" Heiji   - Seattle, Washington.

NISHIMURA, "George" Yasukichi   - Seattle, Washington;
                                       and Yokohama, Japan.

SAKAMOTO, Tamizo   - Seattle, Washington.

TAKAHASHI, Chas. Theodore (Takeo)   - Seattle, Washington.

TAKASAKI, Yaichi (Yoichi)   - Kingston, Washington.

Summary:

    A comprehensive survey of Japanese activity in the U. S. fishing-
canning industry has not yet been made. This present report is merely
an account of such circumstances as were revealed through a study of
the TOKYO CLUB syndicate.

    Reports on hand indicate that Alaskan canneries, whether float-
ing or shore-based, American- or foreign-owned, employ a considerable
amount of Japanese capital and labor. Those modern floating canneries
based in Japan and their companion fishing fleets are, of course, composed entirely of alien personnel and operate in a manner which permits
of very little surveillance on the part of American investigative agencies.
Shore-based canneries, on the other hand, are often American-owned but
employ laborers of foreign birth or ancestry.

    With regard to occupational activity these individuals may be
classified as (1) fishermen; (2) "inside" cannery laborers; and (3) super-
intendents, foremen, carpenters, machinists, etc. In 1939 the above-
mentioned cannery laborer group numbered some 9,680 workers, of whom
the major portion were native Alaskans and Filipinos. The Japanese a-
mong them totaled 685 (about 7%), of whom approximately 300 were believed to have returned to Japan at the conclusion of the season. A
second detailed check, initiated August, 1941, and still unfinished,
shows the proportion of Japanese to be slightly over 6%, or just about
what it was in 1939. This percentage is composed almost equally of
U. S. citizens and aliens.

CONFIDENTIAL

CONFIDENTIAL

American leaders in the fishing-canning industry have endeavored to provide ONI with full information of this situation, stressing the fact that the Japanese involved are scattered in definitely strategic places throughout Alaska, and that there exists the possibility that some of these Japanese, particularly those who go back and forth to Japan, may have Japanese military or naval connections. These allegations are substantiated by reliable reports which specifically refer to suspicious land, sea, and aerial activity in strategic areas by Japanese military or naval officers and others supposedly affiliated with fishing-cannery interests.

Keeping in mind this general background of the situation, one must regard as significant the following data on subject cannery owners and operators and their affiliations. While there is not sufficient evidence to permit of any blanket or categorical conclusions, the information does appear to suggest an entirely logical connection between the Japanese fishing-cannery interests and other known subversive individuals and organizations. It is hoped that further investigation will clarify the affiliations and reveal any major Japanese subversion hook-up which may exist.

Personnel:

ISHIBASHI, "George" Naoichi - Alien, Class "A" suspect. In 1935 was believed to be leader of narcotic smuggling gang as well as a Japanese intelligence agent. Mail communication with Lt. Comdr. Shigeru FUJII of IJN. In 1941 reported as labor contractor, restaurant owner, and head of KOSHIN CLUB, Portland gambling house affiliated with the TOKYO CLUB chain. Active in Buddhist circles. Intimate with Dr. "Benjamin" Masayoshi TANAKA, Portland Japanese intelligence chief and president of suspect SOKOKU KAI; also close to Kanekichi YAMAMOTO and others of the Seattle TOYO CLUB group.

NAGAMATSU, "Henry" Heiji - Alien, Class "A" suspect. Head of H. H. NAGAMATSU AND COMPANY, cannery contractors, also president-manager of the NORTH COAST IMPORTING COMPANY. Was reported to be a frequent visitor of Kanekichi YAMAMOTO and to be intimately associated with him in cannery union affairs.

NISHIMURA, "George" Yasukichi - Alien, Class "A" suspect. Cannery contractor and operator (plant located at Koguang, Bristol Bay, Alaska) and exporter-importer (owner G. Y. NISHIMURA AND COMPANY, Seattle). Leader of Seattle Japanese. Maintains home in Yokohama to which he used to make annual trips. Heavy contributor to Japanese War Fund. Mail communication (1936-37) with Kanekichi YAMAMOTO, Tamizo SAKAMOTO, and Hakuta FUJIOKA. (All three of these are suspects, YAMAMOTO and SAKAMOTO being active leaders in the TOKYO CLUB chain (see case history

CONFIDENTIAL

on same), as well as having cannery interests; and FUJIOKA being cannery superintendent for NISHIMURA.) In addition, NISHIMURA was in 1936-37 closely affiliated with Dr. Seiji KANDA (or KONDA), Takuzo SUZUKI, and Koji UCHIDA, Japanese espionage agents who posed as "fishing school instructors" or KYODO SUISAN KAISHA agents while undertaking Alaskan surveys. In April, 1938, was investigated by U. S. Treasury Department on income tax charges, and is believed to have left the country.

SAKAMOTO, Tamizo - Class "A" suspect. Professional gambler, associated with G. Y. NISHIMURA AND COMPANY cannery (manager; also has financial interest). Prior to 1933 was affiliated with ISHIBASHI and SASAKI in narcotic smuggling. Since 1936 intimate with Lt. Comdr. Shigeru FUJII (IJN; now deceased) and Kanekichi YAMAMOTO. Is reported also as operating a card room in the basement of the L. C. Smith Building, Seattle, said project being backed by the TOYO CLUB (TOKYO CLUB chain) or by YAMAMOTO personally.

TAKAHASHI, Charles Theodore (Takeo) - American-born, Class "A" suspect. Wealthy head of C. T. TAKAHASHI COMPANY, an export-import firm dealing mostly in lumber and scrap metal and formerly known as the ORIENTAL TRADING COMPANY. (Same firm is sometimes called the CHINA IMPORT AND EXPORT COMPANY, probably with the intention of hiding its Japanese ownership.) Also head of RESILIENT MATTER, INC., and C. T. CONTRACTORS, INC., the latter supplying labor to fisheries, lumber camps, and railroads. All of these firms are reported to be fronts for widespread and diversified activity of a subversive nature; contacts and affiliations with known Japanese and Occidental pro-Nazi elements in the U. S. and Mexico have been both consistent and of long standing.

TAKAHASHI himself does considerable travel, frequently to Japan, and acts as go-between in arranging for so-called "inspection trips" to important plants, airports, strategic areas, etc., by visiting Japanese military-naval officers and business men. Over a long period he was in intimate contact with such key men as Colonel Usaburo OKA, Inspector of the Imperial Japanese Army Ordnance Inspector's Office in New York City, Commanders Shigeru FUJII and Taro ISOBE, IJN, and Majors Otoji NISHIMURA and Munemichi TOMIJI (now Lt. Col.). He was also reported to have been a silent partner of Kanekichi YAMAMOTO in the TOKYO CLUB chain prior to the latter's deportation from this country in 1939. Other activities of interest are his recent concentration upon the purchase of apartment houses and hotels in and about Seattle, and his apparent assumption of control of Mitsubishi (Seattle branch) funds for the duration of the "freezing order."

TAKASAKI, Yaichi (or Yoichi) - Alien, Class "A" suspect. During the fishing season is employed as cannery foreman by G. Y. NISHIMURA COMPANY of Seattle. Little else is known of him except for his connection with sumo, or Japanese wrestling.

CONFIDENTIAL

JAPANESE CANNERIES - Supplement

Personnel:

TAKAMOTO, Felix (with aliases Felix QUINAL, Marsek QUINAL) and Mary TAKAMOTO (alias Mary QUINAL) - Felix is believed to be a Malayan with some Japanese blood. Both subjects are known active Communist organizers in the fish canneries at Terminal Island, California. They are also reported to act as go-betweens for certain Japanese organizations and members of the fishing fleet, believed to be engaged in subversive activities off the Mexican Coast.

HOSHI, Hiroshi ("Paul") - An American-born Japanese, age 26, HOSHI is considered a dangerous suspect and has been recommended for custodial detention. In 1933, he was reported to be President of the SEATTLE JAPANESE AMATEUR RADIO CLUB and operator of Station W7CFJ. He was employed in 1937 as operator for the Van Camp Sea Food Company's fishing boat SAN RAFAEL, based at San Diego.

In the summer of 1938 he was reported to be an officer and member of ARTA, American Radio Telegraphists Association (C.I.C.), and also to be acting as a contact man between the Communist Party, the C.I.O. and the Japanese in the fishing industry. At that time, he was employed as radio operator on the Van Camp Co.'s boat DESTINY. In the winter of 1940 he was reportedly employed as radio operator on the SANTA INEZ operating between San Diego and Mexico.

CONFIDENTIAL

-17-

CONFIDENTIAL

ALASKA CANNERY WORKERS UNION
(A. F. of L. Affiliate, Local #2054)
519 Main Street
Seattle, Washington

Officers:

     ARAI, Clarence T.   - One-time leader and organizer (1937).

     OKAZAKI, "Robert" I. - President (1937-38).

     WATANABE, Yozo   - Organizer and president (1937).

             (Recent officers not reported.)

Summary:

     When last reported (1938), the 200-300 membership of this union
was mostly Japanese. Like its rival, the C. I. O. Local #7 (see case
history), the group is apparently connected, through the Japanese Consulates and Japanese labor and cannery contractors (see case history
on JAPANESE CANNERIES), with large-scale fishing-cannery interests
which are known to be deeply involved in various types of subversive
activity. It might also be noted that the A. F. of L. union, in a
test of strength wherein the bargaining agency of the salmon packing
industry was at stake, lost to the C. I. O. group, and has since been
definitely subordinate as a representative group.

     It is felt that description of the interlocking affiliations of
those who once held key positions in the union will do more to identify
the exact nature of the organization than will any further general statement.

Members:

     ARAI, Clarence T. - Class "A" suspect, Captain U.S.A. Reserves
(commission expired 6/1/41). Prominent attorney and civic leader in
Seattle. Local leader (and one-time national head) of the JAPANESE
AMERICAN CITIZENS LEAGUE, also of the ALASKA CANNERY WORKERS UNION, which
union he helped organize. Has had active contacts with influential
Japanese Army, Navy, and consular officials over a long period (Major
TAKAHASHI and Consul OKAMOTO among others) and is reported to travel
extensively. It is also worth noting that a 1936 report records the
belief that ARAI was a member of an exceedingly clever and astute intelligence ring, and that inquiry into the case at that time was not
advisable.

CONFIDENTIAL

CONFIDENTIAL

KANAYA, Richard T. - One of the organizers of the ALASKA CANNERY WORKERS UNION; at present an officer of the ASSOCIATION OF JAPANESE CANNERY WORKERS, which was recently organized to supplant the so-called "JAPANESE EDUCATIONAL SOCIETY." (The ASSOCIATION OF JAPANESE CANNERY WORKERS apparently aims to unite both A. F. of L. and C. I. O. labor union members under Japanese control. See case history on the association.)

MATSUMOTO, Ken - One-time officer in the TOKYO CLUB syndicate (see case history) and interested, with Kanekichi YAMAMOTO and others in the syndicate, in the formation of the ALASKA CANNERY WORKERS UNION.

NAGAMATSU, "Henry" Heiji - Class "A" suspect, Japanese citizen. Head of H. H. NAGAMATSU AND COMPANY, cannery contractors; also president-manager of the NORTH COAST IMPORTING COMPANY, both of Seattle. Was observed to be a frequent visitor of Kanekichi YAMAMOTO and is believed to be involved, through YAMAMOTO and his own work as a labor contractor, in the affairs of the ALASKA CANNERY WORKERS UNION.

NISHIMURA, "George" Yasukichi - Class "A" suspect. Cannery contractor and operator (plant located at Koguang, Bristol Bay, Alaska) and exporter-importer (owner G. Y. NISHIMURA AND COMPANY, Seattle). Leader of Seattle Japanese. Maintains home in Yokohama to which he used to make annual trips. Heavy contributor to Japanese War Fund. Mail communication (1936-37) with Kanekichi YAMAMOTO, Tamizo SAKAMOTO, and Hakuta FUJIOKA. (All three of these are suspects, YAMAMOTO and SAKAMOTO being active leaders in the TOKYO CLUB chain (see case history on same), as well as having cannery interests, and FUJIOKA being cannery superintendent for NISHIMURA.) In addition, NISHIMURA was, in 1936-37, closely affiliated with Dr. Seiji KANDA (or KONDA), Takuzo SUZUKI, and Koji UCHIDA, Japanese espionage agents who posed as "fishing school instructors" or KYODO SUISAN KAISHA agents while undertaking Alaskan surveys. In April, 1938, was investigated by U. S. Treasury Department on income tax charges, and reportedly left this country.

OKAZAKI, "Robert" Iwao - Was president of the ALASKA CANNERY WORKERS UNION in 1937-1938. Nothing known to ONI of his earlier background. In 1939 was contacted in Los Angeles by M. A. AKIYAMA, who was reported as having just come from Japan on a "secret mission."

WATANABE, Yozo - Class "A" suspect. One of the original organizers and one-time president (1937) of the ALASKA CANNERY WORKERS UNION; owner of a Seattle clothes cleaning and pressing shop. In frequent telephonic communication with Kanekichi YAMAMOTO, to whom he is alleged to have reported union affairs.

CONFIDENTIAL

CONFIDENTIAL

YAMAMOTO, Kanekichi - Class "A" suspect. Until 1938 was one of
the leaders in the TOKYO CLUB chain (see case history); was also affiliated with the NICHIBEI KOGYO KAISHA (see case history).

He has long been interested in cannery business and is reported
to have been one of the chief forces behind the formation of the ALASKA
CANNERY WORKERS UNION. Frequently in the company of Lt. Commander Shigeru
FUJII, IJN, and Consul Issaku OKAMOTO. Deported in 1939, and at present
believed to be in Shanghai (perhaps operating the Chinese branches of
the TOKYO CLUB gambling-smuggling syndicate).

CONFIDENTIAL

CONFIDENTIAL

CANNERY WORKERS AND FARM LABORERS UNION
(CIO Affiliate, Local #7)
Seattle, Washington

Officers:

HAMA, Carl (Aliases: YONEDA, Karl or George; HAMA, Kiyoshi; UCHIDA, Tsutomo.)	- Vice President (1939).
ITO, Kenji (or Kenzo)	- Legal representative (1941).
KUMAMOTO, Yukio	- Member Executive Board (1937-1938).
MINATO, "George" Masao	- Delegate (1938) to national convention of the UNITED CANNERY, AGRICULTURAL, PACKING AND ALLIED WORKERS OF AMERICA.
MIYAGAWA, "Dyke" Daisuke	- Member Executive Board (1937-1938) in charge of publicity.
TAKIGAWA, "George"	- Vice President (1937-1938) and delegate to national convention of the UCAPAWA (1938).

Summary:

As stated in the report on JAPANESE CANNERIES (see case history), the interests of cannery laborers are represented by the A.F. of L. ALASKA CANNERY WORKERS UNION and the above-mentioned CIO CANNERY WORKERS AND FARM LABORERS UNION. Of these two unions the latter is by far the larger and more influential; at the same time both groups are related through a newly organized ASSOCIATION OF JAPANESE CANNERY WORKERS (see case history), which ostensibly aims to consolidate the Japanese elements into a united labor front.

While the Japanese membership of subject union (1939 total about 700) is numerically inferior to the Filipino, it is obvious that the Japanese are in control of key positions and have utilized the union as a front for activities far removed from the demands of normal cannery business. An inspection of the attached diagram and a study of the individual affiliations set forth below will indicate that the union's connections with the West Coast Japanese consulates, Army and Navy agents, officials of the TOKYO CLUB chain, and other suspects have been more than coincidental. It must constantly be kept in mind in this connection

CONFIDENTIAL

CONFIDENTIAL

that Japan strove to put into operation in the United States and its
territories a highly integrated and specialized intelligence network
which could "take over" from regular established agencies in wartime.

Under such circumstances, Japanese nationals and pro-Japanese
nisei who are well settled in normal and yet strategic occupations are
likely to be the mainstay of Japanese espionage-sabotage operations in
this country.

Members and Associates:

HADA, Carl (with aliases) - Class "A" suspect. West Coast Communist Party organizer and labor agitator. Editor (1936) of the San
Francisco RODO SHIMBUN, a Communist Japanese-language news organ (no
longer published); contributor (1941) to the Communist DOHO newspaper
of Los Angeles, which is also printed (in English) by Japanese. Credi-
ted with having organized the Los Angeles JAPANESE WORKERS ASSOCIATION
in 1936. Active in AMERICAN LEAGUE AGAINST WAR AND FASCISM. Vice president of subject union in 1939.

ITO, Kenji (or Kenzo) - Nisei (second generation) Japanese, Class
"A" suspect. Active in JACL (1935-). One-time Japanese Consul at New
Orleans and, since October, 1937, legal adviser and "special member"
of the Seattle Consulate assigned to propaganda. Was reported in April,
1941, to be legal representative of subject labor union. Extremely
active since 1937 as propagandist defending Japanese foreign policy;
reported for naval espionage in 1940. He has done extensive traveling in
the U. S. and Latin America as well as in the Orient.

KUMAMOTO, Yukio - A U. S. citizen, Class "A" suspect. Former president of the Seattle chapter of the KIBEI NIKKEI SHIMIN KYOKAI (a society
composed of American-born Japanese who have been brought up and educated
in Japan from childhood until majority). Office manager of Seattle Branch
of MITSUBISHI SHOJI KAISHA until very recently. Member of the Executive
Board of subject CANNERY WORKERS AND FARM LABORERS UNION, Local #7.

MINATO, "George" Masao - Formerly student at University of Washington. In 1938 made unsuccessful bid for office in subject union; was,
however, elected delegate to national convention that year. Has short
wave radio license (W-7-FWG). Treasurer (1941), ASSOCIATION OF JAPANESE
CANNERY WORKERS (see case history).

MIYAGAWA, "Dyke" Daisuke - American-educated nisei, suspected of
membership in the Communist Party. Has for some time been striving to
consolidate the West Coast Japanese into a political bloc to exploit
the power he feels due them. Member (1937-1938) of Executive Board of
subject union, in charge of publicity. President (1941) of ASSOCIATION
OF JAPANESE CANNERY WORKERS (see case history).

CONFIDENTIAL

-22-

CONFIDENTIAL

OKAMARU, "Welley" or "Welly" Shoji - American-educated nisei (with kibei classification), Class "A" espionage suspect. Reported (July, 1941) to have repudiated his American citizenship. For the past six or seven years has been in the Japanese Consular Service (Seattle), first as Secretary, then as Consular Assistant and more recently as Chancellor. Is known to have cooperated closely with Lt. Comdr. Sadatomo OKUDA and Chancellor Kanji KANEKO (both of Seattle) in the local Japanese intelligence system; OKAMARU is reported to head a unit which contacts labor unions, particularly members of the Communist Party in the A. F. of L. and C. I. O.

TAKIGAWA, "George" Kiyoshi - American-educated nisei, active as political and labor leader among West Coast second generation Japanese. Vice president of subject CANNERY WORKERS AND FARM LABORERS UNION, Local #7, and delegate to the 1938 national convention. President of the JAPANESE EDUCATIONAL SOCIETY from 1938 or 1939 until the dissolution of the society in 1941. (TAKIGAWA was actually forced to resign sometime before the group disbanded, having been charged with conduct unsupportable by the organization and specifically with having accepted money in return for job favors. The society was then reorganized and renamed the ASSOCIATION OF JAPANESE CANNERY WORKERS.)

TAKIGAWA (or TAKI), William - Class "B" nisei suspect, brother of "George" Kiyoshi TAKIGAWA. Believed to be either a Communist Party member or a "fellow-traveller;" has done some work among the Negroes. Was an unsuccessful candidate for office in subject union in 1939. Has done some traveling between Seattle and Alaska.

CONFIDENTIAL

CONFIDENTIAL

ASSOCIATION OF JAPANESE CANNERY WORKERS
(Formerly the Japanese Educational Society)
Seattle, Washington

Officers:

MIYAGAWA, "Dyke" Daisuke	— President
KANAZAWA, Hiroshi	— Secretary
MINATO, "George" Masao	— Treasurer
OKAMOTO, Eddie M.	— Trustee
UYENO, Tom	— Trustee
HIRAHARA, Davis	— Member of Advisory Board
KANAYA, Richard T.	— Member of Advisory Board
KAWANO, M.	— Member of Advisory Board
KIKUCHI, Chihiro	— Member of Advisory Board
MIYAMOTO, Frank	— Member of Advisory Board
OKAZAKI, Masayuki	— Member of Advisory Board
WATANABE, Taul	— Member of Advisory Board

Summary:

Subject association was originally known as the JAPANESE EDUCAT-
IONAL SOCIETY, and under that title functioned as a headquarters for
Japanese aliens and nisei connected with the canning business. President
of the JAPANESE EDUCATIONAL SOCIETY during the three years of its existence (1938-1941) was "George" Kiyoshi TAKIGAWA (see case history on
CANNERY WORKERS AND FARM LABORERS UNION, C.I.C. Local #7). He was forced
to resign his office shortly before the group was dissolved, having been
charged with "conduct unsupportable by the organization," and specifically
with having accepted money in return for job favors.

Information is lacking to indicate whether or not the JAPANESE
EDUCATIONAL SOCIETY had membership covering the A. F. of L. ALASKA CAN-
NERY WORKERS UNION as well as the aforementioned C.I.C. group, but the
newly formed organization (viz. The ASSOCIATION OF JAPANESE CANNERY WORKERS)
is definitely known to cover both unions. (It should be noted that, while

-24-

CONFIDENTIAL

these unions are predominantly of native Alaskan and Filipino membership, the Japanese manage to retain a large measure of control. Union affiliation with Japanese consulates and other Japanese offices or agents are described in the case histories of the respective unions.)

<u>Members' Affiliations:</u>

MIYAGAWA, "Dyke" Daisuke - American-educated <u>nisei</u> (second generation Japanese), active in political and labor spheres among the West Coast Japanese. Is suspected of Communist affiliations, though his membership in the CP has not been definitely ascertained. Has been member of the Executive Board of the C.I.O. CANNERY WORKERS AND FARM LABORERS UNION, Local #7, in charge of publicity (1937-1939).

PINATO, "George" Masao - American-educated nisei. Has short wave radio license (W-7-FNG). Delegate of the C.I.O. CANNERY WORKERS AND FARM LABORERS UNION, Local #7, to the international convention of the UNITED CANNERY, AGRICULTURAL, PACKING AND ALLIED WORKERS OF AMERICA at San Francisco (December 1938).

MIYAMOTO, Frank Shotaro - American-educated nisei, instructor in sociology at the University of Washington (1941). Has done considerable research on sociological conditions among Japanese in the Seattle area. Worked in Alaska the summer of 1941 (exact duties unknown). Nothing of a derogatory nature has yet been reported concerning him. (It may be possible that this is not the same Frank MIYAMOTO listed above under "Officers.")

KANAYA, Richard T. - One of the speakers at the first organization meeting of the A.F. of L. ALASKA CANNERY WORKERS UNION.

UYENO, Tom - One of twenty-one delegates of the C.I.O. CANNERY WORKERS AND FARM LABORERS UNION, Local #7, to the Washington State C.I.O. Convention (1938).

-25-

CONFIDENTIAL.

CONFIDENTIAL

HOTELS INVOLVED IN TOKYO CLUB SYNDICATE

HOLLAND HOTEL
504 Fourth Avenue
Seattle, Washington

- MINAMI, S. - Manager prior to 1/14/41
  LARKIN, ---)
  VERNON, ---) - Present managers (1/14/41)

KASHU HOTEL
1701 Laguna Street
San Francisco, California

- NAKANO, Sakutaro - Owner (August, 1941)
  Class "A" suspect

N. P. HOTEL
306 Sixth Avenue, S.
Seattle, Washington

- SHITAMAE, Hiroku "Frank" - Senior partner
  SHITAMAE, Shihei "George" - Brother and
    joint operator (2/27/41)
  N. S. INVESTMENT CC. (believed to be
    operated by SHITAMAE BROS.) - Owner (1/14/41)

OHIO HOTEL
1218 S. W. Front St.
Portland, Oregon

- SUMIDA, James Yoshio - Lessee

OLYMPIC HOTEL
(also referred to as
NEW OLYMPIC HOTEL)
117 N. San Pedro St.
Los Angeles, Calif.

- SAWANO, J. - (Contact man) - Manager (May, 1935)
  WATANABE, Kyohei - (Contact man and agent) -
    Assistant manager (May, 1935)
  FUKUI, Soji (Soki) - Organizer and stock-
    holder (9/15/36)

PORTLAND HOTEL

- Location and management unknown.

S. P. HOTEL
123 West Burnside Ave.
Portland, Oregon

- SUMIDA, James Yoshio - Lessee

STEVENS HOTEL

- Location and management unknown

TACOMA HOTEL
822 Jackson Street
Seattle, Washington

- HARA, Seiichi   )
  KAWAKAMI, Kakuzo) "Hotel partners" (1/30/41)
  (Another report (1/14/41) lists
    HARA, Seiichi - Manager
    WAHLSTROM (Mrs.) - Owner)

U. S. HOTEL
315 Maynard Street
Seattle, Washington

- MIYAGAWA, "Joe" Genke - Manager (6/3/41)
    Is the brother of the MIYAGAWA (probably
    "Dyke" Daisuke) who owns GOLDEN DONUT CAFE
  PRENTISS REALTY CO. - Owner (1/14/41)

CONFIDENTIAL

CONFIDENTIAL

RESTAURANTS, CAFES, CLUBS, AND POOL HALLS INVOLVED
IN TOKYO CLUB SYNDICATE

The FRISCO CAFE
560 Fifth Avenue
San Diego, California

GOLDEN DONUT CAFE   - MIYAGAWA, (probably "Dyke" Daisuke) - Owner (6/3/41)
Seattle, Washington

KOSHIN CLUB   - ISHIBASHI, "George" Naoichi - Manager (1941)
Portland, Oregon

NEW CENTRAL CAFE   - FURUMOTO, S. (Mrs.) - Proprietor (1941)
653 Weller St.
Seattle, Washington

NIPPON POOL HALL   - SAITO, Moriya (Dr.) - Owner (1941)
608 Main Street
Seattle, Washington

The SHINKO CLUB   - YASUMURA, Sadakichi - Manager (4/22/38)
1725 Laguna Street
San Francisco, California

STACY STREET TAVERN -   ASAKURA, Makutaro - Proprietor (1/30/41)
2401 First Ave., S.
(corner of Stacy St.)
Seattle, Washington

The STAR POOL HALL -   ICHIKAWA, Hakui - Proprietor (11/4/41)
517 Jackson Street
Seattle, Washington

The SUN CAFE   -   OBAYASHI, J. U. - Operator (1940)
421 Market Street
San Diego, California

TOKYO CAFE
239 Elm Avenue
Long Beach, California

To: All Naval Districts except ND 16, FBI, MID, COI, State Dept.,
     Special Defense Unit of Dept. of Justice

                                              B-7-J

CONFIDENTIAL

	NICHIBEI KOGYO KAISHA	TOKYO CLUB CHAIN	LOS ANGELES COMMUNIST ACTIVITIES	KAISUN KYOKAI	SAKURA KAI	OTHER SUBVERSIVE GROUPS	CLASS "A" AND "B" SUSPECTS	IJA, IJN CONSULATE CONTACTS	ALASKA CANNERY WORKERS UNION (AFL)	ASSOC. OF JAPANESE CANNERY WORKERS	BUSINESS 'FRONTS'	CANNERY CONTRACTORS	C.I.O. LOCAL #7	EXTENSIVE TRAVEL	ESPIONAGE SUSPECT
KUMAMOTO	+	+		+	+	+	+	+			+			+	+
KIMURA	+	+		+	+	+	+				+			+	
MUKAEDA	+	+		+		+	+	+							+
NARUMI	+	+		+		+	+				+			+	
MASUIKE	+	+		+	+		+				+				
NIDA	+	+		+			+				+				
SAN	+	+				+	+	+							
UYEDA	+	+		+	+						+				
FUMUSAWA	+	+		+	+		+	+							+
NAKAMURA	+	+			+	+	+								
YAMATODA	+	+				+	+	+			+				+
TOMINAGA	+	+				+									
MORI	+	+													
SUZUMI		+					+							+	+
YAMAMOTO	+	+				+		+	+			+		+	
MATSUMOTO		+						+							
ICHIKAWA	+	+				+	+	+			+			+	
ISHIBASHI		+				+	+	+			+	+		+	+
MORII	+	+				+	+	+			+			+	+
MIRAO		+				+									
SUITANI		+					+								+
FUKAO		+					+								
SASAKI		+				+		+							+
WATANABE							+	+			+				
NAMBA			+			+	+						+		+
ARAI							+	+	+					+	+
MIYASAWA			+						+				+	+	
MAGAMATSU							+		+		+	+			
NISMIMURA, Y									+		+	+		+	+
NISMIMURA, G						+		+							
SAKAMOTO		+				+	+	+				+		+	
MINATO						+				+			+		
TAKIGAWA, G						+				+			+		
TAKIGAWA, T			+			+	+						+		
MENO		+				+	+								
KUMAMOTO						+	+				+		+		
TSUDA	+					+	+							+	+
TAKAHASHI		+					+	+			+	+		+	+
ITO						+	+	+					+		+

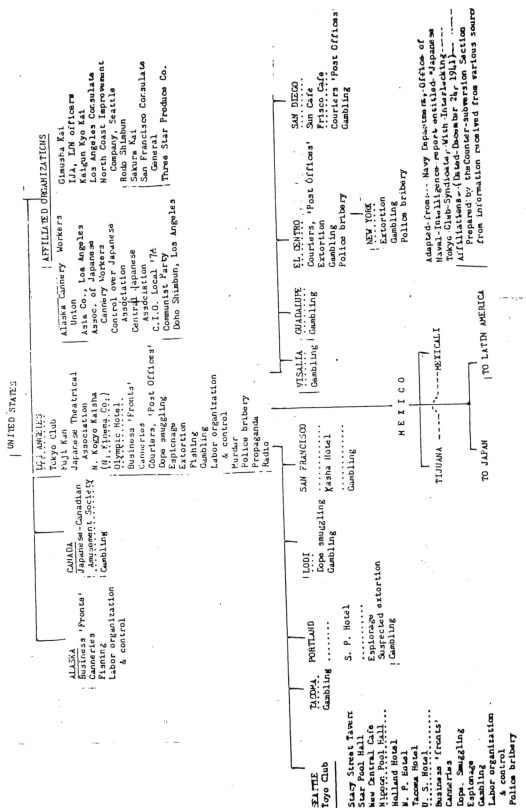

UNITED STATES NAVAL INTELLIGENCE SERVICE

INVESTIGATION REPORT

Confidential

Date: 26 Jan. 1942

Subject: JAPANESE RESIDENTS OF T. H.—LOYALTY OF
Report made at: Honolulu, T. H.
Report made by: C. B. Baldwin, Lt., I–V (S), USNR; R. W. Breed, End., I–V
    (S), USNR.
    USNR.
Period covered: 16 Dec., 1941; 26 Jan., 1942.
Status of Case: Closed.
Origin of Case: Fourteenth Naval District.

Source File No.: 14ND #1798.
ONI File No.:
    SYNOPSIS: Report predicated upon Japanese plane crash on 7 December,
1941, and events subsequent thereto, on Island of Niihau, T. H. Niihau is one
of smallest Hawaiian Islands, its meager population consisting mostly of
Hawaiians and a few Japanese engaged in cattle raising, and communications
with other islands are nil except by boat. Thus the residents of Niihau had no
cognizance of the Japanese attack, or its extent and effect, until several days
after it took place. Pilot of this plane survived and was taken prisoner by local
Hawiians, who confiscated his sidearm and flight papers. Among guards of the
aviator were an American-born Japanese named Harada and an alien Japanese
named Shintani, neither of whom had ever been considered disloyal to the United
States. Shintani attempted unsuccessfully to secure possession of the pilot's
papers by bribery, stating it was a matter of life and death, and that Japan had
forced him to take this action. Shintani, however, later repented and re-joined
the Hawaiians. With the aid of Harada, the pilot recovered his pistol and a
shotgun, set up two machine guns from his plane, and dominated the island.
Pilot was finally killed by an audacios Hawiian couple, and Harada committed
suicide. Shintani is now in custodial detention.
    DEDUCTIONS: The fact that the two Niihau Japanese who had previously
shown no anti-American tendencies went to the aid of pilot when Japanese
domination of the island seemed possible, indicates likelihood that Japanese
residents previously believed loyal to the United States, may aid Japan if further
Japanese attacks appear successful.
    CLOSED.
    RWB/zw
    APPROVED:

MAYFIELD,
Captain, U. S. Navy,
District Intelligence Officer.

Confidential

26 JANUARY, 1942.

Subject: Japanese residents of T. H.—Loyalty of.
    On Sunday, 7 December, 1941, a Japanese fighter plane crashed on the island
of Niihau, T. H. The pilot, who was the sole occupant, was seized by the local
Hawaiians and his pistol and papers were taken from him. He surrendered and
at first was peacable and friendly, speaking English fluently. At the time of
the landing, SHINTANI, a Japanese alien resident on Niihau, held a brief conversation in Japanese with the pilot, the subject of which was not understood
by the Hawaiians. SHINTANI had at this time no record of any subversive
activities or tendencies.
    Niihau is one of the smaller islands, being seventh in size in the Hawaiian
group, and its meager population consists mostly of Hawaiians and a few Japanese. The people of Niihau have very few weapons, and had no means of communication, by radio or otherwise, with the Mainland or the other islands during
the week from 7 December, 1941, to 14 December, 1941, which is the period to
which this report pertains. Thus it is conceivable that the presence of the
Japanese plane gave the inhabitants the impression that the other islands of
the Hawaiian group had been invaded and captured by the Japanese; and the
actions of the inhabitants with respect to the enemy pilot may be noted in the
light of such possible belief, which also may have been fostered by the pilot.
    The aviator was kept under guard pending his dispatch to Kauai, nearest of
the more important islands. When, on Wednesday, 10 December, the islanders
found themselves unable to send the pilot to Kauai, due to the failure of a
motor launch to arrive at Niihau, the aviator was quartered at the home of
YOSHI HARADA, American of Japanese descent. Several Hawaiians remained

to keep guard at the house of HARADA, who up to this time had shown no sign of disloyalty and took his regular turn at guarding the pilot.

On Thursday, 11 December, HARADA sent a messenger to SHINTANI to come and assist him in guarding the pilot, stating that he, HARADA, did not desire the responsibility of being the only Japanese in charge of the pilot. SHINTANI replied that he would join HARADA on the following day, Friday. He did so, and a conversation in Japanese was held between HARADA, SHINTANI, and the pilot. The nature of the conversation is unknown.

On the afternoon of this same day, Friday, 12 December, SHINTANI attempted to secure the pilot's papers and pistol from the Hawaiian who had possession of them, by offering the Hawaiian a bribe of two hundred dollars. SHINTANI said excitedly, in the course of the attempted bribery, that it was a matter of life and death and that Japan had forced him to take this action. The attempt at bribery failed, and SHINTANI took no further action on the pilot's behalf. SHINTANI has since been placed in custody, however.

On the same afternoon, HARADA and the pilot succeeded in obtaining HARADA's shotgun from a building near HARADA's house. With the shotgun, the pilot captured the Hawaiian guard and locked him in a warehouse. About 1730 that afternoon HARADA and the pilot broke into the house of the Hawaiian who had custody of the pilot's papers and pistol. HARADA was carrying the shotgun and covering a Hawaiian prisoner at the time. The pilot recovered only his pistol at this time. The owner of the house had been in hiding during the burglary; and, after the Japanese left, he removed the papers and secreted them elsewhere, after which he warned the community of the pilot's escape.

The pilot and HARADA then secured two machine guns from the plane and set them up in the village. HARADA, brandishing a gun, seized a wagon and horses from some Hawaiians and forced a captive to load machine-gun cartridges from the plane into the wagon. HARADA told a Hawaiian that the cartridges were enough to kill off every man, woman, and child on the island.

That night HARADA and the pilot broke into SHINTANI's house in search of the flight papers. They failed to find them and became furious; and later, when they saw SHINTANI in the village, they pursued him, but he escaped and joined the Hawaiians, who had scattered to the maintains and beaches. Thereupon the pilot and HARADA took as prisoners the few Hawaiians who happened to be in the village at the time, and bound them.

About midnight the pilot attempted to send a radio message from his plane in Japanese. A few Hawaiians heard him, although they did not understand the message; and the residents, now assuming that a war must be going on, were alarmed at the thought that the pilot had sent for aid from the enemy. While the pilot and HARADA were absent from the wagon containing ammunition, the Hawaiians recovered the machine-gun bullets and secreted them. At 3:00 a. m. on 13 December, the aviator burned his plane and the House of the Hawaiian who had custody of the papers. However, the Hawaiians had already sent the pilot's papers to Kauai, via a small boat, under cover of darkness. The pilot and HARADA told the Hawaiian prisoners that they would be released if they disclosed the location of the papers.

On 13 December an audacious Hawaiian couple succeeded in killing the pilot, whereupon HARADA committed suicide. Both men were buried at Niihau. An expedition squad of twelve armed soldiers arrived from Kauai at 1350 that day, having been apprised of he situation by the Hawaiians arriving in the small boat which had left Niihau with the pilot's papers the night before.

CONCLUSIONS: It is worthy of note that neither SHINTANI nor HARADA had previously exhibited un-American tendencies, living docilely so long as the American Government was the established one. Attention is also invited to the fact that the Island of Niihau was isolated as to communication, so it is conceivable that the presence of the Japanese plane induced a belief among the residents that the Hawaiian Islands were under Japanese domination; and the residents were in fact alarmed about the possibility of further Japanese aid for the pilot. These facts indicate a strong possibility that other Japanese residents of the Territory of Hawaii, and Americans of Japanese descent, who previously have shown no anti-American tendencies and are apparently loyal to the United States, may give valuable aid to Japanese invaders in cases where the tide of battle is in favor of Japan, and where it appears to the residents that control of the district may shift from the United States to Japan.

CLOSED.

In reply refer to Initials
and No.

Op-16-B-7-J

NAVY DEPARTMENT
OFFICE OF THE CHIEF OF NAVAL OPERATIONS
WASHINGTON

February 14, 1942

MEMORANDUM for Mr. Tamm

SUBJECT: The Japanese Problem

There is transmitted herewith a copy of a report
on the Japanese Question which was prepared by Lieutenant
Commander K. D. Ringle, U.S.N.

This report was prepared at the request of the
Office of Naval Intelligence following the statement by
Mr. C. B. Munson, in his survey of the Japanese on the West
Coast, that Lieutenant Commander Ringle was particularly
well acquainted with the Japanese problem.

Although it does not represent the final and
official opinion of the Office of Naval Intelligence on
this subject, it is believed that this report will be of
interest to the Federal Bureau of Investigation.

H. B. Keisker,
Commander, U.S.N.R.

I ENCLO.

DECLASSIFICATION CN 5/14/85
BY 1628 REP IAG

Mr. E. A. Tamm
Federal Bureau of Investigation
U. S. Department of Justice
Washington, D. C.

RECORDED
INDEXED   GI-10556-613

Copy to: Military Intelligence Division
           Alien Enemy Control Unit, Department of Justice MAR 11 1942
           Special Defense Unit, Department of Justice

8 MAR 2 1942

Branch Intelligence Office

BIO/ND11/EF37/A8-5   ELEVENTH NAVAL DISTRICT   26 JAN 1942

Serial LA/1055/re   Fifth Floor, Van Nuys Building
                           Seventh and Spring Streets
                           Los Angeles, California

CONFIDENTIAL

From:	Lieutenant Commander K. D. RINGLE, USN.
To:	The Chief of Naval Operations
Via:	The Commandant, Eleventh Naval District.

Subject: Japanese Question, Report on.

Reference: (a) CpNav ltr file (SC)A8-5/EF37 Op-16-B-7/RB A8-5/EF37
                      Serial No. 01742316 of 12/30/41.
                  (b) Reports of Mr. C. B. Munson, Special Representative
                      of the State Department, on Japanese on the West
                      Coast, dated Nov. 7, 1941, and Dec. 20, 1941.
                  (c) NNI 119 Report, file BIO/ND11/EF 37/A8-2, serial LA/861
                      of 3/27/41, subject-NISEI.
                  (d) NNI 119 Report, file BIO/ND11/EF37/A8-2, serial LA/5223
                      of 11/4/41, subject-NISEI.
                  (e) NNI 119 Report, file BIO-LA/ND11/FF37/P8-2, serial
                      LA/6524 of 12/12/41, subject-HEIMUSHA-KAI.
                  (f) NNI 119 Report, file BIO-LA/ND11/FF37/P8-2, serial
                      LA/417 of 1/5/42, subject-KIBEI Organizations and
                      Activities.
                  (g) Dept. of Commerce Bulletin, Series P-3, Number 23,
                      dated 12/9/41.

Enclosures: (A) Transcripts of J. B. Hughes' broadcasts of Jan. 5, 6,
                      7, 9, 15, 19, and 20, 1942.
                  (B) F.B.I.,L.A. Report re Japanese Activities, Los Angeles,
                      dated Jan. 20, 1942.

     1.   In accordance with paragraph 2 of reference (a), the follow-
ing views and opinions with supporting facts and statements are submitted.

     I OPINIONS.

          The following opinions, amplified in succeeding paragraphs,
are held by the writer:

DECLASSIFICATION CN 5/14/85
BY 1678 LEI /4G

BIO/ND11/EF37/A8-5

Serial LA/1055/re

CONFIDENTIAL

Subject: Japanese Question, Report on.
- -

(a) That within the last eight or ten years the entire
"Japanese question" in the United States has reversed itself. The alien
menace is no longer paramount, and is becoming of less importance almost
daily, as the original alien immigrants grow older and die, and as more and
more of their American-born children reach maturity. The primary present
and future problem is that of dealing with these American-born United States
citizens of Japanese ancestry, of whom it is considered that least seventy-
five per cent are loyal to the United States. The ratio of these American
citizens of Japanese ancestry to alien-born Japanese in the United States is
at present almost 3 to 1, and rapidly increasing.

(b) That of the Japanese-born alien residents, the large
majority are at least passively loyal to the United States. That is, they
would knowingly do nothing whatever to the injury of the United States, but
at the same time would not do anything to the injury of Japan. Also, most
of the remainder would not engage in active sabotage or insurrection, but
might well do surreptitious observation work for Japanese interests if given
a convenient opportunity.

(c) That, however, there are among the Japanese both alien and
United States citizens, certain individuals, either deliberately placed by
the Japanese government or actuated by a fanatical loyalty to that country,
who would act as saboteurs or agents. This number is estimated to be less
than three per cent of the total, or about 3500 in the entire United States.

(d) That of the persons mentioned in (c) above, the most
dangerous are either already in custodial detention or are members of such
organizations as the Black Dragon Society, the Kaigun Kyokai (Navy League),
or the Heimusha Kai (Military Service Men's League), or affiliated groups,
The membership of these groups is already fairly well known to the Naval Intelligence service or the Federal Bureau of Investigation and should immediately be placed in custodial detention, irrespective of whether they are alien
or citizen. (See reference (e) and (f).

(e) That, as a basic policy tending toward the permanent solution of this problem, the American citizens of Japanese ancestry should be
officially encouraged in their efforts toward loyalty and acceptance as bona
fide citizens; that they be accorded a place in the national effort through
such agencies as the Red Cross, U.S.O., civilian defense, and even such
activities as ship and aircraft building or other defense production activities, even though subject to greater investigative checks as to background
and loyalty, etc., than Caucasian Americans.

-2-

BIO/MD11/EF37/A8-5

Serial LA/1055/re

CONFIDENTIAL

Subject: Japanese Question, Report on.
- -

      (f) That in spite of paragraph (e) above, the most potentially dangerous element of all are those American citizens of Japanese ancestry who have spent the formative years of their lives, from 10 to 20, in Japan and have returned to the United States to claim their legal American citizenship within the last few years. These people are essentially and inherently Japanese and may have been deliberately sent back to the United States by the Japanese government to act as agents. In spite of their legal citizenship and the protection afforded them by the Bill of Rights, they should be looked upon as enemy aliens and many of them placed in custodial detention. This group numbers between 600 and 700 in the Los Angeles metropolitan area and at least that many in other parts of Southern California.

      (g) That the writer heartily agrees with the reports submitted by Mr. Munson, (reference (b) of this report.)

      (h) That, in short, the entire "Japanese Problem" has been magnified out of its true proportion, largely because of the physical characteristics of the people; that it is no more serious than the problems of the German, Italian, and Communistic portions of the United States population, and, finally that it should be handled on the basis of the <u>individual</u>, regardless of citizenship, and <u>not</u> on a racial basis.

      (i) That the above opinions are and will continue to be true just so long as these people, Issei and Nisei, are given an opportunity to be self-supporting, but that if conditions continue in the trend they appear to be taking as of this date; i.e., loss of employment and income due to anti-Japanese agitation by and among Caucasian Americans, continued personal attacks by Filipinos and other racial groups, denial of relief funds to desperately needy cases, cancellation of licenses for markets, produce houses, stores, etc., by California State authorities, discharges from jobs by the wholesale, unnecessarily harsh restrictions on travel, including discriminatory regulations against all Nisei preventing them from engaging in commercial fishing—there will most certainly be outbreaks of sabotage, riots, and other civil strife in the not too distant future.

    II   BACKGROUND.

      (1) In order that the qualifications of the writer to express the above opinions may be clearly understood, his background of acquaintance with this problem is set forth.

BIO/ND11/EF37/A8-5

Serial LA/1055/re

CONFIDENTIAL

Subject: Japanese Question, Report on.
- -

        (a) Three years' study of the Japanese language and the Japanese people as a naval language student attached to the United States Embassy in Tokyo from 1928 to 1931.

        (b) One year's duty as Assistant District Intelligence Officer, Fourteenth Naval District (Hawaii) from July 1936 to July 1937.

        (c) Duty as Assistant District Intelligence Officer, Eleventh Naval District, in charge of Naval Intelligence matters in Los Angeles and vicinity from July 1940 to the present time.

        (2) As a result of the above, the writer has over the last several years developed a very great interest in the problem of the Japanese in America, particularly with regard to the future position of the United States citizen of Japanese ancestry, and has sought contact with certain of their leaders. He has likewise discussed the matter widely with many Caucasian Americans who have lived with the problem for years. As a result, the writer believes firmly that the only ultimate solution is as outlined in paragraphs I(e) and I(h) above; namely, to deliberately and officially encourage the American citizen of Japanese ancestry in his efforts to be a loyal citizen and to help him to be so accepted by the general public.

    III   ELABORATION OF OPINIONS EXPRESSED IN PARAGRAPH I.

        (1) For purposes of brevity and clearness, four Japanese words in common use by Americans as well as Japanese in referring to these people will be explained. Hereafter these words will be used where appropriate.

        ISSEI (pronounced ee-say) meaning "first Generation." Used to refer to those who were born in Japan; hence, alien Japanese in the United States.

        NISEI (pronounced nee-say) meaning "second generation." Used for those children of ISSEI born in the United States.

        SANSEI (pronounced san-say) meaning "third generation." Children of NISEI.

        KIBEI (pronounced kee-bay) meaning "returned to America." Refers to those NISEI who spent all or a large portion of their lives in Japan and who have now returned to the United States.

BIO/ND11/EF37/A8-5

Serial LA/1055/re

CONFIDENTIAL

Subject: Japanese Question, Report on.
- -

(2) The one statement in paragraph I(a) above which appears to need elaboration is that seventy-five per cent or more of the Nisei are loyal United States citizens. This point was explained at some length in references (c) and (d). The opinion was formed largely through personal contact with the Nisei themselves and their chief organization, the Japanese American Citizens League. It was also formed through interviews with many people in government circles, law-enforcement officers, businessmen, etc., who have dealt with them over a period of many years. There are several conclusive proofs of this statement which can be advanced. These are—

(a) The action taken by the Japanese American Citizens League in convention in Santa Ana, California, on January 11, 1942. This convention voted to require the following oath to be taken, signed, and notarized by every member of that organization as a prerequisite for membership for the year 1942, and for all members taken into the organization in the future:

> "I, _____, do solemnly swear that I will
> support and defend the Constitution of the
> United States against all enemies, foreign and
> domestic; that I will bear true faith and
> allegiance to the same; that I hereby renounce
> any other allegiances which I may have know-
> ingly or unknowingly held in the past; and that
> I take this obligation freely without any
> mental reservation or purpose of evasion. So
> help me God."

(b) Many of the Nisei leaders have voluntarily contributed valuable anti-subversive information to this and other govermental agencies. (See reference (d) and enclosure (B).

(c) That the Japanese Consular staff, leaders of the Central Japanese Association, and others who are known to have been sympathetic to the Japanese cause do not themselves trust the Nisei.

(d) That a very great many of the Nisei have taken legal steps through the Japanese Consulate and the Government of Japan to officially divest themselves of Japanese citizenship (dual citizenship), even though by so doing they become legally dead in the eyes of the Japanese law, and are no longer eligible to inherit any property which they or their family may have held in Japan. This opinion is further amplified in references (c) and (d).

BIO/ND11/IF37/A6-5

Serial LA/1055/re

CONFIDENTIAL

Subject: Japanese Question, Report on.
- -

          (3) The opinion expressed in paragraph I(b) above is based on
the following: The last Issei who legally entered the United States did so in
1924. Most of them arrived before that time; therefore, these people have been
in the United States at least eighteen years, or most of their adult life.
They have their businesses and livelihoods here. Most of them are aliens only
because the laws of the United States do not permit them to become naturalized.
They have raised their children, the Nisei mentioned in paragraph (1) above,
in the United States; many of them have sons in the United States army. Exact
figures are not available, but the local Military Intelligence office estimates
that approximately five thousand Nisei in the State of California have entered
the United States army as a result of the Selective Service Act. It does not
seem reasonable that these aliens under the above conditions would form an
organized group for armed insurrection or organized sabotage. Insofar as numbers go, there are only 46,697 alien Japanese in the eight western states.

          The following paragraph quoted from an Associated Press despatch
from Washington referring to the registration of enemy aliens is considered most
significant on this point: "The group which must register first comprises the
135,843 enemy aliens in the western command—Arizona, California, Idaho,
Montana, Nevada, Oregon, Utah, and Washington. The group includes 26,255
Germans, 60,905 Italians, and 46,697 Japanese." It is assumed that the foregoing figures are based either on the 1940 census or the alien registration
which was taken the latter part of 1940.

          There are two factors which must be considered in this group of
aliens: First, the group includes a sizeable number of "technical" aliens;
that is, those who, although Japanese born and therefore legally aliens, entered
the United States in infancy, grew up here, and are at heart American citizens.
Second, the parents of the Kibei, mentioned in paragraph I(f), should be considered as those who are most loyal to Japan, since they themselves are the ones
who sent their children to be educated and brought up entirely in the Japanese
manner.

          (4) Paragraph I)c) needs no further elaboration.

          (5) Paragraph I(d) has been elaborated at length in references
(e) and (f).

          (6) Elaboration of paragraph I(e). The United States recognizes
these American-born Orientals as citizens, extends the franchise to them,

-6-

BIO/ND11/EF37/AS-5

Serial LA/1055/re

CONFIDENTIAL

Subject: Japanese Question, Report on.
- -

drafts them for military service, forces them to pay taxes, perform jury duty, etc., and extends them to the complete protection afforded by the Constitution and Bill of Rights, and yet at the same time has viewed them with considerable suspicion and distrust, and so far as it is known to the writer, has made no particular effort to develop their loyalty to the United States, other than to permit them to attend public schools. They are segregated as to where they may live by zoning laws, discriminated against in employment and wages, and rebuffed in nearly all their efforts to prove their loyalty to the United States, yet at the same time those of them who grow to about the age of 16 years in the United States and then go to Japan for a few years of education find themselves viewed with more suspicion and distrust in that country than they ever were in the United States, and the majority of them return after a short time thoroughly disillusioned with Japan and more than ever loyal to the United States.

It is submitted that the only practical permanent solution of this problem is to indoctrinate and absorb these people, accept them as an integral part of the United States population, even though they remain a racial minority, and officially extend to them the rights and privileges of citizenship, as well as demanding of them the duties and obligations.

Furthermore, if some such steps are not taken, the field for proselyting and propaganda among them is left entirely to Japanese interest acting through Consulates, Consular agents, so-called "cultural societies", athletic clubs, Buddhist and Shinto priests—who through a quirk in the United States immigration laws may and have entered the country freely, regardless of exclusion laws or quota as "ministers of religion"—trade treaty aliens, steamship and travel agencies, "goodwill" missions, etc. It is well known to the writer that his acquaintance with and encouragement of Nisei leaders in their efforts towards Americanization was a matter of considerable concern to the former Japanese Consul at Los Angeles.

It is submitted that the Nisei could be accorded a place in the national war effort without risk or danger, and that such a step would go farther than anything else towards cementing their loyalty to the United States. Because of their physical characteristics they would be most easily observed, far easier than doubtful citizens of the Caucasian race, such as naturalized Germans, Italians, or native-born Communists. They would, of course, be subject to the same or more stringent checks as to background than the Caucasians before they were employed.

BIO/ND11/EF37/A8-5

Serial LA/1055/re

CONFIDENTIAL

Subject: Japanese Question, Report on.

- -

(7) No elaboration is considered necessary for paragraphs I(f), I(g), and I(h).

(8) Elaboration of paragraph I(i). The opinion outlined in this paragraph is considered most serious and most urgent. There already exists a great deal of economic distress due to such war conditions as frozen credits and accounts, loss of employment, closing of businesses, restrictions on travel, etc. This condition is growing worse daily as the savings of most of the alien-domin ted families are being used up. As an example, the following census, taken by missionary interest, of alien families in the fishing village on Terminal Island is submitted:

"How long can you maintain your family without work?"

Immediate attention	—	9 families
1 month	—	52 families
2 months	—	64 families
3 months	—	61 families
4 months	—	32 families
5 months	—	20 families
6 to 10 months	—	129 families
Over 10 months	—	90 families
Total		477 families.

Large numbers of people, both Issei and Nisei, are idle now, and their number is growing. Children are beginning to be unable to attend school through lack of food and clothing. There have been already incipient riots brought about by unprovoked attacks by Filipinos on persons of the Japanese race, regardless of citizenship. There is a great deal of indiscriminate anti-Japanese agitation stirring the white population by such people as Lail Kane, former Naval Reserve Officer, James Young, Hearst correspondent, in his series of lectures, and John B. Hughes, radio commentator, transcripts of whose broadcasts are submitted as enclosure (A).

There are just enough half truths in these articles and statements to render them exceedingly dangerous and to arouse a tremendous amount of violent anti-Japanese feeling among Caucasians of all classes who are not thoroughly informed as to the situation. It is noted that in these broadcasts, lectures, etc., there are no distinctions made whatever between the actual members of the Japanese military forces in Japan and the second and third generation citizens of Japanese ancestry born and brought up in the

BIO/NDll/EF37/A8-5

Serial LA/1055/re

CONFIDENTIAL

Subject: Japanese Question, Report on.
- -

United States. It must also be remembered that many of the persons and groups
agitating anti-Japanese sentiment against the Issei and Nisei have done so for
some time from ulterior motives--notable is the anti-Japanese agitation by the
Jugo-Slav fishermen who frankly desire to eliminate competition in the fishing
industry. .

It is further noted that according to the local press, Congressman Leland M. Ford has introduced a bill in Congress providing for the removal
and interment in concentration camps of all citizens and residents of Japanese
extraction, which according to the census figures would amount to about 127,000
people of all ages and sexes in the continental United States, plus an additional 158,000 in Hawaii and other territories and possessions, excluding the
Philippines, (see reference (g) for population breakdown). It is submitted
that such a proposition is not only unwarranted but very unwise, since it would
undoubtedly alienate the loyalty of many thousands of persons who would otherwise be entirely loyal to the United States, would add the extra burden of
supporting and guarding these people to the war effort, would disrupt many
essential businesses, notably that of the growing and supplying of foodstuffs,
and would probably cause a widespread outbreak of sabotage and riot.

IV RECOMMENDATIONS.

(1) Based on the above opinions, the following recommendations
for the handling of this situation are submitted:

(a) Provide some means whereby potentially dangerous United
States citizens may be held in custodial detention as well as aliens. It is
submitted that in a military "theater of operations"--which at present includes
all the West coast--this might be done by review of individual cases by boards
composed of members of Military Intelligence, Naval Intelligence, and the
Department of Justice.

(b) Under the provisions of (a) above, hold in custodial detention such United States citizens as dangerous Kibei or German, Italian, or
other subversive sympathizers and agitators as are deemed dangerous to the
internal security of the United States.

(c) Similar procedure to be followed in cases of aliens--not
only Japanese, but other aliens of whatever nationality, whether so-called
"friendly" aliens or not. This suggestion is made since it is believed that

BIO/ND11/FF37/A8-5

Serial LA/1055/re

CONFIDENTIAL

Subject: Japanese Question, Report on.

- -

there exist other aliens--Spanish, Mexican, Portuguese, Slavonian, French, etc., who are active Axis sympathizers.

(d) Other suggestions as listed in reference (a).

(e) In the cases of persons held in custodial detention, whether alien or citizen, see that some definite provision is made for the support of their dependent families. This could be done by:

(1) Releasing certain specified amounts from these people's "frozen" funds monthly for the support of these dependents.

(2) Making definite provisions through relief funds for the support of such dependents, so that they will not become either public charges or embittered against the United States, and themselves dangerous to the internal peace and security of the country.

(f) In the interest of national unity and internal peace and security some measures should be instituted to restrain agitators of both radio and press who are attempting to arouse sentiment and bring about action-- private, local, state, and national, official and unofficial, against these people on the basis of race alone, completely neglecting background, training, and citizenship.

K. D. RINGLE.

Copy to:
DIO(2)

C O P Y   ~~CONFIDENTIAL~~

BIO/ND11/EF37/A8-5

SUBJECT: Japanese Menace on Terminal Island, San Pedro, California.

REFERENCE: (a) Report on subject prepared by Counter Intelligence
                    Section, ONI, January 18, 1942.

PREPARED BY: Lieut. Comdr. K. D. RINGLE, USN.

DATE: February 7, 1942.

- -

I Ownership of Land and Establishment of Colony.

1.   The land on which the Japanese colony on Terminal Island is
established is owned by the City of Los Angeles and administered under the
Harbor Department. This land, including the sites of the various fish canneries and the waterfront and moorings at Fish Harbor, has been leased by
the City of Los Angeles to the fish canneries for many years. The canneries
in turn built the houses and barracks now occupied by the Japanese and sub-
leased them to the cannery employees.

            This was done so that at any hour of the day or night when
fish were brought in, cannery employees could be quickly called to work and
the fresh fish processed before any deterioration or spoilage set in. Also,
the cannery employees engaged in the actual taking of fish at sea were likewise leased dwellings here. These sub-leases are very short-term leases,
subject to quick cancellation if the lessees should cease to be employed by
the canneries. It should therefore be self-evident that this entire colony
has existed since its inception due to the tolerance, knowing or unknowing,
of the Los Angeles city government and the fish packing industry.

II Japanese Population.

1.   The total Japanese population, including both alien and
American born, is at present about 2500. It is interesting to note in this
connection that there are only about 800 aliens, the balance being entirely
American born. Of these 800 about 375 male alien fishermen were taken into
custody by the Department of Justice on 2 February 1942, leaving an alien
population of about 425 at present, largely women.

2.   It will be noted that this is a decrease in Japanese population from that reported in reference (a). Causes for this decrease are as
follows:

            (a) Due to the unsettled political situation between the
United States and Japan during the last two years, a great many of the alien
families have returned to Japan.

            (b) There have been no replacements arriving from Japan for
those who have died or who have moved away.

~~CONFIDENTIAL~~

P

Y

SUBJECT: Japanese Menace on Terminal Island, San Pedro, California.
- -

(c) The American-born children as they came of age have turned to other means of livelihood and have moved away from Terminal Island. This is considered to be a result of the Americanizing influence of their education in the American public schools.

(d) The fish canneries themselves have been gradually replacing a great many of the former Japanese employees, both afloat and ashore by non-Japanese, such as Jugo-Slavs, Filipinos, Negroes, and the like.

3.   There does exist in the present population a large element of what is considered to be the most dangerous class of persons of the Japanese race in the United States. This class is composed of those persons born in the United States, sent to Japan in infancy, raised and trained there, and whohave returned to the United States within the last four or five years as adults, and who have been permitted entry as American citizens because of their American birth. There are several hundred of this type of person presently residing on Terminal Island and engaged either in the taking or processing of fish. It is felt that these persons constitute the greatest menace of the whole colony to the security of the United States.

III The Fishing Fleet.

1.   The menace of the so-called Japanese fish boats has been decreased greatly in the last few years, due to the action of the United States authorities in such cases as that of the fish boat Nancy Hanks. It is quite true that formerly there were a number of actual alien-owned and alien-documented vessels operating out of the Port of Los Angeles, paying so-called "light money" for the privilege of so operating. However, largely due to the rigid enforcement of the customs laws, these vessels have either been withdrawn or have changed their documentation to American ownership. In the case referred to of the Nancy Hanks, the customs instituted a suit against the owners for non-payment of duty on fish brought into the United States and sold in the domestic market, by a foreign-owned vessel.

In order that these vessels could be documented under the laws of the United States, it was required that at least 51% of the vessel be owned by American citizens, and that an American citizen be master of the vessel. These laws were in the past evaded by having the ownership vested in the American-born children of aliens and by having the American-born master be merely a dummy, the real control of the vessel and her crew being vested in the head of the fishing crew who was known as the "fish boss," who directed all movements of the vessel at sea. The latter practice was common even on those vessels owned by the fish packers themselves. Hence, this evasion of the law was done with the tacit consent and connivance of the fish packing companies, although it is exceedingly doubtful if this can be proved in any court of law.

- 2 -

C O P Y   ~~CONFIDENTIAL~~

SUBJECT: Japanese Menace on Terminal Island, San Pedro, California.
- -

In the last two or three years, this situation has gradually been rectified by a more rigid inspection and supervision of these vessels by the Customs and the Coast Guard, until at the present time it is doubtful if any of the documented vessels are actually alien-owned or alien-controlled.

Nevertheless, there are a large number of small undocumented vessels used in inshore fishing which are completely alien-owned and alien-controlled, since they do not come within the documentation laws of the United States. These as a rule are the small one and two-man vessels of less than five tons.

Since the outbreak of the war on December 7, 1941, there has been no Japanese, either alien or citizen, permitted to leave the harbor on any fishing vessel, large or small. This was done by the Department of Justice acting through the Immigration Service by telegram received on December 7th, which is quoted in part as follows: "It is important in addition to prevent departure persons of Japanese race claiming United States citizenship." This restriction is still in effect.

IV   Analysis of the Hazard to the Security of the United States due to this Japanese Colony on Terminal Island.

1.   As has been pointed out, it is very evident that a hazard definitely exists due to the location of this large Japanese colony in the heart of the Los Angeles harbor district. It is considered that this hazard can be broken down as follows:

   (a) Physical observation and espionage - 75%.
   (b) Sabotage - 20%.
   (c) Fifth column activity - 5%. By fifth column activity is meant preparation for and assistance to any attempted attack or invasion from outside sources.

2.   An analysis of the above hazards is as follows:

(a) It is evident that observation and espionage has been going forward for a great many years. Therefore, it is evident that the physical location of all fixed defense works and harbor improvements and the like are already known to the Japanese. These fixed installations would include such items as the exact location and extent of Reeves Field, Naval Operating Base, Fort MacArthur, oil, gas, and power lines, tank farms, marine oil loading terminals, important docks, oil refineries, shipbuilding installations, railway lines and bridges, anti-submarine nets and buoys, harbor approaches, and aids to navigation, and the like.

The items which would be of value to the enemy and which these people are in an unexcelled position to observe and report on, are such items as arrival and departure of convoys, including size, strength of escort, and

CONFIDENTIAL

SUBJECT: Japanese Menace on Terminal Island, San Pedro, California.

----

bulk of cargo; troop movements; arrival and departure of major units of the
fleet; progress of shipbuilding, including launching and commissioning of men-
of-war, as well as merchant marine; progress of construction of Naval Operating
Base, including the new dry dock and the channel approaches thereto; delivery
of new aircraft; the strength or lack of strength of the aerial defenses of
the Naval Air Station and Naval Operating Base; and similar matters.

     As long as this colony, which contains known alien sympathizers,
even though of American citizenship, is allowed to exist in the heart of every
activitiy in the Los Angeles Harbor, it must be assumed that items such as the
above are known, observed, and transmitted to the enemy quickly and easily.

     (b) Sabotage. The only reason that sabotage is considered to
be no more than 20% of the total hazard, is because of the rather rigid and
effective guards and protections which have been placed into effect within the
last six months. These protective measures include the emptying of marine
loading terminals of oil, gasoline, and other inflammables; lights and guards
on ships and docks; constant patrol of the waters of the harbor by the Coast
Guard and recently by the City Police of Los Angeles and Long Beach; the post-
ing of guards on bridges leading to Terminal Island; the fencing and private
guards required under the terms of the contracts by firms engaged in defense
work, such as Bethelehem Shipbuilding Company, Los Angeles Shipbuilding & Dry
Dock Company, etc.; and the presence of troops in the immediate vicinity.

     It should not be inferred from the above that full and adequate
protective measures have been placed into effect—far from it. There still
exists a great need for increased police and fire protection and the reduction
of possible fire hazards due to the tremendous lumber yards, free-flowing oil
wells, exposed water, gas, gasoline, oil and transmission lines, and installations, etc. These hazards are at the moment beyond the control of the naval
and military authorities, but would serve as ideal objectives for saboteurs
having as ready access to them as the Japanese colony on Terminal Island.

     (c) Fifth Column Activity. This hazard is considered to be
only 5% of the whole, for two reasons: First, this colony is quite concentrated and under constant observation, and can be quickly and immediately sur-
rounded by troops on the spot. Second, because in spite of what has been said
previously, there do exist in this colony a great many known and trusted nisei
(American citizens of Japanese ancestry), who would immediately resent and
combat any such attempt and who are at present acting as observers and informers for the Naval Intelligence Service and the F.B.I.

CONFIDENTIAL

PUBLISHER'S NOTE

Information in the following appendices is included as a supplement to David Lowman's manuscript. The appendices contain documents and photographs bearing on issues raised in the book. Excerpts from *Personal Justice Denied* are included so readers can judge for themselves the quality and accuracy of that work.

APPENDIX I

MISCELLANEOUS DOCUMENTS

DOCUMENT SUMMARIES

Page 335   February 19, 1942—Text of Executive Order 9066.

The next four documents concern the Japanese organization Zaibei Heimusha Kai or as the FBI translated the title, "Association of Japanese in America Obligated to Military Duty."

Page 336   February 10, 1940—FBI report describing U.S. Customs' discovery of "approximately 10,000 certificates of thanks issued by the IMPERIAL JAPANESE NAVY, for contributions of money for the relief of officers and men of the Japanese Navy." Of interest in this document is the translated name of the organization, which is shown in the "Title" box of the report and the number of individual certificates involved.

Page 337   October 14, 1941—Military Intelligence Division report. Subject: Japanese Ex-Service Men's Organizations. This document describes the origins of the Zaibei Heimusha Kai, its membership, which includes "military age Nisei" (U.S. citizens), its involvement in "intelligence activities," and its pledge "to do sabotage (railroads and harbors) in the states mentioned above (California, Oregon, Washington and Utah)." Another organization, the Imperial Comradeship Society, is also mentioned as being committed to sabotage.

Page 338   January 30, 1942—FBI letter of transmittal from the Special Agent in Charge, Salt Lake City to the Director of the FBI, with enclosed translation of the April 1938 prospectus of the Utah Heimusha Kai. The stridently militant prospectus includes the statement, "However, in the state of war, we are all Nationals and must be united and recognize our own duties. We are the most patriotic, second to none, but still we are residing in a foreign country and unable to serve the country of our origin directly....We are able to talk and act proudly every day even though in a foreign country. This privilege, needless to say, would never have been granted for us without the background of Japanese might and power in the world."

The war fever among some Japanese in Utah was described by a retired U.S. Army colonel who on Pearl Harbor Day was the only Caucasian working in the Bingham Copper Mine maintenance shop. There he saw Nisei, U.S. citizens, rush to take up arms "to kill Americans." They were luckily stopped by Issei, Japanese citizens, who were older and wiser.

Persons of Japanese ancestry were not evacuated from Utah even though a number of Issei security suspects were arrested and some were interned in Department of Justice camps.

Page 341   September 29, 1942—Memo from FBI Director to Special Agent in Charge, Salt Lake City, subject: THE HEIMUSHA KAI , INTERNAL SECURITY — J. This memo states that the Criminal Division of the Justice Department believes the organization has been effectively broken up by the internment of its officers and workers and that "no purpose of the government would be served by a prosecution...." Modern claims that there were no convictions for disloyal acts fail to take into account that the reason was because there were few prosecutions. Enemy alien suspects were interned instead and citizens were evacuated from areas in which they could cause problems.

Page 342   March 25, 1942—Letter from Japanese American Citizens League of Ogden (Utah) to Governor Herbert B. Maw of Utah. This letter requests that Japanese from the West Coast not be resettled in Utah.

Page 343   July 20, 1983—Letter from John J. McCloy to Senator Charles Grassley describing his experience with the Commission on Wartime Relocation and the Internment of Civilians. McCloy was the Assistant Secretary of War during World War II and served as the High Commissioner of Germany after the war.

Page 345   December 22, 1941—Memo for "THE DIRECTOR" (FBI) from Edward A. Tamm reporting on a meeting between Tamm and Assistant to the Secretary of War Bundy in which Bundy revealed that President Roosevelt told the Secretary of War, Henry L. Stimson, at a cabinet meeting several days earlier that he, the President, wanted "all of Japanese aliens in the Hawaiian Islands interned at once."

One significant aspect of this document is that it shows that the President, based on the knowledge he possessed at the time, less than two weeks after the attack on Pearl Harbor, was prepared to intern approximately 41,000 aliens. There is no indication that this order was based on anything more than what the Commander in Chief considered to be military necessity. That the order was not implemented, also for reasons of military necessity, is described by David Lowman.

Page 346   October 24, 1942—State Department memo reporting on a meeting with ONI officers concerning a second exchange of nationals between the U.S. and Japan. ONI officers are reported saying the prevention of certain "Japanese fishermen" from passing their knowledge to Japan is "worth the loss of all

Americans now in the Far East." At the time there were
approximately 15,000. This equation of 15,000 lives to the
value of information held by a few Japanese residents places
the far more benign evacuation in clear perspective.

Executive Order No. 9066

AUTHORIZING THE SECRETARY OF WAR
TO PRESCRIBE MILITARY AREAS

WHEREAS the successful prosecution of the war requires every possible protection against espionage and against sabotage to national-defense material, national-defense premises, and national-defense utilities as defined in section 4, Act of April 20, 1918, 40 Stat. 533, as amended by the act of November 30, 1940, 54 Stat. 1220, and the Act of August 21, 1941, 55 Stat. 655 (U. S. C., Title 50, Sec. 104):

NOW, THEREFORE, by virtue of the authority vested in me as President of the United States, and Commander in Chief of the Army and Navy, I hereby authorize and direct the Secretary of War, and the Military Commanders whom he may from time to time designate, whenever he or any designated Commander deems such actions necessary or desirable, to prescribe military areas in such places and of such extent as he or the appropriate Military Commanders may determine, from which any or all persons may be excluded, and with such respect to which, the right of any person to enter, remain in, or leave shall be subject to whatever restrictions the Secretary of War or the appropriate Military Commander may impose in his discretion. The Secretary of War is hereby authorized to provide for residents of any such area who are excluded therefrom, such transportation, food, shelter, and other accommodations as may be necessary, in the judgement of the Secretary of War or the said Military Commander, and until other arrangements are made, to accomplish the purpose of this order. The designation of military areas in any region or locality shall supersede designations of prohibited and restricted areas by the Attorney General under the Proclamations of December 7 and 8, 1941, and shall supersede the responsibility and authority of the Attorney General under the said Proclamations in respect of such prohibited and restricted areas.

I hereby further authorize and direct the Secretary of War and the said Military Commanders to take such other steps as he or the appropriate Military Commander may deem advisable to enforce compliance with the restrictions applicable to each Military area hereinabove authorized to be designated, including the use of Federal troops and other Federal Agencies, with authority to accept assistance of state and local agencies. I hereby further authorize and direct all Executive Departments, independent establishments and other Federal Agencies, to assist the Secretary of War or the said Military Commanders in carrying out this Executive Order, including the furnishing of medical aid, hospitalization, food, clothing, transportation, use of land, shelter, and other supplies, equipment, utilities, facilities and services.

This order shall not be construed as modifying or limiting in any way the authority heretofore granted under Executive Order No. 8972, dated December 12, 1941, nor shall it be construed as limiting or modifying the duty and responsibility of the Federal Bureau of Investigation, with respect to the investigation of alleged acts of sabotage or the duty and responsibility of the Attorney General and the Department of Justice under the Proclamations of December 7 and 8, 1941, prescribing regulations for the conduct and control of alien enemies, except as such duty and responsibility is superseded by the designation of military areas hereunder.

Franklin D. Roosevelt
February 19, 1942

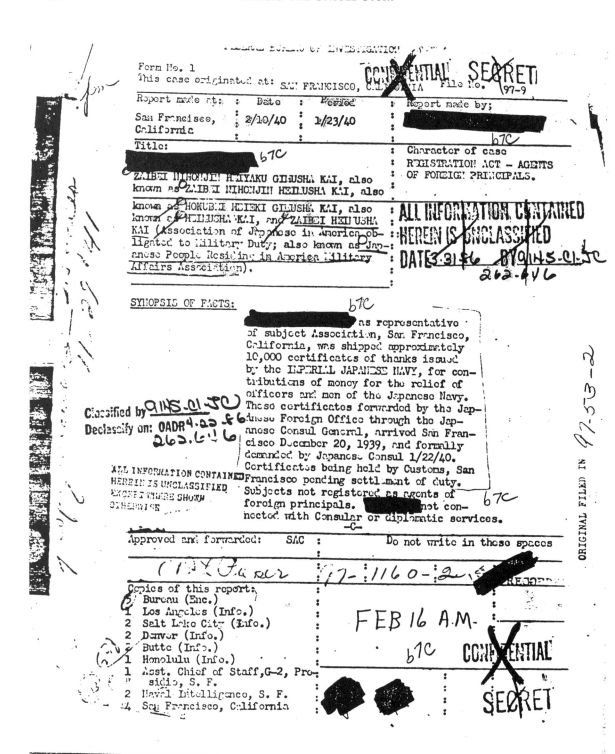

C O P Y

~~CONFIDENTIAL~~ ~~CONFIDENTIAL~~

WAR DEPARTMENT

M. I. D.

MID 336.8 Japan   10-14-41

MILITARY INTELLIGENCE DIVISION
CONTACT OFFICE
205 DIllingham Building
Honolulu, T. H.

14 October 1941.
(Date)

Subject: JAPANESE EX-SERVICE MEN'S ORGANIZATIONS

Summary of Information:

1. ZAIBEI HEINUKAI (Japanese Military Service Men League). This organization was organized in August, 1937, by Tadaaiki Izuka, Assistant Chief of Japanese Foreign Information Bureau Headquarters in San Francisco.

There are 7200 members in northern California, Washington, Oregon and Utah. Each member gives $1.00 to Japanese War Fund, and others engaged in intelligence activities. This includes military age nisei as well as Japanese aliens. ¥650,000 00 were sent to Japan as of May 1941.

2. IMPERIAL COMRADESHIP SOCIETY (Japanese Ex-Service Men League) This organization is headed by Sakutaro Kuboda, owner of Market Hotel, a retired officer. Kuboda visited Japan last year and attended Japanese Overseas Congress. He is especially recognized by Japanese army to carry on the work. His son Takashi is an active member of Japanese American Citizen League; he is also the editor of Shinmin no Tomo (Citizen Friend) This Society raised a fund of ¥1,000,000.00 at the request of Finance Minister, Mr Ikeda, through Yokohama Specie Bank in San Francisco and Los Angeles, Headquarters at Los Angeles.

These two organizations are the same in nature. It is further stated that these two organizations have pledged to do sabotage (railroads and harbors) in the states mentioned above, in time of emergency. Similar organizations are in Hawaii. Sixty-nine local units of these two organizations are said to be carrying on activities.

Distribution:
MID, Washington, D.C.
FBI, Honolulu
ONI, Honolulu
File

~~CONFIDENTIAL~~

	Evaluation	
	—of source	—of information
	Reliable	
	Credible	
	Questionable	
	Undetermined	

3

~~CONFIDENTIAL~~

Federal Bureau of Investigation
United States Department of Justice
Salt Lake City, Utah
January 30, 1942

Director
Federal Bureau of Investigation
Washington, D. C.

Dear Sir: Re: HEIMUSHA KAI OF UTAH
                       INTERNAL SECURITY J

        For the Bureau's information there are enclosed
three copies of a prospectus of the Heimusha Kai of Utah
dated April 1938 recently found in the possession of
████████████ the subject of SLC File 65-516. ████████████

        This office is continuing its investigation of
the persons connected with this organization.

                              Very truly yours,

                              JAY C. NEWMAN
                              Special Agent in Charge

Encl.
AMASD

ALL INFORMATION CONTAINED
HEREIN IS UNCLASSIFIED 262-646
DATE 3/28/86 BY 9145-S1-JC

RECORDED
&
INDEXED

97-1160-15

FEDERAL BUREAU OF INVESTIGATION
19 FEB 4 1942
U. S. DEPARTMENT OF JUSTICE

I ENCLO. 19

COPY

COPIES DESTROYED
293 APR 6 1961

FEB 5 RECD

Prospectus of the Heimusha Kai of Utah dated April 1938
Found in the Possession of ██████████████ b7C
The Subject of SLC File 65-516
██████████████████████████████████████ b7D

*****

"The people of the whole world are acknowledging that the Military
operation by our father country in the Chinese incident is really due to
unavoidable circumstances. However, in the state of war, we are all Nationals
and must be united and recognize our own duties. We are the most patriotic,
second to none, but still we are residing in a foreign country and unable
to serve the country of our origin directly. There are many able-bodied
men of the fatherland fighting around the enemy. Some are shooting the
others with their own human bullets. Others are fighting under the explosives of the bombers and shells and sometimes they are fighting in an
infected land. There are many many of their surviving families suffering
from sickness and even poverty in Japan. These tragic stories we read in
the newspapers every morning and evening, day after day. As you know,
tears are unpreventable under these circumstances. All we Japanese brothers
are expressing our loyalty to our own country, the war relief, comfort letters
and donations. Moreover, we intend to help the war operations to bring
the matter of conflict to a conclusion at the earliest date. This is a
part of our duty since we are unable to serve in action.

We are able to talk and act proudly every day even though in
a foreign country. This privilege, needless to say, would never have
been granted for us without the background of Japanese might and power
in the world.

We demand you to cooperate with this help to the fatherland in
the time of this emergency.

REGULATIONS OF THE HEIMUSHA KAI

1. The name is Utah Heimusha Kai
2. The temporary office is at Morishito & Company, 124 West First
South, Salt Lake City, Utah.
3. Two classes of members.

    1. Regular
    2. Support

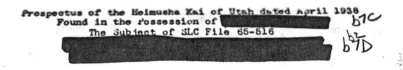

Regular members are from the able-bodied men to 47 years who are
eligible for military conscription but deferred. They pay $1.00 each as
the War Relief until the end of the incident.

4. All the members besides the members who are mentioned in
Section 3 are called support members. They give as much as they wish to.

-2-

5. Our task is direct help for collecting the war relief, comfort bags, donations and other things. We have no connections of any kind with political or religious organizations.

6. The expenses of this organization are paid by the regular members.

7. The appointed officers are as follows:

     1. Honorary Secretary
     2. The treasurers
         1. One from regular member
         2. One from support member

     3. Fourteen Directors

         a. Four Salt Lake City
         b. Two Garfield
         c. Two Murray
         d. Two Bingham Canyon
         e. One Tooele
         f. One Provo
         g. Two Southern Utah

8. The donations should be turned into the Salt Lake City office before the 20th of each month.

9. Changing regulations, officers, and striking of names are made according to the majoritys' wish.

97-1160-30

RECORDED

Date: September 29, 1942

To: SAC, Salt Lake City

From: J. Edgar Hoover - Director, Federal Bureau of Investigation

Subject: THE HEIMUSHA KAI
              INTERNAL SECURITY - J

b7C

          Reference is made to the report of Special Agent ▮▮▮▮▮▮▮▮
          ▮▮▮▮▮▮▮▮ dated April 11, 1942, at Salt Lake City. It is observed
that this report sets out two undeveloped leads.

          The Attorney General has advised that in the opinion
of the Criminal Division, this organization has been effectually broken
up by the internment of officers and workers of the various branch
chapters of this organization, and that no purpose of the Government
would be served by a prosecution for a violation of any Federal Statute
that might be indicated by the facts. It is, therefore, suggested that
this case be closed unless your office feels that specific facts which
may warrant prosecution might be developed by the following out of the
leads in the referenced report.

ALL INFORMATION CONTAINED
HEREIN IS UNCLASSIFIED 162-646
DATE 4-1-86 BY 9148-01-JC

. Tolson_____
. E. A. Tamm_
. Clegg_____
. Glavin_____
. Ladd_____
. Nichols_____
. Rosen_____
. Tracy_____
. Carson_____
. Coffey_____
. Hendon_____
. Kramer_____
. McGuire_____
. Quinn Tamm_
. Nease_____
s Gandy_____

COMMUNICATIONS SECTION
MAILED 2
★ SEP 29 1942 P.M.
FEDERAL BUREAU OF INVESTIGATION
U. S. DEPARTMENT OF JUSTICE

b7C

13 OCT 5 1942

"FOR BETTER AMERICANS IN A GREATER AMERICA"

JAPANESE AMERICAN CITIZENS LEAGUE
OF OGDEN

Ogden, Utah

March 23, 1942

MAR 23 RECD

Honorable Herbert B. Maw
Governor, State of Utah
State Capitol
Salt Lake City, Utah

My dear Governor:

The Japanese residents of Ogden City and Weber
County find it imperative to submit the following
objections to the influx of Japanese evacuees from the
restricted coastal areas:

1- This is the Central Defense Area.
2- Problems of housing, lack of available farming
areas, and all other means of livelihood are
acute.
3- The influx of new Japanese inhabitants would be
a hazard to those already established here.

Weber County and Ogden Japanese of First and Second
generation have established a reputation through industry and good behavior in appreciation of the privileges
given them to contribute to the general welfare of the
community. It appears exceedingly unwise to disturb
and disrupt this status, for this most important reason
the strangers from other localities might be undesirable
in adjustment to these settled conditions.

We, therefore, emphatically and sincerely oppose
the entrance and settlement of these people, at the same
time express our regrets that the war situation compels
our position in this emergency.

Very truly yours,

Jiro Tsukamoto

Jiro Tsukamoto
President, Pro. Tem.

JT:m

483

JOHN J. McCLOY
ONE CHASE MANHATTAN PLAZA
NEW YORK, N. Y. 10005

1983 JUL 26 PH 2: 21

July 20, 1983

Dear Senator:

I understand that the subcommittee, of which you
are Chairman, is to meet on July 27 in Washington on matters
in which I am deeply interested as a citizen of the United
States and as The former Assistant Secretary of War during
the Franklin D. Roosevelt administration when the Japanese
war was taking place.

I was in the War Department on the "Day of Infamy"
on December 7, 1941 and I believe I was the highest senior
civilian official there at the time of the attack. I have
testified before the commission which was appointed by
President Carter to look into the circumstances surrounding
the steps which were taken by our government following the
attack to offset the consequences of the loss of almost our
entire Pacific Battle Fleet and its installations on that
day.

Only as this commission was about to close its
hearings, was I called upon to appear before it in regard to
the relocation program which had been ordered by President
Roosevelt. By that time, a great head of steam had been
built up by news accounts of the hearings largely inspired
by the lobbyists. From my personal experience, at the
hearings of the commission, I believe its conduct was an
horrendous affront to our tradition for fair and objective
hearings. It constituted a serious affront to that
tradition. Whenever I sought in the slightest degree to
justify the action of the United States which was ordered by
President Roosevelt, my testimony was met with hisses and
boos such as I have never, over an experience extending back
to World War I, been heretofore subjected to.   Others had
similar experiences. I do not have the means or the
resources to call witnesses or produce evidence in support
of the action taken by the President of the United States
and his advisors but I was there at the time and it became
clear from the outset of my testimony that the commission
was not at all disposed to conduct an objective
investigation of the circumstances which induced the
President of the United States to issue the order which he
did and as to the significance and purpose of which he was
fully aware. The commission was, in effect, one erected to
build up a case against the propriety of such an order and
the manner in which it had been carried out. No current
officials of the government, so far as I have heard, were
ever called on to produce evidence in support of the action
which the President and his advisors took in their good
judgment as to what the consequences of the attack demanded.

484

Nor were any called to produce any information from the
records of the government as to the motivation for the
order.

Bland statements have been repeated by the
commission to the effect that not a single case of proven
sabotage or disloyalty had been produced either before or
after the attack which would justify the propriety of the
relocation. The fact of the matter is that this evidence
was not sought. Anything which could be educed to show the
reasonableness of the precautions taken by the President
produced these demonstrations or were later called
"irrelevant" by the chair. Comparisons between the manner
in which the ethnic Japanese/Americans were treated in
contrast to the manner in which Japanese ethnics were
treated in the rest of the world including Canada were also
declared irrelevant. The fact that the members of the
Pacific Fleet who were on their ships at the time of the
attack and whose bodies are still entombed in their vessels
at the bottom of the Harbor were never adequately
compensated for their suffering and death was also called
"irrelevant." The extensive amenities made available to the
relocatees in the camps and elsewhere were also deemed
"irrelevant."

I may not be in a position now to cite chapter and
verse this long after the event but given the same amount of
money that this commission had to make its case and with the
paid staffs at its disposal, I could readily have produced
supporting evidence of the threats which then faced the
nation. I could go on and on giving evidence of what I
consider to have been the wholly one-sided nature of the
commission's hearings. It would have presumably been quite
as simple for an objective examiner of the commission to
have dug up again the so-called "MAGIC" revelations as it
was for Mr. Mohr, a reporter on the NEW YORK TIMES to do so.
It is little wonder that this information caused
consternation among the commission as well as in the
editorial offices of Mohr's paper and the feeble attempts
now being made by the commission itself to discount his
research is quite revealing. The truth is really that this
commission simply does not know whether there were any acts
of sabotage or frustrated acts of sabotage committed on the
West Coast.

I have been asked whether I would be prepared to
testify before your committee. I, of course, would be. I
cannot be there on July 27 or 28 as I have a long standing
commitment with my family but I can certainly find a date
convenient to your committee and myself shortly thereafter.

Very truly yours,

/tr

Senator Charles E. Grassley
Subcommittee to the Senate Judiciary Committee
 in charge of Administrative Practice & Procedure
Senate Office Building
Washington, D.C. 20310

JOHN EDGAR HOOVER
DIRECTOR

Federal Bureau of Investigation
United States Department of Justice
Washington, D. C.

LAT:DS

December 22, 1941

MEMORANDUM FOR *THE DIRECTOR*

Mr. Tolson
Mr. E. A. Tamm
Mr. Clegg
Mr. Glavin
Mr. Ladd
Mr. Nichols
Mr. Tracy
Mr. Rosen
Mr. Carson
Mr. Coffey
Mr. Hendon
Mr. Kramer
Mr. McGuire
Mr. Quinn Tamm
Mr. Nease
Tele. Room
Tour Room
Mr. Nease
Miss Gandy

I called upon Assistant Secretary of War Bundy this morning. I explained to Mr. Bundy that the Attorney General had talked to you about the matter of removing certain Japanese aliens from the Hawaiian Islands and that you had instructed me to ascertain the facts in order that the FBI might know what assistance could be rendered.

Mr. Bundy stated that at the Cabinet meeting several days ago the President had told the Secretary of War that he, the President, desired to have all of the Japanese aliens in the Hawaiian Islands interned at once. Bundy said that the President had mentioned particularly removing all of the Japanese aliens from the islands of Oahu and Hawaii, possibly to some other island in the Hawaiian group. I told Mr. Bundy that apparently someone had received the impression that the program contemplated the evacuation of certain Japanese from the Hawaiian Islands to the mainland. Bundy, who did not appear to have much knowledge of what this was all about, left the office, apparently to talk to the Secretary of War, and returned a few minutes later, and after checking with various officers in the War Department by telephone, advised that the present plan of the War Department contemplated leaving the matter in its entirety in the hands of the Commanding General of the Hawaiian Islands.

Mr. Bundy stated that there was consequently no action or assistance which could be rendered by the Bureau at this time, in view of the War Department's plan, apparently in disregard of what the President apparently said at the Cabinet meeting, to allow the commanding general to do as he saw fit with the Japanese aliens in the Hawaiian Islands.

RECORDED

Respectfully,

Edward A. Tamm

DEC 27 1941

COPY

Attachment

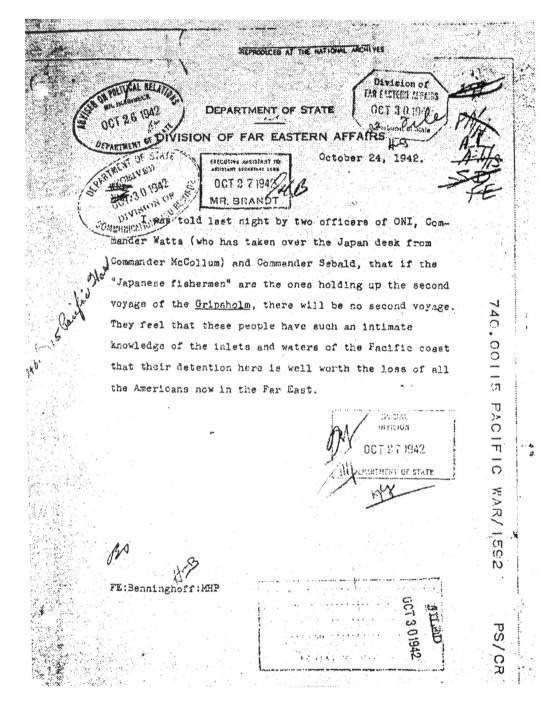

REPRODUCED AT THE NATIONAL ARCHIVES

DEPARTMENT OF STATE

DIVISION OF FAR EASTERN AFFAIRS

Division of
FAR EASTERN AFFAIRS
OCT 3 0 19

October 24, 1942.

I was told last night by two officers of ONI, Commander Watts (who has taken over the Japan desk from Commander McCollum) and Commander Sebald, that if the "Japanese fishermen" are the ones holding up the second voyage of the Gripsholm, there will be no second voyage. They feel that these people have such an intimate knowledge of the inlets and waters of the Pacific coast that their detention here is well worth the loss of all the Americans now in the Far East.

FE:Benninghoff:MHP

APPENDIX II

EXCERPTS FROM *PERSONAL JUSTICE DENIED*

"In its five-hundred-page report, Personal Justice Denied, *the Commission has a ten-page section labeled 'Intelligence.' This contains some of the most curious statements ever to appear in an official document."*

INTELLIGENCE[1]

The intelligence services have the task of alerting and informing the President, the military and those charged with maintaining security about whether, where and when disruptive acts directed by an enemy may be expected. Intelligence work consists predominantly of analytical estimate, not demonstrably comprehensive knowledge—there may always be another, undiscovered ring of spies or a completely covert plan of sabotage. Caution and prudence require that intelligence agencies throw the net of suspicion wide, and take measures to protect vital information or militarily important installations. At the same time, if intelligence is to serve the ends of a society which places central value on personal liberty, even in time of war, it must not

---

[1] *Personal Justice Denied,* pages 51-56 (reference footnotes omitted).

be overwhelmed by rumors and flights of fancy which grip a fearful, jittery public. Above all, effective intelligence work demands sound judgment which is immune to the paranoia that treats everyone as a hostile suspect until his loyalty is proven. In 1942, what credible threat did Japan pose to the internal peace and security of the United States?

It was common wisdom that the Nazi invasions of Norway and Western Europe had been aided by agents and sympathizers within the country under attack—the so-called fifth column—and that the same approach should be anticipated from Japan. For this reason intelligence was developed on Axis saboteurs and potential fifth columnists as well as espionage agents. This work had been assigned to the Federal Bureau of Investigation and the Navy Department but not to the War Department. The President had developed his own informal intelligence system through John Franklin Carter, a journalist, who helped Roosevelt obtain information and estimates by exploiting sources outside the government. None of these organizations operated with the thoroughness of, say, the modern CIA, but they were the best and calmest eyes and ears the government had.

Each of these sources saw only a very limited security risk from the ethnic Japanese; none recommended a mass exclusion or detention of all people of Japanese ancestry.

On November 7, 1941, John Franklin Carter forwarded to the President a report on the West Coast situation by Curtis B. Munson, a well-to-do Chicago businessman who had gathered intelligence for Carter under the guise of being a government official. Carter summarized five points in the report, which may be all the President read; the War Department also reviewed the report at Roosevelt's request. Regarding sabotage and espionage, Munson wrote:

> There will be no armed uprising of Japanese. There will undoubtedly be some sabotage financed by Japan and executed largely by imported agents or agents already imported. There will be the odd case of fanatical sabotage by some Japanese "crackpot". In each Naval District there are about 250 to 300 suspects under surveillance. It is easy to get on the suspect list, merely a speech in favor of Japan at some banquet, being sufficient to land one there. The Intelligence Services are generous with the title of suspect and are taking no chances. Privately, they believe that only 50 or 60 in each district can be classed as really dangerous. The Japanese are hampered as saboteurs because of their easily recognized physical appearance. It will be hard for them to get near anything to blow up *if it is guarded*. There

is far more danger from Communists and people of the Bridges type on the Coast than there is from Japanese. The Japanese here is almost exclusively a farmer, a fisherman or a small business man. He has no entree to plants or intricate machinery.

The Japanese, if undisturbed and disloyal, should be well equipped for obvious physical espionage. A great part of this work was probably completed and forwarded to Tokio years ago, such as soundings and photography of every inch of the Coast.... An experienced Captain in Navy Intelligence, who has from time to time and over a period of years intercepted information Tokio bound, said he would certainly hate to be a Japanese coordinator of information in Tokio. He stated that the mass of useless information was unbelievable. This would be fine for a fifth column in Belgium or Holland with the German army ready to march in over the border, but though the local Japanese could spare a man who intimately knew the country for each Japanese invasion squad, there would at least have to be a terrific American Naval disaster before his brown brothers would need his services. The dangerous part of their espionage is that they would be very effective as far as movement of supplies, movement of troops and movement of ships out of harbor mouths and over railroads is concerned. They occupy only rarely positions where they can get to confidential papers or in plants. They are usually, when rarely so placed, a subject of perpetual watch and suspicion by their fellow workers. They would have to buy most of this type of information from white people....

Japan will commit some sabotage largely depending on imported Japanese as they are afraid of and do not trust the Nesei [sic]. There will be no wholehearted response from Japanese in the United States. They may get some helpers from certain Kibei. They will be in a position to pick up information on troop, supply and ship movements from local Japanese.

For the most part the local Japanese are loyal to the United States or, at worst, hope that by remaining quiet they can avoid concentration camps or irresponsible mobs. We do not believe that they would be at least any more disloyal than any other racial group in the United States with whom we went to war.

Munson sent three or four more reports to Carter between December and February, including a long review of the situation in Hawaii; he did not change his estimate of the West Coast situation. Most of these reports found their way to Roosevelt's desk. After Pearl Harbor, where Japan received no aid from fifth column activity or sabotage, Munson pointedly noted that "[a]n attack is the proof of the pudding," and remained firmly persuaded that the number of people on the West Coast who could reasonably be suspected of a menacing degree of loyalty to the enemy was small—and not demonstrably greater among the ethnic Japanese than other racial groups. In addition, the physical characteristics of the Japanese which made them readily identifiable made it more difficult for them to engage in sabotage unnoticed or to do any espionage beyond collecting public information open to anyone.

Although Munson was an amateur at intelligence, he talked at length to professionals such as the FBI agent in charge in Honolulu and the people in Naval Intelligence in southern California. He was also in touch with British Intelligence in California and reported that they shared his principal views. The British intelligence officer made one point, repeated by other professionals, which gave savage irony to the exclusion program: "It must be kept in mind when considering the 'Security' to be derived from the mass evacuation of all Japanese, that the Japanese in all probability employed many more 'whites' than 'Japanese' for carrying out their work and this 'white' danger is not eliminated by the evacuation of the Japanese."

Munson had also come to respect the views of Lieutenant Commander K. D. Ringle of the Office of Naval Intelligence in southern California. Ringle had spent much time doing intelligence work in both Japan and southern California where he had assisted in breaking a major Japanese spy ring through a surreptitious entry and developed an effective system of Nisei informants (which he shared with the FBI). When Ringle wanted the membership list of the "Black Dragon" society, a super-patriotic Japanese group, for example, the society's original books for the western half of the United States were delivered to him three days later.

In late January 1942, Ringle estimated that the large majority of ethnic Japanese in the United States were at least passively loyal to this country. There were both citizens and aliens who could act as saboteurs or espionage agents, but he estimated the number to be 3% of the total—or 3,500 in the entire United States who were identifiable individually. Many Nisei leaders had voluntarily contributed valuable anti-subversive information to federal agencies, said Ringle, and if discrimination, firings and personal attacks became prevalent, that conduct would most directly incite sabotage and riots. Ringle saw no need for mass action against people of Japanese ancestry. It is difficult to judge how far one should go in equating Ringle's views with those of Naval Intelligence, since there is no single statement of their position, but he claimed that Naval Intelligence sympathized with his opinions.

The third major source of intelligence was the FBI, which assessed any danger to internal security and had plans ready in case of war. Immediately after Pearl Harbor, President Roosevelt signed Proclamation 2525 pursuant to the Alien Enemy Act of 1798, as amended, which gave the government the authority to detain enemy aliens and confiscate enemy property wherever found. The Proclamation permitted immediate and summary apprehension of "alien enemies deemed dangerous to the public health or safety of the United States by the Attorney General or Secretary of War." On December 8, similar proclamations were issued for the summary apprehension of suspect Germans and Italians.

The FBI had already drawn up lists of those to be arrested—aliens "with something in their record showing an allegiance to the enemy." Three categories of suspects had been developed: "A" category—aliens who led cultural or assistance organizations; "B"—slightly less suspicious aliens; and "C"— members of, or those who donated to, ethnic groups, Japanese language teachers and Buddhist clergy. People in the "A," "B," and "C" categories were promptly arrested in early December. Throughout the initial roundup, Attorney General Biddle was concerned that arrests be orderly. He did not want citizens taking matters into their own hands or directing hostility toward American citizens on the basis of descent, and on December 10 issued a press release stating these themes loudly and clearly. The Attorney General was also firm from the beginning that citizens would not be arrested or apprehended unless there were probable cause to believe that a crime had been committed—the usual standard for arrest. Such arrests were not to occur until the FBI was ready to initiate criminal charges, and the same standards applied to those of German, Italian and Japanese nationality or descent.

By December 10, 1942, FBI Director J. Edgar Hoover reported that "practically all" whom he initially planned to arrest had been taken into custody: 1,291 Japanese (367 in Hawaii, 924 in the continental United States); 857 Germans; 147 Italians. In fact, however, the government continued to apprehend enemy aliens. By February 16, 1942, the Department of Justice held 2,192 Japanese; 1,393 Germans; and 264 Italians and arrests continued even after that date. Many arrested in the early sweeps were Issei leaders of the Japanese American community and its organizations.

FBI views on the need for mass exclusion from the West Coast were provided at the Attorney General's request shortly before the Executive Order was signed, and must be read in that context. Hoover did not believe that demands for mass evacuation were based on factual analysis. Although he doubted Nisei loyalty in case of invasion and grasped the obvious point that people excluded from the West Coast could not commit sabotage there, he pointed out that the cry for evacuation came from political pressure. The historical experience of the FBI showed that Japan had used Occidentals for its espionage—which Ringle had learned from his clandestine raid on the Japanese consulate. Hoover balanced his own opinions by sharing with the Attorney General his West Coast field offices' views of evacuation, which varied from noncommittal in Los Angeles to dismissive in San Francisco to vehemently favorable in San Diego and Seattle. Nevertheless, Hoover's own opinion, and thus the Bureau's, was that the case to justify mass evacuation for security reasons had not been made.

These mainland intelligence views were blurred by sensational and inaccurate reports from Hawaii. On December 9, 1941, Secretary of the Navy Knox went to Hawaii to make the first brief examination of the reasons for American losses at Pearl Harbor. He returned to the mainland on December 15 and told the press, "I think the most effective Fifth Column work of the entire war was done in Hawaii with the possible exception of Norway." This laid major blame for the Pearl Harbor defeat at the door of the ethnic Japanese in the United States. Knox's statement was not only unfounded: it ignored the fact that Japanese Americans in large numbers had immediately come to the defense of the islands at the time of the attack.

The Secretary raised the matter again at the Cabinet meeting of December 19, when Attorney General Biddle noted that "Knox told me, which was not what Hoover had thought, that there was a great deal of very active, fifth column work going on both from the shores and from the sampans" in the Pearl Harbor attack.* John Franklin Carter also disputed Knox in a memo to Roosevelt. Nor were his views supported by General Short, who had been in command at the time of the Pearl Harbor attack, and they were contradicted a few days later by the new Commanding General in Hawaii, Delos Emmons, who stated in a broadcast to the islands that there had been very few acts of sabotage at the time of the attack. The basis of Knox's statement has never

---

* Hoover did not believe that fifth column activities were prevalent in Hawaii, having heard from the FBI's special agent in charge in Honolulu as early as December 8, that General Short had reported absolutely no sabotage during the attack and, on December 17, he advised the Attorney General that it was believed that the great majority of the population of foreign extraction in the islands was law-abiding. Hoover directly questioned Knox's opinion, but he did not do so publicly, and it is unknown whether his views were heard outside the Justice Department. Memo, Hoover to Tolson, Tamm and Ladd, Dec. 8, 1941; Memo, Hoover to Attorney General, Dec. 17, 1941. FBI (CWRIC 5786-89; 5830).

been clear; he may have relied on rumors which had not yet been checked, or he may have confused prewar espionage by Japanese agents with fifth column activity. Nevertheless, because military news from Hawaii was carefully censored and the Secretary appeared to speak from firsthand knowledge, Knox's statement carried considerable weight. His accompanying recommendation for the removal of all Japanese, regardless of citizenship, from Oahu is one of the first calls for mass racial exclusion. The alarm Knox had rung gave immediate credence to the view that ethnic Japanese on the mainland were a palpable threat and danger. The damage was remarkable. When Knox's official report came out on December 16, there was no reference to fifth column activities; it described espionage by Japanese consular officers and praised the Japanese Americans who had manned machine guns against the enemy. Nevertheless, the story ran in major West Coast papers headlined "Fifth Column Treachery Told," "Fifth Column Prepared Attack" and "Secretary of Navy Blames 5th Column for Raid." Nothing was promptly done at the highest level of the government to repudiate Knox's initial statement or publicly to affirm the loyalty of the ethnic Japanese, even though Munson (through Carter) emphasized Knox's inaccuracy and urged that such a statement be made by the President or Vice President.

Much calmer (though opaque) views were reported by the first official inquiry into the Pearl Harbor disaster. The Roberts Commission, appointed by the President and chaired by Supreme Court Justice Owen J. Roberts, issued a report on January 23, 1942, which never mentioned sabotage, espionage or fifth column activity in its conclusion. Regarding such activity, the body of the report says in part:

> There were, prior to December 7, 1941, Japanese spies on the island of Oahu. Some were Japanese consular agents and other [sic] were persons having no open relations with the Japanese foreign service. These spies collected and, through various channels transmitted, information to the Japanese Empire respecting the military and naval establishments and dispositions on the island. . . .
>
> It was believed that the center of Japanese espionage in Hawaii was the Japanese consulate at Honolulu. It has been discovered that the Japanese consul sent to and received from Tokyo in his own and other names many messages on commercial radio circuits. This activity greatly increased toward December 7, 1941. The contents of these messages, if it could have been learned, might have furnished valuable information. In view of the peaceful relations with Japan,

and the consequent restrictions on the activities of the investigating agencies, they were unable prior to December 7 to obtain and examine messages transmitted through commercial channels by the Japanese consul, or by persons acting for him.

It is now apparent that through their intelligence service the Japanese had complete information.

Testimony at secret hearings lay behind the conclusions. General Short, in command of the Army on Hawaii at the time of Pearl Harbor, had misinterpreted the warning message of late November as an alert against sabotage and so should have been particularly conscious of it; Short testified that "I do not believe since I came here that there has been any act of sabotage of any importance at all, but the FBI and my intelligence outfit know of a lot of these people and knew they probably would watch the opportunity to carry out something."

Robert L. Shivers, the FBI's Special Agent in Charge in Hawaii (and a man Munson thought highly of) testified that Japanese espionage before Pearl Harbor "centered in the Japanese consulate;" he held responsible the 234 consular representatives who had not been prosecuted in 1941 for failure to register as foreign agents. These men were arrested immediately after Pearl Harbor and kept in custody. Shivers offered documentary proof to support his views, and testified that there were no acts of sabotage in Hawaii during the Pearl Harbor raid.

Despite such telling testimony, the Roberts Report did not use language designed to allay the unease spread by Knox. In fact the Report tended to have the opposite effect; in March a House Committee stated that public agitation in favor of evacuation dated from publication of the Roberts Report. Predictions which the Commission heard in Hawaii may have caused this silence. Besides Roberts, the Commissioners were high-ranking military officers who, at Secretary Stimson's direction, used the Commission's inquiry to look into the future defense of the islands. They asked intelligence staff in Hawaii about the prospects for future sabotage or fifth column activity and received conflicting advice.

Shivers asserted that "just as soon as Japan achieves some temporary decisive victory, the old spirit will begin to bubble forth" and that:

> [If] there should be an out-and-out attack on this island by the Japanese Navy, reinforced by their air arm, I think you could expect 95% of the alien Japanese to glory in that attack and to do anything they could to further the efforts of the Japanese forces.

You would find some second- and third-generation Japanese, who are American citizens but who hold dual citizenship, and you would find some of those who would join forces with the Japanese attackers for this and other reasons. Some of them may think they have suffered discrimination, economic, social, and otherwise, and there would probably be a few of them who would do it.

He also thought the Japanese community in the United States and Hawaii was highly organized, and so in theory had the ability to assist the Axis. Finally, Shivers believed only individuals, not the Japanese in the United States collectively, would become potential saboteurs.

Angus Taylor, the United States Attorney for Hawaii, a man of vehement and strident views, not directly engaged in intelligence work, testified that in the event of subsequent Japanese attack, even the third-generation citizens would "immediately turn over to their own race."

The Intelligence Officer of the 14th Naval District, Irving Mayfield, believed that the Japanese system of spies and saboteurs would not rest on race or ethnicity. This point had, of course, been made repeatedly by Hoover, Munson and Ringle. The professionals largely agreed that the Japanese did not rely on Issei and Nisei for espionage, and there was no reason to believe they would for sabotage. In a 1943 memorandum, Mayfield set out the logic of his position: it had to be the operating premise of counterespionage that Japan's spying operation might be made up of only ethnic Japanese, only non-ethnic Japanese or a combination of the two. A solely ethnic Japanese group might be able to rely on people of known loyalty to Japan with close ties to that country, but American suspicion of such people and the possibility that they might be detained in time of war might well lead Japan to rely entirely on people who were not ethnic Japanese. Variations of these extremes were equally possible:

> For purposes of security, the vital core of the organization might be composed of non-Japanese. . . . On the other hand, the nucleus of the organization may be composed of Japanese, who will make use of non-Japanese as the need and opportunity arises. This group might even have available a non-Japanese whose sole function would be to assume direction of the espionage organization in case the members of the original core are immobilized or rendered ineffective by security or counter-espionage measures.

Mayfield's thorough approach to the problem exposed the flimsy reasoning behind the policy of exclusion—without evidence, there was no sound basis for expecting the Japanese to employ any particular ethnic group as spies or saboteurs. This proved true; in Hawaii one of the few alien residents brought to trial for war-related crimes was Bernard Julius Otto Kuehn, a German national in the pay of Japan, and on the mainland the few people convicted of being illegal agents of Japan were predominantly not ethnic Japanese.

But these views did not reach the topmost level of the War Department. Secretary Stimson recorded in his diary a long evening with Justice Roberts after his return from Hawaii, noting Roberts' expressed fear that the Japanese in the islands posed a major security risk through, espionage, sabotage and fifth column activity. Roberts also visited General DeWitt and one may assume that he presented similar views to the General.

Thus, in the early months of war, the intelligence services largely agreed that Japan had quietly collected massive amounts of useful information over recent years, in Hawaii and on the mainland, a great deal of it entirely legally, and that the threat of sabotage and fifth column activity during attack was limited and controllable. Significantly, the intelligence experts never focused exclusively on ethnic Japanese in the United States: logically the Japanese would not depend solely on the Issei and Nisei, and experience showed that they did not trust the Nisei, employing Occidentals for espionage.

The prophecy about who might conduct future espionage and sabotage was based on a number of factors. No significant sabotage or fifth column activity had helped destroy Pearl Harbor. Insofar as the Japanese would rely on the Issei or other Axis aliens' assistance, those who were at all suspect had been interned by the Department of Justice. Insofar as the Japanese would rely on the Nisei, there was no knowledge or evidence of organized or individual Nisei spying or disruption. Ringle and Munson did not believe there would be any greater disloyalty from them than from any other American ethnic group; Taylor, and perhaps Shivers in Hawaii, dissented. The course recommended by Hoover (Ringle and Munson suggested similar approaches) was one of surveillance but not arrest or detention without evidence to back up individualized suspicion. Hoover recommended registering all enemy aliens in the United States; also, to protect against fifth columnists, he wanted specific authority (either suspension of the writ of habeas corpus or a "so-called syndicalism law") to permit the apprehension of any citizen or alien "as to whom there may be reasonable cause to believe that such person has been or is engaging in giving aid or comfort to the enemies of the United States;" and he backed Department of Justice evaluation of lists of suspect citizens to determine who should be taken into custody under any such extreme authority.

These restrained views did not prevail. Those with intelligence knowledge were few, and they rarely spoke as a body. Navy Intelligence, for instance, felt it had enough on its hands without contradicting or challenging the Army. Whatever its intelligence officers thought, the Navy was intent on moving the ethnic Japanese away from its installations at Terminal Island near Los Angeles and Bainbridge Island in Puget Sound, and Secretary Knox's support of stern measures against the ethnic Japanese seemed unlikely to change. Few voices were raised inside the War Department, which was responsible for security on the West Coast. Stronger political forces outside the intelligence services wanted evacuation. Intelligence opinions were disregarded or drowned out.

The following addendum was hurriedly put together by the General Counsel of the Commission on the Wartime Relocation and Internment of Civilians in an effort to rebut the claim that MAGIC intelligence played a major role in the World War II evacuation decision. During two years of hearings and research the Commission remained ignorant of the existence or implications of MAGIC.

MAGIC ADDENDUM (Addendum to *Personal Justice Denied*)[2]

There have been recent reports in the press which point out that the Commission's report, *Personal Justice Denied*, does not make reference to the multi-volume Department of Defense publication, *The "Magic" Background of Pearl Harbor.* Those volumes contain Japanese diplomatic cables of 1941 which American cryptanalysts deciphered, a small number of which refer to Japan's intelligence efforts in the United States. There is a penumbra to the articles which suggests that if the Commission had been aware that Japan had an intelligence network in this country which involved any American citizens of Japanese ancestry or resident Japanese aliens, it would have reached different conclusions and opinions about Executive Order 9066.

In fact, review of the "Magic" cables does not alter the Commission's position. Rather, it confirms the views expressed by the Commission. *Personal Justice Denied* devoted several pages to analyzing the American intelligence views of Japan's espionage, sabotage, and fifth column capabilities on the West Coast in late 1941 and 1942. Several relevant points were made in that discussion. First, the intelligence sources reviewed assumed that Japan had a modest number of intelligence agents and perhaps potential saboteurs on the West Coast in 1942. Second, people familiar with the intelligence activities of Japan believed that the Japanese intelligence network employed many who were not ethnic Japanese. Third, the intelligence experts believed that any threat of sabotage, espionage or fifth column activity was limited and controllable and did not justify mass exclusion of the ethnic Japanese from the West Coast. Nothing in the "Magic" cables contradicts these basic points.

What the "Magic" cables show is an effort by Japan to develop an intelligence capability in the United States made up of both non-ethnic Japanese and

---

2   *Personal Justice Denied*, pages 471-475 (reference footnotes omitted).

ethnic Japanese. In fact, in sending instructions about who should be used in such an effort, the cables first emphasize groups *other* than the Issei and Nisei:

> (5) Utilization of U. S. citizens of foreign extractions (other than Japanese), aliens (other than Japanese), communists, Negroes, labor union members, and anti-Semites, in carrying out the investigations described in the preceding paragraph would undoubtedly bear the best results.
>
> These men, moreover, should have access to governmental establishments, (laboratories?), governmental organizations of various characters, factories, and transportation facilities.
>
> (6) Utilization of our "Second Generations" and our resident nationals. (In view of the fact that if there is any slip in this phase, our people in the U. S. will be subjected to considerable persecution, and the utmost caution must be exercised).

Among the more than 4,000 "Magic" cables in 1941, only a very small number reflect the collection of intelligence which was not clearly public information or data obtainable by legal observation. The limited number of cables which include sensitive information frequently do not make clear the source of the information, and those that do refer to both persons who were not ethnic Japanese as well as ethnic Japanese. This is shown by what is probably the most complete report from the United States describing Japan's intelligence-gathering effort, a cable of May 9, 1941 from Los Angeles; the cable also demonstrates the difficulty of determining how much, if any, of the information collection was secret or illegal:

> We are doing everything in our power to establish outside contacts in connection with our efforts to gather intelligence material. In this regard, we have decided to make use of white persons and Negroes, through Japanese persons whom we can't trust completely. (It not only would be very difficult to hire U.S. (military?) experts for this work at the present time, but the expenses would be exceedingly high.) We shall, furthermore, maintain close connections with the Japanese Association, the Chamber of Commerce, and the newspapers.
>
> With regard to airplane manufacturing plans and other military establishments in other parts, we plan to establish very close relations with various organizations and in strict secrecy have them keep these military establishments under close surveillance. Through such

means, we hope to be able to obtain accurate and detailed intelligence reports. We have already established contacts with absolutely reliable Japanese in the San Pedro and San Diego area, who will keep a close watch on all shipments of airplanes and other war materials, and report the amounts and destination of such shipments. The same steps have been taken with regard to traffic across the U.S.-Mexico border.

We shall maintain connection with our second generations who are at present in the (U.S.) Army, to keep us informed of various developments in the Army. We also have connections with our second generations working in airplane plants for intelligence purposes.

With regard to the Navy, we are cooperating with our Naval Attache's office, and are submitting reports as accurately and as speedily as possible.

We are having Nakazawa investigate and summarize information gathered through first hand and newspaper reports, with regard to military movements, labor disputes, communistic activities and other similar matters. With regard to anti-Lewis movements, we are having investigations made by both prominent Americans and Japanese who are connected with the movie industry which is centered in this area. We have already established connections with very influential Negroes to keep us informed with regard to the Negro movement.

This cable also illustrates the further problem that it is very difficult to distinguish puffery from truth in the "Magic" documents—certainly later cables do not show the transmission of information which would have given Japan knowledge of anything but a very small part of the items listed in this cable. Of course, information could be transmitted by methods other than "Magic" codes, but there is considerable room to doubt that any program of this sort was fulfilled.

Next, there is no indication in the "Magic" cables of a sabotage or fifth column organization. The likelihood of sabotage and fifth column aid in case of attack were, of course, major arguments advanced in support of the exclusion.

As to the intelligence network being identifiable and controllable, the "Magic" volumes end with the Pearl Harbor attack and do not report whether Japanese agents were picked up by the FBI immediately after December 7th. But an occasional indication is available. One of the few persons with a Japanese name mentioned in the cables in connection with covert activities is one Iwasaki, who had been in touch with William Duciley Pelley, leader of the Silver Shirts, a fascist organization in the United States. The records of the Western Defense Command show that it became fully familiar with Iwasaki's relation to the Silver Shirts and knew that he had returned to Japan before the outbreak of war. Evidence of this sort tends to corroborate the views that intelligence experts, such as Lieutenant Commander Ringle of the Office of Naval Intelligence, expressed in 1942.

The startling news would have been to discover that Japan had no intelligence capability on the West Coast before Pearl Harbor. What has been found in the "Magic" cables only reaffirms the conclusions and opinions the Commission reached in its report.

One reason that the documents were not located and reviewed is that there is no clear evidence that they played any part in the decision to issue Executive Order 9066 or to pursue the policy of exclusion and detention of the West Coast ethnic Japanese. The Commission did not locate references to the "Magic" cables in the extensive documents of the time which deal with exclusion and detention. Within the War Department the impetus for the Executive Order came primarily from General DeWitt on the West Coast, and he was not on the distribution list for "Magic" material. From May to November, 1941, President Roosevelt did not see the "Magic" cables, so that it is a matter of speculation how, if at all, the minor cables dealing with intelligence in the United States were reported to him by those who summarized the cables orally. It is equally difficult to tell what, if any, part of the cable traffic was known to those not on the distribution.

No one who was in the War Department in 1941 and on the distribution for "Magic" information is alive today, so that one cannot demonstrate whether or not these cables had any influence on their thinking when the issue of exclusion was raised. The person still alive who was closest to those who saw the "Magic" cables is John J. McCloy; he testified before the Commission about the basis of the War Department's request for the Executive Order, and in discussing espionage and sabotage made no argument that intelligence from Japanese sources played any part in the decision:

> MR. MACBETH: First, is it your memory that there were no known cases of actual sabotage from Japanese aliens or Japanese American citizens on the West Coast prior to the signing of the Executive Order?
>
> MR. McCLOY: I can't say—I don't know whether there were or whether there weren't. There were rumors that there was violence and some espionage, that everybody was reporting in that there were signals from the Coast and they were close enough to watch the

convoys. Whether it was espionage or not, I can't say. But this wasn't such a motivating factor with us, the possibility was there, and I think the soldiers who were military minded always had—they weren't saying that they wanted—they wanted to try to eliminate as far as possible all potential sabotage or espionage after the attack, and I don't know that they had any records at that time; I didn't know of any record of any convictions; there were suspicions and rumors but that's as far as I can go.

MR. MACBETH: Would it be fair then to say that the decision was made not on the basis of actual events of sabotage or espionage known to the War Department, but on the fear of possible future actions, is that right?

MR. McCLOY: Yes. Except, of course, the Pearl Harbor attack itself.

In sum, the "Magic" cables confirm the basic analysis presented by the Commission.

Much has been made of the sentence in *Personal Justice Denied* which states that "not a single documented act of espionage, sabotage or fifth column activity was committed by an American citizen of Japanese ancestry or by a resident Japanese alien on the West Coast." This statement stands. The "Magic" cables do not identify individuals in those groups who committed demonstrable acts of espionage, sabotage or fifth column activity.

Since it is always possible that such an identification might one day be made, it is worth underscoring that espionage or sabotage by a small group does not justify excluding and detaining the entire ethnic group to which they belong. During World War II the following Caucasians were convicted of espionage on the mainland: William A. Schuler, Dr. Otto Willumeit, Gerhard Kunze, Rev. Kurt B. Molzahn, Nicholine Buonapane, Frederick V. Williams, David W. Ryder, Igor Stepanoff, Arthur C. Read, Mrs. Valvalee Dickinson, John Farnsworth, Harry A. Thompson, Frederick H. Wright, John C. LeClair, Joseph H. Smyth, Walker G. Matheson, Ralph Townsend, and Mimo de Guzman. Such evidence provides no good argument for excluding all German Americans or English Americans from the coasts and detaining them in the interior. Equally, there was no good argument for excluding and detaining the Japanese Americans.

Angus MacBeth
June 1983

APPENDIX III

LOYALTY IN CAMPS

From the beginning of the evacuation there were those among the evacuees who were bent on trouble and who were involved in efforts to pressure individuals loyal to the United States to action contrary to the interests of the war effort. Force, sometimes deadly, was used.

In 1943 an effort was made by the War Relocation Authority to segregate the "troublemakers" from others in the relocation centers. A loyalty questionnaire was the major instrument used to differentiate between those who were and were not loyal to the U.S. In particular, question #28 was considered crucial.

Male U. S. citizens were asked, "Will you swear unqualified allegiance to the United States of America and faithfully defend the United States from any or all attack by foreign or domestic forces, and forswear any form of allegiance or obedience to the Japanese Emperor, or any other foreign government, power, or organization?"

The question was not materially different from the oath required by the Japanese American Citizens League of its members as outlined in the Ringle memo of January 26, 1942.[1]

For many reasons including anger at evacuation, an unwillingness to serve in the armed forces (which would not accept individuals without an affirmative expression of loyalty to the U.S.), and loyalty to Japan and its

---

[1] See Ringle memo, January 26, 1942, page 315. Reference on page 319.

Emperor, 28 percent of U.S. citizen males seventeen and older answered "no" to question #28 or refused to fill out the questionnaire. This 28 percent included a large contingent of Kibei, those who had been educated in Japan and were identified in intelligence reports to be of generally suspect loyalty.

Tule Lake Relocation Center, near Newell, California, where fully 49 percent of citizen males answered "no" to question #28 or refused to fill out the questionnaire, was designated a "segregation center" and those of suspect loyalty from the other nine relocation centers were moved there. With them came many in their families who professed U.S. loyalty but did not want to suffer family separation. There were also many at Tule Lake who professed loyalty to the U.S. but did not want to be moved again. All together there was a total of 18,000 people at the facility and the mix of loyal and disloyal made it a difficult situation.

Agitation by pro-Japan elements soon started and was initially condoned by the War Relocation Authority, which supported a policy of allowing those wishing to return to Japan and others who professed loyalty to Japan, to participate in Japanese educational and cultural programs. The agitation quickly led to militant pro-Japan and anti-American demonstrations and pressure on the loyal segment of the population to support a radical program, a main point of which was to further segregate those truly loyal to Japan into a special facility of their own.

The Justice Department, which had struggled with the issue of citizenship and its inherent rights in regard to controlling disloyal conduct by citizens, sought a solution to the problem by securing legislation that allowed individuals to renounce their citizenship, thereby becoming enemy aliens and subject to strict, yet legal action by the government. By January 1945 fully half of the Nisei and Kibei at Tule Lake, or about 4,600 individuals, had applied to renounce their U.S. citizenship, many no doubt because of pressure from the pro-Japan organizations.

The following letter from John L. Burling, "For the Attorney General," provides a good summary of the situation. The accompanying photographs from the National Archives illustrate the type and magnitude of the pro-Japan and anti-American activity Burling discusses in his letter. One can only wonder what the wartime situation along the West Coast would have been had these fanatics been running loose. Or what threat they would have posed as potential Japanese intelligence operatives. Despite their professed and demonstrated disloyalty to the United States each of them still alive in 1988 was eligible for a $20,000 payment and an apology from the nation.

DEPARTMENT OF JUSTICE
Newell, California

January 10, 1945

Manao Sakamoto
  Chairman, Sokuji Kikoku Hoshi Dan
Tsutomu Higashi
  Chairman, Hokoku Seinen Dan
Tule Lake Center
Newell, California

Sirs:

        Your letter of January 1, 1945 and your telegram of January 6, 1945
to the Attorney General pertaining to the apprehension as alien enemies
of seventy members of your organizations on December 27, 1944 has been
referred to me for reply. Although I have been in some doubt as to whether
the latter merits any reply at all inasmuch as I have questioned both of
you and have found that neither of you is able to write English and therefore
neither could have written the letter himself and since neither of you is
able or willing to tell me who did write it, I have nevertheless determined
to make this reply to your communications so that your two organizations
may have a clear and unequivocal statement as to the attitude and policies
of the Department of Justice toward the organizations and their activities.

        I may say at the outset that the tone of your communications as
well as the tone of the statements made to me by the leadership of the two
organizations suggests that those leaders, possibly because they have for
nearly three years resided in camps safely away from the pressures of
war, have lost all sense of reality. The young men of the Hokoku Seinen
Dan leadership glibly assert their loyalty to the Emperor of Japan and
their desire to fight in the Japanese Army. They have the effrontery to
engage on American soil in semi-military drilling and in Japanese
patriotic exercises to the sound of bugles. They have the impudence to
appear before officials of the American Government wearing their hair
cut short in the manner of Japanese soldiers and having painted on their
shirts a Japanese patriotic emblem with the background of the Rising Sun.
The older men of the Sokuji Kikoku Hoshi Dan do not make such spectacles
of themselves but feel free not only to tell the American Government of
their loyalty to Japan but even to encourage the activities of the young
men.

        All this would be bad enough but what is worse is that the leaders
of these organizations appear to feel that because of these activities
they are entitled to respect and approval not only from persons who are
loyal to Japan but from the American Government itself. The tone of the

- 2 -

communications which the leaders of the two organizations have had with me
indicates that those leaders believe that the organizations are respectable
and reasonable ones entitled to the friendly consideration of this Government.
In thinking that, those leaders have, as I say, lost all sense of reality.

As those of us who have not for years been sheltered behind the
protective fences of this Camp appreciate and as the heroic Nisei of the
100th Battalion know all too well, America is engaged in a terrible war
and is paying for the victory, which is sure, a frightful cost in blood
and lives. The Japanese Army and Navy, to which the leaders of these
organizations profess loyalty, commenced this war against us without
warning and the victories over the Japanese Army and Navy which we have
already won and will continue to win are taking the lives of thousands of
our young men of every ancestry, including your own.

Under these circumstances only children or half-crazy people could
suppose that the American Government can look with friendship or approval
upon organizations openly engaged in activities designed to show loyalty
to the enemy. In my opinion the reason the leadership of those organizations so foolishly fails to understand the attitude which the American
Government must take toward the organizations is that the leaders have
throughout most of the war refused to fight in the American Army, been
unable to fight in the Japanese Army and have sat in safety and even
relative comfort in a Government camp. Tule Lake may not be a delightful
place to live but there is little doubt that the foxholes are worse.
Sheltered as they are, the leaders do not know the meaning of war.

Members of the organizations, particularly the Hokoku Seinen Dan,
tell me that they are anxious to fight for Japan and that they should
receive at least the respect due to enemy patriots. I doubt very much
whether they are entitled even to that consideration. In the first place,
the members of the Hokoku Seinen Dan are almost all American citizens.
They were born in the United States. Even by the Japanese code, loyalty
is a matter of birth; and this country, therefore, is the mother country
of the members of the Seinen Dan. Yet in time of war these young men,
who were born in this country, have betrayed it and have demonstrated their
loyalty to the enemy. They are not patriots, but traitors. They are,
thank God, but a small minority of the young people of Japanese ancestry
born in this country, but they are a disgrace and a shame to their brother
Japanese-Americans who have proved with their blood that they understand
what it means to be loyal to the country of one's birth.

Not only are the leaders of the Hokoku Seinen Dan traitors to the
country of their birth but is very doubtful whether they are
truly loyal to Japan. A very large number of the leaders are Kibei
who left Japan after 1937. In that year Japan commenced the China
Incident which, although it was not a declared war, was nevertheless a

- 3 -

bloody and costly one. Ever since 1937 soldiers of the Japanese Army have
been fighting in China. Ever since that time there has been compulsory
military service in Japan. Of course, few people left Japan who were
actually drafted but many of the young men who were 17, 18 or 19 in those
years left one jump ahead of the draft. If you do not believe this, look
around among your Kibei friends. Ask yourselves why these boys who now
say they are so anxious to fight and die for the Emperor didn't stay and
do so when they had the chance. Ask yourselves why it is only now, when
they are snug and safe in an American camp for the duration of the war,
that they decide that they want to fight for Japan. Is it not that they
know they will go back to Japan after the war and know that the veterans
of the Japanese Army will ask them why they left during the Chinese war
and where they were when the fighting was going on? Is it not their
hope that by this foolish head-shaving and bugle-blowing they will
persuade people of their Japanese patriotism even though when they were
last in Japan they fled from the draft?

Some of the young men admit they left Japan during the fighting in China,
but say they are now going back on an exchange ship and fight. There is
reason to doubt their sincerity. In the first place, while they were
making these assertions it looked to everyone as if there would be no
more exchanges during the war. Although throughout the entire war the
United States government has been anxious to exchange Japanese nationals
desiring to return to Japan for American citizens in the Orient. Japan
has agreed to only two exchanges and had not agreed to any since
October 1943. Thus it seemed perfectly safe for the boys who did not
fight when they had the chance to say that now they wanted to go back
on an exchange ship and fight. In the second place, it is not at all
clear yet what the conditions of the exchange will be, or even if there
will be one. Ordinarily men of military age are not exchanged or, if
they are, an agreement is made between the belligerents forbidding them
to fight. This may be included in the terms of the contemplated exchange.
The boasters still may be safe.

Many of the leaders of the Sokuji Kikoku Hoshi Dan and the Hokoku
Seinen Dan have expressed the view that the activities of these organizations are permissible since residents at this Center were told, when
it was established as a segregation center, that this Camp was to be for
persons who look toward a future in Japan and, in a sense, was to be for
persons who were loyal to Japan. This is wholly wrong. It is true that
this Camp was set aside as a segregation center and that by and large
persons who were denied leave clearance were transferred here. It is also
true that many persons who were segregated here had already declined to
express their loyalty to the United States. Many people, however, came
here to be with their families or for other reasons unrelated to loyalty
to Japan. Thus, it is incorrect to say that this is a camp exclusively
for Japanese patriots and that pro-Japanese activity is therefore permissible. No Government can force inner loyalty. Those Issei who feel
loyal to Japan may live quietly in the Camp and continue to feel that

- 4 -

loyalty. Those Nisei who feel loyal to Japan may, under the new statute, apply for renunciation of their citizenship; and, if it is approved, they, like their elders, may live in a Camp quietly and continue to feel that loyalty. No one, however, has the right to engage in pro-Japanese demonstrations and parades or to publish pro-Japanese newspapers or to wear a semi-military uniform bearing the emblem of the Rising Sun on it. What is even more important, no one loyal to Japan has the right here to seek to convert others to that loyalty. I am well aware that your two organizations have put pressure on residents of this Center to assert loyalty to Japan and that in a number of cases physical violence was employed. There is no more right to engage in Japanese patriotic ceremonies or to publish a pro-Japanese paper in this Center, where some loyal Americans still live, than there is anywhere else in the United States. It is as treasonable to coerce others into asserting loyalty to Japan here as it would be outside. All these activities will stop.

Coming to the specific questions which you asked the Attorney General in your letter of January 1, 1945, you are informed that the seventy men apprehended by the Department of Justice on December 27, 1944 were apprehended as alien enemies pursuant to Section 21 Title 50 United States Code, which authorizes the apprehension of alien enemies who are deemed dangerous to the internal security of the United States. All of these men were alien enemies either because they were Issei to begin with or because they were dual citizens who had renounced their American citizenship, thus leaving only Japanese citizenship. Their internment as alien enemies was deemed in the national interest by the Attorney General because of the subversive activities of the organizations of which they were leaders.

You next state that these men were originally segregated in Tule Lake with their families because of their professed loyalty to Japan and ask why they are now interned and separated from their families. They have not been interned because of their feeling of loyalty to Japan but because they were leaders in subversive organizations which encouraged the pro-Japanese activities to which I have referred. They were apprehended because it was felt to be necessary to remove them to a Department of Justice internment camp where their conduct could be more carefully controlled. At some later date it may or may not be possible to arrange for their internment in a camp where their families may join them. At the present time there are not sufficient family camp facilities to permit this. The Geneva Convention does not guarantee an enemy, whether a prisoner of war or a civilian internee, the right to have his family with him. Internment in family camps is an additional humanitarian procedure provided by this Government which can be provided only as there is space available.

Your third question asks why the men who were apprehended on December 27 were not given time to bid farewell to their families or to pack their belongings. Since the men were apprehended in the middle of the night when they presumably were in their apartments with their families, I should suppose they did in fact have an opportunity to say goodbye. I also understand that they were able to take with them their necessary belongings.

- 5 -

You last state that one of the seventy men was arrested when his mother was ill and you assert that his removal was, therefore, inhuman. It is, of course, unfortunate that this man's mother was ill at the time but there is nothing inhuman about the son's apprehension. Persons who engage in subversive activities may expect to be apprehended and if this apprehension comes at an unfortunate time, that is his own responsibility. In view of the fact that seventy men had to be moved by special train, it was necessary to conduct the operation with speed and efficiency and, although I am unaware of the details of the movement, I assume that there was a practical reason which made it impossible for the apprehended man to visit his mother. The Department of Justice desires to be humane but when dealing with avowed enemies of this country the interests of the United States will, within the safeguards of the Geneva Convention, come first.

In your letter of January 1, 1945 you refer to the apprehension of the seventy men as an "intolerable incident". There is nothing whatever "intolerable" about that incident. What is intolerable is that the activities of your two organizations continue. Since these activities are intolerable, they will not be tolerated but, on the contrary, will cease.

For the Attorney General

John L. Burling

Tule Lake Segregation Center

National Archives

Shaved heads, but not shaved faces, were required of the Hokoku Seinen Dan as evidenced by this alien enemy sent to Santa Fe Internment Camp June 24, 1945 with 399 other anti-American agitators from the Tule Lake Segregation Center in Newell, California.

National Archives

January 26, 1945, Tule Lake Segregation Center, Newell, California—
Members of Hokoku Seinen Dan gather at Gate 1 to give "banzai" send-off
to 171 members of their anti-American organization being sent to the
Department of Justice Internment camp in Santa Fe, New Mexico. White
headband and sweatshirts were the Hokoku uniform.

National Archives

January 26, 1945, Tule Lake Segregation Center, Newell, California—Hokoku
in marching demonstration as part of send-off celebration.

National Archives

January 26, 1945, Tule Lake Segregation Center, Newell, California—"Banzai" salute by members of Hokoku Seinen Dan.

National Archives

February 11, 1945, Tule Lake Segregation Center, Newell, California—Hokoku "right dress" to line up in honor of 650 of their group being sent to Department of Justice Internment camp at Bismarck, South Dakota.

National Archives

Tule Lake Segregation Center, Newell, California—"Banzai" to 650 Hokoku being taken to Department of Justice Internment Camp at Bismark, South Dakota on February 11, 1945

National Archives

Tule Lake Segregation Center, Newell, California—Bugle Corps of Hokoku Seinen Dan gather at Gate 1 to give proper send-off to 125 of their number being sent to Santa Fe Internment Camp on March 4, 1945.

National Archives

Tule Lake Segregation Center, Newell, California—March 18, 1945, Japanese sympathizers watch early morning drill of Hokoku Seinen Dan. Women supporters of Japan were organized in a group called Hokoku Joshi Seinen Dan (Young Women's Organization to Serve Our Mother Country).

National Archives

Tule Lake Segregation Center, Newell, California—February 12, 1945, Charles Rothstein, special assistant to the Attorney General, assists in the raid on Hoshi Dan headquarters in which all property is confiscated. Roger Huff, WRA internal security officer, is in background; two other internal security officials at right.

APPENDIX IV

PROBLEMS WITH EVACUATION RESEARCH

Despite wide-ranging access to historical information under the Freedom of Information Act, there still exist a variety of impediments to obtaining information relating to intelligence operations. These range from an overload of requests on records holding agencies to a requirement to screen and redact portions of reports dealing with security issues and personal privacy.

It presently takes the FBI several years to honor a request for information that has not already been processed and cleared. When released, the information requested may be drastically limited. For example, a request for information from the FBI on the Imperial Comradeship Society, a known subversive Japanese organization on the West Coast before World War II which was reported to be committed to conducting sabotage, took three years to fill and then provided 237 pages of documents from 944 reviewed. One missing section included 185 pages listing membership and biographical data which would have revealed important information on the participation of resident and citizen Japanese. Those pages that were released were often heavily redacted.

Few would argue against the need to protect methods and sources of intelligence information or against the desirability of personal privacy, but without the information used at the time to influence this historical decision, it is impossible to obtain a true picture of the situation .

Unfortunately, FBI reviews, in an effort to make no mistakes, sometimes redact information that is legally releasable. Appeals of such errors also take time to process. Records on citizens can be released if proof of death is provided.

However, this leads to a dilemma. If you don't know who was involved, how can you provide the required death certificates to obtain information on their involvement? And, without general access to this critical information, the work of those with a vested interest in historical revision becomes easier.

Political considerations also affect accessibility. At the California State Archives, for instance, there are seventy-six boxes of records produced by the California Un-American Activities Committee which undoubtedly contain information related to Japanese government espionage efforts and other subversive activities in California before the war. These records are now under the legal control of the State Senate Rules Committee. Why this material needs sealing after sixty years is not quite clear.

California presently appropriates millions of dollars in support of the "official" history of Japanese evacuation while sealing records which may reflect the prudence of evacuation and shed light on the conditions that existed at the time of Pearl Harbor.

The Smithsonian Institution and the National Archives have each taken public positions on the issue of evacuation and in doing so have chosen to ignore information available to them that would more fairly present the event in historical perspective. The permanent Smithsonian exhibit is shot through with exaggeration and in one instance outright fabrication, presenting a picture of evacuation that is factually flawed and more fitting as propaganda than history. That the audio-visual portion of the exhibit was funded by the Japan Shipbuilding Industry Foundation is a matter of wonder in our national museum.

The National Archives, the institution that holds much of the documentation pertaining to the evacuation, has in its public presentations covering the event ignored much of the information that would present a balanced account. It, too, has adopted the findings in *Personal Justice Denied* as its own. Research on this topic is apparently a sensitive matter at the National Archives.

While fastidious in assisting researchers in finding materials, the publisher's efforts in securing photographs dealing with evacuation, which provided a view contrary to the institutionally accepted version of the event, were sometimes met with reluctance on the part of archive employees.

Access to information on evacuation is not only critical to an understanding of an historical event, it has relevance to current legislative initiatives. Italian-Americans are presently seeking review of wartime treatment of individuals of Italian ancestry, and the Congressional Hispanic Caucus is seeking redress payments for Latin American-Japanese who were interned in the United States during the war. In the interest of fair and reasoned handling of these initiatives, complete disclosure and consideration of related documents should be made. German-Americans who were interned in the same Department of Justice camps as Japanese, it is interesting to note, seldom have their experience acknowledged.

The political manipulation of history for the purpose of obtaining money and bestowing the mantle of victimhood on one particular group at the expense of all others is hardly an honorable activity. To use this victimhood as a "currency of power" is hardly worthy of a proud people.

The failure of the U.S. government to present the facts involved in the wartime decision to evacuate the Japanese and to defend the honor of our country and its wartime leaders is nothing short of an outrage. It is dishonest to continue concealing these facts while funding public indoctrination which portrays a flawed accounting of actions taken in the urgency of war.

Greater access to government-held information would place the sad events of Japanese evacuation in perspective and show that those innocents involved were actually victims of the Japanese Empire and its prewar plans and activities. And that those many who were engaged in acts threatening to our country were treated with kindness and magnanimity unknown in Asia during those tragic years.

GLOSSARY

Army G-2
Intelligence staff

BAMS
A complex Allied merchant ship super-enciphered code captured from a merchant ship by the German raider Atlantis and provided to the Japanese. One of two U.S. codes the Japanese were known to have been able to read.

CAST
Cover name for U.S. Navy cryptanalytic unit located in Cavite, Philippines before the war. Involved in interception and decoding of Japanese diplomatic traffic on the Tokyo-Berlin and Tokyo-Moscow circuits.

Central Bureau Brisbane (CBB)
A forward cryptanalytic group formed to support General MacArthur.

cipher
Any system in which arbitrary symbols or groups of symbols represent units of plain text of regular length, usually single letters.

code
Any system of communication in which arbitrary groups of symbols represents units of plain text of varying length.

COMINT
Communications intelligence

COPEK
Highly secure Navy communications circuit used to provide daily PURPLE keys to station CAST in the Philippines.

ELINT
Electronic intelligence derived from emissions such as radar.

enemy alien
Legal status given citizens of enemy countries by Presidential proclamation in accordance with well established law which stripped them of constitutional protections afforded in times of peace and made them subject to summary search, seizure, internment and deportation, among other things, during times of war.

FRUMEL
Fleet Radio Unit Melbourne. A Navy cryptanalytic group located in Melbourne.

HYPO
U.S. Navy cryptanalytic group located at Pearl Harbor

internment
Incarceration of enemy aliens for the duration of the war in Department of Justice camps. U.S. citizens were allowed to live in these camps with their relatives. During the war 10,905 Germans, 16,849 Japanese and 3,278 Italians, citizen family members included, were interned. The number of Japanese includes 5,589 Japanese-Americans who renounced their U.S. citizenship. The decision to intern was generally based on review of individual cases by boards composed of leading, local citizens. Only a small fraction of enemy aliens were interned.

Issei
First generation Japanese emigrants to the U.S.

J-19
Foreign ministry code used primarily by Japanese consulates.

JACL
Japanese-American Citizens League

JICPOA
Joint Intelligence Center Pacific Ocean Area, located in Hawaii.

Kibei
Nisei, or second generation Japanese, born in the United States but educated in Japan.

MAGIC
Intelligence derived from high level Japanese diplomatic traffic

MID
Army Military Intelligence Division

NCJAR
National Council for Japanese-American Redress

Nisei
Children of Issei born in the U.S.

NSA
National Security Agency

ONI
Office of Naval Intelligence

OP-20-G
The Navy cryptanalytic unit within the Office of Naval Communications that worked with the Army Signal Intelligence Service to produce MAGIC intelligence. Located in Washington, D.C.

PURPLE
Cover name given to Japanese crypt system first introduced in March, 1939 and was broken by SIS about eighteen months later.

PURPLE analog
The machine developed in the minds of SIS members which performed the exact functions of the Japanese code machine.

RED
Cover name for the Japanese high-level code that preceded PURPLE.

relocation
Voluntary or enforced movement from the West Coast exclusion area to locations in non-effected states or to government run relocation centers from which movement to jobs and schools in other states was arranged. There were approximately 9,000 who relocated voluntarily, 30,000 who relocated from centers to other states and 4,300 who left centers to attend college.

SIGINT
Signals intelligence

SIS
Signal Intelligence Service, the Army cryptanalytic unit, within the Signal Corps, that broke the Japanese PURPLE code system and built the PURPLE analog machine which gave access to high level diplomatic messages throughout the war. Located in Washington, D.C.

Third Bureau
Japanese Naval Intelligence

traffic analysis
The study of call signs, message routing, volume priorities and frequency allocation to obtain useful information, especially when the code being used cannot be read.

ULTRA
In the Pacific Theater, intelligence derived from Japanese army and navy codes.

WDC
Western Defense Command. The Army command charged with defense of the Western United States.

WRA
War Relocation Authority, the civilian organization charged with the operation of ten relocation centers, the relocation of individuals during the war to eastern states, the securing of jobs and schools for those individuals and the eventual resettlement of all occupants in 1945.

INDEX

Y

Yamagata, Clarence, 60
Yamamoto, Isoroku (Adm.), 51-52, 123
Yardley, Herbert O., 44-48
Yasuo Wakatsuki, 11
Yoshikawa, Takeo, 191-193
Young Women's Organization to serve Our
    Mother Country, See *Hokoku Joshi Seinen*
    Dan

Z

Zaibei Heimusha Kai (Association of
    Japanese in America Obligated to
    Military Duty), 332

This book was produced entirely on a Macintosh PowerBook G3 laptop computer. All scanning and processing of images, including reproduced documents, was done on a Umax 2400S scanner with GraphicConverter, a $30 shareware photoediting program developed in Germany by Thorsten Lemke. Documents and photographs were scanned on location at the National Archives in College Park, Maryland and in Washington, D.C. Additional documents were scanned at the California State Archives in Sacramento and at the Military History Institute in Carlisle, Pennsylvania.